# Innovations
# in Computational
# Intelligence,
# Big Data Analytics,
# and Internet of Things

A volume in
*Emerging Information Technologies: Applications, Innovations, and Research*
Sam Goundar, *Series Editor*

**Emerging Information Technologies:
Applications, Innovations, and Research**

Sam Goundar, *Series Editor*

*Enterprise Systems and Technological Convergence: Research and Practice* (2021)
Sam Goundar

# Innovations in Computational Intelligence, Big Data Analytics, and Internet of Things

*edited by*

## Sam Goundar
*RMIT University*

## J. Avanija
*Mohan Babu University*

## Gurram Sunitha
*Mohan Babu University*

## K. Reddy Madhavi
*Mohan Babu University*

INFORMATION AGE PUBLISHING, INC.
Charlotte, NC • www.infoagepub.com

**Library of Congress Cataloging-in-Publication Data**

A CIP record for this book is available from the Library of Congress
http://www.loc.gov

ISBN: 979-8-88730-559-2 (Paperback)
      979-8-88730-560-8 (Hardcover)
      979-8-88730-561-5 (E-Book)

Printed in the United States of America

# CONTENTS

1   A Systematic Literature Review of Computational Intelligence,
Big Data Analytics, and Internet of Things.................................... 1
*Gurram Sunitha, Sam Goundar, J. Avanija, and K. Reddy Madhavi*

2   Applications of Innovations in Computational Intelligence, Big
Data Analytics, and Internet of Things ............................................ 15
*J. Avanija, Sam Goundar, Putta Vishnu Vardhan, D. Ganesh,
and Gurram Sunitha*

3   Trends and Future Research Directions of Innovations
in Computational Intelligence, Big Data Analytics, and
Internet of Things ............................................................................ 31
*B. Narendra Kumar Rao, Sam Goundar,
Gopireddy Karthik Kumar Reddy, Dudi Sai Hima Sri,
Gundampati Sudheer Kumar, and Gundarapu Vikas*

4   An Intelligent Framework for Traffic Congestion Analysis
System Using Deep Convergence Network......................................... 47
*A. Jafflet Trinishia, S. Asha, and Kanchana Devi V*

5   IoT Security: Securing the Future of Connectivity........................... 75
*David Silva, Travis Hearne, and Theodore Wiard*

6   Implementation of DenseNet Deep Learning Mechanism
for Thorax Disease Classification in Chest X-Ray Images................ 93
*D. Ganesh, K. Suresh, Mohamed Yasin, Gurram Sunitha,
and Thulasi Bikku*

7 An Integrated Comprehensive Security Framework
for Wireless Sensor Networks: A Survey............................................ 113
*V. Jyothsna, P. Bhasha, E. Sandhya, and K. Khaja Baseer*

8 A Feature-Fusion-Based Multimodal Biometric Along With
One-Time Token Authentication System for Increased Security
in Cloud Environments........................................................................ 139
*Reddy Madhavi K., Vijayasanthi Maddela, K. Suneetha,
Ashok Patel, and Karuna G.*

9 A Workload Clustering and Resource Provisioning Framework
for Cloud Using: Adaptive Cat Swarm Optimization and Rule
Based Classification............................................................................. 159
*Gurram Sunitha, Mohammad Gouse Galety, J. Avanija,
K. Reddy Madhavi, and A. V. Sriharsha*

10 IoT Protocols: A Review..................................................................... 179
*Kasarapu Ramani, G. B. Hima Bindu, M. L. Haritha,
N. Pushpa Latha, and I. Suneetha*

11 IoT Enabled Monitoring of Solar Plants in Agri Lands................. 199
*P. Dhanalakshmi, K. Srujan Raju, Nagendra Panini Challa,
B. Hemanth Kumar, and K. P. N. V. Satya Sree*

12 A Simple and Effective Approach for Identification of
Collaborative Concerns and Risks Under Distributed
Version Control.................................................................................... 215
*K. Suneetha, Jabeen Sultana, Reddy Madhavi K.,
Gudavalli Madhavi, and Naga Jyothi*

13 Lung Disease Detection Using Hybrid Machine Learning
Algorithms ........................................................................................... 233
*J. Avanija, K. Srujan Raju, Gurram Sunitha,
Mohammad Gouse Galety, and A. V. Sriharsha*

14 An Investigation of Future Research Directions in Secure
Internet of Things Systems and Applications................................... 249
*M. Bharathi, M. Dharani, Sivaram Rajeyyagari,
and B. M. Rajeswari*

15 An Effective Pedestrian Detection Using Convolutional Neural
Network: Computer Vision Applications .......................................... 265
*N. Ashokkumar, P. T. Kavitha, P. Nagarajan, M. Bharathi,
K. Neelima, and M. Dharani*

**16** Chronic Kidney Disease Prediction Using Hybrid Machine
Learning Models ................................................................. 283
*K. Reddy Madhavi, J. Avanija, Shivaprasad Kaleru,*
*K. Arun Kumar, and R. Hitesh Sai Vittal*

**17** Cyber Security Constrained Power System With TCSC
Under *n*-1 Contingency Condition..................................... 299
*Suresh Babu Daram, Kumar Reddy Cheepati, Killada Sesi Prabha,*
*and Venkatesh P.*

**18** Trending Opportunities and Challenges in Enabling
Technologies of Industry 5.0 ............................................. 323
*S. Sreenivasa Chakravarthi, Jagadeesh Kannan, S. Sountharrajan,*
*Saravana Balaji B., and J. Avanija*

**19** Big Data Analysis to Categorize Agricultural Land According
to Climatic Information...................................................... 343
*M. Sirish Kumar, Kurakula Arun Kumar, Avula chitti,*
*B. Panduranag Raju, and Sivaram Rajeyyagari*

**20** Binaural Hearing Aid Noise Reduction Using
an External Microphone..................................................... 361
*G. Naga Jyothi, K. Vijetha, K. Reddy Madhavi, K. Suneetha,*
*and S. Sreenivasa Chakravarthi*

About the Editors ................................................................ 375

CHAPTER 1

# A SYSTEMATIC LITERATURE REVIEW OF COMPUTATIONAL INTELLIGENCE, BIG DATA ANALYTICS, AND INTERNET OF THINGS

**Gurram Sunitha**
*Mohan Babu University*

**Sam Goundar**
*RMIT University*

**J. Avanija**
*Mohan Babu University*

**K. Reddy Madhavi**
*Mohan Babu University*

*Innovations in Computational Intelligence, Big Data Analytics, and Internet of Things*, pages 1–14
Copyright © 2024 by Information Age Publishing
www.infoagepub.com

## ABSTRACT

Because of continuous innovation and the great importance placed on automation, digital information has become an increasingly valuable driver transitioning all domains. The fundamental focus of this chapter stems from the dynamic interaction between information progression and trending technologies, as well as the growth of real-world concerns, which has been speeding the progress of the digital economy. Those who can acquire, keep, transform, and use data are in control. As a result, intelligence gained through data analysis and learning improves our understanding via computational intelligence, big data analytics and Internet of things. This chapter provides a systematic literature review on computational intelligence, big data analytics, and the Internet of things, focusing on the problems and opportunities presented by domains such as healthcare, smart farming, industry 4.0/5.0, smart cities.

## A SYSTEMATIC LITERATURE REVIEW OF COMPUTATIONAL INTELLIGENCE

CI systems are a collection of human information processing technologies that have been created to address difficult real-world-driven problems that cannot be solved or optimized using traditional methods. It plays an important part in the development of effective intelligent systems, such as games and cognitive developmental systems. Recently, increased emphasis has been placed on artificial intelligence (AI), with CI serving as the foundation for practically all successful AI systems. This section explores and debates the implications of AI and CI in the digital era, providing a comprehensive view of the applications, problems, and opportunities to apply AI and CI.

### Computational Intelligence and Healthcare

Every day, hospitals and the healthcare industry generate vast amounts of data. After a more thorough study of the individual patient's health history, lab, diagnostic, treatment, and financial data, this information may be quite useful for furthering the healthcare (De et al., 2022). In this perspective, all the governments and private healthcare industries/hospitals have been managing the healthcare data digitally online/offline since the past decade (Ahirwal et al., 2022). This supports extensive research to be undertaken by the scientists to design and develop innovative profiles of diagnosis, treatment, and healthcare maintenance for various diseases.

CI and healthcare are an interdisciplinary field of the application of CI techniques and algorithms to foster automated computation, diagnosis, and treatment by medical professionals to provide value-based healthcare (Elngar et al., 2022; Mishra et al., 2022). Various machine learning, deep learning architectures have been investigated, customized and converted into real-time technology for assisting medical professionals in providing timely value-based healthcare (Reshma et al., 2022). Disease diagnosis and detection, severity detection have been tried to be automated efficiently. Various diseases such as cancers, tumors, lesions, abnormalities, fractures, and so forth have been extensively studied and automated assisting systems have been developed. The application of CI to healthcare industry has been felicitous in diagnosing diseases of various medical branches such as hepatology, haematology, nephrology, cardiology, oncology, cytopathology, obstetrics, neurology, gynaecology, intensive care, paediatrics, osteology, radiology, otolaryngology, dermatology, and so forth (Alrafiah, 2022; Dhombres et al., 2022; Qazi et al., 2022).

## Computational Intelligence and Smart Farming

The traditional irrigation management system is challenged by issues such as water insufficiency, unpredictable weather, pollution of water, soil, air, dynamic rainfall, seasonal fluctuations, destructive pests, negative impacts of fertilizers, and so forth. In a greenhouse, the environment can be regulated, but in an open field-cultivation farm, these characteristics are difficult to control. The fluctuating environmental variables must be managed adaptively with precision irrigation systems (De Alwis et al., 2022).

Precision farming is becoming a viable alternative to address the growing need for food and space. An AI driven system requires precision farming to provide an environment conducive to cultivar production. The development of CI-based urban agricultural automation systems is in high demand (Shereesha et al., 2022). Agriculture is a labor-intensive strategy of regulating plant growth and development that makes use of technical advances and inventions. Farming automation systems are frequently used in conjunction with expert systems for detection, prediction, and management, among other things (Kose et al., 2022). AI-enabled technologies empower farmers to increase agricultural productivity, analyze soil, monitor pest attacks, manage water, manage seeds, rotate crops, better control harvesting conditions and timing, manage nutrition, and decrease waste (Altalak et al., 2022). Deploying AI systems for making agriculture smart and précised, involves various ethical, moral, and legal perspectives (Uddin et al., 2022). Technologies have been developed specific to a country, a region, and crop (Strong et al., 2022). As generating a large agricultural database might be a complex task, techniques with few-shot learning have also been investigated (Yang et al., 2022).

## Computational Intelligence and Industry 4.0/5.0

Industry 4.0/5.0 will transform the way we work, live, think, and interact with one another. Industry 4.0/5.0 relies heavily on CI (Tang et al., 2022). It helps machines to think, learn, and make decisions. Enhanced productivity, efficiency, flexibility of operations and maintenance, considerable profitability, personalized product design and services, and a productive economy are all advantages of the fourth/fifth industrial revolution. Economies that aggressively pursue AI technologies have a greater increase in manufacturing value added than other countries.

Industry 4.0/5.0 is a concept used to characterize the transition to a fourth stage of humanity's technological-economic progress, beginning with the first industrial revolution. Industry 4.0/5.0 could boost any industry's competitiveness. AIe is positioned as a major component of this revolution, inextricably tied to the gradual amassing of vast amounts of data, the employment of algorithms in processes, and the massive interconnectivity of digital systems and devices (Peres et al., 2020).

Industry 4.0/5.0 refers to the total digitalization of the value chain, from suppliers to customers, by integrating data processing technology, intelligent software, and sensors to intelligently anticipate, control, plan, and manufacture, generating better value for the entire chain (Javaid et al., 2022). Much interrogation is done for the application of AI for possible automation of the construction industry (Baduge et al., 2022). Other applications include smart product design, smart manufacturing, smart robotics, smart assembly lines, smart inventory, smart design for ships, smart product management, smart operations, smart defect detection and management, smart testing, and so on (Banjanović-Mehmedović & Mehmedović, 2020; Jiang, 2022; Revathy et al., 2022; Wang et al., 2022).

## Computational Intelligence and Smart Cities

In this digital age of instant communication, improvements in developing technologies can be harnessed to create smart cities and intelligent societies. The mandatory prerequisite for becoming a smart city is to achieve sustainable social, environmental, and economic development while also improving societal living standards and AI (Herath et al., 2022). AI plays a critical role in operational management of various elements contributing to the smart cities such as green buildings, smart transport, smart waste and water management, efficient energy generation and distribution and management, smart homes, smart governance, robust IT infrastructure, sustainable environment and disaster management, reliable safety and security, affordable services, smart homes, smart education, value-based healthcare, eco-friendly farming, and so on (Charan et al., 2023; Gomede et al., 2018; Hina et al., 2022; O'Dwyer et al., 2019; Shao, 2022).

The present age is obsessed with increasing efficiency and the ease with which they do tasks. This desire to simplify everything has also permeated their way of life, making smart houses appealing to them. In particular, the commercial market has been in heavy competition in launching smart home devices. The global smart home market is predicted to reach $79.17 billion in 2022, and to $138.9 billion by 2026 and $537 billion by 2030. Smart houses and AI technology are constantly evolving, and many smart home devices have increased the quality of life (Guo et al., 2019).

## A SYSTEMATIC LITERATURE REVIEW OF BIG DATA ANALYTICS

One of the most important parts of any digital transformation strategy is data. There will be no return on investment from company digitization if there is insufficient or untrustworthy data to enable digital services or operations. Aside from data availability and quality, there is also the issue of accessibility and integration. Data stored in a silo may contain immense promise, but it is practically worthless if multiple homogenous or heterogenous data sources cannot be easily accessed and integrated to provide a more holistic perspective of a process or pattern. As a result, any digital transformation strategy should place a strong emphasis on data. It has been proven that the explosion of big data will create an insatiable demand for data scientists who can slice and dice data to help organizations make better informed decisions. Big data analytics supports researchers, sole proprietors, and entrepreneurs, to make well-thought, faster, and more informed business decisions. Also, it supports vastly for operational cost maintenance and in providing innovative and/or personalized products and services.

### Big Data Analytics and Healthcare

The size of the worldwide healthcare analytics market was estimated at $32.08 billion in 2021, reaching over $121.1 billion. By 2022, it was predicted that India's healthcare industry could be worth up to $372 billion, up from a value of about $280 billion in 2020. Various potential sources of healthcare data are government health ministries and agencies, disaster management agencies, hospitals, medical research, wearables, medical devices, and so on.

Big data in healthcare suffers from various issues such as most of it is not digitalized; unstructured data formats; huge in volume; various velocity and veracity; integrity, confidentiality, privacy problems, and so forth. These issues make medical data research an enormously complex task, making it impossible for industry executives to capitalize on its huge promise to change the industry (Shilo et al., 2020). Despite these challenges, novel technological breakthroughs are enabling healthcare data to be converted into actionable information. Big data in healthcare allows radical support for medical professionals in providing value-based healthcare thus transforming and redirecting the future of medicinal practices towards diagnostics, personalized treatment, patient profiling, health predictions, preventative medicine, precision medicine, medical research, communicative disease control, creating effective drugs, and so on (Dash et al., 2019; Galetsi & Katsaliaki, 2020; Mehta & Pandit, 2018; Miah et al., 2022; Pramanik et al., 2022; Rehman et al., 2022).

## Big Data Analytics and Smart Farming

The 21st century will provide humanity with tremendous challenges to sustainability. In these circumstances, humanity is confronted with the major challenge of boosting agricultural production. The pressing need is to ensure food security for the world's rapidly growing population. In these situations, disruptive technologies such as big data analytics are to be efficiently utilized for making precision agriculture or precision farming sustainable (Coble et al., 2018).

As more experience, applications, best practices, and computational capacity become accessible, agriculture big data applications are fast evolving. Big data is now everywhere. When it comes to agriculture, it is clear to see how technological advancements may help not only the farming sector, but society as a whole. The typical issues with conventional farming include greenhouse gas emissions, water use, soil quality degradation, pesticide contamination, decreased yield and quality of yield, labor, and other issues (Osinga et al., 2022). Farmers can take advantage of big data analytics for a whole highly heterogeneous tasks such as farming processes, food supply chain management, livestock management, crop yield prediction and failure risk, livestock feed intake prediction, farm structuring, crop quality, safety and nutritional predictions and maintenance, animal husbandry and aquaculture, and so on (Wolfert et al., 2017).

## Big Data Analytics and Industry 4.0/5.0

Our industrial environment has undergone a phenomenal change as a result of the swift evolution of information and communication technologies (Nayyar et al., 2020). The incorporation of cutting-edge tech-nologies results in a shift in the industrial processes that turns hand produc-tion methods into machine-driven procedures. The industrial revolution is the result of the automation of industrial operations (Goundar et al., 2021). A smart and sustainable industry is being developed in large part thanks to big data analytics. Numerous and ubiquitous applications of big data analytics in production processes, planning and control, operational efficiency, productivity and performance, technologies, and sustainability are worthily proven (Papadopoulos et al., 2022).

## Big Data Analytics and Smart Cities

Smart cities strive to increase the efficiency and efficacy of public ser-vices in order to eventually build self-sustaining communities. Because of the variety of data that was gathered, saved, analyzed, and applied to cre-ate smarter cities, it serves as an example of how big data analytics may be applied (Lohachab, 2022; Zhang et al., 2022). Big data analytics must be revitalized in smart cities in order to meet present and future living ex-pectations. The potential of big data analytics to revolutionize areas like transportation, education, health, and energy to ensure the development and self-sufficiency of smart cities (Barkham et al., 2022; Javed et al., 2022).

## A SYSTEMATIC LITERATURE REVIEW OF INTERNET OF THINGS

Most of the lifestyle changes that occurred in this millennium were brought on by the development of cutting-edge, reasonably affordable and infor-mation technology. The rife use of the Internet, a whole new paradigm of the digital world, has been established. The rapid changes in informa-tion technology, mobile devices and wearable devices are making sense by intruding into various domains making the relevant smart and intelligent applications, devices, systems, and technologies. The motto of Internet of things (IoT) was to integrate physical objects with the Internet and this has marked the beginning of a new age.

## Internet of Things and Healthcare

Integrating IoT into medical equipment has improved quality and effec-tiveness of healthcare, with significant value for the patients with chronic diseases, and those who need constant supervision (Arunachalam et al.,

2023; Sunitha et al., 2021). There is currently study being done on ways to change the healthcare business by improving efficiency, reducing expenses, and refocusing on improved patient care (Sowmya et al., 2023). The healthcare sector will experience a paradigm shift thanks to IoT.

The buzz these days in the field of IoT for the healthcare industry is the "Internet of medical things" (IoMT) which is an interconnection of medical equipment, applications that are linked to healthcare IT systems over the Internet. The machine-to-machine connection that is the foundation of IoMT is made possible by medical equipment that include Wi-Fi. IoMT devices connect to cloud infrastructures that enable the storage and analysis of collected data. Such technology allows for real-time health monitoring of patients by the doctors for providing better healthcare. But yet this technology has to overcome a lot of hurdles related to the patient's privacy, technical, legal, and regulatory issues.

## Internet of Things and Smart Farming

As agriculture has existed since the beginning of civilization, it appears antiquated. However, the use of contemporary technologies is assisting those working in the agribusiness to increase productivity and reduce costs (Sinha & Dhanalakshmi, 2022). IoT in agriculture provides technological support and seems to have limitless potential with major impact on agriculture making it smart and sustainable (Qazi et al., 2022). Through the use of interconnected devices for monitoring the soil, pests, crop, livestock, weather, and so on, IoT improves the efficacy of agrarian and farming methods by minimizing manual labor thereby enhancing yields and cost-effectiveness (Pandey & Mukherjee, 2022).

## Internet of Things and Industry 4.0/5.0

Due to the incorporation of new technology breakthroughs and IoT applications in industrial systems, industrial IoT (IIoT) is expanding. By automating smart devices to sense, gather, process, and share events in industries, IIoT represents a new perspective on IoT in the industrial sector. The primary goal of the IIoT is to improve operational effectiveness, capacity, and the governance of industrial manufacturing processes, operations, and equipment (Khan et al., 2020). IIoT holds great promise for manufacturing in terms of quality control, environmentally friendly practices, supply chain traceability, and overall supply chain effectiveness (Malik et al., 2021). Industrial activities such as predictive maintenance, supply chain management, timely production, increased operational maintenance, maintainable cost variance, better field service, better reach to customer services, energy management, and asset tracking rely on IIoT (Khanna & Kaur, 2020; Younan et al., 2020).

## Internet of Things and Smart Cities

The global trend of urbanization continues to accelerate. Such rapid transformation is likely to bring with it a slew of problems, including pollution, transportation congestion, and crime (Deng & Benslimane, 2022). A smart city is essentially a strategic assemblage of ICTs and an intelligent architecture of cloud-connected assets that can communicate and interact with one another. Parking, lamps, transit, energy, health, buildings, and the environment are all examples of items that can become "smart" in a city thanks to an IoT architecture (Raj et al., 2022).

## CONCLUSIONS

This chapter provides a systematic literature review on CI, big data analytics, and IoT, focusing on the problems and opportunities presented by domains such as healthcare, smart farming, industry 4.0/5.0, and smart cities. The fundamental focus of this chapter stems from the dynamic interaction between information progression and trending technologies, as well as the growth of real-world concerns, which has been speeding the progress of the digital economy. The authors have tried to reconnoiter and debate the implications of CI in the digital era, providing a comprehensive view of the applications, problems, and opportunities to apply AI and CI in the domains of healthcare, smart farming, industry 4.0/5.0, and smart cities. Big data analytics allows radical support for various domains transforming and redirecting the future of the domain. With this perspective, the authors have presented a detailed review of the applications of big data analytics to the fields of healthcare, smart farming, industry 4.0/5.0, and smart cities. With the motto of integrating physical objects with the Internet, IoT has marked the beginning of a new age. The rapid changes in information technology, mobile devices, and wearable devices are making sense by intruding into various domains making the relevant smart and intelligent applications, devices, systems, and technologies. In this regard, this chapter has focused on presenting a detailed review of the status of IoT to the fields of healthcare, smart farming, industry 4.0/5.0, and smart cities. The authors conclude that the development of intelligent applications and technologies to improve the human world requires the integration of the fields of CI, big data analytics, and IoT.

# REFERENCES

Ahirwal, M. K., Londhe, N. D., & Kumar, A. (2022). *Artificial intelligence applications for health care.* CRC Press.

Alrafiah, A. R. (2022). Application and performance of artificial intelligence technology in cytopathology. *Acta Histochemica, 124*(4), 151890. https://doi.org/10.1016/j.acthis.2022.151890

Altalak, M., Ammad uddin, M., Alajmi, A., & Rizg, A. (2022). Smart agriculture applications using deep learning technologies: A survey. *Applied Sciences, 12*(12), 5919. https://doi.org/10.3390/app12125919

Arunachalam, R., Sunitha, G., Shukla, S. K., Urooj, S., & Rawat, S. (2023). A smart Alzheimer's patient monitoring system with IoT-assisted technology through enhanced deep learning approach. *Knowledge and Information Systems, 65,* 5561–5599. https://doi.org/10.1007/s10115-023-01890-x

Baduge, S. K., Thilakarathna, S., Perera, J. S., Arashpour, M., Sharafi, P., Teodosio, B., Shringi, A., & Mendis, P. (2022). Artificial intelligence and smart vision for building and construction 4.0: Machine and deep learning methods and applications. *Automation in Construction, 141,* 104440. https://doi.org/10.1016/j.autcon.2022.104440

Banjanović-Mehmedović, L., & Mehmedović, F. (2020). Intelligent manufacturing systems driven by artificial intelligence in industry 4.0. In I. Karabegović, A. Kovacević, L. Banjanović-Mehmedović, & P. Dasić (Eds.), *Handbook of research on integrating industry 4.0 in business and manufacturing* (pp. 31–52). IGI Global.

Barkham, R., Bokhari, S., & Saiz, A. (2022). Urban big data: City management and real estate markets. In P. M. Pardalos, S. T. Rassia, & A. Tsokas (Eds.), *Artificial intelligence, machine learning, and optimization tools for smart cities* (pp. 177–209). Springer.

Charan, N. S., Narasimhulu, T., Bhanu Kiran, G., Sudharshan Reddy, T., Shivangini Singh, T., & Sunitha, G. (2023). Solid waste management using deep learning. In A. Abraham, T. Hanne, N. Gandhi, P. Manghirmalani Mishra, A. Bajaj, & P. Siarry (Eds.), *14th international conference on soft computing and pattern recognition* (pp. 44–51). Springer.

Coble, K. H., Mishra, A. K., Ferrell, S., & Griffin, T. (2018). Big data in agriculture: A challenge for the future. *Applied Economic Perspectives and Policy, 40*(1), 79–96. https://doi.org/10.1093/aepp/ppx056

Dash, S., Shakyawar, S. K., Sharma, M., & Kaushik, S. (2019). Big data in healthcare: Management, analysis and future prospects. *Journal of Big Data, 6*(1), 1–25. https://doi.org/10.1186/s40537-019-0217-0

De, S., Das, R., Bhattacharyya, S., & Maulik, U. (Eds.). (2022). *Applied smart health care informatics: A computational intelligence perspective.* Wiley.

De Alwis, S., Hou, Z., Zhang, Y., Na, M. H., Ofoghi, B., & Sajjanhar, A. (2022). A survey on smart farming data, applications and techniques. *Computers in Industry, 138,* 103624. https://doi.org/10.1016/j.compind.2022.103624

Deng, D. J., & Benslimane, A. (2022). Innovation and application of Internet of things for smart cities. *Mobile Networks and Applications, 27*(1), 1–2. https://doi.org/10.1007/s11036-020-01715-z

Dhombres, F., Bonnard, J., Bailly, K., Maurice, P., Papageorghiou, A. T., & Jouan-nic, J. M. (2022). Contributions of artificial intelligence reported in obstetrics and gynecology journals: Systematic review. *Journal of Medical Internet Research, 24*(4), e35465. https://doi.org/10.2196/35465

Elngar, A. A., Chowdhury, R., Elhoseny, M., & Balas, V. E. (Eds.). (2022). *Applications of computational intelligence in multi-disciplinary research.* Academic Press.

Galetsi, P., & Katsaliaki, K. (2020). A review of the literature on big data analytics in healthcare. *Journal of the Operational Research Society, 71*(10), 1511–1529. https://doi.org/10.1080/01605682.2019.1630328

Gomede, E., Gaffo, F. H., Briganó, G. U., De Barros, R. M., & Mendes, L. D. S. (2018). Application of computational intelligence to improve education in smart cities. *Sensors, 18*(1), 267. https://doi.org/10.3390/s18010267

Goundar, S., Avanija, J., Sunitha, G., Madhavi, K. R., & Bhushan, S. B. (Eds.). (2021). *Innovations in the industrial Internet of things (IIoT) and smart factory.* IGI Global.

Guo, X., Shen, Z., Zhang, Y., & Wu, T. (2019). Review on the application of artificial intelligence in smart homes. *Smart Cities, 2*(3), 402–420. https://doi.org/10.3390/smartcities2030025

Herath, H. M. K. K. M. B., & Mittal, M. (2022). Adoption of artificial intelligence in smart cities: A comprehensive review. *International Journal of Information Management Data Insights, 2*(1), 100076. https://doi.org/10.1016/j.jjimei.2022.100076

Hina, M. D., Soukane, A., & Ramdane-Cherif, A. (2022). Computational intelligence in intelligent transportation systems: An overview. In R. Tomar, M. D. Hina, R. Zitouni, & A. Ramdane-Cherif (Eds.), *Innovative trends in omputational intelligence* (pp. 27–43). Springer.

Javaid, M., Haleem, A., Singh, R. P., & Suman, R. (2022). Artificial intelligence applications for industry 4.0: A literature-based study. *Journal of Industrial Integration and Management, 7*(1), 83–111. https://doi.org/10.1142/S2424862221300040

Javed, A. R., Shahzad, F., ur Rehman, S., Zikria, Y. B., Razzak, I., Jalil, Z., & Xu, G. (2022). Future smart cities: Requirements, emerging technologies, applications, challenges, and future aspects. *Cities, 129*, 103794. https://doi.org/10.1016/j.cities.2022.103794

Jiang, W. (2022). A machine vision anomaly detection system to industry 4.0 based on variational fuzzy autoencoder. *Computational Intelligence and Neuroscience, 2022*, 1945507. https://doi.org/10.1155/2022/1945507

Khan, W. Z., Rehman, M. H., Zangoti, H. M., Afzal, M. K., Armi, N., & Salah, K. (2020). Industrial Internet of things: Recent advances, enabling technologies and open challenges. *Computers & Electrical Engineering, 81*, 106522. https://doi.org/10.1016/j.compeleceng.2019.106522

Khanna, A., & Kaur, S. (2020). Internet of things (IoT), applications and challenges: A comprehensive review. *Wireless Personal Communications, 114*(2), 1687–1762. https://doi.org/10.1007/s11277-020-07446-4

Kose, U., Prasath, V. S., Mondal, M. R. H., Podder, P., & Bharati, S. (Eds.). (2022). *Artificial intelligence and smart agriculture technology.* CRC Press.

Lohachab, A. (2022). Bootstrapping urban planning: Addressing big data issues in smart cities. In Information Resources Managment Association (Ed.), *Research anthology on big data analytics, architectures, and applications* (pp. 1329–1358). IGI Global.

Malik, P. K., Sharma, R., Singh, R., Gehlot, A., Satapathy, S. C., Alnumay, W. S., Pelusi, D., Ghosh, U., & Nayak, J. (2021). Industrial Internet of things and its applications in industry 4.0: State of the art. *Computer Communications, 166,* 125–139. https://doi.org/10.1016/j.comcom.2020.11.016

Mehta, N., & Pandit, A. (2018). Concurrence of big data analytics and healthcare: A systematic review. *International Journal of Medical Informatics, 114,* 57–65. https://doi.org/10.1016/j.ijmedinf.2018.03.013

Miah, S. J., Camilleri, E., & Vu, H. Q. (2022). Big data in healthcare research: A survey study. *Journal of Computer Information Systems, 62*(3), 480–492. https://doi.org/10.1080/08874417.2020.1858727

Mishra, S., Tripathy, H. K., Mallick, P., & Shaalan, K. (Eds.). (2022). *Augmented intelligence in healthcare: A pragmatic and integrated analysis.* Springer.

Nayyar, A., & Kumar, A. (Eds.). (2020). *A roadmap to industry 4.0: Smart production, sharp business and sustainable development* (pp. 1–21). Springer.

O'Dwyer, E., Pan, I., Acha, S., & Shah, N. (2019). Smart energy systems for sustainable smart cities: Current developments, trends and future directions. *Applied Energy, 237,* 581–597. https://doi.org/10.1016/j.apenergy.2019.01.024

Osinga, S. A., Paudel, D., Mouzakitis, S. A., & Athanasiadis, I. N. (2022). Big data in agriculture: Between opportunity and solution. *Agricultural Systems, 195,* 103298. https://doi.org/10.1016/j.agsy.2021.103298

Pandey, A. K., & Mukherjee, A. (2022). A review on advances in IoT-based technologies for smart agricultural system. *Internet of Things and Analytics for Agriculture, 3,* 29–44. https://doi.org/10.1007/978-981-16-6210-2_2

Papadopoulos, T., Singh, S. P., Spanaki, K., Gunasekaran, A., & Dubey, R. (2022). Towards the next generation of manufacturing: implications of big data and digitalization in the context of industry 4.0. *Production Planning & Control, 33*(2–3), 101–104. https://doi.org/10.1080/09537287.2020.1810767

Peres, R. S., Jia, X., Lee, J., Sun, K., Colombo, A. W., & Barata, J. (2020). Industrial artificial intelligence in industry 4.0-systematic review, challenges and outlook. *IEEE Access, 8,* 220121–220139. https://doi.org/10.1109/ACCESS.2020.3042874

Pramanik, P. K. D., Pal, S., & Mukhopadhyay, M. (2022). Healthcare big data: A comprehensive overview. *Research Anthology on Big Data Analytics, Architectures, and Applications,* 119–147. https://doi.org/10.4018/978-1-5225-7071-4.ch004

Qazi, S., Khawaja, B. A., & Farooq, Q. U. (2022). IoT-equipped and AI-enabled next generation smart agriculture: A critical review, current challenges and future trends. *IEEE Access, 10,* 21219–21235. https://doi.org/10.1109/ACCESS.2022.3152544

Raj, E. F. I., Appadurai, M., Darwin, S., & Rani, E. F. I. (2022). *Internet of things (IoT) for sustainable smart cities.* In E. F. I. Raj, M. Appadurai, S. Darwin, E. F. I. Rani (Eds.), *Internet of things* (pp. 163–188). CRC Press.

Rehman, A., Naz, S., & Razzak, I. (2022). Leveraging big data analytics in healthcare enhancement: Trends, challenges and opportunities. *Multimedia Systems, 28*(4), 1339–1371. https://doi.org/10.1007/s00530-020-00736-8

Reshma, G., Al-Atroshi, C., Nassa, V. K., Geetha, B., Sunitha, G., Galety, M. G., & Neelakandan, S. (2022). Deep learning-based skin lesion diagnosis model using dermoscopic images. *Intelligent Automation of Soft Computing, 31*(1), 621–634. https://doi.org/10.32604/iasc.2022.019117

Revathy, G., Selvakumar, K., Murugapriya, P., & Ravikumar, D. (2022). Smart manufacturing in industry 4.0 using computational intelligence. In N. Thillaiarasu, S. L. Tripathi, & V. Dhinakaran (Eds.), *Artificial intelligence for Internet of things* (pp. 31–48). CRC Press.

Shao, N. (2022). Research on architectural planning and landscape design of smart city based on computational intelligence. *Computational Intelligence and Neuroscience, 2022,* 1745593. https://doi.org/10.1155/2022/1745593

Shereesha, M., Hemavathy, C., Teja, H., Reddy, G. M., Kumar, B. V., & Sunitha, G. (2022, December 15–17). Precision mango farming: Using compact convolutional transformer for disease detection. In A. Abraham, A. Bajaj, N. Gandhi, A. M. Madureira, & C. Kahraman (Eds.), *Innovations in bio-inspired computing and applications* (pp. 458–465). Springer. https://doi.org/10.1007/978-3-031-27499-2_43

Shilo, S., Rossman, H., & Segal, E. (2020). Axes of a revolution: Challenges and promises of big data in healthcare. *Nature Medicine, 26*(1), 29–38. https://doi.org/10.1038/s41591-019-0727-5

Sinha, B. B., & Dhanalakshmi, R. (2022). Recent advancements and challenges of Internet of things in smart agriculture: A survey. *Future Generation Computer Systems, 126,* 169–184. https://doi.org/10.1016/j.future.2021.08.006

Sowmya, T. S., Narasimhulu, T., Sunitha, G., Manikanta, T., & Venkatesh, T. (2023). Vision transformer based resnet model for pneumonia prediction. *4th International Conference on Electronics and Sustainable Communication Systems,* Coimbatore, India (pp. 316–321). IEEE. https://doi.org/10.1109/ICESC57686.2023.10193644

Strong, R., Wynn, J. T., Lindner, J. R., & Palmer, K. (2022). Evaluating Brazilian agriculturalists' IoT smart agriculture adoption barriers: Understanding stakeholder salience prior to launching an innovation. *Sensors, 22*(18), 6833. https://doi.org/10.3390/s22186833

Sunitha, G., Sasikumar, G., Madhan, E. S., Reeba, R., & Supriya, L. P. (2021). Intelligent system to find the health care centers for senior citizens based on disease and nearest locations using GPS. *Turkish Journal of Computer and Mathematics Education, 12*(2), 2140–2150. https://doi.org/10.17762/turcomat.v12i2.1860

Tang, S., Chen, L., He, K., Xia, J., Fan, L., & Nallanathan, A. (2022). Computational intelligence and deep learning for next-generation edge-enabled industrial IoT. *Transactions on Network Science and Engineering, 10*(5), 2881–2893. https://doi.org/10.1109/TNSE.2022.3180632

Uddin, M., Chowdhury, A., & Kabir, M. A. (2022). Legal and ethical aspects of deploying artificial intelligence in climate-smart agriculture. *AI & Society,* 1–14. https://doi.org/10.1007/s00146-022-01421-2

Wang, J., Song, Y., Yuan, C., Guo, F., Huangfu, Y., & Liu, Y. (2022). Research on the training and management of industrializing workers in prefabricated building with machine vision and human behaviour modelling based on Industry

4.0 era. *Computational Intelligence and Neuroscience, 2022,* 9230412. https://doi
.org/10.1155/2022/9230412

Wolfert, S., Ge, L., Verdouw, C., & Bogaardt, M. J. (2017). Big data in smart farming—A review. *Agricultural Systems, 153,* 69–80. https://doi.org/10.1016/j
.agsy.2017.01.023

Yang, J., Guo, X., Li, Y., Marinello, F., Ercisli, S., & Zhang, Z. (2022). A survey of few-
shot learning in smart agriculture: Developments, applications, and challenges. *Plant Methods, 18*(1), 1–12. https://doi.org/10.1186/s13007-022-00866-2

Younan, M., Houssein, E. H., Elhoseny, M., & Ali, A. A. (2020). Challenges and
recommended technologies for the industrial internet of things: A comprehensive review. *Measurement, 151,* 107198. https://doi.org/10.1016/j
.measurement.2019.107198

Zhang, D., Pee, L. G., Pan, S. L., & Cui, L. (2022). Big data analytics, resource or-
chestration, and digital sustainability: A case study of smart city development.
*Government Information Quarterly, 39*(1), 101626. https://doi.org/10.1016/j
.giq.2021.101626

CHAPTER 2

# APPLICATIONS OF INNOVATIONS IN COMPUTATIONAL INTELLIGENCE, BIG DATA ANALYTICS, AND INTERNET OF THINGS

**J. Avanija**
*Mohan Babu University*

**Sam Goundar**
*RMIT University*

**Putta Vishnu Vardhan**
*Sree Vidyanikethan Engineering College*

**D. Ganesh**
*Mohan Babu University*

**Gurram Sunitha**
*Mohan Babu University*

*Innovations in Computational Intelligence, Big Data Analytics, and Internet of Things,* pages 15–30
Copyright © 2024 by Information Age Publishing
www.infoagepub.com

## ABSTRACT

A subset of artificial intelligence (AI) is computational intelligence (CI). A human-like intelligence may be achieved in human-made robots by applying CI to develop intelligent systems. Compared to conventional methods, CI is more resilient, simpler, more efficient in producing tractable answers. When doing statistical computation (data analytics) in the fields of healthcare, social media research, industry, business, and pattern identification, recent technical advancements in CI have shown highly positive results. Big data is sometimes referred to as data that is "high volume, high diversity, and high velocity." Big data is the enormous collection of information that businesses have gathered from a wide range of sources, including mobile applications, radio-wave reading and remote sensing equipment, wireless sensors, smartphones and other multimedia devices, remote sensing and location tracking equipment, and other similar sources. Data analytics is the process of applying analytical methods and code languages to large amounts of data in order to draw meaningful and appropriate conclusions from it.

The Internet of things (IoT) is becoming widely used in almost all facets of contemporary life as a result of innovation in next-generation wireless technology, enabling people to work and live more intelligently. These fields cover a wide spectrum of commercial, military, and civil applications, including smart cities, smart homes, healthcare, the environment, and transportation. This chapter focuses on the various applications of the advancements in Computational Intelligence, big data technologies and Internet of things in various fields such as healthcare, agriculture, industries, business, energy sector, and retail business.

A subset of artificial intelligence (AI) is computational intelligence (CI). CI may be used to find solutions to real-world issues that call for judgment and reasoning. A human-like intelligence may be achieved in human-made robots by applying CI to develop intelligent systems. Compared to conventional methods, CI is more resilient, simpler, more efficient in producing tractable answers. When doing statistical computation (data analytics) in the fields of healthcare, social media research, industry, business, and pattern identification, recent technical advancements in CI have shown highly positive results. CI includes neural networks, genetic algorithms, evolutionary algorithms, fuzzy logic, swarm intelligence, and other things, whereas AI includes an expert system, NLP, machine vision, voice recognition, and many more. When a computational agent acts in a given environment, it is said to be acting in AI. A computational agent, on the other hand, is an agent in CI whose judgements regarding tasks or actions may be articulated in terms of computation (Prabha et al., 2023). The paradigms, concepts, algorithms, and implementations used to create new devices and systems that display intelligent behavior and anticipate accurate outcomes in complicated situations make up the majority of the research field of CI in healthcare

(Sujith et al., 2021). The contribution of CI to healthcare is significant in and of itself (Sadiku & Musa, 2021).

Big data is sometimes referred to as data that is "high volume, high diversity, and high velocity." Big data is the enormous collection of information that businesses have gathered from a wide range of sources, including mobile applications, radio-wave reading and remote sensing equipment, wireless sensors, smartphones and other multimedia devices, remote sensing and location tracking equipment, and other similar sources. According to the international research and consulting organization Gartner, *big data* refers to high-velocity, high-volume, or high-variety information assets that necessitate efficient, cutting-edge methods of information processing in order to improve process automation, decision-making, and insight. Data analytics is the process of applying analytical methods and code languages to large amounts of data in order to draw meaningful and appropriate conclusions from it. Data analytics, then, is the process of using the analytical component of data science on massive data or raw data in order to obtain insightful conclusions and information. It has received considerable attention and practical use for strategic decision-making, theory development, theory testing, and theory debunking across sectors (Chaudhary & Alam, 2022).

Due to the fusion of smart devices and physical items with the Internet, the Internet of things (IoT) has become a well-known technology in the current timeline. IoT is becoming widely used in almost all facets of contemporary life as a result of innovation in next-generation wireless technology, enabling people to work and live more intelligently. These fields cover a wide spectrum of commercial, military, and civil applications, including smart cities, smart homes, healthcare, the environment, and transportation (Azrour et al., 2022). The development of increasingly smarter appliances including refrigerators, stoves, temperature controllers, farming implements, medical gadgets, position trackers, and other items is now possible thanks to this technological innovation.

In this chapter, we discuss the various applications of the advancements in CI, big data technologies, and IoT in various fields such as healthcare, agriculture, industries, business, energy sector, and retail business.

## INDUSTRY 5.0

There is no doubt that various industrial sectors experience differing rates of contemporary technology development. Production must advance along with technological advancements if it wants to remain competitive. It's important to look ahead, even if Industry 4.0 is still the main transition for many industrial executives. Since the launch of the Industrial IoT (IIoT), many changes have been made in the industrial sector, and the IoT is a powerful modern technology that is behind these changes and has substantial advantages for manufacturers across several sectors (Elangovan, 2022).

We can see a glimpse of how small to medium-sized businesses and original equipment manufacturers can best leverage, increasing the process effectiveness, operational effectiveness, and reducing unskilled workforce using "Industry 3.0" to "Industry 4.0" through "Industry 5.0." This will undoubtedly lead to the manufacturing of greater value tasks than ever before, driving optimal results from human-to-machine interactions.

Many of the innovations now in use are reimagined versions of the underlying concepts established by earlier changes. The industrial automation landscape is already including the fifth industrial transition, commonly known as Industry 5.0. Industry 5.0 blends human ingenuity and craftsmanship with the efficiency, uniformity, and speed of robots. Additionally, it stimulates people's imaginations, making them more compliant. Because humans are recovering product design via manufacturing that requires creativity, Industry 5.0 generates even higher-value jobs than Industry 4.0.

As processes become more complex, it will be necessary to strike a balance between giving human operators a space to interact with shop floor equipment and creating an ecosystem that can handle the significant amount of information generated. This will be made possible by the development of digital twins. Industry 5.0 creates a unique alternative that will soon be in demand in the upcoming years by fusing human innovation and robotic accuracy. Industries may and must follow the road map laid out by both Industry 4.0 and Industry 5.0 in order to survive.

Industry 4.0's digital revolution entails smart production facilities with Internet-connected gadgets. Manufacturing companies generate, gather, and analyze data on the whole supply chain to identify ways to promote quality improvement, process optimization, cost reduction, and compliance. Industry 5.0 will combine critical human intelligence thinking with industrial automation's accuracy and speed. It includes long-lasting policies that make even a little amount of waste production significant, cross-cutting practices, and increases the organization's efficiency and environmental friendliness.

## ADVANCEMENTS IN AGRICULTURE AND FOOD INDUSTRY

One of life's fundamental needs is food. Around the world, 60% of the population relies on agriculture to meet their food needs. Managing the food needs of the world's population, which is expanding quickly, is becoming increasingly challenging. Because conventional farming is still prioritized by the majority of farmers today. Traditional agricultural procedures prevent neither the output of agricultural goods nor their quality from being improved. In a similar vein, traditional agricultural practices are to blame for the growing food scarcity as well as the farmer's financial situation. These days, technology is developing more quickly than ever. Increasing the adoption of modern technologies may improve both the output capacity and the quality of the products. As a consequence, in addition to ensuring the quality of food grains, farmers' economic prosperity may also be ensured. Additionally, it is possible to guarantee that food is available for everyone (Pattnaik et al., 2020).

## Agribots

The need for IoT-controlled agribots is significant in the agricultural sector. With the use of sensor and artificial intelligence technology, they received training on their surroundings. Agribots don't just save labor costs; they also boost yield outputs and cut down on waste. The weeding robots are highly useful for quickly and efficiently removing weeds from crops after they have been identified using image processing techniques. As is well known, overuse of pesticides causes productive fields to become wastelands and lowers the quality of the goods produced, both of which have a negative impact on human health. In this case, using agribots to remove weeds not only preserves the health of the soil and crops but also helps farmers save money. IoT-controlled agribots may automatically harvest crops (picking vegetables, fruits, etc.) with the use of image processing and machine learning techniques. Tools for image processing and machine learning not only assist in fruit harvesting, but also in differentiating between ripe and unripe fruits. In addition to assisting in harvesting, plowing, and the replacement of human labor, argibots also assist in the transportation of bulky items, the measurement of plant spacing with high precision, and so on. IoT can also operate drones that can spray toxic canes while being fitted with cameras and sensors (Satapathy et al., 2022).

## Remote Sensing

Remote sensing is another IoT-controlled technology that is extremely beneficial and transformative for farmers. Sensors (such as moisture sensors, heat sensors, health monitoring devices, pest sensors, etc.) can be installed in various fields for various purposes. Data collected by the sensors is stored on cloud-based storage, and big-data and machine learning tools are used to analyze this large volume of diverse data to produce useful insights. The farmer may therefore monitor the crop at various stages and take necessary measures. In agriculture, remote sensing is primarily used to monitor crop, weather, soil quality, irrigation, and harvesting (Abraham et al., 2021).

## Smart Agriculture

The usage of IoT technology in agriculture is sometimes referred to as "smart agriculture." IoT solutions are increasingly being adopted in agriculture, despite the fact that they are still not as common as consumer linked devices. IoT is a logical network of applications and physical devices, as is well known. IoT is used in agriculture through sensors, imaging equipment, robotics, and data analysis technologies including big data, machine learning, drones, GPS, and so on. Farmers must first invest in infrastructure and equipment, including sensors, robots, drones, highly skilled labor, energy, Internet access, equipment installation and maintenance costs, and an effective supply chain.

## Crop Management

One use of IoT in farming is crop management. Sensor-equipped stations are positioned in the field to gather information unique to crops, including information on plant water potential, temperature, humidity, and precipitation. To successfully stop any illnesses or pests, crop growth and any abnormalities may be monitored.

## Cattle Monitoring

One more use is attaching sensors to agricultural animals to track their performance and health is the management and monitoring of cattle. For instance, one device on the market today for farming employs smart collar tags that can transmit information on the livestock as a whole as well as information on the nutrition, activity, health, and temperature of each individual livestock.

## Farm Production Management System

A more sophisticated use of IoT-based agriculture may be shown using the farm production management system, which includes several sensors and communication units installed on field premises along with a UI that includes analytical skills. These solutions enable the user to simplify the farm's commercial operations and monitor it remotely. The automation of greenhouses, truck tracking, and storage management are further IoT-driven agriculture use cases.

Additionally, it is believed that IoT would benefit the environment. There are already devices on the market that provide insights and encourage resource conservation, as well as sensors that monitor radiation, the quality of the air and water, or that look for dangerous compounds. However, there are also more creative applications for IoT, such as the suppression of deforestation and poaching and protecting biodiversity. For instance, 15% of the world's carbon emissions come from deforestation. Some groups have started IoT programs to combat additional deforestation by monitoring and detecting illicit logging and poaching operations remotely by attaching smart sensors to trees.

## REVOLUTIONARY HEALTHCARE TECHNOLOGIES

Healthcare will be guided toward a whole new generation of effective services by IoT services and devices, saving lives and time in the process. Wireless gadgets are a result of ongoing development in the field of remote healthcare. Presently, simulated emergency rooms of the future can be used to get a complete picture of the patient's entire health. IoT technology makes communication easier and may notify medical staff based on a patient's vital signs. It changes the healthcare sector to provide systems that are more effective, affordable, and provide better patient care.

The current age is also characterized by significant advancements in healthcare technology, which have given rise to the big data era. Big data is distinguished by its quantity, diversity, speed, and authenticity. In order to create the next generation of smarter linked products and gadgets, researchers and engineers are focusing on "IoT" and "big data" (Bhatt et al., 2017). Embedded medical devices are also becoming more common, making information available anywhere in the world. Healthcare companies construct a powerful future with the possibilities of continuous engineering. They have close ties to vast Internet-connected objects and machines that produce enormous volumes of data. The main goal shared by all hospitals, clinics, and health institutions in the globe is superior healthcare outcomes.

IoT and healthcare work together to advance medical technology and expand access to healthcare services while lowering costs and increasing accuracy. Healthcare stakeholders have lately concentrated on "big data analysis" to support the healthcare sector rather than only digitizing medical records and developing automated medical systems. By providing healthcare practitioners with the resources they need to provide better treatment, "big data" has the potential to assist healthcare organizations. IoT healthcare devices collect medical data as signals or pictures. For an appropriate diagnosis, the IoT's large data must be analyzed. This gives healthcare institutions the precise data they need to manage population health in an efficient manner. Intelligent systems can gather real-time data at a previously unheard-of degree. Big data, meanwhile, utilizes open-source technology with erratic security protocols. Organizations in the healthcare sector must thus offer exceptional big data security.

Healthcare-related problems can be handled by techniques like BDA, HA, and machine learning techniques (MLT), which also offer solutions for the best possible decision-making (Almagrabi et al., 2022). Several concerns pertaining to the healthcare sector include lowering costs, being aware of cutting-edge technology, and so on.

## SMART WEARABLES EVERYWHERE

The IoT and wearables' capacity to exchange, process, and disseminate information is what drives their operational dynamics. These gadgets include a variety of electrical parts, sensors, actuators, computer technologies, as well as protocols for communication and information.

### E-Textiles

As the IoT develops and more things are connected to one another and the cloud, electronic textiles (e-textile) are set to play a significant role. Our world and everyday lives have been changed by the technical breakthroughs of these gadgets, and in the near future, usage is projected to increase significantly. Our everyday lives have transformed as a result of computers and smartphones' ability to transmit vast amounts of data that keep us connected to our environment. These electronic gadgets have evolved and now take on several forms, but they all have the qualities of portability, intelligent data collection, and a near proximity to the human body. These core requirements have stimulated technical advancement, most notably in the areas of mechanical compatibility, integrating electronics, and communication capability, all of which are currently being applied to the idea of wearable electronics. Due to the growth of IoT and wearable electronics, electronic textiles have been taken into consideration. E-textiles are thought of as a means to add features to common wearable textiles and provide competitive advantages in the market since they can carry out electronic operations (Mokhtari, 2022; Raad, 2020).

The advancements in CI, big data, and IoT combined together with wearable technologies has a wide range of applications in various sectors including healthcare, sports, entertainment, gaming, smart grids, pets, military, travel, fashion, education, aerospace, and many more.

## Healthcare

There are several additional cutting-edge applications for IoT devices in hospitals beyond tracking patients' health. IoT devices are utilized for asset management, such as pharmacy inventory control, as well as tracking the whereabouts of medical devices including "oxygen pumps," "wheelchairs," "defibrillators," and also other monitoring equipment in real time. Real-time monitoring and coordination of the deployment of medical personnel at several sites is also possible. Additionally employed to assist in reducing infections in patients is IoT-driven hygiene monitoring technology.

## Fitness

The market for fitness trackers that offer a variety of sensors and wireless capabilities is expanding quickly. Just a few of the brands on the market now include Fitbit, Apple, Samsung, Jawbone, and Garmin. These trackers record data relating to health and fitness, including heart rate, steps taken or stairs climbed, sleep habits, and stress levels. Nowadays, the majority of trackers can also pinpoint the user's position. The visibility that IoT technology provides is one of the key reasons it has had such an influence on the fitness sector. No matter what the user's workout objectives are, their main goal is to become better and be able to measure that development. IoT gives customers an unmatched level of visibility to monitor their personal development through visualization, analysis, and continuous data gathering.

## Sports

Today, IoT and wearable technology are essential to the growth and safety of athletes as well as the involvement and enjoyment of fans in sports. Organizations are spending billions to build stadiums that are smart and employ IoT in order to enhance fan experiences inside the venue. Fans may interact fully with their preferred teams and sportsmen like never before. IoT is revolutionizing how coaches manage players, coordinate practice sessions, and handle crucial events throughout every game in the field of player development. By fusing modern game analytics with sensors, coaches may easily access vast amounts of information to learn about player performance measures and efficiency as well as opposite team's vulnerabilities to create a more educated in-game plan.

## Entertainment and Gaming

The ways in which we enjoy and create video games, music, and movies are being redefined by technologies like "haptics," "augmented reality" (AR), and "virtual reality" (VR). A VR device called the Oculus Rift, for instance, is being utilized to make immersive movies that are unlike anything we have ever seen. Innovative music is currently created using wearable technology that offers haptic feedback and gesture control. Wearable technology is now being used in several theme parks across the world to improve the visitor experience.

## Military and Public Safety

A key element of the linked soldier system that provides increased safety, tracking, and a tactical advantage is wearable technology. In order to improve army mobility and system scalability, the research and development community is putting more work into this area to develop thin, lightweight devices, tiny antennas, and more efficient radio communication systems. These systems use a range of physiological sensors to keep an eye on things like body temperature, blast effects, breathing patterns, and heart rate. The information would be accessible for instant examination or wireless real-time transfer to headquarters.

## Travel and Tourism

The IoT and wearable technologies have received significant investment from the travel and tourism sector. In 2015, the industry invested around $128.9 million in these technologies. By linking smart devices, systems, and processes, IoT is currently being utilized to help streamline back-end processes and boost the efficiency of travel companies, airlines, and hotels. For instance, by using sensor-enabled cargos, airlines and hotels may manage supply chains more efficiently, allowing businesses to plan for unforeseen events and shield travelers from service interruptions. According to several studies, mobile and wearable technology are beginning to show a significant impact in major facets of the tourist and travel industry. Another area that is utilizing wearable technology is the hospitality sector. For instance, a system created by Starwood Hotels lets their favored guests utilize "virtual room keys" rather than actual room keys. It also provides access to the hotel's bookings and star point balances, as well as directions to the property.

## Aerospace

In the past, astronauts used printed instructions as a backup in case of system failure or emergency. Calling the ground station for assistance is a crew duty because of such problems. The further a spacecraft gets from Earth, the more difficult it is to communicate. Both on the ground and in the air, IoT is changing the aerospace sector. IoT-based "real-time analytics" are already driving advances in this industry's production quality and productivity. For instance, power meters enabled by IoT may offer data on electricity use in the manufacture of airplanes, which might result in considerable cost savings and a business that is more environmentally friendly. Advanced analytics algorithms, as per Airbus, monitor energy consumption and recommend energy-saving solutions that might result in a 20% cost reduction. IoT may provide a deeper understanding of how a whole production line is run. In one airplane manufacturing, information from the equipment and handlers is sent into a real-time visual center, allowing managers to monitor operations in real-time and run extremely realistic simulations to find the best methods to improve operations.

## Education

A growing number of instructors are beginning to understand that new digital technology may present a chance to improve learning rather than be a distraction. In reality, several research support the useful potential of IoT and wearable technologies as teaching aids. IoT might also assist schools in enhancing information access, monitoring vital resources, and enhancing campus security. At a lower running cost, linked gadgets may be utilized to monitor equipment, employees and students. Last but not least, assisting students with disabilities in their academics by employing IoT-enabled gadgets is a successful strategy. Using a system of smartphone or a tablet and smart gloves, students with hearing loss may go from signing to verbal speaking and conversely.

## Fashion

When we talk about wearable gadgetry today, the initial thought that springs to mind are the unattractive fitness monitoring devices and smart wristbands, which, in the eyes of the critics of fashion, have yet to develop "style." As wearable gadgetry advances in popularity, developers are realizing the need of working with fashion designers to produce cutting-edge goods that consumers will really want to purchase.

## Industry

It's anticipated that the market for wearable technology products in industrial settings would grow faster than the market for smart homes in general. Due to the use of camera-based headsets by engineers and technicians when working in the industry, service businesses have already observed the repercussions of wearable computing in action. For instance, Vuzix manufactures a selection of accessories, including glasses and headsets, that offer cutting-edge choices for "WMS" (warehouse management systems). In contrast, Fujitsu is focusing on a smart glove solution designed for industrial maintenance and on-site operations. The glove has a gesture-driven input controller and an integrated "Near Field Communication" (NFC) tag reader. The industrial IoT, often known as IIoT, is a rapidly spreading use of the IoT that is transforming industrial and manufacturing processes by providing faster and more effective data collecting and accessibility. IIoT is achieving significant results in a variety of ways, including by allowing analytics to detect erosive processes inside refinery pipelines, supplying real growth information to locate underused plant capacity, enhancing safety, predicting maintenance, or hastening the advancement of new products by feeding operational data back in the cycle of product design. The IIoT aspires to connect people, management, sophisticated analytics, and machines. It primarily consists of a network of manufacturing facilities linked by communications technologies, producing innovative systems that can monitor, acquire, analyze, and give priceless insights that may aid in guiding wiser and quicker business choices.

## Home Automation and Smart Living

To increase convenience, comfort, and energy economy, home automation might consist of centralized control of appliances, security systems, systems for cooling air, lighting, and other equipment. Home automation has been a notion for many years, and consumers have had access to items for a long time. The earliest iteration of "smart houses" may have had less to do with intelligence and much to do with remote control, frequently via a computer or smartphone, and only a little amount of automation. However, many contemporary homes now include blinds that can change their angle to maintain a specific level of light or thermostats that can learn how to set the proper temperature by studying a user's behaviors and analyzing their usage patterns. The consumers may then micro-personalize their experience with the aid of these insights. This house is undoubtedly "smart." The smart home IoT tool and service industry is huge and quite varied. Some producers concentrate on particular aspects of the indoor environment, such as temperature control and lighting. Others create whole smart home hubs that can link to and converse with a wide range of smart electronics, such the Google Home or Amazon Echo virtual assistants. IoT powered smart home systems provide users visibility into their household, which optimizes utility consumption. Users may quickly discover the energy-wasting areas and behaviors and alter use by using insights obtained from smart home devices on power, gas, and water consumption.

Wearable technologies and IoT are suited for fresh and inventive applications to supplement the ones now in use. They offer an almost limitless number of possibilities for connecting our machinery. This area is open for innovation, and increased connectivity will significantly alter the course of human history in ways we can hardly foresee.

## INNOVATIONS IN ENERGY SECTOR

To decrease the amount of energy used by businesses, transportation, communication networks, and buildings, effective energy management systems must be developed. Since the amount of energy preserved may be equal to the amount of energy generated, energy conservation is just as important as energy production. In situations like consumer and industrial environments, it is vital to preserve energy as much as feasible (El Himer et al., 2022).

In the past 10 years, the green energy industry has advanced significantly because of technological developments. However, there are still a few problems in this field that developing technology can help solve. Machine learning (ML) and AI are examples of technologies that can study history, improve the current timeline, and forecast the upcoming timeline. The majority of the problems affecting green energy and the renewable energy industries could be solved by AI.

Modern green energy management systems should make use of recent technology like IoT and AI to be able to provide cheaper, effective, and smart solutions. IoT enables the system to function with greater flexibility and be wireless, while AI helps the system optimize electricity use, making it more energy-efficient.

Smart energy uses AI innovations such artificial neural networks, fuzzy logic, genetic algorithms, and hybrid systems that combine some of the aforementioned. Some of the application choices include industrial automation, life safety, security, equipment monitoring, fire management, and energy management.

## Smart Grids

One of the best IoT uses in the energy sector, the smart grid, has the potential to significantly aid in the conservation of energy resources (Swathika et al., 2022). The U.S. Department of Energy (DoE) estimates that the present power disruptions and outages result in the United States' citizens spending $150 billion or more annually. The traditional grids won't be able to meet the growing demand as long as earth's population proceeds to increase. By using IoT-driven source rerouting and monitoring when an electrical outage is found, smart grids are intended to save expenses. The IoT architecture, which includes the smart grid, may be used to keep tabs on and control anything from lights, parking spots, traffic signals, and early power influx detection brought on by severe weather or seismic activity. A combination of sensors, substations, smart meters, sensors, transmission lines, and data analytics makes this possible. Technical advancements for the "smart grid" play a key role in creating smart cities and effective energy management strategies. Smart grids outperform the current system due to communication that is two-way between linked devices and systems that can detect and dynamically adapt to user requests. To assist customers in tracking their usage patterns, "smart energy analytics" can collect information on temperature, pressure, water flow, power loads, and other characteristics.

## Smart Buildings

A smart building is a cutting-edge structure with features that enable people to make knowledgeable judgments about the structures based on data from smart meters and IoT sensors (Kolhe et al., 2022). In a web-based system, IoT and big data analytics are combined with IoT and digital sensors to allow for real-time monitoring, control, and action on the building. In relation to smart buildings, many uses of ML and AI) are considered. A smart building can be created as a programmable system that is interconnected and naturally intelligent. The following are included under the umbrella phrase "electric utilities" for a building: movement-sensitive CCTV, cooling components, alarms, the fire detector, irrigation and watering systems, water/electricity measures, monitoring of the elevator, and used systems at the building entry. Traditional systems were created based on the independent performance of these components, and each component has a monitoring indication that satisfies the intended strategies, such as a control diagram, equipment, executive maps, and diagnostic procedures. The goal of designing a smart building is to use an integrated intelligent system as a management core to control and monitor all aforementioned independent elements as a whole and to secure interactions and communication among all these parts.

## CONCLUSION

We can conclude by saying that while doing statistical computation (data analytics) in the fields of healthcare, social media research, industry, business, and pattern identification, recent technical advancements in CI have shown highly positive results which led to many applications. CI contributes majorly to the vast sectors. The advancements in big data analytics contribute in many applications which include crucial sectors for the welfare of human beings such as agriculture, food, and healthcare. Also, IoT is everywhere these days and its applications are very massive from tiny sensors to large smart cities. The recent advancements in these technologies majorly contribute in almost every major sector and have numerous applications.

## REFERENCES

Abraham, A., Dash, S., Rodrigues, J. J., Acharya, B., & Pani, S. K. (Eds.). (2021). *AI, edge and IoT-based smart agriculture.* Academic Press.

Almagrabi, A. O., Ali, R., Alghazzawi, D., AlBarakati, A., & Khurshaid, T. (2022). A reinforcement learning-based framework for crowdsourcing in massive health care Internet of things. *Big Data, 10*(2), 161–170. https://doi.org/10.1089/big.2021.0058

Azrour, M., Irshad, A., & Chaganti, R. (2022). *IoT and smart devices for sustainable environment.* Springer.

Bhatt, C., Dey, N., & Ashour, A. S. (Eds.). (2017). *Internet of things and big data technologies for next generation healthcare.* Springer.

Chaudhary, K., & Alam, M. (2022). *Big data analytics: Applications in business and marketing.* CRC Press.

El Himer, S., Ouaissa, M., Emhemed, A. A., Ouaissa, M., & Boulouard, Z. (2022). *Artificial intelligence of things for smart green energy management.* Springer.

Elangovan, U. (2022). *Industry 5.0: The future of the industrial economy.* CRC Press.

Kolhe, M. L., Karande, K. J., & Deshmukh, S. G. (Eds.). (2022). *Artificial intelligence, Internet of things (IoT) and smart materials for energy applications.* CRC Press.

Mokhtari, F. (2022). *Self-powered smart fabrics for wearable technologies.* Springer.

Pattnaik, P. K., Kumar, R., & Pal, S. (Eds.). (2020). *Internet of things and analytics for agriculture* (Vol. 2). Springer.

Prabha, C., Singh, J., Agarwal, S., Verma, A., & Sharma, N. (2023). Introduction to computational intelligence in healthcare: Applications, challenges, and management. In M. Gupta, S. Ahmed, R. Kumar, & C. Altrjman (Eds.), *Computational intelligence in healthcare* (pp. 1–16). CRC Press.

Raad, H. (2020). *Fundamentals of IoT and wearable technology design.* IEEE Press. Wiley.

Sadiku, M. N., & Musa, S. M. (2021). *A primer on multiple intelligences.* Springer.

Satapathy, S., Mishra, D., & Vargas, A. R. (2022). *Innovation in agriculture with IoT and AI.* Springer.

Sujith, A.V. L. N., Sajja, G. S., Mahalakshmi, V., Nuhmani, S., & Prasanalakshmi, B. (2022). Systematic review of smart health monitoring using deep learning and artificial intelligence. *Neuroscience Informatics, 2*(3), 100028. https://doi.org/10.1016/j.neuri.2021.100028

Swathika, O. G., Karthikeyan, K., & Padmanaban, S. (Eds.). (2022). *Smart buildings digitalization* (Vol. 1–2). CRC Press.

# CHAPTER 3

# TRENDS AND FUTURE RESEARCH DIRECTIONS OF INNOVATIONS IN COMPUTATIONAL INTELLIGENCE, BIG DATA ANALYTICS, AND INTERNET OF THINGS

**B. Narendra Kumar Rao**
*Mohan Babu University*

**Dudi Sai Hima Sri**
*Sree Vidyanikethan Engineering College*

**Sam Goundar**
*RMIT University*

**Gundampati Sudheer Kumar**
*Sree Vidyanikethan Engineering College*

**Gopireddy Karthik Kumar Reddy**
*Sree Vidyanikethan Engineering College*

**Gundarapu Vikas**
*Sree Vidyanikethan Engineering College*

*Innovations in Computational Intelligence, Big Data Analytics, and Internet of Things*, pages 31–45
Copyright © 2024 by Information Age Publishing
www.infoagepub.com

## ABSTRACT

As the number of devices linked to the Internet rises, terabytes of data are produced daily by contemporary information systems, cloud, and digital technologies. However, the examination of these enormous data takes extensive work at several levels in order to extract knowledge and make decisions. Consequently, big data analytics is a current research and development topic that is becoming significant.

This chapter examines cutting-edge research projects analyzing data from the Internet of things, big data analytics, and innovations in computational intelligence. This article's main goal is to examine the potential effects of big data difficulties, research activities focused on IoT data analysis, and various technologies related to such analysis. In order to examine big data in various stages and better comprehend the knowledge we may derive from the data, this article presents trends and future research areas of innovations. This opens a new prospect for researchers to create solutions based on open source research challenges and subjects. Internet of things, cyber security, data loss, prevention, connectivity, cyber threat, and cyber actor are some related terms.

## BIG DATA ANALYTICS

Data is now available in a wide range of formats, including sensor data, which is an output from a device that can detect changes in the real-time environment, semi-structured data, which is in the form of structured data but shun conforms to the structure of data models as seen in RDBMS, and unstructured data and lacks uniform structure. Structured data is organized for a high degree of organization. Semi-structured data is also a form of structured data. However, as digitalization spreads, more data are being produced every day, increasing the difficulty of managing and analyzing the data. The management of such data primarily consists of three tasks (Al-Fuqaha et al., 2015, Lundberg et al., 2021, Roh et al., 2019):

1. Data acquisition: This process entails gathering data from numerous sources by specifying data types, sources, templates, setups, and so forth. Texts, documents, tables (from relational databases), audio, images, and video are all examples of sources.
2. Data preparation: This process involves storing, cleaning, enhancing, and validating data with a focus on guaranteeing accountability and dependability.
3. Data distribution: This covers both the sharing and protection of data, as well as the maintenance of data security and privacy (Vassakis et al., 2018).

Big data is a developing field that has drawn the interest of many academics and professionals from the fields of agriculture, finance, business, health-care, and cybernetics.

## Big Data–10 Vs

1. *Variety:* Various types of structured data, such as names, phone numbers, and addresses; unstructured data, such as tweets, videos, and images; and semi-structured data, such as HTML documents.
2. *Velocity:* Rapid generation, transmission, collection, and analysis of huge amounts of information.
3. *Volume:* Huge quantities of data are produced every second from a variety of sources, including social media, credit cards, internet transactions, sensors, movies, and images.
4. *Veracity:* This describes how trustworthy data is, that is, how exact, precise, and reliable the data is.
5. *Value:* It primarily denotes the value of the data in terms of the expenses and advantages of gathering and analyzing a specific set of data.
6. *Variability:* The variability of multitude data is due to the disparate multiple sources and data types. Variability is referred to as the inconsistent speed of loading a big data into the database.
7. *Vulnerability:* Protect users from vulnerabilities and protect data access.
8. *Volatility:* How long is the historic data to be retained?
9. *Visualization:* There are different ways to visualize the data such as data clustering, circular network diagrams, and parallel coordinates.
10. *Value:* Acquaintance with customers and targeting them to improve business and machine processes (Ahirwal et al., 2022; De et al., 2022, Zahid et al., 2020).

## TRENDS IN BIG DATA ANALYTICS

### Explore and Interpret Data

In the past, visualization has been used to convey information between machines and people. This visualization typically takes the pictorial representation of graphs and charts in dashboards that represents the important findings and guide our understanding of what the data indicates needs to be done.

The problem was that not everyone is able to spot potentially significant information hidden in a sea of reading. New methods for communicating these insights are constantly emerging as it becomes more important for organizations to act on data-driven insights.

Human language use is one area where significant progress has been made. The availability of information is significantly increased and the amount of information in the organization is significantly improved with the help of analytical tools. The technology used in this field is called natural language processing (Elngar et al., 2022).

Modern technology allows us to immerse ourselves in information to better understand it and gain a better visual perspective. Innovation in this field is undoubtedly driven by augmented reality (AR). While AR can immediately show that the outcome of data analysis affects the world in real time, virtual reality (VR) can be used to develop recent types of visualization techniques that give more meaning to the data. For example, to diagnose a car problem, a mechanic can look at the engine while wearing AR glasses and get predictions about which parts are likely to be troublesome and potentially replaceable. In the near future, we can foresee new data visualization or communication techniques that increase the availability of insights through analysis.

## Hybrid Cloud and the Edge

Cloud computing is a technological development that has had a major impact on big data analysis (Kannan et al., 2022). The capacity to retrieve massive information is fueled by the explosion of businesses and apps on real time data. It is not the feasible strategy to rely on public cloud providers. The security issues are unavoidable when the entire data operations are entrusted to outside parties.

Many businesses nowadays are turning their businesses to hybrid cloud-based architectures, in which some of the data is stored in the form of AWS, Azure, or Google Cloud servers whereas additional, possibly private or sensitive data, resides inside the company's proprietary network storage. Cloud service providers are taking up this development and providing "cloud on premises" solutions which may offer the entire robustness and high-end characteristics of public clouds while data owners are still having full control over their data.

Another significant trend that will have an impact on how big data and analytics are used in our daily lives during the coming year is edge computing. In essence, this refers to hardware that is designed to process data locally rather than transferring it to the cloud for archival analysis. Some part of data requires to be used fast to run the risk of sending it back and forth. The information collected from the sensors on autonomous vehicles is a good example of this. In other cases, when references can be gathered from the devices without having them to send data to others, consumers can be comforted that they have extra privacy. For instance, the "now playing" feature on Android smart phones constantly searches the environment for various activities in order to provide us with the song names playing in the store or movies being watched. With a solely cloud-based approach, this would not be feasible because consumers would object to feeding Google a continuous 24/7 stream of their auditory surroundings (Mishra et al., 2022).

## The Rise of DataOps

A methodology and approach called DataOps draws on the DevOps framework, which is frequently used in the software development industry. DataOps is focused with the end-to-end data flow in business, whereas DevOps positions are concerned with managing continuous technical processes surrounding service delivery. In particular, this entails the removal of barriers that restrict the applicability or availability of data and the implementation of data tools provided "as a service" by third parties.

Working with DataOps requires no formal training. Due to the role's development, it has become a fantastic chance for anyone with IT knowledge or is interested to put effort in innovative and interesting projects. Companies that offer end-to-end administration of data processes and pay as you go, or "DataOps as a service," will grow in popularity (Qazi et al., 2022). The entrance hurdles for small and startup businesses will continue to be reduced as a result. These companies frequently come up with innovative concepts for the newest data driven services, but they might not have access to the infrastructure required to turn those ideas into reality.

### Responsible and Smarter Artificial Intelligence

Smarter artificial intelligence (AI) will result in evolving of new algorithms which are capable of learning with short-time-to-market. Process formulation will be possible through such AI systems (Alrafiah, 2022; Dhombres et al., 2022).

### Dark Data and Data Fabrics

Dark data in a company is the one that is not used in any analytical system. This is collected from network operations that are not directly used to find insights in business. As the size of this data grows, the industry should understand the security risk from unexplored data.

Data fabric includes data storage in the cloud and its environments. It provides the access and data sharing options in a distributed environment. It also offers a consistent data management framework.

## FUTURE TRENDS OF BIG DATA ANALYTICS

### The Increasing Velocity of Big Data Analytics

The weekly or monthly data export followed by analysis are long gone. Later on big data analytics will have a more effect on the current data with the focus on real-time analysis, enabling effective decisions and conclusions.

Gaining real time processes data in streams rather than batches, but performing so has ramifications for preserving data quality because acting on more recent data can increase the risk of missing data.

### Real-Time Data/Insights

Some people might think that having access to real-time data for analysis is excessive. Posting your tweets based on what was popular a month ago or trading Bitcoin based on its value last week sectors like finance and social media have already been transformed by real-time knowledge, but its ramifications go far beyond these (De Alwis et al., 2022; Reshma et al., 2022).

### Real-Time, Automated Decision-Making

AI and machine learning (ML) are profitably used in the manufacturing and health care related sectors where system intelligence monitors component damages. Whenever a part is about to fail, the assembly line may be automatically switched to another location.

That's just one use case, but there are a ton more. For instance, email marketing software that can identify the A/B test winner and apply it to other emails. Organizations can continue to require manual approval as a final step if they don't feel comfortable fully automating decisions yet.

### The Heightened Veracity of Big Data Analytics

It becomes more challenging to ensure data's accuracy and quality as we collect more of it. For additional details on this, see our latest post on the data management future.

### Democratization and Decentralization of Data

Business analysts, executives have long had to rely on their own data scientists to collect and interpret data. In 2022, things will be radically different, thanks to tools and services that let non-technical audiences interact with data.

Tools like dbt which focuses on "data modeling is a way to empower the end users to answer their own queries," analytics engineering is becoming more and more important. In other words, empowering stakeholders rather than doing their analysis or projection modeling.

A more visual approach is also frequently discussed; on their websites, contemporary business intelligence (BI) tools like Tableau, dashboards. The democratization of data movement is well and fully underway.

## INTERNET OF THINGS

IoT offers a framework for seamless communication between sensors and devices in an intelligent environment and makes it possible to share data between platforms in a practical way. IoT is now the next revolutionary technology to capitalize on all the prospects provided by Internet technologies as an outcome of the recent adoption of various wireless technologies.

## TRENDS IN INTERNET OF THINGS

### Smart Homes

Quality of life of users has been directly affected by smart homes. One of the most popular and desired applications of IoT is smart homes. The scope of IoT appliances in smart home peripherals has expanded beyond automation devices to now store and use data to individually customize technology for users. Based on a variety of sensors, gadgets, and appliances at its disposal, IoT movement not only makes life easier but also more productive and successful. Appliances which are IoT driven use sophisticated algorithms to comprehend user characteristics before using those insights to tailor the appliances' outputs. This has enormous stability to expand future development.

### Security

The threats related to IoT devices grow as they proliferate. Since the majority of these devices communicate with one another, they frequently transmit far more data and information than we are able to process. Therefore, lapses in its work processes can be all that hackers need to cause havoc. As the physical and digital are two different worlds converging in IoT, adequate care and money must be invested in ensuring their security. IoT security technologies can assist in preventing security breaches and dangers as well as repairing network flaws. This IoT movement is not just a need, but rather a necessity given that the majority of transactions now take place online. Therefore, it is imperative that block chain-like technologies be developed and used to secure IoT networks in banks, financial institutions, corporations, and so on.

## Healthcare

IoT has assisted hospitals in streamlining operational procedures and increasing patient outcomes by organizing the effective allocation of their resources through the integration of infrastructure and cutting-edge technologies (Arunachalam et al., 2023). Aside from its indisputable contribution to the creation of tools for the treatment and care of patients, technology has been assisting many doctors in managing the time and effort in an optimal way. To give patients a more individualized experience, most hospitals now use chatbots.

However, the majority of these figures relate to cloud transitions in the back-office and financial sectors. These numbers are also expected to rise due to the recent post-pandemic international demand for greater healthcare infrastructure and expertise.

## Industrial IoT

The maintenance and control of the manufacturing lines were one of the major difficulties for enterprises throughout the COVID-19 pandemic. Other factors that demanded ongoing attention from manufacturers across industries included changing competition and client demands. They have benefited from effective resilience and agility in business processes thanks to IoT technology, particularly the cloud solutions for industrial manufacturing.

According to a Statista estimate, the global Industrial Internet of things (IIoT) market size in 2024 is expected to surpass $100 billion. Supply chain management and other IoT trends, along with smart factory solutions, ensure that production units operate lean and meanly, generating maximum profits with the least amount of risk.

## Edge Computing

Data is growing at an unfathomable rate. With each passing day, businesses are seeing the value of its storage and agile analysis. As a result, they prefer a local storage location to a cloud server operated by a third party. Edge computing is the term for this. This new IoT trend aids in reducing potential bandwidth and data bottlenecks, enabling quicker information retrieval. Faster analysis and data transfer makes IoT smarter.

## Governance and Regulation

The EU is anticipated to draft a bill mandating smart device operators and manufacturers to adhere to stricter guidelines about how data can be collected, maintained, and what needs to be done to defend against breaches. Additionally, it is anticipated that EU law would address issues related to edge computing, which makes use of hardware intended to process data right where it is being collected rather than transmitting it back to centralized cloud servers for analysis. Asia's 3-year plan to put policies in place to support the widespread use of IoT technology will be completed in 2023, according to the Chinese government. Like everywhere else in the globe, the IoT is considered as having the ability to propel rapid corporate growth in China. However, it is recognized that this expansion must be regulated to prevent potential conflicts with personal rights and privacy concerns.

The global edge computing market can be anticipated to reach $250.6 billion dollars by 2024, according to Statista.

## IoT Technology: A More Connected World

Production is made simpler when machines get smaller. A recent movement in technology philosophy has seen industry abandon the monolithic, single-device paradigm in favor of a more modular, microservices-based strategy. A network of devices can handle all calculations and measurements in place of a single device. Additionally, each device might have a unique utility that helps the network as a whole. The foundation of IoT technology is this.

## Artificial Intelligence and IoT Technology

One of the most captivating uses of IoT technology is the ability to support AI software. AI and IoT complement each other well. AI benefits from distributed data from IoT and advanced management from IoT.

## IoT Connectivity—5G, WiFi 6, LPWAN, and Satellites

In recent years the key obstacle is the wireless data rates to IoT. Components of IoT such as sensors, edge computing, and smart homes will improve as the technologies improve (Mohan et al., 2021). Newer connectivity are methods of connectivity, such as satellites, WiFi 6, and 5G.

## Edge Computing—Low Latency and Security

Edge computing is necessary for real-time applications. Edge networks process information which is close to the user and lessen the strain on the entire network for all users as opposed to processing everything at a central location. Edge computing is advantageous in any situation where quick decisions are required. This is relevant in situations requiring safety and security in particular. By automatically shutting down machinery when someone enters a restricted area of a factory, IoT edge computing will be used to protect the people from danger.

## Wearable IoT Technology

Although many IoT technology solutions depend on sensors and edge devices, wearable IoT devices shouldn't be disregarded. Wearable IoT devices including smart watches, headphones, and headsets for AR and VR will continue to advance in 2022.

## Smart Homes

The growth of digital assistants like Apple's Siri, Google Assistant, and Amazon Echo has changed the smart home market. In 2022, at home IoT technologies appear to have reached appliances, lighting, and security systems. In spite of this, there is still a ton of space for growth, which we shall see all over the upcoming years. A smart phone app that lets users monitor the security of their home network and the security of IoT smart home devices was created by MobiDev and CUJO AI.

## COMPUTATIONAL INTELLIGENCE

The theory, design, implementation, and advancement of computing paradigms driven by biological and linguistic motivations is known as computational intelligence (CI). Evolutionary computation, fuzzy systems, and neural networks have historically been the three main foundations of CI. However, over time, various computing models that were inspired by nature have emerged. Since CI is a young area, it already encompasses a variety of computer paradigms in addition to the three core ones, such as ambient intelligence, artificial life, cultural learning, artificial endocrine networks, social reasoning, and artificial hormone networks.

Soft computing and AI approaches and techniques for imagining the essence of intelligence inherent in the real-world, CI is an area that has expanded rapidly during the past 5 years. Because of the inherent uncertainty, redundancy, and imprecision in real-world processes and practices, which was previously unreachable, is embedded in the systems under evaluation thanks to the development of the discipline of computational intelligence.

With advances in signal processing, smart manufacturing, predictive control, robot navigation, smart cities, and sensor design, to mention a few, CI is no longer just confined to certain computational domains. The implementation of this computational paradigm in a variety of applied disciplines that deal with meaningful information is explored in recent developments in CI (Kuraparthi et al., 2021; Reddy et al., 2022).

## RECENT TRENDS IN COMPUTATIONAL INTELLIGENCE

### Fuzzy Logic

As previously stated, measurements and process modeling designed for the complicated processes found in real life, make up fuzzy logic, one of the key ideas, which requires precise information, it can deal with incompleteness and, significantly, ignorance of facts in a process model.

This method frequently works in a variety of areas, including control and decision-making. However, it is extensively used in the home appliances sector, including cleaning machines and microwaves. We experience it while using a video camera, when it aids in image stabilization when holding the camera erratically. Aside from the many uses of this idea, other fields include business strategy selection, foreign currency trading, and medical diagnostics.

Fuzzy logic lacks learning abilities, a skill that humans are highly valued for having and is only good for approximative thinking. They are able to become better versions of themselves by reflecting on their past errors.

### Neural Networks

Artificial neural networks has been developed based on biological data is what CI experts are working on because biological neural networks can be broken down into three main parts: the cell body, which is an information processor; the axon, that allows the signal transmission; and the synapse regulates signals. As a result, distributed information processing systems are dotted with artificial neural networks, facilitating experimental data by learning and processing (Charan et al., 2023). One of the key advantages of this principle is that it functions like human beings and is fault tolerant.

Because biological neural networks can be divided into mainly three components they are the cell body which is used to process the information; the next component is the axon which is a device that allows the signal transmissions in the body; and the last component is the synapse which regulates the signals in the human body. CI experts are working on the expansion of artificial neural networks (ANNs) which are based on natural ones. ANNs are therefore scattered throughout dispersed processing the systems information, enhancing learning and procedure of the experimental data. The principal's ability to function like a human and be error tolerant is one of its main benefits.

## Evolutionary Computation

The evolutionary computation, which is based on Charles Robert Darwin's initial introduction of the process of natural selection, involves using the power of natural evolution to develop new artificial evolutionary paradigms. The principal applications of this theory are in optimization and multi-objective optimization which are no longer sufficient to solve a variety of issues like DNA analysis and scheduling issues.

## Learning Theory

Learning theory is one of the key CI techniques as it continues to search for a method of "reasoning" similar to that of humans. Learning, according to psychology, is the process of acquiring, enhancing, or altering knowledge, skills, attitudes, and worldviews by combining cognitive, emotional, and environmental consequences and experiences. Understanding theories aids in processing the impacts and experiences, which aids in taking up predictions based on past knowledge.

## Probabilistic Methods

Probabilistic approaches, one of the key components of fuzzy logic that was first developed by Paul Erdos and Joel Spencer in 1974, attempt to assess the outcomes of a computational intelligent system that is primarily characterized by randomness. In light of this, probabilistic approaches highlight the potential answers to an issue.

## LIST OF RECENT TRENDS IN COMPUTATIONAL INTELLIGENCE

- sensor cloud optimization: taxonomy, issues, and survey;
- computational intelligence methods for wireless sensor localization and clustering;
- resource management strategies using computational intelligence in wireless sensor networks;
- MSMOPSO for IoT resource provisioning optimization based on swarm intelligence;
- accessing healthcare data from the IoT via DNA-based authentication;
- cancer diagnostics using CI techniques;
- CI technique-based methods for IoT security and privacy;
- automatic augmentation of coronary arteries using path-based metaheuristics and convolutional gray-level templates;
- theft management of public vehicles through image analysis and a cloud network in smart cities;
- new detection of malignant cells utilizing principal component analysis and image segmentation;
- using soft computing techniques, classifying the operational spectrum for the embedded optical communication system with RAMAN amplifier;
- geopositioning of fog nodes in a cloud network depending on the location of user devices and a framework for game-theoretic applications;
- based on distribution (statistically) of isolated objects, segmenting the retinal blood vessel structure;
- mobile sink in wireless sensor network with energy-efficient rendezvous point routing;
- using handmade features to detect violent events in videos;
- multiclass unbalanced data-based and deep learning-based detection of diabetic retinopathy;
- securing the transmission of homeopathic e-medicines by chaotic key formation is part of the IoT's e-health revolution;
- using the IoT, intelligent irrigation systems based on smart farming and water conservation will be implemented (Sunitha et al., 2023);
- usage in smart enabling technologies for advanced applications;

- using technology in healthcare while maintaining access to individual patient records to improve health and wellbeing; and
- gastric endoscopic biopsies with enhanced alterations in the architecture of the foveolar.

## REFERENCES

Ahirwal, M. K., Londhe, N. D., & Kumar, A. (2022). *Artificial intelligence applications for health care*. CRC Press.

Al-Fuqaha, A., Guizani, M., Mohammadi, M., Aledhari, M., & Ayyash, M. (2015). Internet of things: A survey on enabling technologies, protocols, and applications. *IEEE Communications Surveys & Tutorials, 17*(4), 2347–2376. https://doi.org/10.1109/COMST.2015.2444095

Alrafiah, A. R. (2022). Application and performance of artificial intelligence technology in cytopathology. *Acta Histochemica, 124*(4), 151890. https://doi.org/10.1016/j.acthis.2022.151890

Arunachalam, R., Sunitha, G., Shukla, S. K., Pandey, S. N., Urooj, S., & Rawat, S. (2023). A smart Alzheimer's patient monitoring system with IoT-assisted technology through enhanced deep learning approach. *Knowledge and Information Systems, 65*(12), 5561–5599. https://doi.org/10.1007/s10115-023-01890-x

Charan, N. S., Narasimhulu, T., Bhanu Kiran, G., Sudharshan Reddy, T., Shivangini Singh, T., & Sunitha, G. (2023). Solid waste management using deep learning. In A. Abraham, T. Hanne, N. Gandhi, P. Manghirmalani Mishra, A. Bajaj, & P. Siarry (Eds.), *14th International Conference on Soft Computing and Pattern* (pp. 44–51). Springer. https://doi.org/10.1007/978-3-031-27524-1_5

De, S., Das, R., Bhattacharyya, S., & Maulik, U. (Eds.). (2022). *Applied smart health care informatics: A computational intelligence perspective*. Wiley.

De Alwis, S., Hou, Z., Zhang, Y., Na, M. H., Ofoghi, B., & Sajjanhar, A. (2022). A survey on smart farming data, applications and techniques. *Computers in Industry, 138*, 103624. https://doi.org/10.1016/j.compind.2022.103624

Dhombres, F., Bonnard, J., Bailly, K., Maurice, P., Papageorghiou, A. T., & Jouannic, J. M. (2022). Contributions of artificial intelligence reported in obstetrics and gynecology journals: Systematic review. *Journal of Medical Internet Research, 24*(4), e35465. https://doi.org/10.2196/35465

Elngar, A. A., Chowdhury, R., Elhoseny, M., & Balas, V. E. (2022). *Applications of computational intelligence in multi-disciplinary research*. Academic Press.

Kannan, K. S., Sunitha, G., Deepa, S. N., Babu, D. V., & Avanija, J. (2022). A multi-objective load balancing and power minimization in cloud using bio-inspired algorithms. *Computers and Electrical Engineering, 102*, 108225. https://doi.org/10.1016/j.compeleceng.2022.108225

Kuraparthi, S., Reddy, M. K., Sujatha, C. N., Valiveti, H., Duggineni, C., Kollati, M., Kora, P., & Sravan, V. (2021). Brain tumor classification of MRI images using deep convolutional neural network. *Traitement du Signal, 38*(4). https://doi.org/10.18280/ts.380428

Lundberg, L., Grahn, H., Cardellini, V., Polze, A., & Shirinbab, S. (2021). Editorial to the special issue on big data in industrial and commercial applications. *Big Data Research, 26,* 100244. https://doi.org/10.1016/j.bdr.2021.100244

Mishra, S., Tripathy, H. K., Mallick, P., & Shaalan, K. (2022). *Augmented intelligence in healthcare: A pragmatic and integrated analysis.* Springer.

Mohan, E., Rajesh, A., Sunitha, G., Konduru, R. M., Avanija, J., & Ganesh Babu, L. (2021). A deep neural network learning-based speckle noise removal technique for enhancing the quality of synthetic-aperture radar images. *Concurrency and Computation: Practice and Experience, 33*(13), e6239. https://doi.org/10.1002/cpe.6239

Qazi, W., Sharma, A., & Qazi, S. (2022). Computational intelligent systems in oncology: A way toward translational healthcare. In K. Raza (Ed.), *Computational intelligence in oncology* (pp. 55–). Springer.

Reddy, M. K., Kovuri, K., Avanija, J., Sakthivel, M., & Kaleru, S. (2022, September). Brain stroke prediction using deep learning: A CNN approach. In *2022 4th International Conference on Inventive Research in Computing Applications* (pp. 775–780). IEEE. https://doi.org/10.1109/ICIRCA54612.2022.9985596

Reshma, G., Al-Atroshi, C., Nassa, V. K., Geetha, B., Sunitha, G., Galety, M. G., & Neelakandan, S. (2022). Deep learning-based skin lesion diagnosis model using dermoscopic images. *Intelligent Automation & Soft Computing, 31*(1), 621–634. https://doi.org/10.32604/iasc.2022.019117

Roh, Y., Ho, G., & Whang, S. E. (2019). A survey on data collection for machine learning: A big data-AI integration perspective. *IEEE Transactions on Knowledge and Data Engineering, 33*(4), 1328–1347. https://doi.org/10.1109/TKDE.2019.2946162

Sunitha, G., Sudeepthi, A., Sreedhar, B., Shaik, A. B., & Farooq, C. (2023). Retinanet and vision transformer-based model for wheat head detection. In *5th International Conference on Inventive Research in Computing Applications* (pp. 151–156). IEEE. https://doi.org/10.1109/ICIRCA57980.2023.10220614

Vassakis, K., Petrakis, E., & Kopanakis, I. (2018). Big data analytics: Applications, prospects and challenges. In G. Skourletopoulos, G. Mastorakis, C. Dobre, & E. Pallis (Eds.), *Mobile big data* (pp. 3–20). Springer.

Zahid, H., Mahmood, T., Morshed, A., & Sellis, T. (2020). Big data analytics in telecommunications: Literature review and architecture commendations. *IEEE/CAA Journal Automatica Sinica, 7*(1), 18–38. https://doi.org/10.1109/JAS.2019.1911795

CHAPTER 4

# AN INTELLIGENT FRAMEWORK FOR TRAFFIC CONGESTION ANALYSIS SYSTEM USING DEEP CONVERGENCE NETWORK

**A. Jafflet Trinishia**
*Vellore Institute of Technology*

**S. Asha**
*Vellore Institute of Technology*

**Kanchana Devi V**
*Vellore Institute of Technology*

## ABSTRACT

The evaluation of smart city infrastructure focuses on all areas of development, especially on the intelligent management of transportation. Smart traffic congestion management systems are demandable in the current scenario to provide hassle free instructions and alerts to make the smart move. Cities

*Innovations in Computational Intelligence, Big Data Analytics, and Internet of Things*, pages 47–73
Copyright © 2024 by Information Age Publishing
www.infoagepub.com

are not always overloaded with heavy traffic. Roads are less congested in certain time frames and seem highly congested in the peak timings. Development of smart traffic management systems confines the intelligent management of such time variations. It is required to control the traffic light during the low congestion time, high congestion time, and moderate congestion time. In the case of emergency vehicles passing into the junctions, the traffic lights are required to get the adaptive changes and make the controls appropriately. In similar cases, the location where the usual traffic system is changed into an emergency change needs to be updated to the traffic maintenance control room to alert the upcoming junctions. The planning and execution of dynamic status based congestion update and emergency vehicle passing update is mandatory in smart city executions. In the proposed system, real-time datasets are collected from open source as publicly available websites. The dataset consists of traffic congestion information in the form of recorded values of vehicle count, duration of congestion, location information with time stamps. The raw data is collected from the dataset window and preprocessed. In the preprocessing module, data is down sampled and framed into 1,000 samples of independent packets. The proposed model is initially developed by making the training process with the given dataset. To design the model, the given data is divided into 75% training set and 15% testing set, 10% validation set. Based on the performance measure of the proposed deep convergence network (DCN) in terms of accuracy, precision, recall, and F1 Score, of the trained model, further live data split up into test data is fetched into the system. DCN is considered as the dynamic and robust neural architecture that iteratively repeats the learning process until a very low error rate is obtained. The tested data is further evaluated by making the performance evaluations using the confusion matrix. The confusion plot is formulated with predicted results with the actual results using true positive rate, true negative rate, false positive rate, false negative rate, and so on. In case of higher correlation between the traffic congestion data of testing data with training data, then higher the accuracy will be reflected in the results. Further, the proposed system also included with emergency vehicle alert to the traffic control center. In case of emergency vehicle passed into the real time scenario, then immediate alert of vehicle information, with location data is transmitted into the traffic control room. In such cases, the fore coming junctions get immediate adaptations on traffic lights that will be highly helpful in making the route cleare to the emergency vehicle. The route optimization depends on the pattern analysis done with gradient stochastic optimizer in neural toolbox. The proposed model is developed with MATLAB 2021 Software.

## Need for Traffic Management

Smart traffic control management systems using the Internet of things (IoT) integrated platforms are emerging nowadays in order to provide efficient signal systems and intelligent handling of traffic throughout the city.

The drawback of having the fixed period of signaling system in many cities makes traffic management crucial. Respective of traffic flow on emergency vehicles passing the traffic signal and system follows a fixed flow of instructed work that directly impacts the traffic flow management and control (Kamdar & Shah, 2021). In order to create an effective traffic management system that adopts the environment and makes the signaling according to the flow of traffic and passing of emergency vehicles is considered. The following are some of the components used in traffic control systems.

## Central Processing System

The central processing and control system acts as a basic unit for creating the integrated traffic control environment. The system is integrated with the traffic light signal, wireless cameras, and system controllable queue detectors. In the current scenario artificial intelligence based systems can analyze real time data by collecting and analyzing the previously existing traffic flow recordings. Using artificial intelligence based cameras the vehicles are accurately detected and fetched to the information center in case of any malfunction done by the vehicle and drivers. Artificial intelligence enabled cameras are also helpful in finding out the emergency vehicle passing through the signal that provides prior information to the signaling center to clear the traffic for easy passage (Lakshna et al., 2021). The system is also formulated by passing an optimized data to the hardware functional unit of traffic lights control and signal henceforth, free flow of traffic is performed during less congestion time. Because of the smart traffic control and management system, the information collected by the unit is also helpful for surveillance and security purposes.

## Smart Signal Lights Integration

Smart traffic light systems and signal management systems reduce the efficiency of a manual operation that is adapted during the heavy congestion time (See Figure 4.1). The intelligent light manages the queue and clears the traffic appropriately based on the traffic congestion ratio and adaptive information provided by the main control unit (Mushtaq et al., 2021). All the traffic management systems are connected with the central data management system that handles the data, stores the data, and analyzes the data for further interpretation.

Intelligent cameras and the queuing system updates the information to the traffic control unit for real time updating of traffic conditions. The real time information is helpful for the traffic control management team

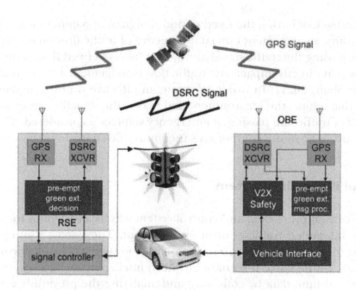

**Figure 4.1**   Smart traffic light integration (Jiri et al., 2020).

to handle the traffic effectively in case of heavy congestion and overcrowding situations, and so on. The cameras with artificial intelligence enabled services also helpful for analyzing the misbehaviors happening during the unmanned situation (Guo et al., 2018). The camera also integrated with analysis modules in which traffic violations also are recorded. The other advantage of smart cameras and queuing systems is to provide the license plate number for the vehicle that malfunctions and violates the traffic. Special cases are also considered while the emergency vehicles cross the traffic—political vehicles, fire engines, and public safety vehicles cross the traffic signal that is detected and informed to all other traffic signals to clear the flow without disturbing the public.

## Smart Traffic Monitoring System

The system empowered with IoT works in various regions—health environments, congestion, home automation, and smart street lamps—are all well known uses of IoT in smart urban communities. Residents will remain in a city for a longer period assuming they can get the desired lifestyle, with the help of smart city infrastructure, best medical care facilities, and creative technology for their family and income growth.

The data connected from each traffic unit is the accumulated information of numerous stampings of time and technical information stored in the database. The massive database is handled by the enabled software analytical tools and IoT enabled smart communication platforms that access part of the traffic management and monitoring system. Smart elements that handle the traffic management system are traffic lights, roads, public transportation, smart parking, guided parking, and guided traffic sign with alerts, artificial intelligence cameras, tracking systems, and IoT-enabled communication assistant. Traffic management systems cannot be discussed without the concept of sensors and integrated cameras to provide security and record all the information related to the driving of a vehicle (Tang et al., 2021).

Smart roads under smart highways are a dream of upcoming city developments that handle lots of AI applications in the roads and highways occupied with the sensors that monitor the vehicle speed, efficiently detect the accidents, accurately detect the license plate of the vehicle, and transmit all the information to the owner and traffic management system for further analysis. Smart parking also comes under the category of traffic management system in which smart applications are developed using mobile to reduce the difficulty in parking. These are all part of the smart city developments (Zhu et al., 2020). Guided parking is also one kind of smart evaluation that assists the drivers to make the parking accurately without disturbing the other vehicles and make secure parking.

Geo special traffic optimization system is an integrated version of GIS models, GPS modules, and radio frequency devices that is helpful to monitor the vehicle using geographical information. It provides 3D visualization of the geographical location in which the vehicle is traveling (Kazi et al., 2018). GPS is currently used for the efficient route guidance [21] particularly to reach certain destinations within less time. GPS plays a major role in the current scenario. The geo-spatial technology can advance the system by providing, learning the location information, guiding the user, showing the traffic flow, showing the traffic heavy consumption, and also suggesting the various smart roots to reduce the time construction.

Smart way of physical infrastructure exploration is a predominant solution for traffic management in many areas of the world. The task is to complete the time consuming complex and distributed work in a precise environment. In spite of assigning technology as a key monitoring system and management tool to overcome the obstacles in the smart traffic management system, intellectual solutions are provided using machine learning algorithms and deep learning algorithms. Artificial intelligence plays a major role in evolving the creation of smart environment and smart infrastructure creation for traffic management [4] rules that can adopt the environment and provide better solutions helpful for the public and traffic management department. Everyday numerous pieces of information are collected from traffic signals that can be stored, filtered, and analyzed with a smart analysis platform using machine learning models.

## VANET-Based Traffic Congestion Management System

Real time path planning and traffic congestion management systems using traffic information sharing via VANET is implemented in the presented system (Figure 4.2). The challenging part of path planning is updating of real time information during a dynamic environment. The presented system discusses the distributed transportation system (DTS) on roadsides. Considering the current traffic information, the redundancy framework is formulated and the required matrix for path planning is mapped. The proposed system is based on a real time path planning algorithm and is compared with the traffic congestion system that exists available formulas the static path plan algorithm for urban mapping.

## SDN Enabled Traffic Congestion Updating

Software defined network enabled social our vehicular adhoc network is created for making the efficient traffic congestion management system.

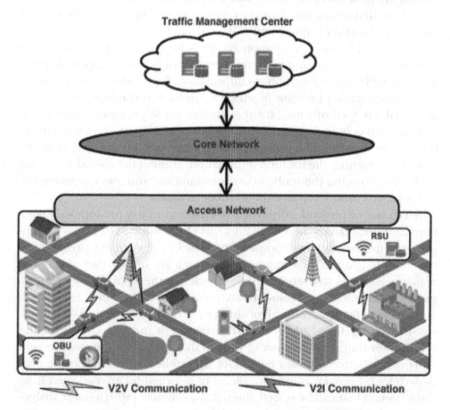

**Figure 4.2**   VANET based traffic congestion management (Prakash et al., 2018).

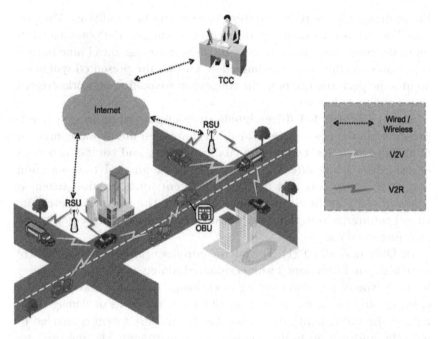

**Figure 4.3**  Privacy preserving authentication in VANETS (Qi et al., 2018).

The 5G enabled VANET structure exploits the social pattern of vehicles and its moving pattern distribution function and clustering of vehicle attributes related to speed distance vehicle attributes. The other presented as a traditional clustering algorithm to show the low level of communication of vehicles in a dynamic environment and to create an adaptive VANET based management system to provide discrete time homogeneous application.

## Privacy Preserving Solutions With VANET

Li et al. (2020) proposed a lightweight privacy preserving authentication model for vehicular communication systems using VANET. Creation of optimization models that communicate the vehicles during heavy congestion is discussed. The 5th generation secure protocol is evaluated for optimization of vehicular networks. Privacy preserving model is evaluated. Figure 4.3 shows the privacy preserving authentication mechanism implemented with software developed vehicular adhoc networks.

## BACKGROUND STUDY

Li et al., 2019. In a metropolitan city the demand of meeting the flexible traffic congestion is a difficult task. The author presented a system in which the traffic signals are regulated using dynamic traffic conditions. The proposed model utilized multi-agent systems that mitigate the potential effect on traffic congestion and minimize the drivers average travel time in metropolitan cities due to heavy congestion. Further the presented system examines the performance of traffic congestion adaptation networks created with a real time data set.

Zhu et al., 2020. IoT driven intelligent transport monitoring system is presented in the given paper. The other developed theory was composed of artificial societies, computational experiments, and parallel processes of executions. The effective demonstration of physical transportation systems in computers and the real intelligent transportation system is analyzed using artificial intelligence networks. The author achieved the virtual counterparts in the cyber world by analyzing the presented traffic environment data.

De Oliveira et al. (2021). The microcontroller firmware enabled control logic platform is developed with customized timing and traffic light safety for each type of junction crossing to exchange the time between specific crossings. In case of any emergency situations, accidents or damage happens to the traffic lights, then immediately the alert system is enabled to send the information to the nearby safety department. The sensors integrated into the embedded platform follows the communication protocol to transit the information at regular instances of time.

Kumar et al. (2021). The author presented a software defined network (SDN) enabled traffic light scheduling framework to balance the traffic flow during normal transport flow and heavy congestion time. Deep reinforcement learning (DRL) is proposed with the presented system in which real time environmental traffic flow is recorded. The vehicle count, speed, and traffic density is recorded to formulate the pattern of traffic at certain instances and validation of similar occurrences during heavy congestion is focused. Using an open-source simulator, the proposed solution offers better understanding on traffic pattern and offers less wait time, average queue with constant intervals (de Oliveira et al., 2021).

DRL is presented by the author, in order to optimize the flow of traffic during congested periods. A smart programming rerouting technique is implemented in which the automated rerouting mechanism is done. Without disturbing the existing flow of vehicles, a smart control of traffic signals after the formulation of optimized route suggestion, the simulation is implemented here. The two phases of approach implemented here reduce the unnecessary delays and reduce traffic overheads to the proposed model using intelligent rerouting mechanisms to reduce the long traffic queues and provide an efficient and balanced traffic control in real time (Kumar et al., 2021).

## Virtual Sensors

The other innovative idea that enables the traffic congestion monitoring to the next level is the usage of virtual sensors for smart traffic (Shankaran R., & Rajendran, 2021) pattern analysis. Virtual sensors are imaginary sensors in which the regular pattern of data sensed by the real time sensor is helpful to make a significant learning pattern to the virtual sensors. Continuous learning and prediction strategies enable the virtual sensors to perform better on making decisions on particular instances. The real time sensors such as flow sensor, distance measurement sensors, obstacle sensors, and vibration sensors enable the system to read, analyze and interpret detection values and iteratively adjust the learning weights. Further the learnt model is implemented for prediction of unknown instances. Further prediction of traffic congestion in specific locations helpful for the safety department and traffic control department.

## SYSTEM DESIGN

## The Software Tool Selection

The software tool selected for the purpose of the proposed traffic congestion detection and smart analysis system is developed using MATLAB 2017 software. MATLAB is a high-level computing language designed for high-performance integrated computations, visualization, and programming within an easy-to-use environment. Its syntax allows users to express and solve complex problems using mathematical notations that are familiar to practitioners in various fields. MATLAB finds typical applications in diverse areas such as algorithm development, modeling and simulation, and the manipulation of data. Artificial intelligence and neuron creation work is used for making the specific traffic management system. It provides a scientific and engineering graphical representation of systems application development that includes dedicated graphical user interface building applications integrated with the MATLAB environment. Inter interactive system was basic data available in the form of a matrix. The software allows you to solve many technology solutions, especially ones that handle the matrix in a faster way and enable the solution attainment in a more interactive way. MATLAB has been in use for several years for many users in all departments especially for constructing model creation analysis data science mathematical computing machine learning artificial intelligence. The features of MATLAB are used for application Facebook solutions and it contains specific tool boxes for all applications. The language commands the work environment handling the graphics mathematics functions and libraries and the application program interface API.

## About Dataset

Traffic congestion is increasing in urban communities all over the globe. Contributing elements incorporate extending metropolitan peoples, course of action, congested and constant traffic light planning and an absence of continuous information. The effects are critical. Given the physical information around building numerous smart streets, urban areas should adopt newer evaluations and innovations to further develop traffic conditions.

Content: This dataset contains 48.1k perceptions of vehicles that pass every hour in four unique intersections:

1. date time act as an attribute
2. the location where the junction is selected
3. number of vehicles
4. vehicle ID

The sensors on every traffic signal detect the vehicle passage and find out the restricted frames, providing immediate alert. Every frame of detection is analyzed to detect the anomaly passage of the vehicles. A part of correlated data is helpful to analyze the similar pattern occurrence hence the traffic signals are continuously given information.

## Existing Drawbacks

Manual handling of traffic during passage of emergency vehicles and emergency situations need a lot of time consuming arrangements that disturb the public as well. To provide a solution for this, a smart routing and learning model using deep neural networks is developed.

Deep cross neural network: A deep cross network is a type of specialized neural network that helps to handle more sophisticated deep learning tasks and models. It has received quite a bit of attention at recent IT conventions, and is being considered for helping with the training of deep networks.

## DESIGN METHODOLOGY

## System Architecture

The system architecture of a proposed deep convergence network for traffic analysis is presented in Figure 4.4.

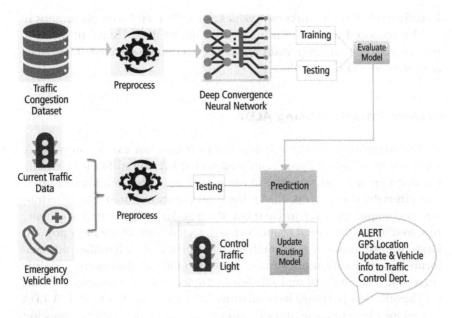

**Figure 4.4**  System architecture of proposed deep convergence network for traffic analysis.

## Preprocessing

This module is used to read the raw information from the dataset and formulate the data into a constant scaled matrix. The dataset is cleaned

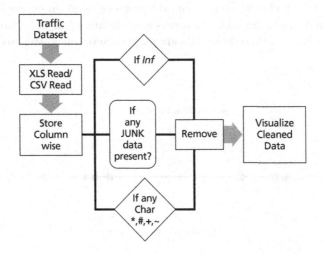

**Figure 4.5**  Preprocessing steps.

initially to remove the unknown values, junk data, and symbols present in it. The recorded information is the unbalanced data. Hence in order to process the data, the important attributes need to be selected. These data are vectored and visualized.

## Feature Extraction Using ALDA

The preprocessed dataset is fetched to feature an extraction process. Here adaptive linear discriminant analysis (ALDA) algorithm is used. Linear discriminant analysis is the linear model for classification and dimensionality reduction process. LDA is the most commonly used feature extraction technique in order to correlate the regular patterns that are being repeated in the presented framework is detected. One of the most popular kinds of classification algorithm that works linear in data handling and performs binary classification. In case multiple modality data occurs, logistic regression may not respond efficiently. Hence instead of using the LDA for classification purposes here adaptive LDA framework is model. A LDA is used for extracting the unique features present in the traffic congestion dataset fixed at the current instant. It is being assumed that the data is being distributed normally or Gaussian distribution hence the data associated with the class with the identical covariance matrix. LDA depends on the analysis of initial projections that carry out with calculation of main values of the inputs. The scatter matrix is formed to estimate the covariance matrix. From the given random distributor data the initial segregation of data relevancy is being plotted and shown in Figure 4.6.

Between each class scattered data the distance needs to be measured in order to make the relevance. If there is more relative data occurring in the neighborhood plot then those data are mapped separately. Analysis is made

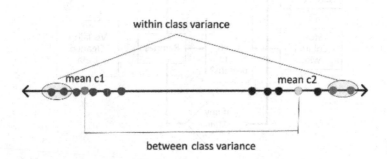

**Figure 4.6**  LDA variance projections.

by the scatter analysis of numerator and the denominator within the same class. The numerator is given by the formula below:

$$\arg\arg J(W) = (M_1 - M_2)^2 / S_1^2 + S_2^2 \tag{4.1}$$

The denominator is calculated by the class cater formula and projection of samples as mentioned below. Analysis for multiple classes can be generated and a relativity graph can be formed as per the formula given:

$$(M_1 - M_2)^2 = (W^T m_1 - W^T m_2)(W^T m_1 - W^T m_2)^T$$
$$= W^T (m_1 - m_2)(m_1 - m_2)^T W = W^T S_b W \tag{4.2}$$

$$S_b = \text{Between class scatter}$$

From the given data set higher the number of relativities occurring within the random distributed data then higher the correlation occurs. The intermediate values are considered as the unique features of the given data and that is further processed to deep convergence neural architecture for classification and prediction. The benefits of linear discriminant analysis is highly utilized here in terms of lightweight normalization and feature extraction that adopt to the unique agent factors within the distributed data.

Class scatter before projection

$$S_i = \sum_{x(n)\in i}^{n} \left(x(n) - m_i\right)\left(x(n) - m_i\right)^T \tag{4.3}$$

Scatter for projected samples

$$s_i^2 = \sum_{x(n)\in i}^{n} \left(W^T x(n) - M_i\right)\left(W^T x(n) - M_i\right)^T \tag{4.4}$$

$$M_i = W^T m_i$$

With little re-arrangement, will get the following equation

$$s_i^2 = W^T \sum_{n(n)\in i}^{n} \left(x(n) - m_i\right)\left(x(n) - m_i\right)^T W \tag{4.5}$$

$$s_i^2 = W^T S_i W$$

## Implementation Summary

Traffic data are not linear in nature. Traffic congestion may occur at any kind of circumstances based on the behavior of the driver, the transport, and the emergency situation people are facing. Traffic congestion in urban areas has become significant issue for many years. Because of traffic congestion people spend a productive time traveling and need to be avoided by smart traffic congestion analysis. In current smart city developments, most of the vehicles are connected through IoT. Traffic congestion is monitored by employing the concept of IoT, which involves the use of diverse traffic sensors, distance measurement sensors, speed measurement sensors, and intelligent cameras. GPS modules in the vehicles are helpful for analyzing the moment strategy of the traffic using crowd sensing techniques. The concept of detecting the anomaly traffic patterns is called traffic anomaly detection in smart cities. Deep understanding of an analysis of traffic congestion, the vehicular dynamics and traffic patterns helpful for the city planets to make decisions to provide flexible solutions. Utilization of smart sensors may use for data driven and model driven methodologies to focus the traffic congestion videos call late with the traffic sense are data to avoid accidents. Vehicular adhoc of networks are created for monitoring the behavior of the vehicles in the traffic congestion that will be helpful to predict the recurrent occurrence of traffic congestion in the particular environment. Deep convergence neural (DCN) network architecture is proposed here for the purpose of analyzing the traffic pattern with respect to the same occurrence and soft traffic congestion pattern in a particular environment.

Here the data set is collected from kaggle.com. The preprocessing of the nonlinear data is cleaned up and its features are extracted using adaptive linear discriminant model. The future extracted dimensionality reduced data is divided into training data on testing data. The training data and testing data is initially used to create robust models using DCN. In case of non-training data, the performance of the system is validator using main square error and the performance measures are calculated using accuracy. The created model is used further to analyze the test data which is nothing but the unknown data recorder in the live traffic congestion. In case a better correlation pattern occurs with the training data on the testing data the DCN architecture predicts the occurrence with next instant of time and depicts the performance of the analyzed system using a confusion matrix.

Another special scenario of the presented system is derived through detection of emergency vehicles during the traffic congestion. The traffic lights are controlled through the presented system to provide flexible adaptation of the traffic lights based on the environmental condition and traffic congestion ratio. The emergency vehicles such as ambulance, medical emergency, fire engine vehicles, and safety and security department vehicles are detected by the camera present with the traffic signal junction then immediate adaptation rule is performed by the presented module to change the timing delay of the traffic signals. In case heavy congestion occurs, the traffic signal detects the emergency vehicle and immediately clear the traffic for a certain period of time then set back to the normal traffic congestion flow. In case no traffic congestion occurs with the camera but still the emergency vehicle occurs immediately the traffic light changes the condition to normal and opens the traffic for allowing the emergency vehicles. Adopting the traffic lights depends on the environmental situation to avoid accidents and abnormal occurrence of emergency situations that will help the traffic police officers and public to adapt to the changing situation more freely without any hesitation.

## Dataset Separation

The preprocessed data is divided into training data and testing data and fetched into deep learning analysis module (Figure 4.7).

## Dataset Visualization

The timestamps of data collected based on hourly traffic count and speed of the vehicle are presented in Table 4.1.

## Deep Convergence Neural Network

The DCN consists of an artificial neural network (ANN) modified for the purpose of complex data analysis of traffic congestion data. It contains multiple layers of neurons that connect between the input and the output.

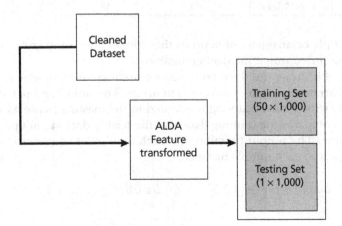

**Figure 4.7** Data preparation.

**TABLE 4.1 Time Stamps of Data Collected With Based on Hourly Traffic Count and Speed of the Vehicle With Circularity of the Vehicle**

| Timestamp | Hourly_Traffic_Count | Speed | Circularity |
|---|---|---|---|
| 10/4/2015 0:00 | 6 | 22 | 48 |
| 10/4/2015 0:05 | 0 | 25 | 41 |
| 10/4/2015 0:10 | 8 | 13 | 50 |
| 10/4/2015 0:05 | 4 | 19 | 41 |
| 10/4/2015 0:20 | 4 | 22 | 44 |
| 10/4/2015 0:25 | 4 | 33 | 57 |
| 10/4/2015 0:30 | 2 | 29 | 43 |
| 10/4/2015 0:35 | 5 | 70 | 43 |
| 10/4/2015 0:40 | 3 | 52 | 34 |
| 10/4/2015 0:45 | 1 | 29 | 44 |
| 10/4/2015 0:50 | 3 | 54 | 36 |
| 10/4/2015 0:55 | 2 | 70 | 34 |
| 10/4/2015 1:00 | 3 | 51 | 46 |
| 10/4/2015 1:05 | 0 | 33 | 42 |
| 10/4/2015 1:10 | 5 | 67 | 49 |
| 10/4/2015 1:15 | 2 | 31 | 55 |
| 10/4/2015 1:20 | 1 | 34 | 41 |
| 10/4/2015 1:25 | 4 | 34 | 36 |
| 10/4/2015 1:30 | 2 | 58 | 54 |
| 10/4/2015 1:35 | 1 | 24 | 56 |
| 10/4/2015 1:40 | 4 | 11 | 47 |
| 10/4/2015 1:45 | 3 | 43 | 37 |

The multiple occurrences of neurons that connect the input layer with the output layer determine the deeper analysis.

Figure 4.8 shows the deep convergence architecture contains multiple layers of accumulated are converged neurons. The multi-level perceptron determines the equivalent weight assigned to the existing networks and iteratively compares the training data with the testing data at multiple intervals of time. The output function acts as the multiples of updated weight with respect to each sample instance.

$$output = f(x) = \left\{ 1 \; if \; \sum \; w_1 x_1 + b \geq 0 \; 0 \; if \; \sum \; w_1 x_1 + b < 0 \right. \qquad (4.6)$$

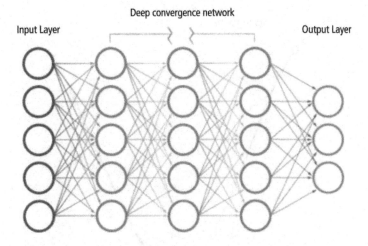

**Figure 4.8**   Deep convergence neural network architecture.

The cost function determines the performance measure of the updated process, here the cost function is validated by calculating mean square error (MSE) is given by,

$$\text{cost function} = MSE = \frac{1}{2m} \sum_{i=1}^{m} (\underline{y} - y)^2 \tag{4.7}$$

The point of convergence of the related values helpful to determine the required correlation factors of the given traffic pattern analysis (see Figure 4.9).

## Performance Metrics

The statistical measures are helpful to validate the performance of the developed model in which the better prediction quality is determined by the accuracy. It is determined by plotting the confusion matrix as shown below:

$$\text{Accuracy} = TP + TN / (TP + TN + FP + FN)$$

$$\text{Precision} = TP / (TP + FP)$$

$$\text{Recall} = TP / (TP + FN)$$

$$F_1 \text{ Score} = 2TP / (2TP + FP + FN)$$

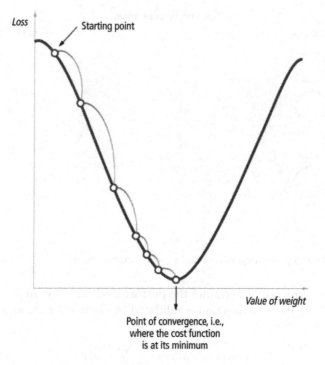

**Figure 4.9** Convergence of the weights.

## RESULTS AND DISCUSSIONS

### Preprocessing

Figure 4.10 shows the flow rate of input data packets collected from the recorders in the highways. The graph is plotted as the number of test cases in the x-axis and standard flow of packet rate that is the number of recordings obtained in the highway recorders.

Figure 4.11 shows the input raw data and data transformed after the LDA process. The dataset contains the frequently occurring vehicle type, the time stamps and duration of the congestion with current instants, and so on.

### Time-Series Plot of Observations vs. Vehicle Count

The time series plot of observations for the longer frame of time vs. the vehicle count recorded on an average (see Figure 4.12). Further the traffic

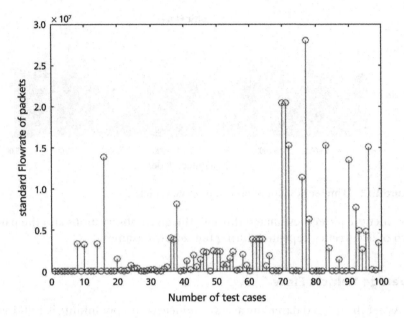

**Figure 4.10**   Flow rate of the data packets.

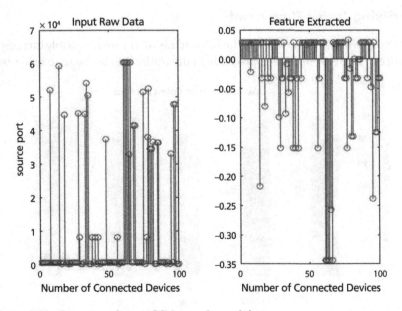

**Figure 4.11**   Input raw data vs. LDA transformed data.

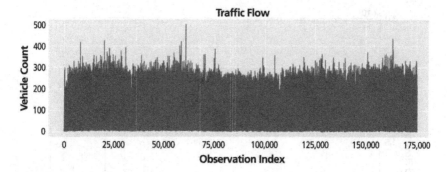

**Figure 4.12**   Time-series plot of observations vs. vehicle count.

flow identification is estimated through the given observations and the pattern of occurrence repeated during the selective frames.

## Average Vehicle Flow

As per the given dataset, the average vehicle count per minute is 100–180 based on the yearly recorded information. The chart shown in Figure 4.13 is the visualization of average information gathered from the dataset.

## Verifying Traffic Flow Trend

*Claim:* With increase in time, the inhabitants of the area probably increase. Hence, a rising trend can be probable in the traffic flow as the time drives by.

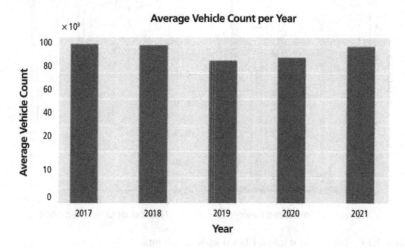

**Figure 4.13**   Time-series plot of observations vs. vehicle count.

*Null Hypothesis:* Upward trend exists alternative hypothesis: Upward trend does not exist.

## Average Traffic Flow of the Day

Figure 4.14 shows the average vehicle flow in a week at every time stamp holds the peak time to normal congestion time.

Average vehicle flow for each day of the week at per minute ratio is displayed in the graph shown in Figure 4.15.

## Prediction Result for the Upcoming Month

Figure 4.16 shows the average vehicle flow expected per minute ration in the upcoming month is predicted by the proposed deep convergence network system.

## Confusion Matrix

Figure 4.17 presents the confusion matrix of a deep convergence network (DCN).

## Notification on Emergency Vehicle Detection

In Figure 4.18, the alert notification on emergency vehicle detection. In case of any emergency vehicle such as ambulance, fire engines, safety department, and army vehicles detected over the camera then, immediate alert will be generated and notified. Further the information transferred to the traffic department for clearing the traffic in next traffic signal junctions. Once the camera detects the emergency vehicle it triggers the control unit of the traffic light section to automatically change the signal to immediate opening and further to clear the traffic the timer is reduced.

Graphical representation of accuracy comparisons of existing systems with proposed DCN performance in terms of accuracy. Lakshna et al. (2021) researched on smart congestion prediction using hardware approach, using logistic regression achieved 91% of accuracy. Ruzicka et al. (2020) denoted the 75% accuracy on neural network based smart traffic prediction analysis using dedicated smart applications. Akoum et al.'s (2017) automatic prediction is focused here using the traffic videos of the live video streaming in the junctions. Using image enhancement

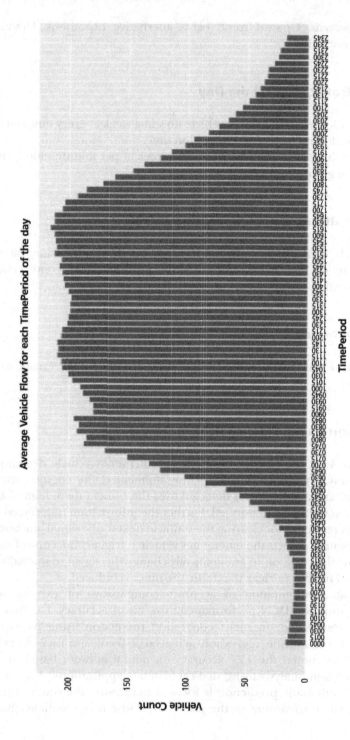

**Figure 4.14** Average vehicle flow of the week.

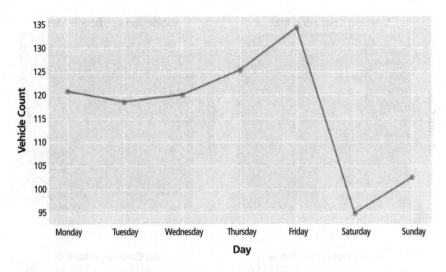

**Figure 4.15** Average vehicle flow for each day of the week.

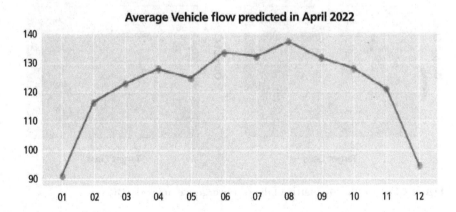

**Figure 4.16** Average vehicle flow prediction in upcoming month (April 2022).

techniques and classification methods, a number of vehicles are counter to detect traffic congestion in real time. 90% accuracy is achieved using the presented system by the author.

Figure 4.19 shows the comparison of existing algorithm with proposed deep convergence network in terms of accuracy as statistical measurement. Further in the proposed work using deep convergence network, Smart traffic congestion detection and emergency vehicle detection is done with the accuracy of 92%.

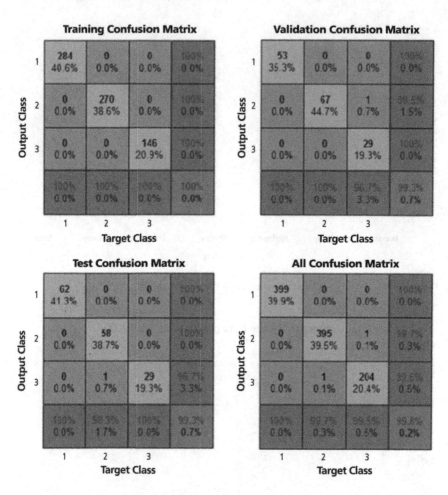

**Figure 4.17**   Confusion matrix of deep convergence network (DCN).

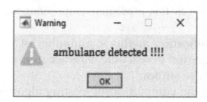

**Figure 4.18**   Alert message on emergency vehicle detection.

**TABLE 4.2  Comparison of Existing Implementations**

| S. No. | Reference | Research Description | Methodology | Accuracy (in %) |
|---|---|---|---|---|
| 1 | A. Lakshna et al., 2021 | Smart congestion prediction hardware approach | Logistic Regression | 91 |
| 2 | Ruzicka et al., 2020 | Smart application for traffic prediction | Neural Networks | 75 |
| 3 | Akoum et al., 2017 | Automatic traffic using image processing | Image Processing | 90 |
| 4 | Proposed work | Smart traffic congestion detection and emergency vehicle detection | Deep Convergence Network | 92 |

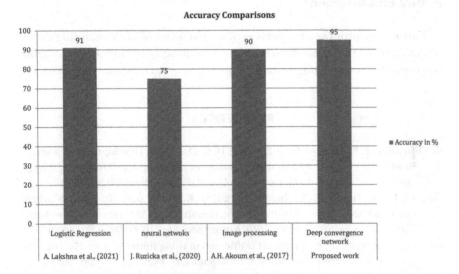

**Figure 4.19**  Accuracy comparisons.

## CONCLUSION

Smart traffic congestion management systems are most demandable in current scenarios to provide the public to save time in heavy traffic congestion situations. The proposed approach uses image processing based emergency vehicle detection systems as well as deep analysis of traffic patterns to predict the traffic congestion to be expected in upcoming days. Deep convergence neural network is used to analyze the existing pattern of traffic congestion from Kaggle dataset, in which the dataset contains enormous patterns of traffic records, number of vehicles crossed, and the emergency vehicle and related behavior on traffic adjustments. Here the dynamic system detects the emergency vehicle through a camera also incorporated with the previous analysis of traffic patterns to optimize the further route on upcoming signals. Currently during the emergency vehicle detection, automatically the traffic signaling is changed to clear up the existing congestions. The proposed DCN based system achieved an accuracy of 92%.

## Future Enhancement

Further the proposed model is explored in terms of understanding more parameters on traffic prediction environment, sensors, and analysis methods towards deep learning transfer learning approach to improve accuracy.

## REFERENCES

de Oliveira, L. F. P., Manera, L. T., & Luz, P. D. G. D. (2021). Development of a smart traffic light control system with real-time monitoring. *IEEE Internet of Things Journal, 8*(5), 3384–3393. https://doi.org/10.1109/jiot.2020.3022392

Guo, C., Li, D., Zhang, G., & Zhai, M.-L. (2018). Real-time path planning in urban area via VANET-assisted traffic information sharing. *IEEE Transactions on Vehicular Technology, 67*(7), 5635–5649. https://doi.org/10.1109/tvt.2018.2806979

Kamdar, A., & Shah, J. (2021). Smart traffic system using traffic ow models. *2021 International Conference on Artificial Intelligence and Smart Systems* (pp. 465–471). https://doi.org/10.1109/icais50930.2021.9396002

Kazi, S., Nuzhat, S., Nashrah, A., & Rameeza, Q. (2018, January 1). Smart parking system to reduce traffic congestion. *2018 International Conference on Smart City and Emerging Technology* (pp. 1–4). https://doi.org/10.1109/ICSCET .2018.8537367

Kumar, N., Mittal, S., Garg, V., & Kumar, N. (2021). Deep reinforcement learning-based traffic light scheduling framework for SDN-enabled smart transportation system. *IEEE Transactions on Intelligent Transportation Systems, 23*(3), 1–11. https://doi.org/10.1109/tits.2021.3095161

Lakshna, A., Ramesh, K., Prabha, B., Sheema, D., & Vijayakumar, K. (2021). Machine learning smart traffic prediction and congestion reduction. *2021 International Conference on Innovative Computing, Intelligent Communication and Smart Electrical Systems* (pp. 1–4). https://doi.org/10.1109/icses52305.2021.9633949

Li, X., Liu, T., Obaidat, M. S., Wu, F., Vijayakumar, P., & Kumar, N. (2020). A lightweight privacy-preserving authentication protocol for VANETs. *IEEE Systems Journal, 14*(3), 3547–3557. https://doi.org/10.1109/jsyst.2020.2991168

Li, Z., Al Hassan, R., Shahidehpour, M., Bahramirad, S., & Khodaei, A. (2019). A hierarchical framework for intelligent traffic management in smart cities. *IEEE Transactions on Smart Grid, 10*(1), 691–701. https://doi.org/10.1109/tsg.2017.2750542

Mushtaq, A., Haq, I. U., Usman, M., Khan, A., & Shafiq., O. (2021). Traffic flow management of autonomous vehicles using deep reinforcement learning and smartr. *IEEE Access, 9*, 51005–51019. https://doi.org/10.1109/access.2021.3063463

Prakash, U. E., K Vishnupriya, Athira Thankappan, & Balakrishnan, A. A. (2018). Density based traffic control system using image processing. *2018 International Conference on Emerging Trends and Innovations in Engineering and Technological Research* (pp. 1–4). https://doi.org/10.1109/icetietr.2018.8529111

Qi, W., Song, Q., Wang, X., Guo, L., & Ning, Z. (2018). SDN-enabled social-aware clustering in 5G-VANET systems. *IEEE Access, 6*, 28213–28224. https://doi.org/10.1109/access.2018.2837870

Shankaran R., S., & Rajendran, L. (2021, January 1). Real-time adaptive traffic control system for smart cities. *2021 International Conference on Computer Communications and Informatics*, 1–6. https://doi.org/10.1109/ICCCI50826.2021.9402597

Růžička, J., Purkrabkova, Z., & Korec, V. (2020). Smart application for traffic excess prediction. *2020 Smart City Symposium Prague*, 1–5. https://doi.org/10.1109/scsp49987.2020.9133935

Tang, C., Hu, W., Hu, S., & Stettler, M. (2021). Urban traffic route guidance method with high adaptive learning ability under diverse traffic scenarios. *IEEE Transactions on Intelligent Transportation Systems, 22*(5), 2956–2968. https://doi.org/10.1109/tits.2020.2978227

Zhu, F., Lv, Y., Chen, Y., Wang, X., Xiong, G., & Wang, F.-Y. (2020). Parallel transportation systems: Toward IoT-enabled smart urban traffic control and management. *IEEE Transactions on Intelligent Transportation Systems, 21*(10), 4063–4071. https://doi.org/10.1109/tits.2019.2934991

# CHAPTER 5

# IOT SECURITY

## Securing the Future of Connectivity

**David Silva**
*Algemetric*

**Travis Hearne**
*Titanium Leadership Consulting*

**Theodore Wiard**
*New Earth Institute of Southwestern*

## ABSTRACT

Technological advancements have created a communication environment that is seemingly limitless, thanks largely to the concept of the Internet of things (IoT). Communication devices, endpoints, and everyday appliances are now connected seamlessly to networks, cloud servers, and other endpoints around the globe, making it easier to communicate and engage with technologically advanced appliances. IoT technology is highly prevalent in healthcare, leading several other industries in implementation and advancement (Malhotra et al., 2021). Patel and Patel (2016) describe the IoT as the concept of everyday things autonomously sharing information and connect-

*Innovations in Computational Intelligence, Big Data Analytics, and Internet of Things*, pages 75–91
Copyright © 2024 by Information Age Publishing
www.infoagepub.com

ing to the Internet through connections with public or private Internet protocol (IP) networks. The IoT concept and the data within this concept continue to evolve, become more technologically advanced and increasingly more complicated to protect.

Data-centric technologies play a fundamental role in the security and privacy of IoT as perimeter-less architectures, such as those in the zero trust security model, and are now considered the new norm. Security and privacy solutions must be defined and enacted at the data level, not over-relying on the security of any given environment. Well-defined, properly implemented, actively managed, and (preferably) automatically executed identity and access management (IAM) policies are required for enabling secure communication between IoT devices. The right operational balance between cloud, fog, and edge computing and compliance with several privacy regulations are rapidly becoming strong requirements for secure, efficient, and interoperable solutions. The question then becomes, how do we protect these highly important and sensitive data from malicious cyber-actors and data-loss events?

## IOT SECURITY: SECURING THE FUTURE OF CONNECTIVITY

The term *Internet of things* (IoT) first appeared in a presentation at Proctor & Gamble in 1999 by Kevin Ashton (Ashton, 2009). However, the concept of smart device communication precedes the Internet itself. From 1966 to 1990, the Advanced Research Projects Agency Network (ARPANET), the precursor of the Internet, enabled communication between remote computers (wide range) for the first time. In 1982, a Coke vending machine at Carnegie Mellon University became the first device connected to the ARPANET (Lane, 2017).

Since then, the notion of an IoT has achieved a ubiquitous status, a phenomenon perfectly aligned with Mark Weiser's remark that "the most profound technologies are those that disappear. They weave themselves into the fabric of everyday life until they are indistinguishable from it" (Weiser, 1991, n.p.), which is indeed an undeniable reality nowadays. Fast forwarding to 2022, we have myriads of companies injecting code in a wide variety of devices so they can efficiently perform tracking, accelerate operational procedures, monitor and reduce errors, control inventory, increase transparency, and enable entirely new businesses around IoT, all of which was anticipated would happen a couple of decades ago (Ferguson, 2002).

The relevance and groundbreaking nature of IoT and its effects on modern society seem to be irrefutable. From convenient smart homes to impressive robots, IoT technology continues to evolve at an extremely challenging pace. IoT is certainly one of these profound technologies that just "disappear" before our eyes, that is, most of the time we don't even think about them anymore and yet, they are there.

However, with great power comes great responsibility. By observing the development of IoT over the past decades we notice an explosion in utilities followed by the unleashing of new vulnerabilities, attacks, risks, and threats to individuals and organizations increasingly involved with and even dependent on IoT.

In this chapter we discuss powerful security and privacy strategies for IoT to address the complex but possible goal of reconciling utility with security and how to pave the way to a new generation of IoT technologies established on the foundation of security and privacy by default and by design.

## THE GREAT APPEAL OF INCREASED CONNECTIVITY

IoT is considered by many one of the most important technologies of the 21st century and it is not hard to understand why. Consider the 1982 Coke vending machine example we mentioned earlier, which resulted in questions such as:

- What if the Coke vending machine could report the current status of its inventory? That would allow its replenishment right on time so the machine would never run out of any specific product.
- What if the Coke vending machine could tell if drinks were cold or not? That would allow users to select colder drinks.
- What if the Coke vending machine could tell for how long each drink is there? Some users could prefer newly loaded drinks as opposed to another drink that was sitting there for a long period of time.

That was exactly what the Coke vending machine from the computer science department at Carnegie Mellon University did. If these features remain interesting today, imagine back in 1982. Once we have one practical example of one "thing" connected to one or more computers and providing information about itself, a new stream of connected things is inevitable. Imagine more people asking, "What if we do the same to refrigerators, cabinets, gates, windows, lights, storage units, cars, etc.?" And this is exactly what happened.

Once we have a large number of devices connected to the Internet, providing data in real-time without human intervention and at a low-cost of computation, not only do we have the immediate benefit of connectivity (standard monitoring, reminders, critical alerts, conditional actions, schedule self-maintenance, automatic reports, etc.), but we also open the doors to apply big data, data analytics, and business intelligence methodologies. This can be accomplished in such a way that organizations can learn more about their customers, which gives immediate insights about their current habits and preferences as well as their willingness to consume new products and services. So clearly

IoT can do much more than just collect and transmit data: It can serve as a fundamental technology in the strategic efforts of any organization.

## The Discrepancy Between Utility and Security

There can be an alarming number of security issues associated with increased connectivity. In this section we discuss some of the most common problems the IoT industry faces with serious implications to society in general.

### Inconsistent Standards

As remarked by Al-Qaseemi et al. (2016), there are numerous concerns and challenges that limit the usefulness and performance of IoT. This paper is focused on those related to architecture—communication issues, data management, zero-entropy systems, scalability, massive data collection, real-time data processing, security and privacy, interoperability, lack of standardization, and so on (Al-Qaseemi et al., 2016). Al-Qaseemi et al. (2016) further remark that standardization enables interoperability, which improves the successful integration and sharing of information amongst distributed systems. This necessitates the use of standard protocols and platforms to link devices from multiple suppliers to communicate with one another. Unifying IoT standards could also improve overall security by making it easier to secure connected devices from different manufacturers.

### Device Hijacking/Ransomware

A ransomware attack in the IoT, unlike typical malware attacks, can be more severe since it can damage an entire landscape of security services, such as confidentiality, integrity, and availability, which can result in not just cash losses but also crucial data leaks (Yaqoob et al., 2017).

Syed Zahra classifies the combination of IoT and ransomware attacks as a new security nightmare. According to Zahra, ransomware is one of the most prevalent dangers today, and cybersecurity professionals, law enforcement agencies, and IoT devices appear to be unprepared to deal with it. IoT devices collect vital and frequently sensitive data, making it critical to provide them with the capacity to maintain data integrity and confidentiality within the owner's premises. Traditional security measures are inadequate in IoT due to the specific characteristics of IoT devices such as resource restrictions, heterogeneity, and mobility (Zahra, 2019).

## Security and Privacy Implications

Back to the 1982 Coke vending machine example. Imagine the excitement at that time when researchers and industry professionals were envisioning the possibilities of turning rudimentary objects into smart devices. What serious implications with respect to privacy would such a venture impose? It would be hard to tell at that time. Today it is actually easy to identify these implications.

To illustrate the relationship between increased functionality and privacy issues, let us imagine that Alice and Bob are married and have two babies. The couple recently bought a new house after years of renting an apartment. They are excited about their new home and promised each other that they would do any home improvement and technological upgrades they could. The house has three levels. They decide to buy baby monitors to check on their little ones and are pleased by the fact that now they can connect the monitors to the Internet and watch their babies by using phones, tablets, and laptops. They buy a virtual assistant and decide to integrate it with smart lights, garage door, indoor and outdoor cameras, including the baby monitors so everything can be controlled by voice command. Encouraged by the possibilities and in the attempt to turn their house into a full-blown smart home, Alice and Bob buy kitchen appliances that can also be integrated to the virtual assistance. Finally, they integrate the central heater and air conditioning, as well as their security system. Alice and Bob could not be more proud of their new smart home.

One day, as Alice is leaving for work, she notices the garage door is open. She asks Bob if it was him, but he has no idea what happened. Alice closes the door and moves on with her day. Later in the same week, they are woken up in the middle of the night by the TV in the master bedroom, which has apparently turned on by itself. Alice and Bob think something weird is going on, but they don't know what exactly. A couple of weeks pass by and Bob notices that their security system has been turned off and that one of the baby monitors is zooming in and out, apparently by itself. Alice and Bob are terrified, so they decide to hire a security company to investigate. The security company quickly discovers that someone hacked their wifi network and has access to all devices connected to their smart system, including their personal phones, tablets, and laptops.

Alice and Bob now realize that for an unknown period of time, an equally unknown number of people could see, hear, and control virtually everything happening in their house. It is uncertain what data was leaked and what kind of information was shared with other parties during this time. Once an unauthorized party is controlling the house's security systems, as well as doors, kitchen appliances, and the house heater, their family was at risk in many terrifying ways. The security company offers to fix the problem by installing security measures, but Alice and Bob are now too scared to try again so they decide to undo all improvements done in the house to turn it into a full-blown analogue home.

Alice and Bob's story is extremely common, worldwide. The temptation is just too big and there is not enough awareness of the risks of increasing connectivity without the proper security measures in place.

Privacy violations don't require devices to be hacked. Smart sensors can collect sensitive personal data which identify, as an example, detailed household energy consumption profiles. When this type of information is released to a third party, the chances of data breach occurring (even unintentionally) are high (Ukil et al., 2014).

### Data Breach

Data breaches in healthcare expose patients to many risks such as privacy violations, identity theft, health insurance fraud, and even death (Moganedi, 2018). A study by Masemovic et al. (2015) shows the most common healthcare data breach types include theft, unauthorized access and disclosure, IoT device loss, system hacking and/or IT incidents, and improper disposal of healthcare information.

### IoT-Enabled Crimes

The IoT is now universal as it continues to expand and become more common. Private companies and governments of every size are increasingly relying on IoT for both providing and consuming a large number of products and services. Consequently, cybercrimes pose many threats to business and governments worldwide with the potential of causing unprecedented damage in an immeasurable number of ways (Kagita et al., 2021).

Nayyar et al. (2020) remarks that IoT is making our lives easier but less secure. Since connectivity is unproportionally and uncarefully prioritized over security, the adoption rate of IoT devices is very high. However, a report by Nayyar et al. (2020) indicated that 70% of these devices are easy to attack. In this sense, the more unsafe devices that connect to unsafe networks and other devices create a sea of new opportunities for malicious adversaries everywhere.

## THREATS TO PUBLIC SAFETY

Any security and privacy incident that affects the life of individuals is a deplorable act. However, there are certain threats that can rapidly escalate to problems of even greater proportions. One example is the smart/electric cars, and more particularly semi or fully autonomous cars. These types of vehicles are hackable (Jafarnejad et al., 2015) and the implication of malicious access to these vehicles can be catastrophic. If an attacker can take control of someone's car, it could be the beginning of a crime spree that includes assault, murder, and even terrorism.

## Security and Privacy for IoT

Learning about the severity of cyberthreats to any IoT ecosystem is one of the first steps towards adopting and/or implementing effective counter-measures that are able to reconcile utility with security and privacy. Thankfully, there are options available. Understanding what these options are, their main characteristics and direct benefits, can help one to identify their suitability for each specific scenario related to IoT.

## IDENTITY AND ACCESS MANAGEMENT

IAM is a framework of technologies, methodologies, recommendations, standards, and policies to ensure reliable identification of human and non-human entities, as well as their access privileges.

To properly address the security and privacy challenges in IoT, modern IAM solutions must include these key concepts: (a) least privilege, (b) separation of duties, and (c) zero trust. Each of these concepts offer unique benefits in addressing vulnerabilities in any application directly or indirectly associated with IoT.

## Least Privilege

Least privilege permissions associated with an account should be limited to the minimum required to perform any given task. In this context, an account can be a user account, application account, or any other type of account (e.g., hybrid). For every account, a set of required access must be specified. Different responsibilities imply different permissions. As we are going to see in the continuation of this discussion, each key IAM concept is beneficial on its own. That means that implementing the principle of least privilege helps to decrease cybersecurity risks.

Unfortunately, most organizations do not implement least privilege, and the reason is understandable. Implementing least privilege is an involved process. It requires constant monitoring of the identity credentials and access needs for each user, application, machine, service, and so on, until they are valid.

Consider a system composed of ten machines, each one executing a distinct task. These machines must be periodically accessed for maintenance, software and firmware updates, data collection, error corrections, and other routines. If a certain entity is responsible for collecting data in a given directory, that entity must be properly identified and allowed to just collect the data in the previously specified directory. In this case, least privilege implies that an entity such as this won't be able to collect data from any other directory and won't be able to execute any other task. Now imagine that this data collection is conducted by a vendor. When the contract between that vendor and the organization (or individual) that owns the machine comes to an end, the vendor must not be able to access the machine, much less collect any data.

The fact that most organizations do not implement least privilege means that they routinely grant more permissions than they have users and applications. Without least privilege implemented, how can one be certain that users and machines are not accessing unauthorized data? Under the least privilege concept, minimizing permissions leads to minimizing risks.

In the Alice and Bob example we discussed previously, under the least principal concept, different accounts with different access privileges should handle different tasks. For instance, access to checking the temperature (read only), possibly something less critical, could be granted to an account used by a contractor responsible for the heater and AC. It should never, however, allow access to the baby monitors or any other feature of Alice and Bob's smart home.

## Separation of Duties

Separation of duties (SOD) relates to the notion that no user should be granted sufficient privileges to independently exploit any given system. For instance, the person who authorizes a request should not also be able to make the request. SOD can be achieved statically by establishing distinct roles that cannot be executed by the same account, or dynamically through the establishment of rules at access time (NIST Computer Security Resource Center, n.d.).

To succeed against processes that require the active participation of many users/accounts, attackers need to deceive multiple parties. The probability of success in this case is much smaller than in the case where there is only one party. Therefore, responsibility over high-risk processes should be split over multiple parties. By doing so, not only are security and privacy issues reduced, but it also reduces the potential for error. The chances that two parties will overlook some critical procedures are lower than in the case of just one-party handling everything.

SOD also decreases vulnerabilities related to social engineering attacks and it helps to protect against insider threats. SOD could help Alice and Bob with critical tasks in their smart home. Alice and Bob should have different accounts and implement the dynamic version of SOD. For instance, for deactivating the security system of their home, if Alice requested the deactivation, Bob would be required to confirm, and vice-versa.

## ZERO TRUST

Not so long ago, security was seen as a matter of perimeter. Organizations would work as some type of fortress protecting everyone inside from all the threats on the outside. More specifically, anyone within the organization would be trusted by default. This notion assumes that all threats are exclusively originated from the outside. Contrary to this idea, cybersecurity statistics show insider threats are very real and extremely common (Sarkar, 2010), whether malicious or unintentional. Another concerning idea is that perimeter defenses can always protect outsiders from getting inside.

Zero trust (ZT) is a new security paradigm that assumes there is no trust established based on physical or network location, or on asset ownership. ZT is one answer to the changes happening in the workplace, such as remote and hybrid work where employees are using their own device and services running in the cloud. ZT focuses on protecting resources, wherever they are, every time access is requested. Verification of identity and access privileges are checked at every request. One successful request does not imply that future requests will be also successful.

ZT is strongly based on least privilege per request access decisions. SOD is also a notion strongly related to ZT. Zero trust architecture (ZTA) is a cybersecurity plan for an organization that incorporates zero trust concepts and includes component relationships, workflow planning, and access controls (Rose et al., 2020).

In practice, ZTA ensures that all data and services are resources, and all communication is secured regardless of physical or network location. Access to resources is granted on a per-session basis and is determined dynamically depending on the context. Additional verifications might apply, such as behavioral and environmental analysis. Resources are constantly monitored, and identity and access privileges are rigorously and dynamically checked before access is granted. At all times, the state of the application is constantly logged, including events, accesses granted and/or denied, the actors involved, the tasks executed, and whatever else is necessary for a clear view of the overall operation.

Due to the rigorous and yet dynamic nature of ZT, the overall approach associated with the zero-trust philosophy is commonly referred to as "never trust, always verify" (Samaniego & Deters, 2018). ZT can be applied to secure Alice and Bob's smart home. One simple example could be dynamic verification of habits and behavior. Imagine that an attacker manages to obtain control over Bob's account. Alice and Bob go to work, and their children stay with Bob's parents during the day. The entire family doesn't return to the house until after 6:00 p.m. If the attacker uses Bob's account to request deactivation of the security system either at an unusual time of the day or from an atypical location, the system can alert Alice that something might be wrong. Alice could then rely on additional verifications (such as video calling Bob) to make sure the request is legitimate.

## IAM Processes

Effective IAM is built upon good processes and procedures aiming to minimize the probability of errors making sure policies are constantly fulfilled. There are three main processes in IAM: (a) provisioning, (b) administration, and (c) enforcement (Cameron & Williamson, 2020). Provisioning is the process of onboarding users into the access management system including all procedures from validating an accounts need, to accessing any given resource, to assigning appropriate permissions.

Administration is an ongoing effort and the most complex of all IAM processes. This includes all procedures from the specification of the IAM blueprint that will be applied in any given scenario to implement and continue maintenance.

Enforcement is a measure that allows IAM policies to be effective. IAM policies can only provide proper protection if they cannot be bypassed or overcome. Monitoring and auditing is part of enforcement, which is done to ensure that the application under consideration will work as expected.

As part of IAM enforcement, we have three critical procedures:

- Authentication: An identity verification mechanism for validating an entity (either a human or a machine) is indeed who/what they say they are according to the informed credentials.
- Authorization: A mechanism that takes place once identity is properly verified, to identify the permissions assigned to the entity. This way access can be either granted or denied.
- Accounting: A constant monitoring and review mechanism of all access control decisions and all activities associated with authentication, authorization, and resource access. Accounting offers the ability to quickly detect strange events and trigger a call for remediation in a timely fashion.

All three of the above IAM processes would be instrumental in Alice and Bob's smart home. Provisioning would allow devices to be properly identified and equipped with additional authentication and authorization mechanisms, where access could only be granted to specific accounts under the concepts of least privilege and separation of duties. Administration would ensure that pre-defined and pre-allowed routines, under strict conditions, would be allowed and that any incident would be promptly analyzed and used to update the existing policies. Enforcement would be essential to provide Alice and

Bob reasonable security assurances via authentication and authorization per-request (under the zero-trust security model), and accounting for raising red flags and triggering remediation whenever necessary.

If any or even all of the measures above sound inconvenient, here is something to consider: convenience, security, and privacy are, by nature, conflicting ideas. A door without a lock and a computer without a password are examples of conveniences that would just make life easier whenever we are tired or in a hurry.

There are ways to alleviate security procedures. We can replace physical keys and passwords through biometric identification. However, it is impor-tant to keep in mind that the more secure a system is, the less convenient it will be. And if it is inconvenient for you, it will probably be even more inconvenient for an attacker.

Should we enable all possible security measures at once, in every single case? Probably not, but here's something to consider when weighing your options. The more critical a particular resource or task is, the greater the need for more restricted security and privacy solutions and vice-versa.

## Modern Standards

Historically, ad-hoc security and privacy solutions have been less than successful. The assumption that world changing technology developed by a particular company behind closed doors will address every threat is a mis-take that can have serious implications. Standards exist to ensure that the knowledge, experience, and collaboration between the most prominent players in any given industry are taken into consideration when designing and providing products and services. Moreover, standards allow a common language and common components to exist as the foundation that makes product and services interoperable. This is true for every industry, and it is critical for security and privacy.

For example, the Office of Management and Budget (OMB) recently developed a federal zero trust strategy in support of the executive order on improving the nation's cybersecurity, urging civilian agencies to imple-ment zero trust concepts in their enterprise security architecture. The pres-idential order and the OMB memorandum are worth reading in full but highlighted here are several areas that have a direct influence on how to implement, deploy, and operate IAM. The main point of the OMB memo-randum's "identity" section is to highlight that agency employees should utilize enterprise-managed identities to access the apps they use. They should deploy phishing-resistant MFA to safeguard employees against ad-vanced online threats.

Agencies must utilize robust multifactor authentication (MFA) through-out their company as part of the measures to achieve this objective, which must be enforced at the application layer rather than the network layer. In addition, when approving users to access resources, agencies must evaluate at least one device-level signal in addition to the authenticated user's identity information.

In terms of phishing-resistant authenticators and MFA techniques, the federal plan recommends the World Wide Web Consortium's open "Web Authentication" standard, as well as Fast Identity Online (FIDO2), as viable options for meeting the Federal Zero Trust Strategy's standards. One of the consequences of the Federal Zero Trust Strategy is that it allows agencies to use FIDO instead of personal identity verification authentication (PIV) or public-key infrastructure (PKI).

Understanding what modern security standards for security and privacy are, who is behind them, and how they actively create a foundation for interoperable, reliable, and secure technologies is a great first step towards secure and futureproof IoT solutions.

## WebAuthn

The Web Authentication API (WebAuthn) is a specification jointly created by the World Wide Web Consortium (W3C) and the FIDO Alliance based on public key cryptography as a strong method for authentication. WebAuthn serves to integrate with devices equipped with built-in authenticators. Instead of passwords, WebAuthn uses a public key and a private key pair, together with a randomly generated credential ID. While public keys are stored in the server (with no special concern), private keys are securely stored on the user's device. WebAuthn is part of a set of technologies that enable passwordless authentication between servers, namely FIDO2.

## The W3C

The World Wide Web Consortium (W3C) is an international organization that works with internal member organizations, composed of full-time staff and the general public to define Web standards. Led by Web inventor and Director Tim Berners-Lee and CEO Jeffrey Jaffe, the W3C's mission is to help the World Wide Web realize its full potential by establishing protocols and norms that ensure the Web's long-term viability. Below, we'll go through some of the most important aspects of this goal, all of which contribute to the W3C's One Web vision.

According to the design principles that guide W3C's work, the Web's social value is that it encourages human communication, trade, and opportunities to exchange information. One of the W3C's primary goals is to ensure that these benefits are available to everyone, regardless of their hardware, software, network infrastructure, native language, culture, geographic location, or physical or mental ability.

In addition, the number of different sorts of gadgets that can connect to the Internet has exploded. Mobile phones, smart phones, PDAs, interactive television systems, voice response systems, kiosks, and even some household goods can now connect to the Internet. The W3C's vision for the Web includes global involvement, knowledge exchange, and trust building.

## The FIDO Alliance

The Fido Alliance, an open industry organization, is transforming the nature of authentication by supporting the development, usage, and compliance of authentication and device attestation standards to help eliminate the world's over-reliance on passwords.

The FIDO Alliance was created in 2012, and major technological companies such as PayPal, Google, Samsung, Microsoft, Intel, Arm, Facebook, Amazon, and Apple are all members of the alliance. The FIDO Alliance is working to transform authentication with open standards that are more secure than passwords and SMS OTPs, easier to use for consumers, and easier to install and maintain for service providers. The FIDO Alliance strives to achieve its goals by creating technical specifications that create an open, scalable, and interoperable collection of procedures that eliminate dependency on passwords.

## PRIVACY-ENHANCING TECHNOLOGIES

Security and privacy is a niche with great concerns, risks, and opportunities. Until recently, modern cryptographic tools and protocols could only address security concerns. However, the desire of using data while encrypted (without requiring prior decryption) is an increasing demand causing companies to adjust their offerings accordingly. Moreover, privacy regulations are taking the world by storm. Any individual or organization that intends to access and use third-party personal data is subject to overwhelmingly demanding privacy laws. The penalties for a single violation can reach millions of dollars, which could lead a small- to medium-sized organization into bankruptcy. Privacy-enhancing technologies (PETs) are a modern set of technologies for addressing the need for computing over encrypted data (COED) and statistical techniques. PETs are then categorized as follows:

- COED Techniques
  - Multiparty Computation
  - Fully Homomorphic Encryption (FHE)
  - Knowledge Proof (ZKP)
- Statistical Techniques
  - Differential Privacy
  - Synthetic Data Generation
  - Federated Machine Learning

Next, we review the basics of homomorphic encryption and multiparty computation and how these technologies can be explored for advancing the security of IoT.

## Homomorphic Encryption

Homomorphic encryption (HE) is a technology first envisioned in the late 1970s (Rivest et al., 1978) and first demonstrated as a general-purpose solution for computing over encrypted data in 2009 (Gentry, 2009). The key point of HE is that the decryptor must be different from the computing entity. If they were the same, the person computing on encrypted data could just decrypt the data and compute in the clear, which is unsecure.

There are efficient linear homomorphic encryption schemes which allow one to compute linear functions (such as averages). Non-linear functions (such as standard deviations) require fully homomorphic encryption (FHE) schemes. An FHE scheme allows both homomorphic addition and multiplication over encrypted data and from these operations we can compute a circuit to evaluate any function.

With current technology, homomorphic encryption can generally compute "low multiplicative depth circuits," that is, functions with low computational complexity. As an example, most algorithms applying existing machine learning models are relatively low in depth in nature.

## Multiparty Computation

Secure computation, also known as multiparty computation (MPC), achieves the same goals as FHE (i.e., to compute over encrypted data) using a different strategy. Instead of requiring a single computing party, it uses multiple computing parties (who could be data owners). In MPC, security comes from the use of multiple parties. If they collude, all security is lost, but you trust a subset of them not to collude. If you are one of the computing parties, you trust yourself, so your security is guaranteed. MPC usually works by secret sharing data.

While FHE requires large amounts of computation to compute nonlinear functions, MPC requires large amounts of communication. In practice, MPC is always faster than FHE by a few orders of magnitude (two or three). MPC is currently deployed in a number of situations, usually bespoke solutions for a specific problem or for a highly repeatable problem space.

### FHE Versus MPC

Even MPC and FHE may require differential privacy protection on the results. Just because you compute the output of a function in a secure manner does not mean that revealing the function output is not going to break privacy. The DP noise needs to be computed within the MPC/FHE computation before the result is revealed, otherwise it could just be peeled off. One could apply MPC/FHE to perform the merging of models in federated machine learning, thus each party produces a local model and then only this is merged using MPC.

Attacks are still possible if the data set is used more than once, for example, how do you know the other party is using the same data set or has not tweaked their local model to try to reveal information about your data/local model?

There is a key difference between MPC and FHE. In FHE you trust the computing party to do the correct thing. However, what if they compute the wrong function? Such an attacker is called an "active" attacker. In MPC if one of the party's deviates from the proscribed function in this way it is detected by most deployable protocols. Thus, MPC easily provides protection against active attacks. Active attacks are not just a problem in getting the wrong result. They can lead to a privacy breach. To secure FHE against active attacks one needs to deploy a different form of PET technology.

## CONCLUSIONS

The tremendous transformative potential of the IoT in the current technological landscape is undeniable. A world of machines communicating with each other, generating, transferring, processing, and analyzing data in real time is an inspiring reality, a true ecosystem for the continuous development of increasingly autonomous and ubiquitous technological solutions. It's not all good news, however, and the indiscriminate increase in connectivity has turned out to be a security and privacy issue with more serious implications than any IoT enthusiast would like to admit. It is necessary to understand the concrete dangers constantly threatening the world of IoT so that possible solutions can also be identified, evaluated, and properly implemented where and when appropriate. Although corrections in existing applications are extremely necessary to guarantee satisfactory levels of security and privacy, the ideal is that IoT solutions are developed based on security and privacy by design and by default.

## REFERENCES

Al-Qaseemi, S. A., Almulhim, H. A., Almulhim, M. F., & Chaudhry, S. R. (2016). IoT architecture challenges and issues: Lack of standardization. *Future Technologies Conference, 1*(1), 731–738. https://doi.org/10.1109/FTC.2016.7821686

Ashton, K. (2009). That 'Internet of things' thing. *RFID Journal, 22*(7), 97–114. https://www.rfidjournal.com/that-internet-of-things-thing

Cameron, A., & Williamson, G. (2020). Introduction to IAM architecture. *IDPro Body of Knowledge, 1*(6). https://doi.org/10.55621/idpro.38

Ferguson, G. T. (2002). Have your objects call my objects. *Harvard Business Review, 80*(6), 138–144. https://hbr.org/2002/06/have-your-objects-call-my-objects

Gentry, C. (2009). *A fully homomorphic encryption scheme* [Unpublished doctoral dissertation]. Stanford University. https://crypto.stanford.edu/craig/craig-thesis.pdf

Jafarnejad, S., Codeca, L., Bronzi, W., Frank, R., & Engel, T. (2015). A car hacking experiment: When connectivity meets vulnerability. *2015 IEEE Globecom Workshops*, 1–6. https://doi.org/10.1109/GLOCOMW.2015.7413993

Kagita M. K., Thilakarathne, N., Gadekallu, T. R., Maddikunta, P. K. R., & Singh, S. (2021). A review on cyber crimes on the Internet of things. In A. Makkar & N. Kumar (Eds.), *Deep learning for security and privacy preservation in IoT* (pp. 83–98). Springer.

Lane, T. (2017). *The "only" Coke machine on the Internet.* Carnegie Mellon University. https://www.cs.cmu.edu/~coke/history_long.txt

Maksimović, M., Vujović, V., & Perišić, B. (2015, June 17–20). A custom Internet of things healthcare system. In *Proceedings of the 10th Iberian Conference on Information Systems and Technologies* (pp. 1–6). IEEE. https://doi.org/10.1109/CISTI.2015.7170415

Malhotra, P., Singh, Y., Anand, P., Bangotra, D. K., Singh, P. K., & Hong, W. C. (2021). Internet of things: Evolution, concerns and security challenges. *Sensors, 21*(5), 1809.

Moganedi, M. (2018, June 28–29). *Undetectable data breach in IoT: Healthcare data at risk [Paper presentation].* 17th European Conference on Cyber Warfare and Security, Oslow, Norway. https://researchspace.csir.co.za/dspace/handle/10204/10485

Nayyar, A., Rameshwar, R. U. D. R. A., & Solanki, A. (2020). Internet of things (IoT) and the digital business environment: A standpoint inclusive cyber space, cyber crimes, and cybersecurity. In D. G. Chowdhry, R. Verma, & M. Mathur (Eds.), *The evolution of business in the cyber age* (pp. 111–152). Apple Academic Press.

NIST Computer Security Resource Center. (n.d.). Separation of duty (SOD). In *Glossary*. Retrieved May 7, 2022, from https://csrc.nist.gov/glossary/term/separation_of_duty

Patel, K. K., Patel, S. M., & Scholar, P. (2016). Internet of things—IOT: Definition, characteristics, architecture, enabling technologies, application & future challenges. *International Journal of Engineering Science and Computing, 6*(5).

Rivest, R., Len, A., & Dertouzos, M. L. (1978). On data banks and privacy homomorphisms. In R. A. Demillo, D. P. Dobkin, A. K. Jones, & R. J. Lipton (Eds.), *Foundations of secure computation* (pp. 169–180). Academic Press.

Rose, S., Borchert, O., Mitchell, S., & Connelly, S. (2020). *Zero trust architecture (NIST Special Publication 800-207)*. National Institute of Standards and Technology. https://doi.org/10.6028/NIST.SP.800-207

Samaniego, M., & Deters, R. (2018, July 2–7). Zero-trust hierarchical management in IoT. In *Proceedings for the IEEE International Congress on Internet of Things* (pp. 88–95) . IEEE. https://doi.org/10.1109/ICIOT.2018.00019

Sarkar, K. R. (2010). Assessing insider threats to information security using technical, behavioural and organisational measures. *Information Security Technical Report, 15*(3), 112–133. https://doi.org/10.1016/j.istr.2010.11.002

Ukil, A., Bandyopadhyay, S., & Pal, A. (2014, April 27–May 2). IoT-privacy: To be private or not to be private. In *Proceedings for the 2014 IEEE Conference on Computer Communications Workshops* (pp. 123–124). IEEE. https://doi.org/10.1109/INFCOMW.2014.6849186

Weiser, M. (1991). The computer for the 21st century. *Scientific American, 265*(3), 94–105. https://www.lri.fr/~mbl/Stanford/CS477/papers/Weiser-SciAm.pdf

Yaqoob, I., Ahmed, E., ur Rehman, M. H., Ahmed, A. I. A., Al-garadi, M. A., Imran, M., & Guizani, M. (2017). The rise of ransomware and emerging security challenges in the Internet of things. *Computer Networks, 129*(1), 444–458. https://doi.org/10.1016/j.comnet.2017.09.003

Zahra, S. R. (2019). Ransomware and Internet of things: A new security nightmare. In Proceedings for the *2019 9th international conference on cloud computing, data science & engineering* (pp. 551–555). IEEE. https://doi.org/10.1109/CONFLUENCE.2019.8776926

# CHAPTER 6

# IMPLEMENTATION OF DENSENET DEEP LEARNING MECHANISM FOR THORAX DISEASE CLASSIFICATION IN CHEST X-RAY IMAGES

**D. Ganesh**
*Sree Vidyanikethan Engineering College*

**K. Suresh**
*Jain (Deemed-to-be University)*

**Mohamed Yasin**
*Sultan Qaboos University Alkhoudh, Oman*

**Gurram Sunitha**
*Mohan Babu University*

**Thulasi Bikku**
*Vignan's Nirula Institute of Technology
and Science for Women*

*Innovations in Computational Intelligence, Big Data Analytics, and Internet of Things*, pages 93–112
Copyright © 2024 by Information Age Publishing
www.infoagepub.com

## ABSTRACT

One of the most readily available diagnostic methods for chest problems is thorax radiography. Deep learning has been developed drastically these days and its algorithms are steadily more utilized to improve the accuracy of detection of the abnormalities related to the thorax disorders on chest X-ray pictures. It's crystal clear that the correlation of deep convolutional neural networks (DCNNs) on comparing to single networks helps in outperforming chest X-ray picture categorization performance. Here, we put forward DenseNet-169 to study the features with abnormalities for the classification of thorax disease on the results of the radiography on the upper body. A training technique is also developed to combine the loss contributions of the participating classifiers into a single loss. A blend of the discriminative functions in DenseNet helps to enhance the performance of the thorax disorder class in chest X-ray images. We carry out our trials on the CheXpert dataset that exhibits the productiveness of the proposed technique when compared to its previous proposals.

As one of the most widely available radiographic tests for diagnosing and evaluating a wide range of lung and cardiac heart conditions, the chest X-ray (CXR) is an excellent tool. Most of the human beings die every 12 months from chest ailments, together with lung infections, pulmonary disease, and lung cancer. A test can assist in early prognosis. In general, every CXR picture may also comprise one or extra anomalies.

The vast majority of CXRs made are examined entirely via visible survey, finished by a specialist. For this, an excessive diploma of talent and attention is required, it's a possibility to apply automatic computational techniques together with computer-aided diagnosis (CAD). Developing a solid and strong computer-aided disorder evaluation device is essential to help disorder prognosis and treatment (Prabhakar et al., 2021). For the thorax disorder type problem, one of these devices is vital to recognition at the capacity lesion regions and suppress the noise added with the aid of using the inappropriate regions. Additionally, exploring the intrinsic correlations of more than one illness is likewise useful to enhance the overall performance of the computer-aided device.

One of the most pressing concerns and challenges in medical image analysis is the need to accurately classify medical images (Sowmya et al., 2023). The categorization process is worn to assign diagnostics to photos based on what they contain. Computer-aided diagnosis of thorax illnesses appears to include two steps: identifying pathological anomalies and classifying those anomalies. Detecting anomalies is difficult because of the complexity and variety of thoracic illnesses, as well as the low quality of chest radiography. The vast majority of publicly accessible chest radiograph databases include the classifications, but not the locations of anomalies in each case. CXR pictures pathological anomalies are challenging to classify since a chest radiograph might comprise a variety of thoracic illnesses, and their locations and sizes are sometimes extremely variable.

Many CXR scans contain non-chest regions that are not necessary, for example, neck and arm locations (Murthy et al., 2022). Instead of focusing on the overall image, on each CXR picture, we must concentrate on the lesion region. When confronted with a problem to locate lesion with the help of a feature learning process directed by attention, the model must be more flexible than previously. Several state-of-the-art techniques, such as ResNet (He et al., 2016) and DenseNet (Huang et. al 2017) have created significant attempts to design a much more intricate architecture in order to grow more meaningful characteristics. In this work, we propose DenseNet-169 as the backbone for a system of lesion attention for the categorization of thoracic pathology, which is inspired by these designs and methodologies.

We sum up the commitments of this work as follows:

- For CXR picture class, we present a DenseNet-169 that learns discriminative features.
- When compared against state-of-the-art techniques, experimental results on the CheXpert dataset show that the DenseNet-169 outperforms them.

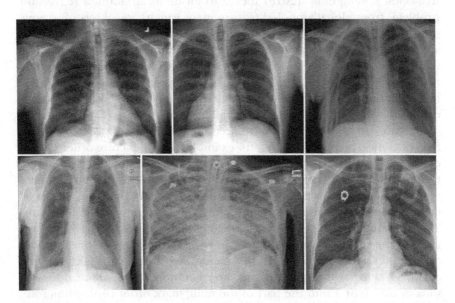

**Figure 6.1** Examples of CheXpert dataset. The first row represents some CheXpert images with no thorax; the second row represents CheXpert images with thorax disease.

- The judgments of the three different classifiers are combined to provide a unified loss value using a training approach based on a single loss function.

## LITERATURE SURVEY

### Medical Malady Diagnosing

Zhang et al. planned a dual-attention paradigm of victimization pictures and alternative texts to form correct predictions (Zhang et al., 2017). Xie et al. (2017) planned an associate degree model of image-to-text to ascertain an instantaneous matching from medical pictures to analysis reports. Every model that is being proposed so far was assessed using a dataset of cancer pictures and correlated with the diagnostic information. Wang et al. (2017) used the benefit of wide-ranging CXR information to generate reasons for the affliction to the body and drawbacks in the diagnosis as multi-label classification and many more. They additionally used novel technique to aspect map image in every category and extracted the spring box for every malady. Concerned outcomes of utmost quality revealed that the model's bounding boxes were frequently far larger than the actual ones. Hwang et al. (2018) meant to locate localization, a regression problem, from globally pooled feature maps which are subsets of various individual classes supervised by image labels using a self-transfer learning architecture. Category activating mapping (Zhou et al., 2016) handles natural images in these works, which have a consistent essence. There was no direct development of the scenario annotation information into the loss function in any of those works. The malady regions were not properly captured by pooling focused mostly on location.

Deep learning procedures have accomplished critical advances in the field of clinical picture handling, for example, clinical picture order (Wang et al., 2017 ), clinical picture division (Zhang et al., 2019), and clinical picture union. For the chest X-beam picture grouping issue, the greater part of the current works is geared toward presenting extra bouncing boxes or medical records regarding it as an old-style multi-mark issue (Wang et al., 2017). Joining with worldwide picture highlights, limiting the injury regions in the chest X-beam picture, or presenting the related clinical report data could serve for analysis. In this paper, we just spotlight CXR picture characterization with picture marks, however, don't think about different sorts of oversight. From the part of the multi-mark order issue, numerous preliminaries have been suggested to characterize the upper body X-Ray beam picture. Wang et al. (2017) constructed an infection expectation standard with the exemplary CNN designs and confined the illness sore regions in light of the weighted initiation maps proposed by Zhou et al. (2016). Rajpurkar et al. (2018) adjusted the DenseNet (Huang et al., 2017) design with a 14-yield completely associated layer and made an exhibition examination between profound learning calculation and the radiologists. In this work, we suggest noticing the disease through DenseNet-169 (Huang et al., 2017) which gives better results than DenseNet-121 that is being used in the paper, which we have considered as our reference paper.

## METHODOLOGY

### Understanding Datasets Followed by Cleaning Data

We planned on using datasets that contain wide-ranging x-rays of the chest of various patients and finally landed at CheXpert released by Stanford. Since most of the data that is used for disease analysis is imbalanced, we need to make sure that no anomalies are present to avoid further problems from being generated. So, we perform validation as well to check the quality of data and the accuracy being generated using this dataset. Here we usually segregate the data into two different classes, that is, normal and thorax class and we use this class-specific data to train the model. We start pre-processing by resizing the shape of the images into one specific format, that is, 1/255 which means, initially all because our original photos have RGB values in the range of 0–255, they are too strong to train our system on, therefore we scale the images down to ranging between 0 and 1. So, it's easier to process them further. We also convert them into grayscale to study them clearly. We use data augmentation that involves cropping, padding, and horizontal flipping which not only helps in cleaning the data but also helps us in generating more data that will be useful in the training model when the dataset alone is insufficient.

### Problem Motivation

The classification based on CXR figure experience from the abundant quantity of noisy areas outside the abnormality area and explicit mechanism lacks in capturing the relationships among distinct diseases. So correspondingly The DenseNet can accomplish both of these goals at the same time. DenseNet structure is shown in Figure 6.2. Given a CXR picture, we extract its features with a DenseNet, that is, DenseNet-169 (Alemi et al., 2017). We classify them based on the training done with class-specific datasets that are used in the process of model development. Based on this learning it classifies the CXR into illness related or healthy persons.

## Dense Net—The Preferred CNN Architecture

Let's take a single image i0 and allow it to pass through a convolution network. This system consists of $N$ levels, where every one of the layers contributes to the implementation of a nonlinear transfiguration $G\ell(\cdot)$, where $\ell$ indicators the sub caste $G\ell(.)$ can be an aggregated variable of procedures which are just such as regularization, rectified straight lines (ReLU), accumulating, or convolution (Conv; Rudrakumar et al., 2023). We indicate the issue of a $\ell$th lower castes as $i\ell$. ResNets. Conventional feed-forward systems connect the $\ell$th subcaste's affairs as input to the $\ell$1st sub caste, resulting in the following sub caste transition. $i\ell = G\ell(i\ell - 1)$. ResNets architecture usually works with these skip-connections concept that bypasses the non-linear conversion with an identity function.

$$i\ell = G\ell(i\ell - 1)i\ell - 1 \qquad (6.1)$$

Recurrent Neural Networks (ReNets) offer their own unique set of advantages, such as allowing gradients to flow straight through their identity functions from the layers in front to those in back (Avanija et al., 2022). This may cause issues with network information flow, as the identification functions and the $G\ell$ result are both mixed.

### Dense Connectivity

To advance the details in between the layers we put forward a distinct connectivity pattern: Here we establish a connection between each of its previous layers with its next layers. Figure 6.2a explains the working procedure of DenseNet pictographically. It sends the feature maps produced by its previous layers as an input to its next layers. $i0, \ldots, i\ell - 1$, as input:

$$i\ell = G\ell\big((i0, i1, \ldots, i\ell - 1)\big) \qquad (6.2)$$

where $(i0, i1, \ldots, i\ell - 1)$ refers to the summation of the outcomes of the previous layers, that is, feature maps, and these layers are numbered as follows: $0, \ldots, \ell - 1$. We refer to this system armature as a Dense Convolutional Network because of its extensive connection. To reduce the complexity and to perceive information easily we chain up the multiple inputs of $G\ell(\cdot)$ in Equation 6.2 into a single tensor.

### Composite Function

On analysis of various papers prior, we define $G\ell(\cdot)$ as a function that is blended of the following operations like batch normalization, followed by a (ReLU) and a $4 \times 4$ complexity.

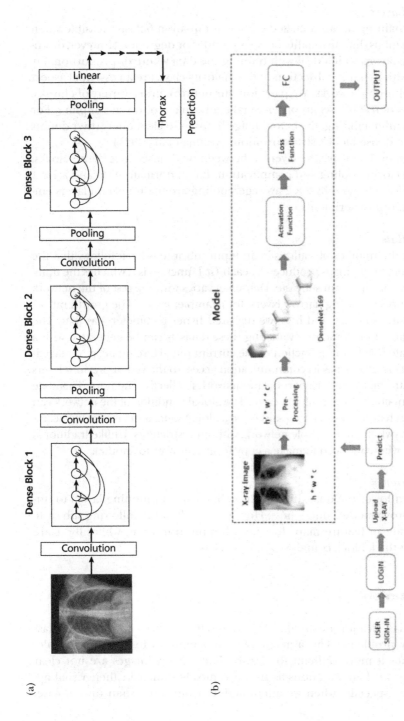

**Figure 6.2** (a) Deep dense net with 3 dense blocks. Transition layers are the layers that are present in between 2 consecutive dense blocks; (b) Overview of the proposed system. Given an image, with the help of DenseNet169, we extract features, then identify the disease correlated features.

*Pooling Layers*

The chaining up as discussed earlier in Equation 6.2 isn't feasible when attribute maps dimensionality or size upgrades or degrades. However, down-sampling layers, which deal with training the data where disproportionality is dealt with in a tiny subsection of the majority class, are an essential aspect of convolution networks. We partition our network into a variety of chunks, known as dense blocks, in order to take advantage of down-sampling. For further understanding, the below image helps us to clear out further doubts about the dense block's structurization (Avanija et al., 2021).

Transition layers are the layers in between two consecutive dense blocks, which perform pooling and complication. Batch normalization and a $1 \times 1$ convolution followed by $2 \times 2$ average pooling are the transition layers employed in our experiments.

*Growth Rate*

When the number of stations in an input subcaste is k0, it follows that the number of feature maps produced by each $G\ell$ 1 function is $k$, which is the number of lines in the input subcaste. DenseNet varies with the rest of the network architectures by having narrow layers, for example, $k = 18$. The growth rate of the network is crucial and here we declared hyper parameter $k$ as that. The state-of-the-art outcomes in evaluating these datasets can be generated with a growth rate that is only a fraction of the current rate. Here we need to make it clear that each layer has its communication access to the rest of previous layers and feature maps that are part of the network's collective memory. This state has $k$ point-charts from each sub caste. The global condition of the network can be seen in feature maps. Being said to be a global state, it means having access from everywhere in the whole network, without restrictions. Unlike traditional networks where we need to make a copy from one layer to another.

*Compression*

We can lower the quantity of points-charts at transitioning layers to further improve model conciseness. However, we allow the following sub caste to generate m feature maps for the following transition, where $0 < 1$ are used. If a thick block contains $m$ point charts.

## Optimization

The classification of the data in these datasets faces a lot of inter-class similarity problems. The availability of few samples for certain pathologies makes it more difficult to classify. These X-ray images are not clear in displaying their variations as they are mostly similar in their visual appearance especially when a patient suffers from more than one disease.

This commonness leads to overfitting when a large scale of parameters is taken into consideration (Avanija et al., 2022). So this may create ambiguity which results in the network getting confused and not accurate as well.

To handle this issue we have utilized the optimizers that are available in various forms. Whereas here we preferred using "Adam" as our optimizer and calculated the loss using loss functions which let us improve the efficiency and quality of data to be trained and the model to be developed.

## IMPLEMENTATION

Here, we assess the effectiveness and performance of the algorithm that we have proposed so far. We will start with the dataset introduction, cleaning of data that is actually known to be pre-processing, and later the training of the model and its functionality and parameters that are involved in it.

### Collections of Data

We tend to evaluate our technique on the CheXpert (Irvin et al., 2019) datasets. The foreign terrorist organization scores for every study of the disease and therefore the average foreign terrorist organization scores overall pathologies square measure accordingly.

CheXpert (Irvin et al., 2019) is a pack of huge datasets necessary for the thorax disease identification project and thanks to Stanford for making it available for free online. For the sake of the dataset, they have gathered around 224,316 chest radiographs from 65,240 patients. We use this dataset for training, testing, and finally evaluating the performance of the model that is built using DenseNet-169 architecture.

### Implementation of the Proposed Model

For better usability, we have created a user interface using web technologies, where a registration form for a new patient is made available with a login option side by and on logging into the website, an option to upload the X-ray image, and predict option to diagnose the presence of the disease are the fragments of the user interface that we have created.

When coming to the development of the model, which plays a crucial role in the whole project we made an experiment with DenseNet-169 and implemented it using PyCharm IDE. PyCharm is an IDE that is a better source available online for the development and execution of the code where Python is opted as its main coding language. PyCharm makes it easier to debug errors in the code with its highly qualified debuggers and testers which are part of it and also its support for web development simplifies the development of the user interface.

Since the data is imbalanced, we have added validation along with training and testing. We have pre-processed the data and performed the data augmentation technique which involves reshaping, cropping, flipping, and various other techniques involved in it. We have used global average pooling, a type of pooling that helps in reducing the complexity of the model. We planned the optimization of the network using Adam with a batch size of 64 and training as many as 50 epochs. In order to grasp the complex patterns in the data, we have applied a few activation functions like ReLU and softmax (Avanija et al., 2021). To quantify the performance of the model we used loss functions like categorical cross-entropy. Finally, we trained the model with the data and calculated the accuracy and visualization of the model with a tensor board.

In machine learning, to enhance one thing you regularly have to be compelled to be ready to live it (Reddy et al., 2022). Tensor Board is the tool we preferred for visualization of the model we have developed. It not only supports visualization but also helps in calculating the accuracy and loss generated by the model.

Tensor Board offers us the visualization of data both on accuracy and loss over scalars, time series, and many more. So, let's learn about each one of them on a summary basis (Reddy et al., 2022). Scalars dashboard helps in visualizing the switching in the values of loss and accuracy of the model during each epoch. We can also use it to envision the learning rate.

The distributions and histograms dashboards let us visualize how the tensor is distributed over time which is used to examine the weights that are associated with biases and examine that they are dynamical in the manner we initially expected them to be.

As the number of epochs escalates, the accuracy and the efficiency of the model shoot up as high as possible.

## RESULTS

The DenseNet-169 (Huang et al., 2017) is adopted as our baseline on the dataset named as "CheXpert" which is downloadable on the Kaggle website. The design is not completely the same as the paper that we have considered to be our reference paper. There they used a ConsultNet along with DensetNet-121 as part of their model, whereas here we replaced this whole part with DenseNet-169 and used global average pooling instead.

We wanted to experiment with the architecture that outperforms DenseNet-121 and we are glad to have the expected results (Figure 6.9). We

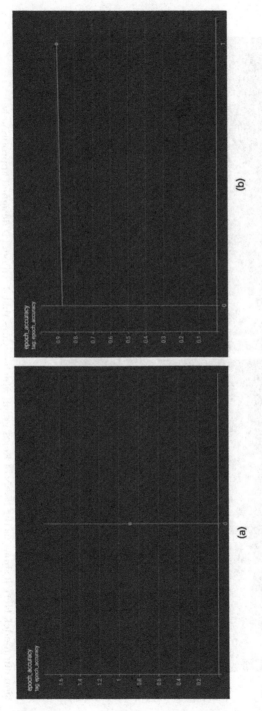

**Figure 6.3** Accuracy of the model on the Scalar Dashboard during 1 epoch (a) and 2 epochs (b).

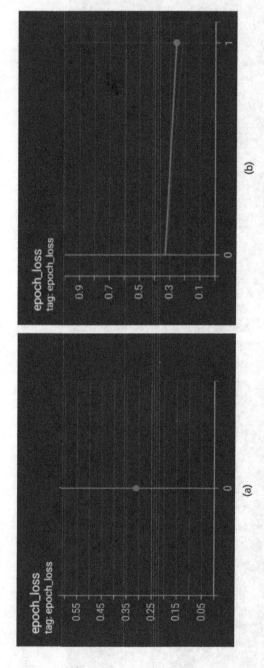

**Figure 6.4** Loss of the model on the Scalar Dashboard during 1 epoch (a) and 2 epochs (b). The Graphs dashboard lets us envision our model. Here it shows us the layers of Keras graph which ensures that the model is designed appropriately.

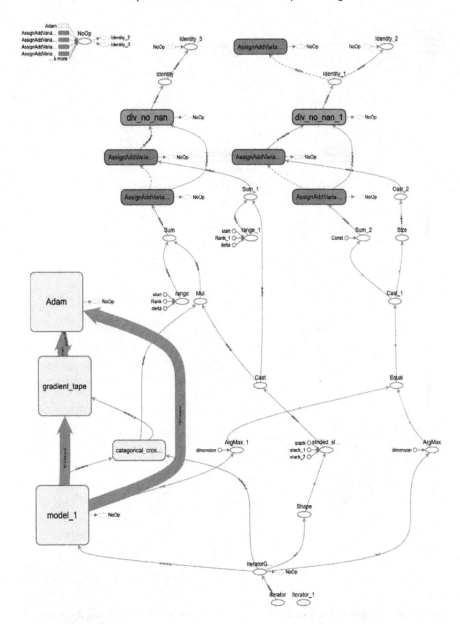

**Figure 6.5**  Design of the model generated using Tensor Board during 1 epoch.

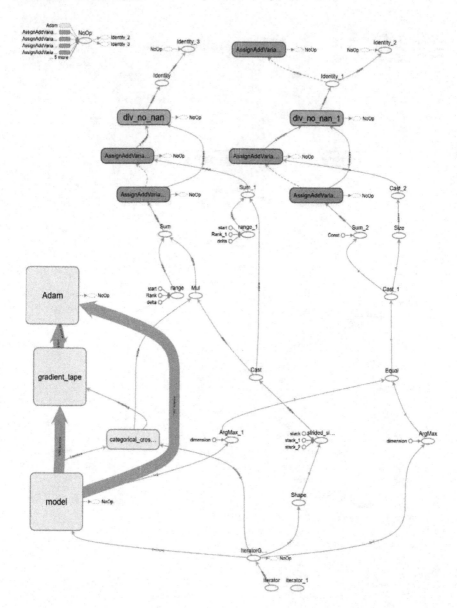

**Figure 6.6** Design of the model generated using Tensor Board during 2 epochs.

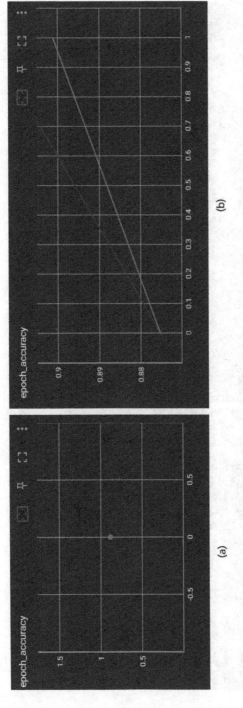

**Figure 6.7** Accuracy of the model on the Time Series Dashboard during 1 epoch (a) and 2 epochs (b).

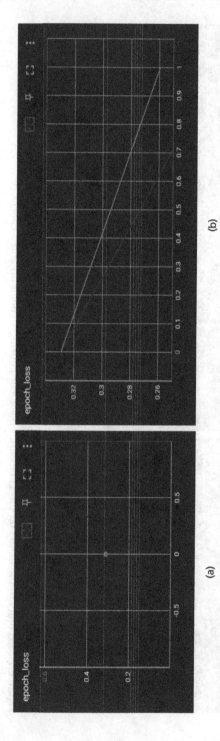

(a)

(b)

**Figure 6.8** Loss of the model on the Time Series Dashboard during 1 epoch (8a) and 2 epochs (8b).

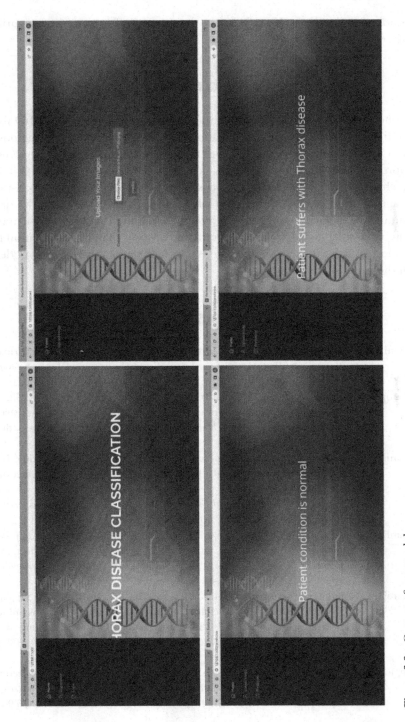

**Figure 6.9**  Output of our model.

can observe that DenseNet-169 has its dominant performance in categorizing certain pathologies.

## CONCLUSION

We hereby conclude that we show and describe a novel DenseNet-169 for multilabel thoracic disease classification that focuses on the lesion regions' most discriminative properties. From the same input image, the proposed approach learned complementary features. This method includes the mechanisms and techniques that focuses on the regions of the thorax X-ray images that are related to the goal label and highlights the network's discriminative elements. Here the architecture follows cumulative passage of outcomes of all nodes to the next node that ensures that the information is not lost and also makes sure that there is less impact of error-causing nodes on the rest of the network.

## REFERENCES

Alemi, A. A., Fischer, I., Dillon, J. V., & Murphy, K. (2017). Deep variational information bottleneck. In *Proceedings of the International Conference on Learning Representations (ICLR)* (pp. 1–19). https://doi.org/10.48550/arXiv.1612.00410

Avanija, J., Konduru, S., Kura, V., NagaJyothi, G., Dudi, B. P., & S., M. N. (2022). Designing a fuzzy q-learning power energy system using reinforcement learning. *International Journal of Fuzzy System Applications, 11*(3), 1–12. https://doi.org/10.4018/IJFSA.306284

Avanija, J., Mohan Reddy, C. C., Chandan Reddy, C., Harshavardhan Reddy, D., Narasimhulu, T., & Napa Venkata Hardhik. (2023). Skin cancer detection using ensemble learning. In *Proceedings for the 2023 International Conference on Sustainable Computing and Smart Systems (ICSCSS)*. IEEE. https://doi.org/10.1109/ICSCSS57650.2023.10169747

Avanija, J., Sunitha, G., Reddy Madhavi, K., & Hitesh Sai Vittal, R. (2021). An automated approach for detection of intracranial haemorrhage using densenets. In K. A. Reddy, B. R. Devi, B. George, & K. S. Raju (Eds.), *Data engineering and communication technology* (pp. 611–619). Springer.

Avanija, J., Sunitha, G., Reddy Madhavi, K., Sreenivasa Chakravarthi, S., & Sai Vittal, R. H. (2022). Prediction and analysis of cervical cancer: An ensemble approach. In *Proceedings of the 2022 4th International Conference on Inventive Research in Computing Applications (ICIRCA)*. IEEE. https://doi.org/10.1109/ICIRCA54612.2022.9985601

He, K., Zhang, X., Ren, S., & Sun, J. (2016). Deep residual learning for image recognition. In *Proceedings of the IEEE Conference on Computer Vision and Pattern Recognition (CVPR)* (pp. 770–778). IEEE. https://doi.org/10.1109/CVPR.2016.90

Huang, G., Liu, Z., Van Der Maaten, L., & Weinberger, K. Q. (2017). Densely connected convolutional networks. In *Proceedings of the IEEE Conference on Computer Vision and Pattern Recognition (CVPR)* (pp. 4700–4708). IEEE. https://doi.org/10.1109/CVPR.2017.243

Irvin, J., Rajpurkar, P., Ko, M., Yu, Y., Ciurea-Ilcus, S., Chute, C., Marklund, H., Haghgoo, B., Ball, R., Shpanskaya, K., Seekins, J., Mong, D. A., Halabi, S. S., Sandberg, J. K., Jones, R., Larson, D. B., Langlotz, C. P., Patel, B. N., Lungren, M. P., & Ng, A. Y. (2019). CheXpert: A large chest radiograph dataset with uncertainty labels and expert comparison. In *Proceedings of the AAAI Conference, 33*(1), 590–597. https://doi.org/10.1609/aaai.v33i01.3301590

Murthy, D. S., Prasad, V. S., Aman, K., Reddy, M. P. K., Madhavi, K. R., & Sunitha, G. (2022, December). An investigative study of shallow, deep and dense learning models for breast cancer detection based on microcalcifications. In *Proceedings of the 2022 International Conference on Data Science, Agents & Artificial Intelligence (ICDSAAI)* (Vol. 1, pp. 1-6). IEEE. https://doi.org/10.1109/ICDSAAI55433.2022.10028840

Prabhakar, T., Sunitha, G., Gudavalli Madhavi, J. A., & Madhavi, K. R. (2021). Automatic detection of diabetic retinopathy in retinal images: A study of recent advances. *Annals of the Romanian Society for Cell Biology*, 15277–15289. http://annalsofrscb.ro/index.php/journal/article/view/5011

Rajpurkar, P., Irvin, J., Ball, R. L., Zhu, K., Yang, B., Mehta, H., Duan, T., Ding, D., Bagul, A., Langlotz, C. P., Patel, B. N., Yeom, K. W., Shpanskaya, K., Blankenberg, F. G., Seekins, J., Amrhein, T. J., Mong, D. A., Halabi, S. S., Zucker, E. J., Ng, A. Y., & Lungren, M. P. (2018). Deep learning for chest radiograph diagnosis: A retrospective comparison of the CheXNeXt algorithm to practicing radiologists. *PLoS Medicine, 15*(11), e1002686. https://doi.org/10.1371/journal.pmed.1002686

Reddy, M. K., Kovuri, K., Avanija, J., Sakthivel, M., & Kaleru, S. (2022). Brain stroke prediction using deep learning: A CNN approach. In *Proceedings of the 2022 4th International Conference on Inventive Research in Computing Applications (ICIRCA)* (pp. 775–780). IEEE. https://doi.org/10.1109/ICIRCA54612.2022.9985596

Reshma, G., Al-Atroshi, C., Nassa, V. K., Geetha, B., Sunitha, G., Galety, M. G., & Neelakandan, S. (2022). Deep learning-based skin lesion diagnosis model using dermoscopic images. *Intelligent Automation & Soft Computing, 31*(1), 621–634. https://doi.org/10.32604/iasc.2022.019117

Rudra Kumar, M., Natteshan, N. V. S., Avanija, J., Reddy Madhavi, K., Charan, N. S., & Kushal, V. (2023). SMOTE-TOMEK: A hybrid sampling-based ensemble learning approach for sepsis prediction. In *Proceedings of the 2023 2nd International Conference on Edge Computing and Applications (ICECAA)* (pp. 724–729). IEEE. https://doi.org/10.1109/ICECAA58104.2023.10212208

Sowmya, T. S., Narasimhulu, T., Sunitha, G., Manikanta, T., & Venkatesh, T. (2023). Vision transformer based ResNet model for pneumonia prediction. In *Proceedings of the 4th International Conference on Electronics and Sustainable Communication Systems (ICESC)* (pp. 316–321). IEEE. https://doi.org/10.1109/ICESC57686.2023.10193644

Wang, X., Peng, Y., Lu, L., Lu, Z., Bagheri, M., & Summers, R. M. (2017). ChestX-ray8: Hospital-scale chest x-ray database and benchmarks on weakly-supervised classification and localization of common thorax diseases. In *Proceedings of the 2017 IEEE Conference on Computer Vision and Pattern Recognition (CVPR)* (pp. 3462–3471). IEEE. https://doi.org/10.48550/arXiv.1705.02315

Xie, Y., Zhang, Z., Xing, F., McGough, M., & Yang, L. (2017). *MDNet: A semantically and visually interpretable medical image diagnosis network.* https://doi.org/10.48550/arXiv.1707.02485

Zhang, Z., Chen, P., Sapkota, M., & Yang, L. (2017). Tandemnet: Distilling knowledge from medical images using diagnostic reports as optional semantic references. In M. Descoteaux, L. Maier-Hein, A. Franz, P. Jannin, D. L. Collins, & S. Duchesne (Eds.), *International Conference on Medical Image Computing and Computer-Assisted Intervention–MICCAI 2017* (pp. 320–328). Springer.

Zhang, Z., Fu, H., Dai, H., Shen, J., Pang, Y., & Shao, L. (2019). ET-Net: A generic edge-attention guidance network for medical image segmentation. In *Proceedings of the International Conference on Medical Image Computing and Computer-Assisted Intervention* (pp. 442–450). https://doi.org/10.48550/arXiv.1907.10936

Zhou, B., Khosla, A., Lapedriza, A., Oliva, A., & Torralba, A. (2016). Learning deep features for discriminative localization. In *Proceedings of the IEEE Conference on Computer Vision and Pattern Recognition (CVPR)* (pp. 2921–2929). https://doi.org/10.48550/arXiv.1512.04150

CHAPTER 7

# AN INTEGRATED COMPREHENSIVE SECURITY FRAMEWORK FOR WIRELESS SENSOR NETWORKS

## A Survey

**V. Jyothsna**
*Mohan Babu University*

**P. Bhasha**
*Sree Vidyanikethan Engineering College*

**E. Sandhya**
*Madanapalle Institute of Technology & Science*

**K. Khaja Baseer**
*Mohan Babu University*

*Innovations in Computational Intelligence, Big Data Analytics, and Internet of Things,* pages 113–137
Copyright © 2024 by Information Age Publishing
www.infoagepub.com

## ABSTRACT

Wireless sensor networks are highly disseminated networks containing small and light weighted sensors located densely to monitor and estimate the physical parameters of the deployed area. It is used in many real time applications in the area of military, environmental, healthcare, home warehouse, and threat detection, and so on. Due to its diversity deployment, it faces security as a major issue. Due to small and light weighted features of the sensor networks and constraints of power and energy, the cryptographic algorithms derived from symmetric or public keys are not appropriate for sensor networks. Researchers are focusing on providing the solutions for the security issues in the sensor networks, either providing the solution for the attacks at a particular layer or solution for a particular type of attacks. In this chapter, an integrated comprehensive security framework is proposed which provides security services in the sensor networks. This security framework consists of five components such as link layer communication protocol, key management scheme, credential management, integrity mechanism, and intrusion detection system.

## INTRODUCTION TO WIRELESS SENSOR NETWORKS

Wireless sensor networks (WSN) are highly disseminated networks containing tiny and light weighted sensors located densely to monitor and estimate the physical parameters of the deployed area (Singh et al., 2009). The recent advancements in the micro-electro mechanical systems (MEMS) technology are due to the sensor networks. Each and every node in the sensor networks has the capability of sensing, processing, and communicating. As sensor nodes are tiny and light weighted, it can sense only a limited area and have less processing power and energy (Kannan et al., 2022). The area of sensing can be wider by networking the sensors which leads to robust, reliable, and fault tolerable networks.

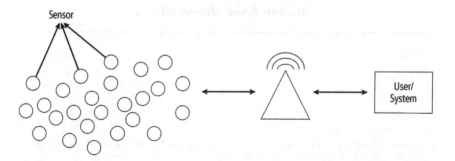

**Figure 7.1** Structure of sensor networks.

Further, the accuracy of data of sensors can be increased by providing cooperation and collaboration among sensor nodes. The other two main operations performed by the sensor networks are data dissemination and data gathering. The process of gathering and transferring sensed data from individual sensor nodes to the base station is known as data gathering, whereas the process of spreading data or queries throughout the network is known as data dissemination. To monitor the different ambient conditions a variety of sensors like seismic, thermal, visual, and infrared, and so forth are used (Bhasha et al., 2020).

## APPLICATIONS OF WIRELESS SENSOR NETWORKS

The following are a few applications for wireless sensor networks (Rashid & Rehmani, 2016):

- Military applications: It is used for monitoring and the surveillance of the battlefield and missiles.
- Environmental applications: It is used for monitoring nature, such as to detect fire in the forest area, detect floods, and monitor pets.
- Healthcare applications: Monitoring the patient's heartbeat, sugar levels, blood pressure, and so on, and sending these reports to the concerned doctors regularly (Silpa et al., 2022a). The doctors can suggest the appropriate treatment by suggesting the medicine and thus avoiding the movement of patients to the hospital (Arunacha-lam et al., 2023).
- Home applications: The sensors make homes a smart home. Today, all homes have appliances like ovens, air conditioners, freezers, and vacuum cleaners that allow them to communicate with one another and be operated remotely. Baby monitoring, door unlocking are also other applications of smart homes.
- Warehouse applications: It is used to monitor the stock in the inventory and helps to track the goods and products.
- Threat detection: It is used to monitor the threats in the system or network and alert the administrator regarding it. Additionally, it is utilized to prevent mass destruction strikes using chemical, biological, or nuclear weapons (Silpa, Niranjana & Ramani, 2022).

## COMPARISON WITH AD-HOC WIRELESS NETWORKS

- When compared to the quantity of nodes in an ad hoc network, the density of nodes deployed in sensor networks is enormous.

- As sensor nodes are very tiny, the energy draining will be very fast and mostly the battery cannot be replaceable or rechargeable (Baseer et al., 2022).
- The failure of nodes in sensor networks is more when compared to the nodes in ad hoc networks.
- There will not be any unique global identifiers (ID) for the sensor nodes, so the feasibility of proving unique addressing for sensor nodes is difficult.
- WSN works with the principle of data-centric, whereas ad-hoc networks work on the principle address-centric.
- One of the major tasks performed by the sensor nodes is data fusion/aggregation (Chakraborty & Das, 2017). It is the process of combining the information collected from different sensors before communicating to the base station. Data fusion's primary objective is to lower communication-related bandwidth, media access time, and power consumption.

## Wireless Sensor Network Architectures

The sensor network architectures are broadly divided into two types. They are (a) layered based architecture and (b) clustered based architecture.

### Layered Based Architecture

Layered architecture (Singh & Singh, 2018) is multi-hop infrastructure network architecture. It is mostly used in military and in-building wireless backbones. A base station (BS), which serves as an access point to a wired network, is part of the layered architecture. The network's sensor nodes received the beacon signals emitted by the BS. All nodes that are able to hear the BS's beacon signals will record the ID of the BS and broadcast the beacon signal back to the BS with their own IDs. Those nodes whose beacon signals can be heard by the BS form layer one as these nodes are one hop distance to the BS. After formation of layer one, the layer one nodes again emit the beacon signal. Since they are one hop away from layer one nodes, the layer one nodes build layer two with these nodes by recording the IDs of the nodes they hear. Now, the layer one nodes transmit the beacon signals to the BS to tell the layer two nodes' creation, and the layer two nodes then disseminate the information to the whole network. The layered structure's subsequent layers are constructed using the same method. Periodically beacon signals are transmitted in the network to provide the information about alters in the layer structure if any node is dead or moves out of range (Baseer et al., 2021).

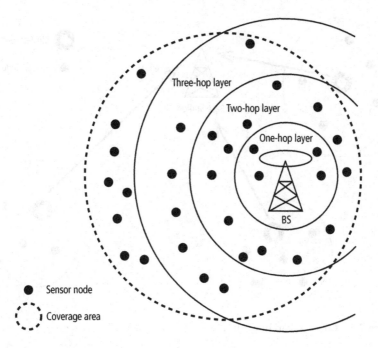

**Figure 7.2**  Layered architecture.

### Clustered Based Architecture

In clustered architecture all the nodes in the network are grouped into clusters and each group is headed with cluster head (Kabashkin, 2019). The exchange of data from the BS to the cluster nodes or from the cluster nodes to the BS is done by the cluster-head. The greater depth of hierarchy can be extended in clustering architecture. Mostly the clustering architecture is used in the applications where the data fusion is intrinsic. The cluster head gathers all the information from the members of the cluster and aggregate it and the resultant information is kept in correspondence to the BS. As sensor networks are self-organizing, formation of clusters and selecting the cluster-heads must be an autonomous, disseminated process.

The organization of the chapter in the remaining sections is as follows: Section 2 summarizes the security requirements and vulnerable features of WSN and layer wise security attacks in the WSNs. Section 3 presents the security framework which consists of five components such as link layer communication protocol, key management scheme, credential management, integrity mechanism, and intrusion detection system and also discusses major algorithms used in each component. Finally in Section 4, the chapter is concluded.

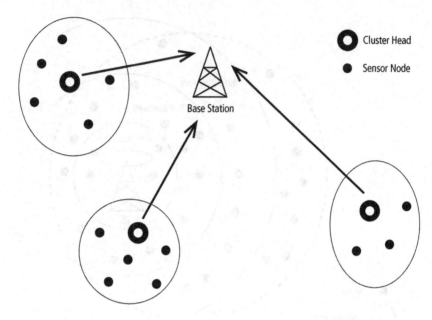

**Figure 7.3**  Clustered architecture.

## SECURITY IN WIRELESS SENSOR NETWORKS

Attackers attempt to exploit the limitations of WSNs, such as node limitations and network limitations, and cause significant performance deterioration in these networks, which are far more open to security threats than wired networks. Security is one of the primary goals of sensor networks (Veeramreddy et al., 2019) because the nodes trust each other to do all the operations such as data fusion, data gathering, data dissemination, and routing in the network. The aggregated information by all sensor nodes is finally communicated to the BS, so the communication links should also be secure. The cryptographic techniques based on symmetric or public key cryptography are not appropriate for sensor networks because of their tiny size and low weight (Silpa, Niranjana, & Ramani, 2022).

## SECURITY REQUIREMENTS

The following specifications should be met by a security protocol created for WSNs (Goyal et al., 2019). These specifications should be met by any security protocol created for other types of networks as well.

## Confidentiality

The information transmitted from the sender node should be under-standable only to the destination node. Attackers should not be able to extract any relevant information from the data transported from source to destination if any other hacker or attacker tries to get it. Data encryption is one of the most used cryptographic methods for ensuring secrecy.

## Integrity

When the data is transmitted from source, it should reach the destina-tion without tampering the data during transmission. If the attacker modi-fies the data, the destination should be able to identify whether it is tam-pered or not. The cryptographic algorithm used for providing the integrity is MAC and hash code algorithms (Silpa, Niranjana, & Ramani, 2022).

## Availability

At all times the network should be in operational condition and pro-vide services to the user when and then required. The network should be capable of fault tolerance and provide robustness in case attacks rise on it.

## Non-Repudiation

When the sender or receiver deny that they have not sent the message nor received the message in the network, then non-repudiation mechanism will help to identify whether they have really performed the above said ac-tivity or not. The commonly used mechanism for non-repudiation is digital signatures.

## Access Control

This mechanism prevents unauthorized people from accessing the re-sources. It will help control who can access the resource, under what con-ditions they can access, and from what resource they are allowed to access (Hima Bindu et al., 2021).

## Authentication

When two parties are communicating in the network, each entity should provide the assurance that the entity it is communicating is the one that it claims to be and also provide the assurance that the data transmitted is from the actual source that the receiver claimed to be.

## VULNERABLE FEATURES OF WSN

Some of the common vulnerable characteristics which may compromise the security requirements of the sensor network are as follows:

### Wireless Medium

Depending on the type of application and the environment, WSNs use different frequencies for communicating with each other and transmit the information from the nodes to the BSand from the BS to nodes and gateways (Naeem & Loo, 2009). In Europe, the sensor nodes communicate with the frequencies 315 MHz, 433 MHz, 868 MHz, whereas North America uses 915 MHz for communication. Initially, the WSNs were developed for military and disaster rescue operations. The 2.4 GHz industrial, scientific, and medical (ISM) band, a widely used radio frequency band, has enabled these networks to develop public applications.

### Cooperative MAC

When any nodes want to communicate it requires medium access. The hidden and exposed dilemma must be taken into consideration while creating the protocols at the MAC layer (Raviraj et al., 2005). Consider three

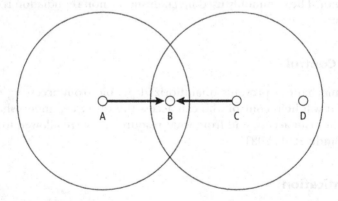

**Figure 7.4** Hidden terminal problem.

sensor nodes A, B, and C. The sensing range of Sensor A is till Sensor B only and the sensing range of Sensor C is till Sensor B only. That is, Sensor A does not know that there is Sensor C and vice versa as they are out of the sending bound for each other. In this situation, if Sensor A wants to transmit the data to Sensor B it will sense the medium and start transmitting if it is free. At the same time if Sensor C also wants to transmit the data to Sensor B it will sense the medium and if it is free it starts transmitting it. Even though both the Sensors A and C are transmitting the data to the same Sensor B, when they sense the medium they get the information that it is free because Sensor A and C are out of their sensing area. This is called a hidden problem and it leads to collisions.

When Sensor C is transmitting the information to another node in the range of B and C, if B wants to transmit the data to another node, say Sensor Node A, and it senses the medium, it will hear it as busy. This leads to unnecessary delay even when the Sensor node B and C is communicating to two different nodes A and D respectively. This is specified as an exposed problem.

In order to avoid the hidden and terminal problem, a cooperative MAC is used at the MAC layer at the data link layer. In cooperative MAC, if any node wants to send the information to any node in the network it will first send the RTS (request-to-send) signal to the destination node and also broadcast the same to all the nodes in its range. If the destination is willing to accept the data it will send the CTS (clear-to-send) signal to the source node and also broadcast the same to all the nodes in its range. With this, if any nodes want to transmit the information to the destination node will get to know that it is transmitting the information and keep waiting such that the hidden problem can be avoided. At the same time, as all nodes are receiving the information about the nodes which are involved in

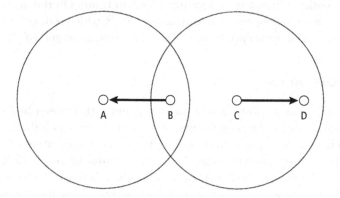

**Figure 7.5** Exposed terminal problem.

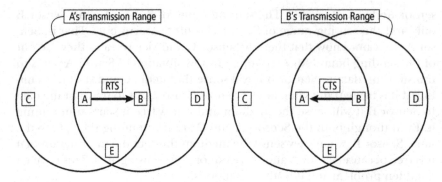

**Figure 7.6** Cooperative MAC.

communication other nodes can communicate with other nodes without any waiting if the medium is free through which the exposed problem can be avoided (Bhasha et al., 2020).

## Multi-Hop Environment

WSNs work with multi-hop principles. In multi-hop principle, the information is exchanged from source to destination through the intermediate nodes passing information to the next node till it reaches the final node. In order to provide easy and rapid transmission of information over the network, multi-hop networks are best suitable (Amanjot et al., 2019). The nodes in the multi-hop architecture have the features of self configuring which leads to reduce the deployment cost and increase the reliability. In the event that the communication path between the source and the destination fails, these networks will assist us in locating a backup route. On the other hand, these multi-hop systems result in routing overheads, which reduce bandwidth throughout and raise security threats (Shaik & Venkatramana, 2022).

## Power Limitations

One of the main constraints of the sensor network is power and energy. This is mainly due to the environmental conditions in which these sensors have been deployed where there will be less or no intervention of human beings. In such situations, mostly the battery cannot be replaceable or rechargeable (Yang et al., 2019). At each tier of the reference model, efficient protocols should be developed in order to operate these battery-powered nodes with the limited energy available. Three general categories may be used to categorize the power sources utilized in sensor networks.

## Replenishable

In this category, sensors can be charged when the power source of the existing sensor is completely drained. The best example of such sensors is sensors used in wearable devices.

## Non-Replenishable

In this category, sensors power sources cannot be replenished once deployed in the network. The only solution in such a type of network is replacing the existing source drained sensors. The best examples of such sensors are the sensors deployed in remote and risky environments.

## Regenerative

This category includes sensors that can recover energy from the physical parameter being measured. The best examples of such sensors are the sensors deployed in power plants to generate power through the transducers.

## DIFFERENT TYPES OF ATTACKS

The action that makes the system compromised is said to be a security attack (Jyothsna et al., 2020). Security mechanisms is the process used to recognize, stop, or recover from the assault. To improve the security of systems and the information shared among them, security services may employ one or more security methods (Jyothsna, Kumar Raja, et al., 2022).

The broadly classification of attacks in the wireless sensors are shown in Figure 7.7. Attackers are of two types—passive and active. Passive attackers intercept the message being communicated from source to destination with the motive of reading and analyzing the message without altering it. Identifying the passive attacker is very difficult (Patel & Aggarwal, 2013).

## Snooping

It is one of the attacks that comes under the category of passive attacks. The process of secretly trying to find out something private without a person's permission is called a snooping attack. In sensor attacks the information is carried out from source to destination through the hop-by-hop mechanism. So, snooping is one of the easy attacks that can be launched in

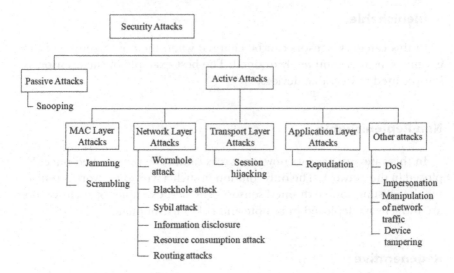

**Figure 7.7** Classification of attacks in the wireless sensors.

the sensor networks. In order to avoid an opponent acquiring the contents of transmissions, confidentiality service should be enabled.

The active attackers intercept the message being communicated from source to destination with the motive of modifying or altering the message. There are many cryptographic algorithms through which an active attacker can be identified.

## MAC Layer Attacks

Jamming and scrambling attacks are the most frequent ones at the MAC layer. In jamming, attackers use specialized devices to create interference in the communication channels such that the actual signals are lost and no communication can be done. In short periods of interference the signals are called scrambling. It makes the medium work for some time and jam for a period.

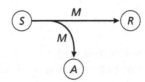

**Figure 7.8** Snooping.

## Network Layer Attacks

The following are the most frequent network layer attacks:

### Wormhole Attack

An attacker compromises the nodes in the network and creates a tunnel between the compromised nodes and transmits the information to another location in the network. The tunnel established between the compromised nodes (wormhole nodes) is said to be a wormhole (Figure 7.9).

### Blackhole Attack

In this attack, the compromised node will falsely advertise the shortest paths in the network during the route discovery or routing table updating process (See Figure 7.10). The attacker's primary goal is to obstruct the route-fining process and interrupt the regular flow.

### Sybil Attack

In this attack, a compromised sensor node in the network will try to create the loops in the routing paths or route the packets in the non-optimal paths or will selectively drop the packets routing through it (See Figure 7.11). Identifying this type of attack is very difficult as it seems normal operating to the other nodes in the network though it is exhibiting Sybil behavior.

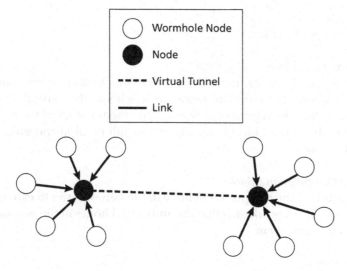

**Figure 7.9** Wormhole attack..

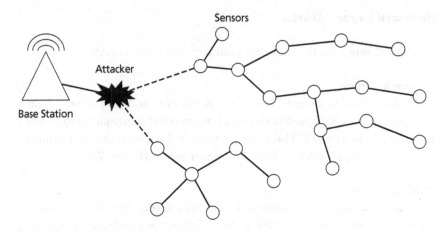

**Figure 7.10**   Blackhole attack.

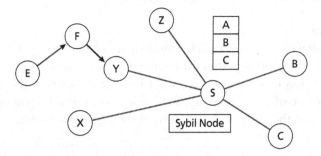

**Figure 7.11**   Sybil attack.

### Information Disclosure

Malicious nodes in the network will intentionally disclose the confidential information transmitted in the network or about the network to unauthorized nodes. The information may include the topology of the network, shortest paths in the network, the control or information transmitted between the nodes.

### Resource Consumption Attack

In this attack, the compromised node in the network tries to exhaust the resources of the network such that the authorized nodes in the network will not be able to use them.

### Routing Attacks

The following are a few of the attacks that have been made against the routing protocol to impede the network's regular operations:

**Routing table overflow.** A malicious node in the sensor network advertises the routes to nodes which are really not part of the network.

**Routing table poisoning.** A malicious node in the sensor network advertises the false routes or modifies the route in such a manner that the packets are routed to the unauthorized nodes.

**Packet replication.** In order to exhaust all of the available bandwidth and battery power for the sensor nodes as well as to confuse the network, malicious nodes in the sensor network duplicate the packets and respond to them in it.

**Route cache poisoning.** Each and every node preserves a route in cache. The attacker tries to poison the routes such that the packets transmitted will not route in the actual path.

**Rushing attack.** When a legitimate user is trying to find the route by sending the RouteRequest message, malicious node will catch hold the request message and flood the request quickly in the network before the other nodes receive it from the actual sender. Now if the nodes receive it from the actual sender they consider it as a duplicate request they discard it. A malicious node will make it as one of the intermediate nodes for any route discovered by the one node to any node in the network. It is enormously hard to detect this type of attack in WSNs.

## Transport Layer Attacks

The specific attack targeted in the transport layer is session hijacking.

### Session Hijacking

In most of the protocols authentication is carried out only at the start of the session. Once the session is established the attacker creates and sends a link to one of the session nodes to fetch the session information. As soon as the node clicks the link, the complete information is fetched by the attacker and then the attacker takes control of the session and starts performing the malicious activities.

## Application Layer Attacks

The most common attack associated with the application layer is repudiation.

### Repudiation

The sender or receiver denies that they have not sent the messages nor received the messages in the network. The non-repudiation is the only mechanism that helps to identify whether they have really performed the above said activity or not.

## Other Attacks

Cross-layer attacks could also occur in the protocol stack. They are as follows:

### Denial of Service

In this attack, the attacker attacks the network or resources unavailable to the legitimate nodes of the network. DoS attackers achieve this by flooding the network or resources with unwanted traffic. This attack dispossesses legitimate users to access the service or resource they needed (Jyothsna, Munivara Prasad, et al., 2022).

### SYN Flooding

The unauthorized node of the network transmits SYN packets to a targeted node and completes the handshake. It makes all open ports with requests and makes legitimate users unable to connect to the network.

### Distributed DoS Attack

When multiple nodes try to impose DoS attack at the same time it is referred as a distributed DoS attack (Veeramreddy, Mukesh, et al., 2019).

### Impersonation

Unauthorized users pretend to be authorized users, enter into the network, and are involved in all the activities in the network and disturb the normal activities.

### Device Tampering

Stealing or damaging the sensors in the area where it is deployed is referred to as device tampering (Bhasha et al., 2021).

## THE SECURITY FRAMEWORK

The security framework consists of five components:

1. link layer communication protocol
2. key management scheme
3. credential management
4. integrity mechanism
5. intrusion detection system

*Link layer communication protocols* provide the competence to save energy for the sensor nodes which is especially important for nodes in the sensor networks which rely on battery power (Singh & Loo, 2009).

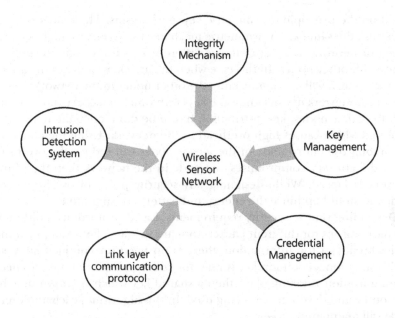

**Figure 7.12** Integrated security framework for wireless sensor networks.

*Key management* helps to solve the problem of unauthorized nodes entering into the network in the process of networking. Key management is always a key mechanism in WSNs (Xiaoa & Rayi, 2007). An efficient key management mechanism should be adopted in sensor networks as each of the sensor nodes rely on battery power.

*Credential management* is the technique used by the sensor network to issue, track, update, and revoke credentials of sensor nodes.

*Integrity mechanism* will provide the assurance of accuracy and consistency of data that is communicated among the nodes in the sensor networks.

*Intrusion detection system* (Jyothsna et al., 2021) analyzes the sensor network by gathering the adequate information and detects any abnormal behavior of the nodes and network.

## ALGORITHMS USED IN THE INTEGRATED SECURITY FRAMEWORK FOR WIRELESS SENSOR NETWORKS

### Localized Encryption and Authentication Protocol

A key management system called Localized Encryption and Authentication Protocol ([LEAP]; Zhu et al., 2003) is primarily used to distribute the keys used in cryptographic methods. This protocol distributes the keys based on the principle of symmetric key mechanisms. The sender and receiver use the same key in symmetric mechanisms. To ensure high security in sensor networks it is better to use different keys for a node to communicate with other nodes. In this case when the attacker launches the attack on one node, it will not compromise the other nodes in the network. But as the sensor network doesn't know the keys with which it has to communicate with the other nodes, key distribution has to be done once the network is deployed which causes high overhead in the network. Using the common key among the entire node in the sensor nodes will reduce the overhead but if the attacker compromises one node in the network then the whole network is lapsed. While designing any security protocol on the sensor nodes, it should optimize the energy and battery consumption.

Depending on the security requirements, LEAP protocol uses different key mechanisms for different packets to share the keys. For example, if the nodes broadcast the information, there is no need for confidentiality, so in this situation a common key is used for communication. If peer to peer communication is taking place then a shared key which is known only by the source and destination is being used. In this algorithm, each and every node will maintain four keys.

1. A key used to communicate between sensor node and base station.
2. A common key used by a sensor node to communicate with all other nodes in the sensor networks and also the base station.
3. A key used in the cluster to communicate with its nodes of the cluster and its cluster head and vice versa.
4. A pair of keys to communicate with each of its neighboring nodes in the sensor networks.

In LEAP, each and every node is preloaded with a common initial key before deploying into the network. Every node generates a master key from the initial common key and their unique identifier. After generating the master key, nodes will send hello messages to its neighbors. The neighboring nodes authenticate the above said hello message by generating the master key of the sender as it knows the common key and the identifier of the sender. After the nodes have established the network, they delete the common key and generate shared keys based on the master keys of each node. In this way all the remaining keys discussed above are generated and secure communication is performed among the nodes. Until the malicious node gets the common key, it is not possible for it to inject the false data into the network or decrypt the messages communicated among the nodes in the cluster or outside the cluster or to and from the BS.

## Intrusion Tolerant Routing in Wireless Sensor Networks (INSENS)

One of the algorithms that enable secure routing of packets in WSNs is INSENS (Deng et al., 2003). In this algorithm, each and every node in the network will maintain the routing table which contains the shortest path from one sensor node to all the other nodes in the network by evading malicious nodes. This algorithm will not completely avoid the attacks in the network but can minimize the harm caused by the malicious nodes in the network. It also minimizes the number of computations and communications in the network. The necessity of bandwidth at each node can also be reduced. This algorithm can mainly be used to prevent the launching of DoS and its attacks in the network. Only the BS has the capability of broadcasting the packets. Strong one way hash algorithms are used to avoid any node in the network that can masquerade as the BS. To reduce the computations at each node, control information related to routing is computed at the BS and broadcast routing tables by authenticating the nodes. INSENS algorithm is designed in such a way that if an attacker compromises the node in the sensor network, multipath routing is used such that the packets are routed to the destination without passing through the compromised

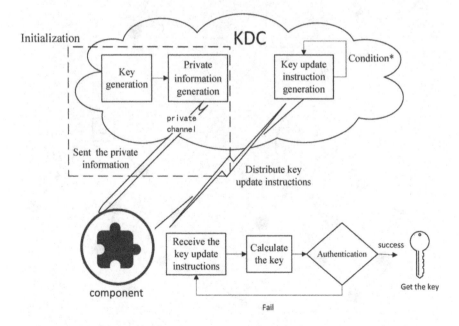

**Figure 7.13**   Secure key establishment mechanism for LEAP.

node. INSENS algorithm works in two phases—route discovery and data transmission.

During the phase of route discovery, the BS uses a hop to hop algorithm to forward the request message to all nodes in the sensor networks. After receiving the request message, the sensor nodes record the identity of the source and forward it to all its immediate neighbors. By using the request message each and every node in the network will be able to identify its subsequent neighbors. This algorithm avoids the flooding of packets, but

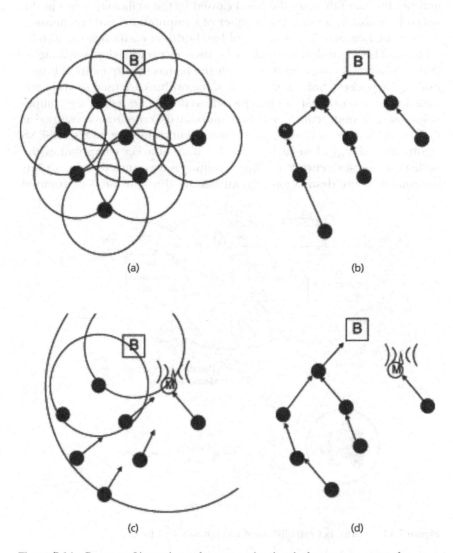

(a)                    (b)

(c)                    (d)

**Figure 7.14**   Process of intrusion tolerant routing in wireless sensor networks.

instead forwards the packet by analyzing the topology and by sending feedback packets. Integrity mechanisms are used to protect the messages by using an energy efficient shared key encryption mechanism. Finally, the BS computes the routing tables with multipath for all nodes and securely transmits the same for every node in the network. In the second phase, the actual data is transmitted with the help of data routing tables computed and transmitted by the BS.

## Security Protocols for Sensor Networks

Security protocols for sensor networks ([SPINS]; Perrig et al., 2001) is a suite of algorithms mainly designed to provide the security services such as authentication, confidentiality, and integrity by optimizing the resources in the sensor networks. Two primary protocols make up this suit—sensor network encryption protocol (SNEP) and a micro-version of timed, efficient, streaming, loss-tolerant authentication protocol (µTESLA).

SNEP protocol is mainly designed to defeat the cryptanalysis and replay attacks in the network. Cryptanalysis is a process of identifying the plain text or the keys used to compute the encrypted message with the information available with the attacker. In replay attack, the data transmitted by the authorized users is captured by the attacker and tries to retransmit the captured packet again and again in the networks or delays its transmission in the network. The messages are embedded with time-stamp, to protect from replay attacks. µTESLA mainly used to provide the integrity and confidentiality of the message. It uses MAC to provide the integrity of the message. While transmitting the message, source embed a MAC code computed on the original data and sends to the receiver.

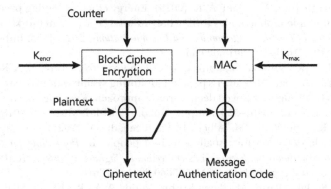

**Figure 7.15** Process of security protocols for sensor networks (SPINS).

The receiver upon receiving the message computes the same on the data it received. If the code computed is the same as the code transmitted by the source, the message is accepted, otherwise it indicates there is some modification in the message. These MAC codes are so strong that small changes in the message leads to a lot of deviation in the code. To provide confidentiality, the messages have been encrypted by using the shared keys among the specific nodes. The BS periodically generates the pair of keys and transmits the same to the nodes in order to avoid the same key being used by the node throughout its existence. If any of the nodes has been compromised by the attacker, the key available now with the attacker is valid only for a particular time. Upon the validity, the key expires and a new key is communicated to the nodes by the BS in a secure manner such that the compromised node can be identified.

## CONCLUSION

Wireless Sensor networks are highly disseminated networks containing of small and light weighted sensors located in dense to monitor and estimate the physical parameters of the deployed area. It is used in many real time applications. Researchers are focused to provide the solutions to security issues in the sensor networks either providing the solution for the attacks at a particular layer or solution for a particular type of attacks by considering the power and Energy constraints. Even many protocols are designed to solve the open issues of the wireless sensor networks, till there is a necessity of providing an integrated comprehensive security framework.

## REFERENCES

Amanjot Singh Toor, A., & Jain, A. K. (2019). Energy efficient routing protocol using multiple mobile nodes (MEACBM) in wireless sensor networks. AEU–*International Journal of Electronics and Communications, 102*, 41–53. https://doi.org/10.1016/j.aeue.2019.02.006

Arunachalam, R., Sunitha, G., Shukla, S. K., Pandey, S. N., Urooj, S., & Rawat, S. (2023). A smart Alzheimer's patient monitoring system with IoT-assisted technology through enhanced deep learning approach. *Knowledge and Information Systems, 65*(12), 5561–5599. https://doi.org/10.1007/s10115-023-01890-x

Baseer, K. K., Jahir Pasha, M., Albert, D. W., & Sujatha, V. (2021). Navigation and obstacle detection for visually impaired people. In *Proceedings for the 2021 4th International Conference on Microelectronics, Signals & Systems (ICMSS)*, 1–3. https://doi.org/10.1109/ICMSS53060.2021.9673618

Baseer, K. K., Jahir Pasha, M., Rama Krishna Reddy, A. V., Rekha, M., Shaheda Begum, M., & E. Sandhya. (2022). Smart online examination monitoring system.

*Journal of Algebraic Statistics, 13*(3), 559–570. https://publishoa.com/index.php/journal/article/view/661

Bhasha, P., Pavan Kumar, T., & Baseer, K. K. (2020). A simple and effective electronic stick to detect obstacles for visually impaired people through sensor technology. *Journal of Advanced Research in Dynamical & Control Systems, 12*(6), 18–27. https://doi.org/10.5373/JARDCS/V12I6/S20201003

Bhasha, P., Pavan Kumar, T., Baseer, K. K., & Jyothsna, V. (2021). An IoT-based BLYNK server application for infant monitoring alert system to detect crying and wetness of a baby. In S. Bhattacharyya, J. Nayak, K. B. Prakash, B. Naik, & A. Abraham (Eds.), *International Conference on Intelligent and Smart Computing in Data Analytics, 1312* (pp. 55–65). Springer.

Chakraborty, I., & Das, P. (2017). Data fusion in wireless sensor network-a survey. *International Journal of Scientific Research in Network Security and Communication, 5*(6), 9–15. https://doi.org/10.26438/ijsrnsc/v5i6.915

Deng, J., Han, R., & Mishra, S. (2003, May). *INSENS: Intrusion tolerant routing in wireless sensor networks* [Poster presentation]. IEEE International Conference on Distributed Computing Systems.

Goyal, A. K., Tripathi, A. K., & Agarwal, G. (2019). Security attacks, requirements and authentication schemes in VANET. In *Proceedings 2019 International Conference on Issues and Challenges in Intelligent Computing Techniques (ICICT)* (pp. 1–5). IEEE.

Hima Bindu, G. B., Ramani, K., & Shoba Bindu, C. (2021). Multi-objective dynamic resource scheduling model for allocating user tasks in cloud computing. *Turkish Journal of Computer and Mathematics Education, 12*(9), 509–515. https://turcomat.org/index.php/turkbilmat/article/view/3107

Jyothsna, V., Kumar Raja, D. R., Hemanth Kumar, G., & E, D. C. (2022). A Novel Manifold approach for intrusion detection System (MHIDS). *Gongcheng Kexue Yu Jishu/Advanced Engineering Science, 54*(02), 2043–2076.

Jyothsna, V., Munivara Prasad, G. GopiChand, & Bhavani, D. D. (2022). DLMHS: Flow-based intrusion detection system using deep learning neural network and meta-heuristic. *International Journal of Communication Systems, 35*(10), e5159, 1–17. https://doi.org/10.1002/dac.5159

Jyothsna, V., Prasad, K. M., Rajiv, K., & Others. (2021). Flow-based anomaly intrusion detection system using ensemble classifier with feature impact scale. *Cluster Computing, 24*, 2461–2478. https://doi.org/10.1007/s10586-021-03277-5

Jyothsna, V., Sreedhar, A. N., Mukesh, D., & Ragini, A. (2020). A network intrusion detection system with hybrid dimensionality reduction and neural network based classifier. In M. Tuba, S. Akashe, & A. Joshi (Eds.), *ICT Systems and Sustainability: Proceedings of ICT4SD 2019, Volume 1* (pp. 187–196). Springer.

Kabashkin, I. (2019, April 29–May 2). Reliability of cluster-based nodes in wireless sensor networks of cyber-physical systems [Paper presentation]. *10th International Conference on Ambient Systems, Networks and Technologies (ANT)*, Leuven, Belgium. https://doi.org/10.1016/j.procs.2019.04.044

Kannan, K. S., Sunitha, G., Deepa, S. N., Babu, D. V., & Avanija, J. (2022). A multi-objective load balancing and power minimization in cloud using bio-inspired algorithms. *Computers & Electrical Engineering, 102*(5), 108225. https://doi.org/10.1016/j.compeleceng.2022.108225

Naeem, T., & Loo, K. K. (2009). Common security issues and challenges in wireless sensor networks and IEEE 802.11 wireless mesh networks. *International Journal of Digital Content Technology and its Applications, 3*(1), 88–93. https://doi.org/10.4156/jdcta.vol3.issue1.naeem

Patel, M. M., & Aggarwal, A. (2013, March 1–2). Security attacks in wireless sensor networks: A survey. In *Proceedings of the 2013 International Conference on Intelligent Systems and Signal Processing (ISSP)* (pp. 329–333). IEEE.

Perrig, A., Szewczyk, R., Wen, V., Culler, D. E., & Tygar, J. D. (2001). SPINS: Security protocols for sensor networks. In *Proceedings of the 7th Annual International Conference on Mobile Computing and Networking* (pp. 189–199). https://doi.org/10.1145/381677.381696

Rashid, B., & Rehmani, M. H. (2016). Applications of wireless sensor networks for urban areas: A survey. *Journal of Network and Computer Applications, 60*, 192–219. https://doi.org/10.1016/j.jnca.2015.09.008

Raviraj, P., Sharif, H., Hempel, M., & Ci, S. (2005). MOBMAC–An energy efficient and low latency MAC for mobile wireless sensor networks. In *Proceedings of the 2005 Systems Communications* (pp. 370–375). IEEE. https://doi.org/10.1109/ICW.2005.56

Shaik, J. B., & Venkatramana, P. (2022). Investigation of crosstalk issues for MWCNT bundled TSVs in ternary logic. *ECS Journal of Solid State Science and Technology, 11*(3), 4508–4514. https://doi.org/10.1149/2162-8777/ac5c85

Silpa, C., Niranjana, G., & Ramani, K. (2022). Securing data from active attacks in IoT: An extensive study. In *Proceedings for the International Conference on Deep Learning, Computing and Intelligence advances in intelligent systems and computing*. Springer. https://doi.org/10.1007/978-981-16-5652-1_5

Silpa, C., Srinivasa Chakravarthi, S., Gopi Kumar, J., Baseer, K. K., & Sandhya, E. (2022a). Health monitoring system using IoT sensors. *Journal of Algebraic Statistics, 13*(3), 3051–3056. https://publishoa.com/index.php/journal/article/view/984

Silpa, C., Srinivasa Chakravarthi, S. S., Gopi Kumar, J., Baseer, K. K., & Sandhya, E. (2022b). Securing data from active attacks in IoT: An extensive study. In *Proceedings of the International Conference on Deep Learning, Computing and Intelligence. Advances in Intelligent Systems and Computing*, Springer, Singapore, vol 1396, 2022.

Singh, H., & Singh, D. (2018). Concentric layered architecture for multi-level clustering in large-scale wireless sensor networks. In *Proceedings for the 2018 First International Conference on Secure Cyber Computing and Communication (ICSCCC)* (pp. 467–471). Jalandhar, India. IEEE. https://doi.org/10.1109/ICSCCC.2018.8703282

Singh, J., (2009). A survey on wireless sensor network security. *International Journal of Communication Networks and Information Security, 1*, 55–78. https://arxiv.org/pdf/1011.1529.pdf

Singh, T. N., & Loo, K. K. (2009). Common security issues and challenges in wireless sensor networks and IEEE 802.11 wireless mesh networks. *International Journal of Digital Content Technology and its Applications, 3*(1), 88–93. https://doi.org/10.4156/jdcta.vol3.issue1.naeem

Veeramreddy, J, Mukesh, D., & Sreedhar, A. N. (2019). A flow-based network intrusion detection system for high-speed networks using meta-heuristic scale. In S.-L. Peng, N. Dey, & M. Bundele (Eds.), *Computing and Network Sustainability: Proceedings of IRSCNS 2018* (pp. 337–347). Springer.

Xiaoa, Y., & Rayi, V. K. (2007). A survey of key management schemes in wireless sensor networks. *Computer Communications, 30*(11–12), 2314–2341. https://doi.org/10.1016/j.comcom.2007.04.009

Yang, G., Tay, W. P., Guan, Y. L., & Liang, Y. (2019). Optimal power allocation for diffusion-type sensor networks with wireless information and power transfer. *IEEE Access, 7,* 32408–32422. https://ieeexplore.ieee.org/stamp/stamp.jsp?arnumber=8664158

Zhu, S., Setia, S., & Jajodia, S. (2003). LEAP: Efficient security mechanisms for large-scale distributed sensor networks. In *Proceedings of ACM Conference on Computer and Communications Security*, 62–72. https://www.cse.psu.edu/~sxz16/papers/leap.pdf

# CHAPTER 8

# A FEATURE-FUSION-BASED MULTIMODAL BIOMETRIC ALONG WITH ONE-TIME TOKEN AUTHENTICATION SYSTEM FOR INCREASED SECURITY IN CLOUD ENVIRONMENTS

**Reddy Madhavi K.**
*Mohan Babu University*

**Vijayasanthi Maddela**
*Sree Vidyanikethan Engineering College*

**K. Suneetha**
*Jain (Deemed-to-be University)*

**Ashok Patel**
*University of Massachusetts*

**Karuna G.**
*GRIET*

*Innovations in Computational Intelligence, Big Data Analytics, and Internet of Things*, pages 139–157
Copyright © 2024 by Information Age Publishing
www.infoagepub.com

## ABSTRACT

Due to the advancement of modern innovations such as distributed computing, information may now be accessed from anywhere at any time. Meanwhile, maintaining information security is basic. Validation is essential for keeping up with security through different access control procedures. Organic data of a single customer is presently being utilized as a check component for the affirmation approach, which is a relatively fresh fad. Fingerprints, iris, ear, and palm prints are all used to identify people and are common examples used to create ID frameworks. In any instance, multiple qualities are combined to expand the intricacy of client approval and guarantee incredible security. This article combines the elements of distinctive marks, iris, and palm print features with one time token (OTT) to create a multimodal differentiating evidence framework. Every trademark has been subjected to the preceding image management methods, such as pre-handling, standardization, and element extraction. A fantastic mystery key is framed from the recovered elements by connecting the properties in two phases. The FAR and FRR assessments are used to choose the construction's energy. To evaluate the model's show, three standard symmetric cryptographic procedures, as advanced encryption standard (AES), data encryption standard (DES), and Blowfish, are used. In a cloud environment, our proposed viewpoint further develops information security and board access.

Considering resource interest, dispersed processing is a state of the art development that grants clients to utilize organizations without managing them by and by (Kushida et al., 2015). It's adaptable, trustworthy, and gives you admittance to your information whenever, from anyplace. In a cloud environment, it considers the execution of precise, large-scale exercises. The main benefit of this innovation is that it takes into account more advanced asset management, security, and access control. Subsequently, the quantity of people utilizing cloud organizations keeps on developing. The data may be saved in various cloud administrations, which the client could get to remotely at whatever point they required it. The data is subject to malicious assaults because it is stored on a distant server and can be hacked at any time. As a result, making a profoundly protected information confirmation and access control framework system is unavoidable. In any case, modern PC innovations are incredibly sophisticated, and they may make most frameworks established before a decade think again about their security. To further develop security in the cloud climate, various techniques have been presented (Latha & Sheela, 2019).

The estimating and calculation of the human body is alluded to as "biometrics." The viewpoints, or modalities, of an individual can be straightforwardly connected with these ways of behaving. These KPIs are additionally utilized by far most of organizations access control framework verification calculations

(Asthana et al., 2014). Finger impressions, iris, palm prints, retina, DNA, voice, step, and different highlights have been found.

Enlistment is the most typical method for collecting, managing, and storing the characteristics of each individual in a data set. During the confirmation cycle, the client is validated using an entrance control system such as a unique mark verification. The significance of biometrics emerges from the way that every individual's model is extraordinary. Biometric developments that are separated from the remainder of the world are obsolete, contain a couple of imperfections, and are generally used in circumstances where security is certainly not a main issue. More than one component is combined in a multimodal biometric framework. The multimodal validation technique improves the framework's vitality.

In any scenario, cryptography is important. The most popular method of transforming plain text from an understandable organization to a jumbled mess is cryptography (Ranjith et al., 2016). Encryption is the term for this system. Interpreting is a comparative cycle's reversal approach. Severe key cryptography (SKC), wrong key cryptography (AKC), and hashing are instances of cryptographic calculations capabilities, to name a few. In SKC, the source and recipient share an analogous mystery key to scramble and translate correspondences. Anyone with the mysterious key might be able to see the message. Be that as it may, two keys are utilized in the AKC crypto approach: general society and secret keys (Kamalakannan et al., 2015).

The public key has been uncovered, yet the confidential key has stayed a secret. The correspondence can be unscrambled if both keys are confirmed. To switch data over completely to an irregular assortment of letters or numbers that can't be changed back to its unique design, use hashing. Hashing is a kind of "one-way encryption" that guarantees the correspondence stays private from being unscrambled. The second section of this chapter delves into the issues surrounding this project. The third section discusses how the organization depicts the proposed model's work process from top to bottom. The fourth section portrays the result of the request and examines its importance. The final section sums up the discoveries and wraps the survey up.

## BACKGROUND RESEARCH

Multimodal biometric validation frameworks are utilized in an assortment of fields, including cryptography, picture handling, and PC associations. By joining stand-apart finger engraving and palm print, a multimodal biometric structure-based check system is made. To standardize pixel power, histogram evening out is utilized. Extraction of features is done with PCA, and the inclusion combination is done with the Gabor wavelet technique.

This concept was developed in order to work on the security of the client affirmation system. A hash key based cryptographic technique is provided to further strengthen cloud security by mixing the highlights acquired from multimodal biometrics. Unique finger impression in this framework, the modalities of the eye, iris, and face are merged.

To extract elements of discrete modalities, several image handling calculations are used. To improve the recovered attributes, a multi-information appraisal strategy known as the *artificial fish swarm* (AFS) is utilized. The information to be saved in the cloud is mixed utilizing *advanced encryption standard* (AES) gauges and a client-created hash key.

A multimodal biometric-based cloud security improvement procedure is planned by incorporating three modalities. The binarized merging vectors are then, at that point, XORed with the adjusted element vectors. Before being stored in the cloud, the information is encrypted with AES using the most recent key (Mansour et al., 2015). To provide a thorough validation framework for client check, face and iris modalities are used.

The image's element vectors are identified using machine learning methods. This technique employs complex perceptron and self-coordinated map brain networks. In a cloud environment, the multimodal biometric technique (MFA-MB) is used to put out a complex verification framework (Ahmad et al., 2017). Because of secret word-based client checks, information security in the cloud is fragmented.

In this system, different steps of client distinguishing proof, like passwords and multimodal biometric data are also used to strengthen security. A two-way check component cloud security on portable correspondence is marketed along these lines. The iris and unique mark modalities are used in this technique to validate the client's identity (Nair et al., 2017).

To empower access control and information security, a biometric-based cloud confirmation framework is demonstrated, along with a few processes for diverse cloud geographies. To protect against slope climbing attacks, a multimodal biometric architecture is used to protect the cloud. Two-way encryption is employed in this project. Uni-modular or multimodal biometric encryption is completed in sync 1 for the underlying level of verification. The successor stage occurs after the most typical method of processing information involving the Euclidean distance metric at a higher level.

A decision-level mix method for various biometric cryptosystems is well-known for ensuring secure data transfer in the cloud. While managing this technology gives incredible security in terms of approval and integrity in terms of access control when it comes to data.

To establish mindful models to safeguard cloud-enabled frameworks, multimodal biometric techniques are used. The underlying innovation in this framework's technique is the integration of MFA-class MB's affiliation requirements. After that, another action is taken to review the client experience with this framework, and finally, cloud validation on paas and saas service is improved.

This work promotes a local binary pattern strategy for eliminating highlights from multimodal ascribes that is based on entropy. Individuals with a low FAR and a high FRR can be identified using the determined features.

Various specialists have attempted to work on the security and helpfulness of different designated network conditions since the creation of the principal secret key based validation framework. To safeguard remote sensor organizations (WSNs), symmetric and deviated key cryptography as well as cryptographic hash capabilities have been oftentimes utilized. To get the climate of WSNs, Wong et al. (2006) proposed a secret key based lightweight and dynamic client validation system. Kong et al. (2006), then again, found that the arrangement set forth is unreliable and recommended a two-factor client validation method and attested that their technique offers dependable validation.

Sadly, Kong et al. (2006), as well as Jia et al. (2017), demonstrate that the method is unsafe and susceptible to a number of well-known attacks, including impersonation, privileged-insider assaults, and bypassing the gateway node. The system therefore does not provide reciprocal authentication between the associated sensor nodes and the gateway node. Kong et al. (2006) proposed a better two-factor user authentication approach to address these security flaws. According to Kong et al. (2006), their plan accomplished a number of security aspects.

Kong et al. (2006) inspected the procedure, found various imperfections, and introduced a pristine client validation framework that utilizes brilliant cards and elliptic curves cryptography (ECC) and affirmed that their arrangement is suitable for further developed security with regards to WSNs. Nonetheless, Kong et al. (2006) exhibited that the proposed approach is inefficient as far as additional stockpiling above and that it requires additional handling assets. Then Inani, Singh, and Saxena (2018). at that point, for remote sensor organizations, proposed another transient accreditation based verification procedure with common validation and key arrangement.

Jia et al. (2017) presented an enhanced lightweight mutual authentication mechanism to accord with these security challenges, achieving essential security features and lightweight attributes using hash functions and bitwise exclusive-OR (XOR) operations. In 2016, Farash et al. (2016) pointed out the security flaws in the scheme of Turkanović et al. (2014) and showed that the scheme does not ensure sensor node anonymity and, moreover, does not provide untraceability. Farash et al. (2016) recommended another client verification and key understanding procedure for heterogeneous remote sensor organizations, with their plan being explicitly appropriate for the Internet of things (IoT) setting, to address these security defects.

The method set forth by Farash et al. (2016) was analyzed in 2017 by Kumari et al. who found that it didn't give client or sensor-hub namelessness and couldn't endure a few notable assaults. At the point when the secret word is broken or a brilliant gadget is lost, run of the mill two-factor validation techniques are shaky. Khalsanet et al. (2022) laid out an original client verification method utilizing an ECC-based computerized signature for the IoT climate around the same time. Their plan offers characteristics like user anonymity and untraceability.

Their arrangement offers qualities like client obscurity and untraceability. Notwithstanding, this plan brings about higher above costs for calculation and correspondence at the associated IoT units. Specialists bring likewise as of late proposed new procedures and ways to deal with the table for a scope of safety arrangements, including a secretive correspondence framework in light of blockchain (Wang & Su, 2020), information protection in brilliant horticulture (Song et al., 2020), and defending savvy lattice (Wang et al., 2020). An as of late proposed verified key understanding method for cloud-supported digital actual frameworks was made by Kong et al. (2020).

Be that as it may, May et al. (2018) guarantee that their arrangement contains a huge plan issue. In a cloud-based IoT setting, Krishna Prasad and Aithal (2018) fostered a new, lightweight verification component. They stated that their arrangement is successful, versatile, and equipped for giving IoT sensors ongoing information access through relating entryway hubs in assorted groups. Krishna Prasad and Aithal's (2018) plan was analyzed by Shen et al. (2019), who found that it is as yet unsound and doesn't scale as expected when new passage hubs are added. Moreover, the technique misses the mark on approval instruments, making private data defenseless against interruption.

In the setting of many enrolled clients, Panchal et al. (2017). showed that Sarier (2017) can't empower common confirmation between framework components. To the extent that we know, most of the at present utilized confirmation techniques are not great for use with appealing cloud-based applications in IoT and WSN settings.

## MATERIALS PROCEDURES

For each of the three categories, social affair biometric picture tests from 100 people were used to build the data set for this study. The photographs are altered to a comparable $m * n$ size to maintain pixel integrity. In the areas beneath, we'll go through every technique in additional profundity as we go over photographs taking care of.

*Structure for a multimodal biometric verification framework proposed design extraction from an assortment of traits*

## Finger Impression

The most significant biometric highlight utilized for confirmation is the interesting finger impression. To a great many people, the finger impression configuration is astounding. Subsequently, these attributes are considered all through the affirmation discussion.

The sensor's distinctive mark picture could include commotion and hindrance (Schaefer, 1996). To get rid of these issues, some picture data preparation approaches are employed to address these concerns.

Follow the steps to remove a component location from the provided unique finger imprint data:

1. Picture standardization and division: The dark level picture is modified in the scope of values to normalize the power of the image.
2. Direction assessment: For every pixel in the picture, the slant is first processed. Finding the assortment turn in the image's slants likewise decides the local direction. The heading field of the picture is then smoothed utilizing the Gaussian low pass channel strategy. Figure 8.1 portrays the multimodal biometric confirmation structure framework.
3. Morphological treatment: Before obtaining the minute details focused from the unique finger impression, the image is reduced. The element focuses are planned, and the edges are highlighted. The development of a skeleton example of edges occurs at this step.
4. Extracting the area of interest (ROI): The components centered from the skeletal picture are recovered utilizing two morphological methodologies: ERODE and OPEN. The extraordinary finger impression.

## Iris

The iris is a critical part of the natural eye. The natural eye's life systems differ from one person to the next. This is likely the most reliable approach for validating an individual's identity in really dangerous situations.

There have been numerous approaches for eliminating areas of interest from the iris that have shown to be effective. This framework employs a

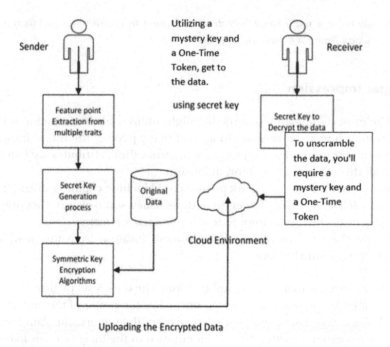

**Figure 8.1** Blueprint of work for a multimodal biometric approval structure.

number of techniques, which are listed below. Their strategy for separating highlight focuses is depicted in Figure 8.3.

1. Binarization: The information is binarized utilizing the threshold-ing technique as the iris picture's basic handling adventure.
2. The image's bended edges are extremely long when using the watchful edge detection approach.
3. The hue change is utilized to decide the picture's limits.
4. To eliminate features from the iris portion, gabor partition is utilized.

## A Palm Prints

In view of the rattle, intra-class shakiness, and little edges, following the palm locale from the hands is testing (Schneier 1993). Regardless, because of its one-of-a-thoughtfulness, this procedure keeps up with the respectabil-ity of the affirmation structure.

This component can be produced in the way framed in the accompany-ing advances. Figure 8.1 tells the best way to separate feature focuses from palm prints.

## OTT

1. A one-time secret phrase token (OTP token) is a piece of security equipment or software capable of delivering a single-use secret key or PIN passcode.
2. In many circumstances, one-time secret phrase tokens are used as part of two-factor and multidimensional validation. The use of one-time secret key tokens adds another, strong certification to a traditional ID and secret key system.
3. An OTP token can generate a PIN simultaneously or non concurrently, depending on the supplier. To create a one-time secret word, coordinated tokens use a mystery key and time. A test reaction confirmation system is used using offbeat tokens (CRAM).
4. OTP security tokens used to be pocket-sized coxcombs with a little screen that displayed a number. The number varied depending on how the token was created, every 30 or 60 seconds and the client had to provide their client name and secret word in addition to the token's number.
5. Today, most OTP tokens are based on programming, and the pass code generated by the token is displayed on the client's screen. Token programming allows portable clients to enter verification data without having to monitor a separate piece of equipment.

The time-based OTP (TOTP) algorithm, which is depicted as follows, is an example of this OTP age:

- The mystery key is generated by one backend server.
- The server gives the secret key to the person who generates the OTP.

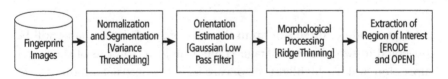

**Figure 8.2** Extraction of unique finger impression highlight focuses utilizing a technique.

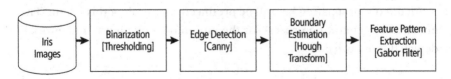

**Figure 8.3** Iris highlight point extraction method.

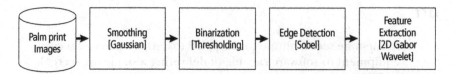

**Figure 8.4** Extraction of element focuses from palm prints utilizing a technique.

- The picture caught by the sensor is first smoothed utilizing Gaussian procedures.
- Using thresholding approach, the image is binarized.
- To locate palm segments on a binarized image, the Sobel edge recognition algorithm is used.
- Utilizing the 2D—Gabor wavelet strategy, the component centers from the palm area are recuperated.

*XOR and hashing algorithms are used to generate keys.*

## Binarization

The qualities' element focuses are all taken and then turned into a parallel example. It will be replaced by a value of 0 or 1 for each pixel in the perceived highlights, depending on the edge incentive. The last element vector will be converted to a double worth sequence entirely.

## XOR

In this module, three still up in the air from each brand name will be converged in two phases. In Stage 1, the twofold reciprocals of the finger impression and iris highlight vectors are used to construct another vector using the XOR algorithm.

The newly calculated esteem is then XORed with the second element's twofold partner, palm print.

An uncommon paired key will be produced as a result of this system. The mystery key generating process for the multimodal biometric framework is depicted in Figure 8.5.

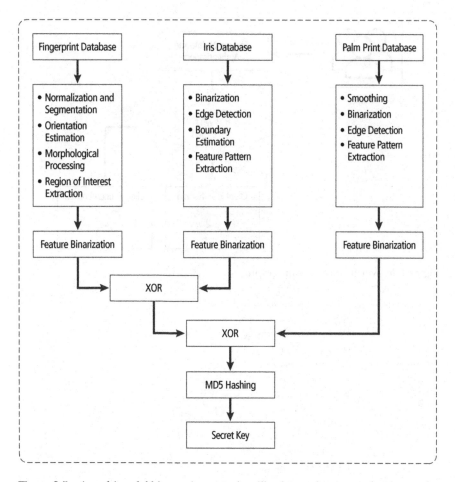

**Figure 8.5**   A multimodal biometric system is utilized to make a secret key in a cycle.

## MD-5 Hashing

The most often used hashing method is the MD-5 strategy, also known as the message-digest computation. It creates a key with a length of 265 pieces. It's normally used to guarantee the trustworthiness of check cycles like mystery key encryption. At last, MD-5 is used to generate the accompanying XOR consideration vector that yields a 128-cycle hash string. In a cloud setting, this hash key is a conclusive secret key utilized for data encryption and translating.

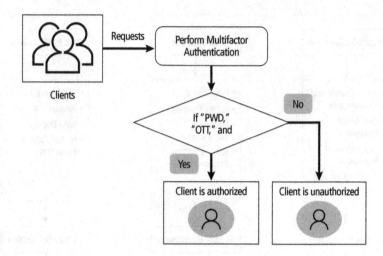

**Figure 8.6**  Verification stream graph.

**Step 1:** Input image $i_{L\_100\,11-3}$ in m*n pixels

$$\text{Norm}_i \sim T\{0,1\}, i = \{0,255\}$$
$$O_s = G_{lpf}(\text{Norm}_i)$$
$$T_{m,n} \sim \text{Morph}(O_{m,n})$$
$$F_{v1} = V_i \{f_{a1}, f_{a2}...f_{an}\} <-T_{m,n\,(Erode,open)}$$
$$\text{Bin}_c \sim \text{Otsu} \{0,1\}, i = \{0,255\}$$
$$E_c = \text{Can}_c(\text{Bin}_c)$$
$$T_{m,n} \sim \text{HT}(E_c)$$
$$Tr_i = (T_{m,n})^T$$
$$T_{m,n} \sim \text{Gab}_i(O_{m,n})$$
$$I_{v2} = V_i \{f_{b1}, f_{b2}...f_{bn}\}$$
$$\text{Sm}_p \sim G_{lpf}(Z_a)$$
$$\text{Bin}_p \sim \text{Otsu} \{0,1\}, i = \{0,255\}$$
$$E_p = \text{Sob}_p(\text{Bin}_p)$$
$$P_{v3} = V_i \{f_{c1}, f_{c2}...f_{cn}\} <-T_{m,n}\,\text{Gab}_i(E_p)$$
End for

**Step 2:** for $z_{m,n}$ in i do:

**Step 3:** $\{F_{vb3}, I_{vb2}, P_{vb3}\} <-\text{Bin}\{F_{v1}, I_{v2}, P_{v3}\}, T\{0,1\}$

**Step 4:** $K_1 <- \text{XOR}(F_{vb3}, I_{vb2})$

**Step 5:** $K_2 <- \text{XOR}(P_{vb3}, K_1)$

**Step 6:** $S_{fin} <- \text{MD5\_Hash}(K2) \{56 > = \text{Key\_Len}(S_{fin}) < = 128\}$

Step 7: S$_{fin}$ login to clients

Stage 8: The cloud server generates OTT and ships it to the customer.

((S$_{Ga}$== S$_{fin}$) && (OTT==OTT1))

Step 9: if ((S$_{Ga}$== S$_{fin}$) && (OTT==OTT1))

Client is verifiable individual.

Else

Client is made-up name for a real person.
if; end if

if you've reached step 10 (The shopper has been given consent.)

Clients can secure required information administrations by encrypting and decrypting data.
Clients are not permitted to view or access information if this is not the case.
if;
end if;

## CRYPTOGRAPHIC CALCULATIONS' PRESENTATION ON BIOMETRIC KEY AGE

### DES

The NIST settled on the data encryption standard ([DES]; Kundu & Sarker, 2016). Symmetric encryption is a sort of encryption that utilizes two key schemes that was commonly used before AES (Sajay et al., 2019). The DES computation is built on top of the Feistel figure. The Feistel structure, which consists of 16 circular patterns, is utilized in DES. There are 64 pieces in the block. Regardless, 56 is the perfect key length. DES doesn't need eight pieces all through the encryption cycle since it utilizes a 64-bit key. The cyclical work, key timetable, and first/last change are the three core features of DES. One of DES' most confusing characteristics is that it is helpless against complete key chase, which is utilized to direct a cryptanalytic assault on the framework.

### AES

AES is a notable symmetric key encryption calculation that is frequently used to boost the security of any security application. It is significantly faster than the triple DES calculation. The DES key size limitation is a drawback. In AES, the data is scrambled using a 128-digit key. The framework proves to be harder to break due to the large size of the key. Iterative development is key to the AES interaction. The AES working relationship relies heavily on replacement and staging. AES utilizes bytes instead of parts to make its

**TABLE 8.1 Misleading Acceptance Rate**

| Picture Count | Fingerprint | Iris | Palm Print | Fused Features |
|---|---|---|---|---|
| 1–20 | 0.39 | 0.36 | 0.36 | 0.11 |
| 21–40 | 0.42 | 0.29 | 0.32 | 0.14 |
| 41–60 | 0.36 | 0.35 | 0.35 | 0.13 |
| 61–80 | 0.33 | 0.26 | 0.39 | 0.16 |
| 81–100 | 0.38 | 0.41 | 0.31 | 0.21 |
| Average | 0.376 | 0.334 | 0.346 | 0.15 |

**TABLE 8.2 Bogus the Level of Individuals Who Are Dismissed**

| Image Count | Fingerprint | Iris | Palm Print | Fused Features |
|---|---|---|---|---|
| 1–20 | 92.26 | 94.60 | 92.62 | 97.86 |
| 21–40 | 91.05 | 96.85 | 91.56 | 94.58 |
| 41–60 | 88.92 | 93.28 | 89.95 | 96.25 |
| 61–80 | 90.23 | 91.35 | 91.96 | 91.36 |
| 81–100 | 89.98 | 93.67 | 90.30 | 92.65 |
| Average | 90.488 | 93.95 | 91.278 | 94.54 |

**TABLE 8.3 Three Algorithms' CPU Execution Time (in milliseconds)**

| File size/algorithm | DES (key size = 56 bits) | AES (key size = 128 bits) | Blowfish (key size = 128 bits) |
|---|---|---|---|
| 512 KB | 22 | 26 | 23 |
| 1 MB | 25 | 29 | 26 |
| 3 MB | 31 | 38 | 35 |
| 5 MB | 37 | 44 | 40 |

computations. Thus, it is easy to draw near to the cross section. How much adjustment on the key is still hanging out there. The quantity of rounds expected for a key with 128 parts is 10. There are 12 rounds in a 192-piece key and 14 rounds in a 256-cycle key.

## Blowfish

Blowfish is a symmetric key cryptography algorithm calculation that was created to supplant the DES calculation. The key could be anything between 32 and 446 pieces long. A 64-bit block size is used in this method. It is based on the Feistel figure and has 16 rounds in all. In symmetric computing, it is one of the quickest block figures. This approach utilizes a 64-digit block size, which is not exactly the AES block size. Subsequently, at times, it is exposed to cryptanalytic assaults. With a similar guideline, Twofish, a cryptographic approach that replaces the Blowfish calculation, was created.

In advised focus on using specific innovative picture handling methods, the attributes from three independent credits are retrieved first. The component focuses are then totally switched over to parallel reciprocals to play out a XOR activity between the quality. XOR is directed via a unique finger impression and iris information.

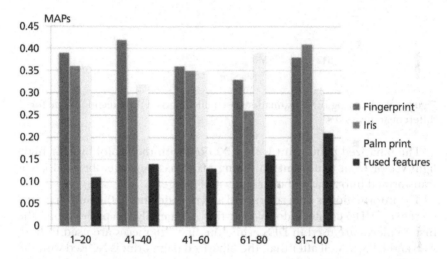

**Figure 8.7**  FAR was utilized to inspect the display of different modalities.

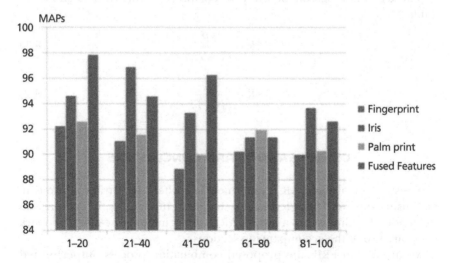

**Figure 8.8**  FRR was utilized to research the presentation of different modalities.

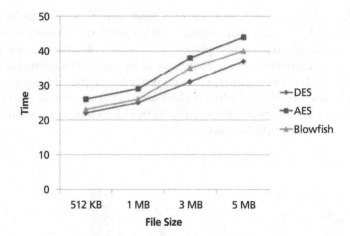

**Figure 8.9** Utilizing three estimations, we benchmarked the execution time for different archive sizes.

The binarized palm print is then XORed with the twofold vector highlight vector from that point on. Using MD-5 hashing, the obtained key is transformed into a hash of characters and integers.

The information is then scrambled and decoded using the newly created secret key. MD-5 creates a double key that is generally 256 pieces long. The first 56 pieces are used in DES, while the first 128 pieces are used in both AES and DES, as well after that, the binarized palm print is XORed with the twofold vector.

The execution season of three calculations in the CPU is shown in Table 8.3.

$$FAR = \frac{FP}{FP + TN} \tag{8.1}$$

$$FRR = \frac{FN}{FN + TP} \tag{8.2}$$

## CONVERSATIONS AND CONCLUSIONS

The results reveal that FAR is extremely low when the attributes are coupled using the cycle depicted in the suggested model. Iris, in comparison to blended highlights, has a lesser FAR. Palm print and one-of-a-kind mark packs are two of the accompanying sections.

Meanwhile, in FRR, the proposed combination process outperformed uni-modular solutions. When compared to the objective of this venture is to keep up areas of strength for security zones in a cloud climate. AES is the most dependable of the three methodologies because of its broad computational strategies. Blowfish is right behind them, with DES acquiring the last opening. Attestation is a significant piece of utilization security. Scattered handling is an electronic methodology of offering a gathering of clients with data improvement administrations.

Cloud companies are becoming increasingly popular since they provide clients with a lot of opportunity. Furthermore, it expresses clear worries about data security.

The multimodal biometric structure further strengthens the affirmation part's unity due to its inborn exceptional normal models. It precisely isolates people in light of the model obtained from their attributes and the OTT determined by the assessment.

Moreover, this system can be utilized to help the construction's decency for an assortment of capacities, for example, safeguarding human hereditary code and flourishing data saved for future reference utilizing an electronic health record (EHR) board, robotized record supervisors, and alternate ways. From that point forward, the information is encoded utilizing three symmetric key encryption calculations: DES, AES, and Blowfish using the mystery key. DES, for example, creates opportunities for execution, while AES outperforms it with better performance.

It outperforms the other two techniques in terms of the encryption process's strength. This approach demonstrated its power in information security because the arrangement for a security framework incorporates the combination of human modalities. Every individual's capacity and execution on the given secret key technique as far as execution time under different record measures. On account of its more modest key and block sizes, DES takes less time, whereas AES takes most of the day because of its larger key size. Between the two, the Blowfish calculation maintains a consistent execution pattern. AES, on the other hand, proves to be the finest in terms of a sense of safety and trustworthiness as shown in Figure 8.9, where three methodologies were used to look at the execution seasons of reports of fluctuating sizes.

## REFERENCES

Ahmad, A., Paul, A., Khan, M., Jabbar, S., Ullah Rathore, M. M., Chilamkurti, N., & Min-Allah, N. (2017). Energy efficient hierarchical resource management for mobile cloud computing. *IEEE Transactions on Sustainable Computing, 2*(2), 100–112. https://doi.org/10.1109/tsusc.2017.2714344

Asthana, R., Verma, N., & Ratan, R. (2014, February 21–22). Generation of Boolean functions using genetic algorithm for cryptographic applications. In

*Proceedings for the 2014 IEEE International Advance Computing Conference*, Gurgaon, India (pp. 1361–1366). https://doi.org/10.1109/iadcc.2014.6779525

Chang, V., & Ramachandran, M. (2016). Towards achieving data security with the cloud computing adoption framework. *IEEE Transactions on Services Computing*, *9*(1), 138–151. https://doi.org/10.1109/tsc.2015.2491281

Farash, M. S., Turkanović, M., Kumari, S., & Hölbl, M. (2016). An efficient user authentication and key agreement scheme for heterogeneous wireless sensor network tailored for the Internet of Things environment. *Ad Hoc Networks*, *36*, 152–176.

Inani, A., Singh, M., & Saxena, R. (2018). A secure mobile cloud computing framework based on data classification using asymmetric key cryptography. *SSRN Electronic Journal*, 831–838. https://doi.org/10.2139/ssrn.3170521

Jia, W., Zhang, B., Lu, J.-T., Zhu, Y., Zhao, Y., Zuo, W., & Ling, H. (2017). Palmprint recognition based on complete direction representation. *IEEE Transactions on Image Processing*, *26*(9), 4483–4498. https://doi.org/10.1109/tip.2017.2705424

Kamalakannan G., Balajee J., & SrinivasaRaghavan, S. (2015). Superior content-based video retrieval system according to query image. *International Journal of Applied Engineering Research*, *10*(3), 7951–7957. https://www.researchgate.net/publication/274543426

Khalsan, M., Machado, L. R., Al-Shamery, E. S., Ajit, S., Anthony, K., Mu, M., & Agyeman, M. O. (2022). A survey of machine learning approaches applied to gene expression analysis for cancer prediction. *IEEE Access*, *10*, 27522–27534. https://doi.org/10.1109/ACCESS.2022.3146312

Kong, A., Cheung, K.-H., Zhang, D., Kamel, M., & You, J. (2006). An analysis of Bio-Hashing and its variants. *Pattern Recognition*, *39*(7), 1359–1368. https://doi.org/10.1016/j.patcog.2005.10.025

Krishna Prasad, K., & Aithal, P. S. (2018). A study on fingerprint hash code generation based on MD5 algorithm and Freeman chain code. *International Journal of Computational Research and Development*, *3*(1), 13–22. https://doi.org/10.5281/zenodo.1144555

Kundu, S., & Sarker, G. (2016). A new RBFN with modified optimal clustering algorithm for clear and occluded fingerprint identification. *IEEE Xplore, 2016, 125–129*. https://doi.org/10.1109/CIEC.2016.7513668

Kushida, K. E., Murray, J., & Zysman, J. (2015). Cloud computing: From scarcity to abundance. *Journal of Industry, Competition and Trade*, *15*(1), 5–19. https://doi.org/10.1007/s10842-014-0188-y

Latha, K., & Sheela, T. (2019). Block based data security and data distribution on multi cloud environment. *Journal of Ambient Intelligence and Humanized Computing*. https://doi.org/10.1007/s12652-019-01395-y

Mansour, A., Sadik, M., & Sabir, E. (2015, November 17–20). Multi-factor authentication based on multimodal biometrics (MFA-MB) for cloud computing. In the *Proceedings for the 2015 IEEE/ACS 12th International Conference of Computer Systems and Applications*, Marrakech, Morocco (pp. 1–4). https://doi.org/10.1109/aiccsa.2015.7507257

Masala, G. L., Ruiu, P., & Grosso, E. (2018). Biometric authentication and data security in cloud computing. In K. Daimi (Ed.), *Computer and network security essentials* (pp. 337–353). Springer.

Nair, V. S., Reshmypriya, G. N., Rubeena, M. M., & Fasila, K. A. (2017, March 16–17). Multibiometric cryptosystem based on decision level fusion for file uploading in cloud. In *Proceedings for the 2017 International Conference on Recent Advances in Electronics and Communication Technology*, Bangalore, India (pp. 29–32). https://doi.org/10.1109/icraect.2017.19

Panchal, G., Samanta, D., & Barman, S. (2017). Biometric-based cryptography for digital content protection without any key storage. *Multimedia Tools and Applications, 78*(19), 26979–27000. https://doi.org/10.1007/s11042-017-4528-x

Ranjith, D., Balajee, J., & Kumar, C. (2016). In premises of cloud computing and models. *International Journal of Pharmacy & Technology, 8*(3), 4685–4695

Sajay, K. R., Babu, S. S., & Vijayalakshmi, Y. (2019). Enhancing the security of cloud data using hybrid encryption algorithm. *Journal of Ambient Intelligence and Humanized Computing*, https://doi.org/10.1007/s12652-019-01403-1

Sarier, N. D. (2017). Privacy preserving multimodal biometric authentication in the cloud. In M. H. A. Au, A. Castiglione, K.-K. R. Choo, F. Palmieri, & K.-C. Li (Eds.), Green, pervasive, and cloud computing: Lecture notes in computer science (pp. 90–104). Springer. https://doi.org/10.1007/978-3-319-57186-7_8

Schaefer, E. F. (1996). A simplified data encryption standard algorithm. *Cryptologia, 20*(1), 77–84. https://doi.org/10.1080/0161-119691884799

Schneier, B. (1993, December 9–11). Description of a new variable-length key, 64-bit block cipher (blowfish). In R. Anderson (Ed.), *Fast software encryption: Lecture notes in computer science* (pp. 191–204). Springer. https://link.springer.com/chapter/10.1007/3-540-58108-1_24

Shen, C., Wang, X., Song, J., Sun, L., & Song, M. (2019). Amalgamating knowledge towards comprehensive classification. In *Proceedings of the AAAI Conference on Artificial Intelligence, 33*, 3068–3075. https://doi.org/10.1609/aaai.v33i01.33013068

# CHAPTER 9

# A WORKLOAD CLUSTERING AND RESOURCE PROVISIONING FRAMEWORK FOR CLOUD USING

## Adaptive Cat Swarm Optimization and Rule Based Classification

**Gurram Sunitha**
*Mohan Babu University*

**Mohammad Gouse Galety**
*Catholic University Erbil*

**J. Avanija**
*Mohan Babu University*

**K. Reddy Madhavi**
*Mohan Babu University*

**A. V. Sriharsha**
*Mohan Babu University*

*Innovations in Computational Intelligence, Big Data Analytics, and Internet of Things*, pages 159–178
Copyright © 2024 by Information Age Publishing
www.infoagepub.com

## ABSTRACT

Nowadays, cloud has become a new way of life for any organization to provide online services to their clients and to bring in a competitive advantage to their businesses. Cloud computing targets at providing a diversity of paid online information technology (software and hardware) services to the user on a demand basis via the Internet. The workload balancing and resource provisioning are the crucial strictures that change the dynamics of cost, scalability, and availability of cloud resources and services. Many frameworks have been proposed for uncluttering various problems encountered through the tasks of workload balancing and resource provisioning. This chapter is targeted to probe the competence of using adaptive cat swarm technique for optimizing the workload clustering and the usage of rule-based classifier for resource provisioning in cloud environments. After an extensive study of the simulation results, it has been verified that the proposed methodology has been considerable in performing workload clustering and resource provisioning. The proposed methodology has showcased on an average of more than 3% improvement in terms of cloud service time and a reduction of cloud service cost on an average of 1.8% when compared with optimization techniques—particle swarm and cat swarm.

Cloud computing targets at providing a diversity of paid online information technology (software and hardware) services to the user on a demand basis via the Internet. All the major players in the market are efficiently utilizing the cloud services for their data management, service deployment, maintenance, and provisions. Utilizing cloud services from the third-parties relieves companies from the stressful scenarios of installation and management of computing centers, memory rack servers, software applications, and so on which is the process of creating a company-owned infrastructure at their physical sites, and is excruciatingly slow and expensive. Hosting software applications on cloud provides the pros of scalability (elasticity), portability, availability, agility, flexibility, reliability, capacity, speed, cost, enhanced user experience, and so on. Nowadays, cloud has become a new way of life for any company to provide online services to their clients and to bring in a competitive advantage to their businesses.

In the cloud computing context, the method of dispensing workloads across various computing resources in a balanced manner and carefully managing network traffic to those resources is termed as load balancing. On cloud, the end goal is to prevent cloud servers from malfunctioning or becoming overcrowded. Balancing the traffic and workload among the cloud servers is a mammoth task to handle for providing timely and equitable services to cloud users. Also, assigning appropriate resources to serve workloads is a key feature. The workload balancing and resource provisioning are the crucial strictures that change the dynamics of cost, scalability, and availability of cloud resources and services. Load balancing shall be done at both software level and hardware level, and at both network level and application level to manage the distribution of work traffic among cloud servers. Cloud load balancing is an issue to be investigated when scale out is the strategy undertaken to handle heavy traffic into the cloud. In the cloud, load balancing needs to be done across the cloud servers that are physically located across the globe. This enhances the uptime and service time of the cloud in the scenarios of server failures if any. The benefits of cloud load balancing include high availability, balancing cloud traffic, efficient resource utilization, and so on. Dynamic load balancing algorithms are those that look for the network's lightest server and then place the proper load on it. The workload is split between the processors during runtime. Various algorithms have been designed and developed for the purpose of dynamic load balancing in the cloud. The dynamic algorithms shall monitor the dynamic traffic in and out of the cloud and shall appropriately distribute it across the cloud resources for the purpose of achieving cloud stability and productivity. Such algorithms are also expected to prevent thrashing of the cloud. Resource provisioning is a challenging task for upkeeping the cloud with the dynamic service requests from the users. Efficient provisioning of existing resources to service the user requests has been extensively studied but it still has scope for investigation and advancement.

This chapter is targeted to probe the competence of using adaptive cat swarm technique for optimizing the workload clustering and the usage of rule-based classifier for resource provisioning in cloud environments. This book chapter content is systematized as follows. The second section quotes the literature survey on workload clustering and resource provisioning in cloud environments. Next, the adaptive cat swarm optimization technique is discussed in detail. Then we propose a novel methodology for cloud environments to the purpose of optimized workload clustering based on adaptive cat swarm technique and resource provisioning done by using rule-based classifiers. Next, the proposed methodology has been extensively simulated using a cloud simulation tool and the results are detailed. Finally, we have given our findings and potential directions for further research.

## LITERATURE SURVEY

The taxonomy, issues and challenges related to workload clustering and resource provisioning techniques in cloud environments have been studied and have been documented with attention to detail (Afzal & Kavitha, 2019; Kumar & Kumar, 2019; Shafiq et al., 2021; Wang et al., 2020). Many studies have been performed on developing approaches for improving the efficiency of the workload clustering and resource provisioning techniques in cloud environments (Jena et al., 2020; Kumar et al., 2021; Priya et al., 2019;

Shafiq et al., 2021; Shahidinejad et al., 2021). Various optimization techniques have been customized and applied to make cloud workload clustering more efficient (Ghobaei-Arani, 2021; Ghobaei-Arani & Shahidinejad, 2021; Sumalatha & Anbarasi, 2019). Frameworks have been proposed for workload clustering on cloud through multi-objective optimization and hybridization to support autonomic resource provisioning and load balancing on cloud (Devaraj et al., 2020). Suitability of machine learning methods for the problem has been surveyed (Duc et al., 2019). Also, the application of bio-inspired algorithms and genetic algorithms for the chosen problem have been investigated (Kannan et al., 2022).

## ADAPTIVE CAT SWARM OPTIMIZATION TECHNIQUE

The adaptive cat swarm optimization is grounded on the stalking and pouncing habits of cats for preying (Ji et al., 2020). They intensely stalk their prey so as to understand the movement patterns of their prey. They approach their prey very slowly and smoothly by lurking and sneaking. This strategy of cats preying behavior has been embedded into the cat swarm optimization technique as two steps—seeking mode and tracing mode. Every cat at any instant of time can be in either one of the modes. The cats will be continuously shifting between the modes—seeking and tracing. The cat moves and searches to find its prey in seeking mode. The cat moves around by changing its position with a certain velocity. Once the cat finds its prey, it shifts into tracing mode. The cat traces the prey and constantly moves towards the prey in the tracing mode.

Let the search space be a $D$-dimensional space. Each cat is represented by $D$ dimensions where $D = \{d_1, d_2, \ldots\}$. The current mode of $Cat_i$ is maintained as $Mode_i$. Let $SMP_i$ represent the Seeking Memory Pool of $Cat_i$. Let the change range of each dimension $d_j$ be represented by the $SRD_{dj}$. Let the mutation of the maximum number of dimensions for $Cat_i$ be specified by the parameter $CDC_i$. $CDC_i$ values range $[0, 1]$. The details of the $Cat_i$ path in the search space is also maintained so as to support backtracking. Every cat $Cat_i$ is evaluated by the fitness function whose value is computed based on the current position of the cat. Let $FV_i$ represent the current fitness value of $Cat_i$. Let $FV_{max.i}$ represent the maximum fitness value among all the candidates in the seeking memory pool of $Cat_i$ and let $FV_{min.i}$ represent the minimum fitness value among all the candidates in the seeking memory pool of $Cat_i$. Let $P_i$ represent the selection probability value of '$Cat_i$. Let $X_{i.d}(t)$ represent the current position of $Cat_i$. Let $V_{i.d}(t)$ and $V_{i.d}(t+1)$ represent the velocity of $Cat_i$ at time instants $t$ and $t+1$, respectively. Let $V_{max}$ represent the maximum velocity. $Vmax$ restricts the maximum speed of cat's movement in the search space. At any point of time, the maximum number of cats that can be in seeking mode and/or tracing mode is restricted by the parameter *mixture ratio* represented as *MR*.

The adaptive cat swarm optimization (ACSO) algorithm can be recapitulated as below.

## Adaptive Cat Swarm Optimization Algorithm

1. Initialize the population of cats, where each individual in the population is represented by $D$ dimensions.
2. Initialize the parameters $V_{max}$, $SRD_{dj}$, $CDC_i$, $MR$.
3. Repeat the following steps until the stopping convergence criteria is met:
   - i. Randomly set the initial state of the cats as either seeking mode or tracing mode by considering the parameter *MR*. Also, set the initial position and velocity.
   - ii. For each $Cat_i$
     - a. If $mode_i$ = seek, then
        Call seek($Cat_i$)
     - b. Else If $mode_i$ = trace, then
        Call trace($Cat_i$)

## Seeking Mode Algorithm

For each $Cat_i$ in seeking mode
   - a. Let $X_{i.d}$ represent the current position of $Cat_i$. Let the next position of $Cat_i$ be $X_{i.d+1}$. If the next position is already visited by $Cat$ then return to position $X_{i.d}$.
   - b. Randomly change the current position of $Cat_i$ based on $CDC_i$ and $SRD_d$ to create multiple candidates in the seeking memory pool.
   - c. Compute the fitness of each candidate in the seeking memory pool.
   - d. The candidate with the highest fitness value will be retained and other candidates will be ignored. The selection probability value for each candidate can be used for conflict resolution if any.

$$P_i = \frac{|FV_i - FV_x|}{FV_{max} - FV_{x\,min}}$$

## Tracing Mode Algorithm

For each $Cat_i$ in tracing mode:

1. Update the velocity of $Cat_i$. Restrict the maximum velocity of $Cat_i$ after updation to $V_{max}$. Let $V_{i,d}(t)$ and $V_{i,d}(t+1)$ represent the velocity of dimension $d_j$ of $Cat_i$ at time instants $t$ and $t+1$, respectively. Then,

$$V_{i,d}(t+1) = w \times V_{i,d}(t) + c_1 \times r_1 \times \left(p_{d,best}(t) - x_{d,i}(t)\right) + c_2 \times r_2 \times (Fi)$$
$$+ f \times F_i + e \times E_i$$

where $r_1$ and $r_2$ are random numbers in the range $[0, 1]$, $c_1$ and $c_2$ are the acceleration coefficients, $w$ is the inertial weight of the cat, $f$ is the weights moving towards the global optima and $e$ is the weights moving away from the local optima, $F_i$ represents the friend of the $Cat_i$ and $E_i$ represents the enemy of the $Cat_i$, $g_{i.best}$ is the global optimal position of $Cat_i$, $p_{i.best}$ is the local optimal position of $Cat_i$, $X_{i,d}$ is the current position of $Cat_i$. The values of $f$, $F_i$, $E_i$, $c_1$, $c_2$ can be determined as follows.

$$f = 0.1 - i \times \frac{0.2}{MaxIter}$$

$$e = 2 \times rand$$

$$F_i = g_{i.best}(t) - x_{d,i}(t) \text{ when } dist2gbest \le radius$$

$$E_i = p_{i.best}(t) - x_{d,i}(t) \text{ when } dist2gbest \le radius$$

where *radius* defines the tracing radius range for the cat's search position.

$$r_p = \frac{1 - \left(\sqrt{c_p} + 1\right) \times rand \times i}{c_p \times MaxIter}$$

for the first half iterations of MaxIter

$$r_p = \frac{1 - \left(\sqrt{c_p} + 1\right) \times (1 + rand) \times i}{c_p \times MaxIter}$$

for the second half iterations of MaxIter

where MaxIter is the maximum number of iterations for searching. It will act as stopping criteria for the search process. The parameter r is adaptive adjusted.

2. Update the position of $Cat_i$

$$X_{i.d}(t+1) = \tfrac{1}{2}\big(y \times X_{i.d}(t) + (1-y) \times X_{i.d}(t-1) + y \times V_{i.d}(t+1) + (1-y)V_{i.d}(t)\big)$$

where $y$ is the memory factor.

The parameters *radius*, *r*, and $y$ in ACSO are observed to be easily learned in order to break out of local optimums and hasten the convergence to the global optimums. The strategy for computing $r1$ and $r2$ lies in the objective to support strong search ability for global optima in the first half iterations and to support stability in the later half iterations to achieve convergence. It means that the ACSO increases the ability of fast convergence to a globally optimal solution.

## PROPOSED METHODOLOGY

The bottleneck to provide cloud services efficiently and effectively is to regulate the process of associating workloads with resources in terms of load sharing, resource allocation, and resource provisioning. To do so, providers need to understand the behavior of the applications running on their cloud platforms. Providing the right amount of resources at the right time at the right location is the key to success. It is a critical challenge to understand the behavior of the application and decide the types and number of resources required for the application to run in a cost-efficient way. The client's service requests shall be analyzed in terms of its size, complexity, quality of service, computing power, network bandwidth, cost package, and so on, and the client's request shall allocate resources appropriately. For seeking this challenge, it is beneficial to cluster similar client requests and allocate such workload clusters to a suitable cloud cluster center which can handle and service the workload cluster.

The proposed methodology for autonomic load sharing and resource provisioning for providing cloud services is based on the multi-objective ACSO technique. The ACSO technique provides better understanding of the uniformity of the distribution, compared to conventional optimization techniques, the algorithm's efficiency and convergence are maintained (Jiang & Zhang, 2019). The ACSO in association with K-means clustering algorithm is used to competently identify the similar services as requested by the client from the cloud and cluster them. Further, rule-based classifier is used for resource provisioning so as to assign a cluster of similar services to suitable cloud cluster centers.

The ACSO technique is a combination of two classical optimization techniques—adaptive particle swarm optimization and cat swarm optimization. The advantages of the ACSO technique are its fast convergence and fast search abilities. The ACSO technique is used as a meta-heuristic in k-means clustering method.

Figure 9.1 presents the proposed model with the objective of efficient workload sharing and resource provisioning in a cloud environment using the techniques—workload clustering and rule-based classification. Multiple users will be simultaneously raising their requests for cloud services which will be received, handled, and logged by the workload manager. As the next step, each service request will be authenticated and it will be verified for integrity. Every service request will be validated against the service level agreement of the service provider with the client. The authenticated and validated service requests will only be considered for providing the cloud services.

Further the service requests will be clustered and then workload clusters will be classified for the need of assigning them to suitable cloud centres for providing services.

### Adaptive Cat Swarm Optimization Technique Based K-Means Algorithm for Workload Clustering

The proposed approach uses ACSO technique as meta-heuristic for K-Means based workload clustering. The optimal centroids for the K clusters are determined by using ACSO technique.

Let there be $N$ cloud service requests. Let cloud service requests be represented as $[req_1, req_2, \ldots req_N]$. The service requests act as the population for the clustering. Initially, all the service requests are considered as a single cluster. Let K represent the number of clusters to be formed. Among the $N$ cloud service requests, any K requests will be randomly selected to act as initial centroids for the K clusters. Each centroid is represented by two parameters—position and velocity.

In the search space, *position* represents the centroid's position in the search space and *velocity* represents the speed with which the centroid's changes its position. In each iteration of K-means clustering, the adaptive cat swarm optimization technique paves way towards finding an optimal centroid. Each centroid shall find its way to the best solution space by following the trend of its local optimum and the trend of its cluster's global optimum.

The algorithm for the proposed methodology is as shown in Figure 9.2. Figure 9.2a shows the parameters for the algorithm and their description.

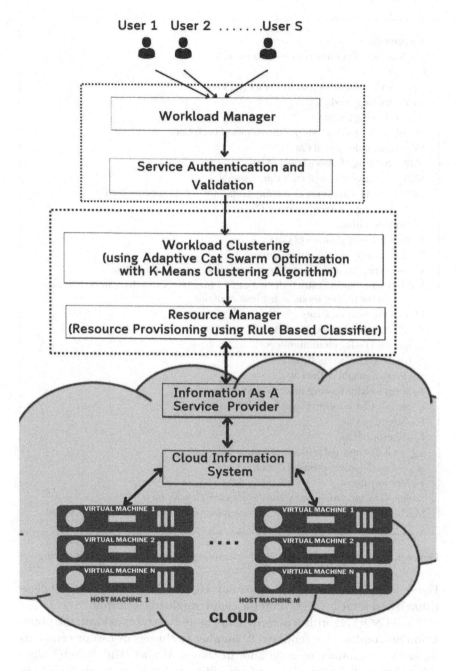

**Figure 9.1** Proposed model for workload sharing and resource provisioning on cloud.

**Parameters:**

$K$ – Number of clusters (or cats or centroids)

$Cat_i$ – $i$th Cat

$mode_i$ – Current mode (seek or trace) of $Cat_i$

seek – Seeking mode

trace – Tracing mode

$D = \{d_1, d_2, \ldots\}$ – Number of dimensions of each Cat

$FV_i$ – Current Fitness of $Cat_i$

$SMP_i$ – Seeking Memory Pool of $Cat_i$

$SRD_{dj}$ – Change range of each dimension $d_j$

$CDC_i \in [0, 1]$ – Mutation of maximum number of dimensions for $Cat_i$

$P_i$ – Selection probability value of $Cat_i$

$t$ – $t$th time instant

$X_{i.d}(t)$ – Current position of $Cat_i$

$V_{i.d} t)$ – Velocity of Cati at time instants $t$

$V_{max}$ – maximum velocity, restricts the maximum speed of any $Cat_i$

MR – Mixture Ratio, restricts the maximum number of cats that can be in seeking and/or tracing mode at any instant of time

PCats – Population of cats

P – Pool of cloud service requests

$r_1, r_2 \in [0, 1]$ – Random numbers

$c_1, c_2$ – Acceleration coefficients

$w$ – Inertial weight of the cat

$f$ – Set of weights moving towards global optima

$e$ – Set of weights moving away from local optima

$F_i$ – Friend of $Cat_i$

$E_i$ – Enemy of $Cat_i$

$g_{i.best}$ – Global optimal position of $Cat_i$

$p_{i.best}$ – Local optimal position of $Cat_i$

$y$ – Memory factor

radius – Tracing radius range for the cat's search position

MaxIter – Maximum number of iterations (stopping criteria for search process)

**Figure 9.2a** Proposed ACSO based K-means algorithm for workload clustering.

Figure 9.2b shows the ACSO algorithm. Figure 9.2c shows the ACSO algorithm based K-means algorithm for cloud workload clustering.

The ACSO() algorithm presented in Figure 9.2b takes as input the population of cloud service requests 'P,' number of clusters or cats or centroids 'K,' and the number of maximum iterations *MaxIter*. The ACSO() algorithm returns 'K' optimal cats which will be taken as centroids for the K-means clustering algorithm. As the first step, K-random cloud service requests are pulled from 'P' to form the initial population of cats *PCats*. The

**AdaptiveCatSwarmOptimization() Algorithm:**
*Input:*
P – Population of cloud service requests
K – Number of clusters (cats or centroids)
MaxIter – Maximum number of iterations
*Output:* Optimal Centroids

1:   K random cloud requests will form the initial population of cats.
                PCats ← random (P, K)
2:   Initialize $V_{max}$, $SRD_{dj}$, CDCi, MR.
3:   Repeat $r$ in 1 to MaxIter in steps of +1
4:        for each $Cat_i$ in PCats :
5:               $mode_i$ ← random ({seek, trace}, constraint: MR)
6:        end for
7:        for each $Cat_i$ in PCats :
8:               if $mode_i$ = seek, then
9:                     $Cat_i$ ← call Seek($Cat_i$)
10:              else if $mode_i$ = trace, then
11:                    call Trace($Cat_i$)
12:              end if
13:       end for
14:  end repeat
15:  return PCats

**Seek() Algorithm:**
*Input:* $Cat_i$ – A cat
*Output:* A Cat with improved fitness value

1:   if !visited($X_{i,d}$) then
                $X_{i,d}$ ← $X_{i,d}$ + 1
2:   end if
3:   SMPCati ← GenerateSMP($Cat_i$)
4:   maxFitCat ← maxFitnessCat($SMPCat_i$)
5:   return maxFitCat

**Figure 9.2b**   Proposed ACSO based K-means algorithm for workload clustering.
*(continues)*

parameters $V_{max}$, $SRD_{dj}$, $CDC_i$, MR are initialized. The mode of each cat in
*PCats* is initialized to either *seek* or *trace* ensuring that the constraint *MR* is
satisfied. The process of searching for *K* optimal centroids will be repeated
for *MaxIter* number of iterations. For each $Cat_i$ in *PCats*, depending on its
current mode the following operations are performed:

**Trace() Algorithm:**

*Input:*

$Cat_i$ – A cat

*Output:*

$Cat_i$ with updated position and velocity

1: Update position of $Cat_i$

$$X_{i.d}(t+1) = \tfrac{1}{2}\big(y \times X_{i.d}(t) + (1-y) \times X_{i.d}(t-1) + y \times V_{i.d}(t+1) + (1-y)V_{i.d}(t)\big)$$

2: Update velocity of $Cat_i$

$$V_{i.d}(t+1) = w \times V_{i.d}(t) + c_1 \times r_1 \times \big(p_{d.best}(t) - x_{d.i}(t)\big) + c_2 \times r_2 \times (Fi) + f \times F_i + e \times E_i$$

where

$$f = 0.1 - i \times \frac{0.2}{MaxIter}$$

$$e = 2 \times rand$$

$$F_i = g_{i.best}(t) - x_{d.i}(t) \text{ when } dist2gbest \leq radius$$

$$E_i = p_{i.best}(t) - x_{d.i}(t) \text{ when } dist2gbest \leq radius$$

$$r_p = \frac{1 - \left(\sqrt{c_p} + 1\right) \times rand \times i}{c_p \times MaxIter}$$

for the first half iterations of MaxIter

$$r_p = \frac{1 - \left(\sqrt{c_p} + 1\right) \times (1 + rand) \times i}{c_p \times MaxIter}$$

**Figure 9.2b (continued)** Proposed ACSO based K-means algorithm for workload clustering. *(continues)*

a. *Cat_i* is in *seek* mode—Seek() algorithm performs the following operations:

   i. Move the *Cat_i* to a new position (new position should not be visited already).

   ii. Generate the candidate cats for the *Cat_i* to form the seeking memory pool.

**maxFitnessCat() Algorithm:**
*Input:*
SMPCat$_i$ – Seeking Memory Pool of Cat$_i$

*Output:*
maxFitCat – the cat with highest fitness value in Seeking Memory Pool of Cat$_i$

1:  K random cloud requests will form the initial population of cats.
            maxFitCat ← Cat$_1$
2:  for each Cat$_i$ in SMPCat$_i$ :
3:          if FVi > FV$_{maxFitCat}$, then
4:                  maxFitCat ← Cat$_i$
5:          end if
6:  end for
7:  return maxFitCat

**GenerateSMP() Algorithm:**
*Input:*
Cat$_i$ – A cat

*Output:*
SMPCat$_i$ – Seeking Memory Pool of Cat$_i$

1:  SMPCat$_i$ ← ∅
2:  do
3:          newCat ← X$_{i,d}$ + random ({-1, +1}, constraints: CDC$_i$ , SRD$_d$ )
4:          SMPCat$_i$ ← SMPCat$_i$ ∪ newCat
5:  while !full(SMPCat$_i$)
6:  return SMPCat$_i$

**Figure 9.2b (continued)**    Proposed ACSO based K-means algorithm for workload clustering.

      iii.  From the candidate cats from the seeking memory pool, determine *maxFitCat* (the cat with highest fitness value).
      iv.  Replace *Cat$_i$* with *maxFitCat*.
  b.  Cat is in *trace* mode—Trace() algorithm performs the following operations:
      i.  Update the position of *Cat$_i$*
      ii.  Update the velocity of *Cat$_i$*

Given the seeking memory pool for any $Cat_i$, the candidates in the seeking memory pool are evaluated and the most fittest cat is determined by the maxFitnessCat() algorithm. Algorithm GenerateSMP() generates the seeking memory pool for any given $Cat_i$ ensuring the constraints $CDC_i$, $SRD_d$.

The ACSO-K-Means() algorithm presented in Figure 9.2c takes as input the pool of cloud service requests and clusters them based on ACSO technique based K-means clustering algorithm. Once cloud service requests are clustered, further they can be assigned to a suitable cloud cluster center which can handle and service the workload cluster.

For resource provisioning the proposed methodology uses the pre-defined rule-based classification. The proposed methodology assumes that the cloud clusters have already been classified based on varying parameters and the rules have been generated. Let the cloud clusters be termed as CC1, CC2, etc. Let each cluster centre $CC_i$ be represented by one rule $R_i$. Figure 9.3 presents the resource provisioning of workload clusters to cloud centers based on rule-based classification.

---

**ACSO-K-Means() Algorithm:**

*Input:*
P – Population of cloud service requests
K – Number of clusters

*Output:*
OptimalWorkloadClusters – Optimal Workload Clusters

```
1:   Initialize MaxIter
2:   Repeat !(stopping condition = true)
3:        OptimalCentroids ← AdaptiveCatSwarmOptimization(P, K, MaxIter)
4:        for each CloudRequest in P:
5:             OptimalWorkloadClusters ← Reassign CloudRequest to similar
                  cluster if required;
6:        end for
7:   end repeat
8:   return OptimalWorkloadClusters
```

---

**Figure 9.2c** Proposed ACSO based K-means algorithm for workload clustering.

**ResourceProvisioner() Algorithm:**

*Input:*

OptimalClusters – Optimal Clusters

CC = {CC$_1$, CC$_2$, . . . CC$_n$} – Cloud clusters

R = {R$_1$, R$_2$, . . . R$_n$} – Classifier Rules

*Output:*

Resource Provisioning of workload clusters to cloud clusters

```
1:   for each WorkloadCluster in OptimalClusters:
2:       for each R_i in R:
3:           If RuleFires (WorkloadCluster, R_i) = true
4:               Assign (WorkloadCluster, CC_i)
5:           end if
6:       end for
7:   end for
```

**Figure 9.3**  Proposed rule-based classification for resource provisioning.

## EXPERIMENTATION AND RESULTS

The experimentation is done on an Intel i5 processor with 12GB memory, 1TB hard disk. The operating system is Cloud Linux. The number of virtualization machines considered for experimentation is four. The proposed methodology of adaptive cat swarm optimization based workload clustering and rule-based classification for resource provisioning has been simulated using the CloudSim tool. The environment setup is tabulated in Table 9.1. The simulation is done ensuring that service level agreements are not

| TABLE 9.1 | Details of Environment Setup for Simulation |
|---|---|
| Parameter | Description |
| Cloud Bandwidth | 3,000 bps |
| Network Bandwidth | 1,500 MIPS |
| Number of VMs | 4 |
| Cost per cloud service | 100–250 units |
| Number of workloads | 50–175 |
| Number of resources | 5–25 |

violated. The simulation results are interpreted, analyzed, and inferences were drawn. The proposed approach is evaluated against particle swarm optimization based K-means (PSO-K-Means) algorithm and cat swarm optimization based K-means (CSO-K-means) algorithm in the context of workloads, resources, waiting time and service cost. The evaluation results have been represented in the Figures 9.4 to 9.7.

Figure 9.4 presents the evaluation of the fitness of the optimal centroids generated by the workload clustering methods—ACSO-K-Means, CSO-K-Means, and PSO-K-Means. The speed of convergence of the three algorithms has been plotted in Figure 9.4. It has been noted that the suggested strategy ACSO-K-Means based workload clustering provided optimal centroids with better fitness values than the CSO-K-Means based workload clustering and PSO-K-Means based workload clustering. Also, the proposed approach converged faster (within lesser number of iterations) than the other two approaches.

Figure 9.5 presents the evaluation of the proposed methodology against the other two algorithms in terms of number of workloads and the ratio of waiting time. The number of resources were kept constant at 50. The proposed methodology handled the workloads with less waiting time thus enhancing the user experience. The proposed methodology demonstrated reduced waiting time by almost 3.2% and 4.26% when matched with the CSO-K-Means based workload clustering, PSO-K-Means based workload clustering respectively.

Figure 9.6 presents the evaluation of the proposed methodology against the other two algorithms in terms of number of resources and the ratio of

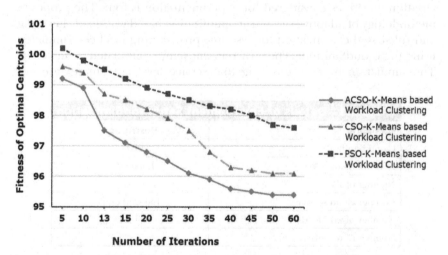

**Figure 9.4** Evaluation of the fitness of the optimal centroids generated by the workload clustering methods—ACSO-K-means, CSO-K-means, PSO-K-means.

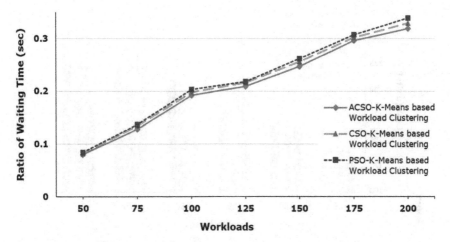

**Figure 9.5** Comparison of the workload clustering methods—ACSO-K-means, CSO-K-Means, PSO-K-means in terms of number of workloads vs ratio of waiting time.

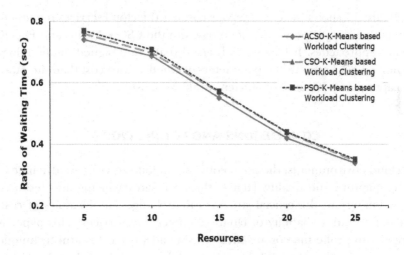

**Figure 9.6** Comparison of the workload clustering methods—ACSO-K-means, CSO-K-means, PSO-K-means in terms of number of resources vs ratio of waiting time.

waiting time. The number of workloads were kept constant at 100. Inherently, as the number of resources were increased, the workloads were handled efficiently. The proposed methodology handled the resources with less waiting time thus enhancing the user experience. When compared to the K CSO-K-means based workload clustering and the PSO-K-means based workload clustering, the suggested methodology showed reduced waiting times of about 2.63% and 3.68%, respectively.

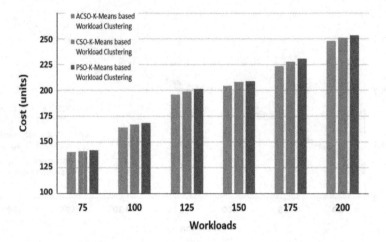

**Figure 9.7** Comparison of the workload clustering methods—ACSO-K-means, CSO-K-means, PSO-K-means in terms of number of resources vs service cost.

Figure 9.7 shows the cloud service cost per the cloud services requested, comparing the proposed methodology with the CSO-K-Means and PSO-K-Means approaches. It has been observed that the designed methodology achieves 1.8% better in the parameters of cloud service cost than the other two approaches because of efficient workload clustering.

## CONCLUSIONS AND FUTURE WORK

In cloud environments, the user requests for cloud services are dynamic in time, quantity, and quality. Hence, the workload balancing and resource provisioning are the crucial strictures that change the dynamics of cost, scalability, and availability of cloud resources and services. This paper is targeted to probe the competence of using adaptive cat swarm technique for optimizing the workload clustering and the usage of rule-based classifier for resource provisioning in cloud environments. After an extensive study of the simulation results, it has been verified that the proposed methodology has been considerable in performing workload clustering and resource provisioning. The proposed methodology has showcased on an average of more than 3% improvement in terms of cloud service time and a reduction of cloud service cost on an average of 1.8% when compared with optimization techniques—particle swarm and cat swarm. Further, more efficacious multi-objective optimization techniques considering various complex parameters can be designed and developed for providing quality cloud service.

# REFERENCES

Afzal, S., & Kavitha, G. (2019). Load balancing in cloud computing—A hierarchical taxonomical classification. *Journal of Cloud Computing, 8*(1), 1–24. https://doi .org/10.1186/s13677-019-0146-7

Devaraj, A. F. S., Elhoseny, M., Dhanasekaran, S., Lydia, E. L., & Shankar, K. (2020). Hybridization of firefly and improved multi-objective particle swarm optimization algorithm for energy efficient load balancing in cloud computing environments. *Journal of Parallel and Distributed Computing, 142*, 36–45. https:// doi.org/10.1016/j.jpdc.2020.03.022

Duc, T. L., Leiva, R. G., Casari, P., & Östberg, P. O. (2019). Machine learning methods for reliable resource provisioning in edge-cloud computing: A survey. *ACM Computing Surveys, 52*(5), 1–39. https://doi.org/10.1145/3341145

Ghobaei-Arani, M. (2021). A workload clustering based resource provisioning mechanism using Biogeography based optimization technique in the cloud based systems. *Soft Computing, 25*(5), 3813–3830. https://doi.org/10.1007/ s00500-020-05409-2

Ghobaei-Arani, M., & Shahidinejad, A. (2021). An efficient resource provisioning approach for analyzing cloud workloads: A metaheuristic-based clustering approach. *The Journal of Supercomputing, 77*(1), 711–750. https://doi .org/10.1007/s11227-020-03296-w

Jena, U. K., Das, P. K., & Kabat, M. R. (2020). Hybridization of meta-heuristic algorithm for load balancing in cloud computing environment. *Journal of King Saud University-Computer and Information Sciences, 34*(6), 2332–2342. https:// doi.org/10.1016/j.jksuci.2020.01.012

Ji, X. F., Pan, J. S., Chu, S. C., Hu, P., Chai, Q. W., & Zhang, P. (2020). Adaptive cat swarm optimization algorithm and its applications in vehicle routing problems. *Mathematical Problems in Engineering, 2020*, 1291526. https://doi.org/ 10.1155/2020/1291526

Jiang, T. H., & Zhang, C. (2019). Adaptive discrete cat swarm optimisation algorithm for the flexible job shop problem. *International Journal of Bio-Inspired Computation, 13*(3), 199–208. https://doi.org/10.1504/IJBIC.2019.099186

Kannan, K. S., Sunitha, G., Deepa, S. N., Babu, D. V., & Avanija, J. (2022). A multi-objective load balancing and power minimization in cloud using bio-inspired algorithms. *Computers and Electrical Engineering, 102*, 108225. https://doi.org/ 10.1016/j.compeleceng.2022.108225

Kumar, M., Kishor, A., Abawajy, J., Agarwal, P., Singh, A., & Zomaya, A. Y. (2021). ARPS: An autonomic resource provisioning and scheduling framework for cloud platforms. *IEEE Transactions on Sustainable Computing, 7*(2), 386–399. https://doi.org/10.1109/TSUSC.2021.3110245

Kumar, P., & Kumar, R. (2019). Issues and challenges of load balancing techniques in cloud computing: A survey. *ACM Computing Surveys (CSUR), 51*(6), 1–35. https://doi.org/10.1145/3281010

Priya, V., Kumar, C. S., & Kannan, R. (2019). Resource scheduling algorithm with load balancing for cloud service provisioning. *Applied Soft Computing, 76*, 416–424. https://doi.org/10.1016/j.asoc.2018.12.021

Shafiq, D. A., Jhanjhi, N. Z., & Abdullah, A. (2021). Load balancing techniques in cloud computing environment: A review. *Journal of King Saud University-Computer and Information Sciences, 34*(7), 3910–3933. https://doi.org/10.1016/j.jksuci.2021.02.007

Shafiq, D. A., Jhanjhi, N. Z., Abdullah, A., & Alzain, M. A. (2021). A load balancing algorithm for the data centres to optimize cloud computing applications. *IEEE Access, 9,* 41731–41744. https://doi.org/10.1109/ACCESS.2021.3065308

Shahidinejad, A., Ghobaei-Arani, M., & Masdari, M. (2021). Resource provisioning using workload clustering in cloud computing environment: A hybrid approach. *Cluster Computing, 24*(1), 319–342. https://doi.org/10.1007/s10586-020-03107-0

Sumalatha, K., & Anbarasi, M. S. (2019). A review on various optimization techniques of resource provisioning in cloud computing. *International Journal of Electrical & Computer Engineering, 9*(1), 2088–8708. https://doi.org/10.11591/ijece.v9i1.pp629-634

Wang, B., Wang, C., Song, Y., Cao, J., Cui, X., & Zhang, L. (2020). A survey and taxonomy on workload scheduling and resource provisioning in hybrid clouds. *Cluster Computing, 23*(4), 2809–2834. https://doi.org/10.1007/s10586-020-03048-8

CHAPTER 10

# IoT PROTOCOLS

## A Review

**Kasarapu Ramani**
*Mohan Babu University, Tirupati*

**G. B. Hima Bindu**
*The Apollo University, Chittoor*

**M. L. Haritha**
*RMK Engineering College, Chennai*

**N. Pushpa Latha**
*Annamacharya Institute of Technology and Sciences, Tirupati*

**I. Suneetha**
*Annamacharya Institute of Technology and Sciences, Tirupati*

## ABSTRACT

Today the Internet has enabled the Internet of Things (IoT) to become ubiquitous and has affected human life with sophisticated applications. The interaction among smart devices such as sensors, gateways, servers, and user

*Innovations in Computational Intelligence, Big Data Analytics, and Internet of Things*, pages 179–197
Copyright © 2024 by Information Age Publishing
www.infoagepub.com

applications in IoT will be through IoT protocols. These protocols not only enable communication between devices, but also ensure security of data being exchanged by the devices. Different IoT protocols are available, each offering specific features and capabilities and suitable for a specific IoT deployment as individual or combination. Many factors will influence the selection of IoT protocol such as power consumption, specific location, battery based operation, environment, and cost. This chapter provides a state-of-art survey on taxonomy of IoT protocols used for various purposes.

## IOT ARCHITECTURE

IoT connects smart devices to the internet using variety of networking technologies. Therefore, it is difficult and complex to manage IoT structure, without any architecture. The architecture of IoT is a framework defining what network's physical components are involved, their functions, configurations, operational principles and procedures, and data formats to be used for effective operations. The IoT architecture depends on the application domain and the technologies used. The most commonly used architecture comprises of the five layers as shown in Figure 10.1 (Pallavi et al., 2017).

### Five Layered IoT Architecture

*Perception Layer*
   This layer mainly comprises of sensors and actuators which are helpful to gather sensed information like temperature, humidity, event detection,

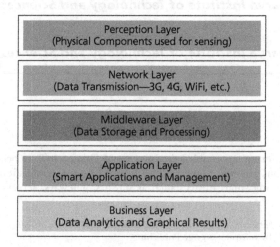

**Figure 10.1**   Five layered IoT architecture.

distance, vibration, acceleration, movement, and so on. Hence, it is also called a sensor layer. The physical quantities sensed are converted into analog or digital signals. This layer is to get information from the target environment and to send data to the network layer.

### Network Layer

This layer transmits data from perception layer to middleware layer through different network technologies-3G, 4G, Wi-Fi, Bluetooth, RFID, NFC, Infrared, and so on. Hence, this layer is also called communication or transmission layer. The required data privacy and confidentiality is also ensured by this layer.

### Middleware Layer

This layer provides data storage based on the device's address, and processing capabilities. It combines data collected from different sources. Also, it reconciles different data formats. It enables data aggregation and accessing. Also, it makes decisions based on computations performed on data-set received from sensors.

### Application Layer

This layer manages application processing based on information received from the middleware layer. It provides application specific services to the users. This application may involve sending emails, raising alarm, securing a system, smart watch functioning, controlling devices, smart agriculture, smart home, smart city, and so on.

### Business Layer

The application logic related to data retrieval, processing, transformation, and management is provided by this layer. Simply, it ensures business rules and policies, while ensuring data validity and consistency. This layer provides analysis results through flowcharts and graphs.

## IoT Communication and Its Parameters

Protocols enable reliable and secure communication. The following factors influence the communication:

### Speed/Data Rate

Speed/data rate determines the amount of information that can be transferred in a given unit of time. The units for this are bits per second (bps), kilobits per second (Kbps), megabits per second (Mbps), and gigabits per second (Gbps).

### Range

Range is the maximum communication distance between two nodes. Transmitting power, frequency band, environment, and kind of modulation technique are the factors that influence the range of communication.

### Power Consumption

Power consumption is the energy required to a node. Either fixed power supply or battery is needed to provide such power to a node. As most of the IoT applications are mobile in nature, they work on batteries and hence, power supply becomes a critical parameter, as battery lifetime is limited. Also, power consumption depends on the number of sensors and other communication equipment used in IoT application building. Finally, this power supply impacts the availability and maintenance strategy of the given application.

### Interoperability

To support a wide range of IoT applications in multiple domains, IoT ecosystem needs cross platform hardware and software to make connectivity among sensors, gateways, and Cloud. A scalable IoT system should support seamless data flow with such interoperability. In general, IoT systems need four kinds of interoperability such as foundational, organizational, semantic, and structural. Providing such interoperability is a critical issue.

### Scalability

To ensure, the given IoT application should be able to support additional devices, features, users, storage, and processing capabilities without degrading quality of service (QoS).

### Cost

The installation and maintenance cost are involved with IoT applications as they depend on specific technology. The scalability, and power consumption adds on network cost.

### Network Topology

Type of topology such as mesh, star, bus, point-to-point, point-to-multipoint influences the communication between IoT nodes.

### Security

Security ensures data protection between sender and receiver nodes. Also, communication should ensure data arrives at the intended destination nodes. The ubiquitous nature of IoT technology demands protection of sensitive information from third parties.

## IoT Devices Connectivity With Networks

The IoT protocol choice depends on the type of devices, their functionality, distance of communication, and usage.

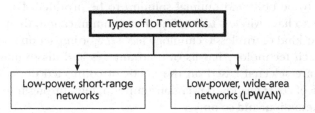

The connectivity of IoT is a tradeoff in bandwidth, range, and power consumption. An ideal IoT network should consume low power, cover high range, and allow high data with low bandwidth. The cellular or satellite communication covers a high range, but requires more bandwidth and consumes more power. The non-terrestrial networks such as satellite and UAV cover approximately 700 km. The networks such as 4G/5G, LTE-M, and NB-IoT, cover approximately 100 km. The low power, wide area networks (LPWAN) work at lower power and support local communication with low data rate, WiFi, the wide area networks such as LoRa and Sigfox cover an area of 5 km. Ethernet and Bluetooth enable communication that covers a small range with power requirement, but requires high bandwidth.

### Low Power and Short Range Networks

These types of networks are suitable for small coverage areas such as homes, offices, restaurants, and so on. They work on small power supplies such as small capacity batteries.

*Example:* Near field communication (NFC), Bluetooth, Z-wave, Zigbee, Wi-Fi/802.11

### Low Power and Wide Area Networks

These networks cover a communication area of about 500 meters and work with minimal power requirement.

*Example:* 4G LTE IoT, 5G IoT, Cat-0, Cat-1, LoRaWAN, LTE Cat-M1, Narrowband or NB-IoT/Cat-M2, Sigfox

## OVERVIEW OF IOT PROTOCOLS

IoT protocols enable devices to exchange data in a structured and meaningful manner and hence play a key role in IoT technology stack. Different technical groups such as the Internet Engineering Task Force (IETF),

World Wide Web Consortium (W3C), Institute of Electrical and Electronics Engineers (IEEE) EPCglobal, and the European Telecommunications Standards Institute (ETSI) have developed various protocols to support IoTs (Al-Fuqaha, 2015). The selection of protocol depends on functional prototype to be built and optimal solution to be provided. For example, our goal is to have wireless technology for communication, then choosing a particular kind of wireless technology has a major impact on application, because each technology has its own advantages and disadvantages. The protocols are selected based on the needs of connected devices such as long range of coverage, low power consumption, high throughput and ease of implementation, and so on.

## PHYSICAL AND NETWORK LAYER PROTOCOLS

The perception layer represents the physical layer which is used to sense and gather the information about the environment. The protocols used at physical and data link layer are as follows:

1. *Ethernet:* It is a networking technology based on IEEE 802.3 and used to connect devices in a personal area network (PAN), home area network (HAN), and local area network (LAN). It is used to connect sensors in industry, home or office automation systems through appliance control, and so on. It supports a data rate up to 10 Gbits/sec.
2. *Bluetooth Low Energy:* It is a wireless technology standard used to exchange data between fixed and mobile devices over short distances They create a personal area network (PAN) covering a distance of 100 meters and provide high security for communication. Bluetooth Smart, also known as Bluetooth Low Energy, was proposed by the Bluetooth special interest group. It can transfer data at a rate of 1 Mpbs and can be connected to many devices in star topology. There are many applications of Bluetooth such as measuring blood pressure profile, health thermometer profile, glucose profile, cycling speed and cadence profile, location and navigation profile, weight scale profile, environmental sensing profile, and so on (Postscapes, 2020).
3. Wi-*Fi:* The wireless fidelity is 802.11 standard and used to form wireless local area networks. It is available in a, b, c, g, n versions and operates in different radio frequency bands: 2.4, 3.6, 5 and

60 GHz. It supports 2 Mbps to 1.73 Gbps of data rate. It can cover up to 100 meters, but has two drawbacks: latency and security.

4. *Wi-Fi Direct:* It provides peer-to-peer connection and gives instance Internet connection through smart mobiles without any access point.

5. *WPA/WPA2/WPA3:* Wireless protected access is a kind of security protocol for Wi-Fi. It uses 64-bit/128-bit/192-bit encryption for data security.

6. *ZigBee:* It operates at 2.4 GHz, and covers 10–100 meters distance communication. It is used to cater commercial/industrial needs as it is cheaper. It enables both star and mesh topologies. It uses three bands of radio frequency: industrial, medical, and scientific. It is based on IEEE 802.15.4 and supports wide-area communication with a low power requirement. It works at a low bandwidth of 250 kpbs. It is used in short range communication with low data rate, in home automation, industrial automation, and data collection in medical devices.

7. *Radio Frequency Identification (RFID):* It has two components called tags and readers and uses radio waves for communication. Passive RFIDs are enabled with readers, but work without batteries; whereas active RFIDs need a battery in order to work. They are portable and enabled with storage capability. It is widely used for inventory tracking, personal tracking, patient health monitoring, and so on.

8. *Z-Wave:* It is a type of low power and long range IoT technology and it covers a distance of up to 100 m in a single hop.

9. *6LoWPAN:* 6LoWPAN represents a IPv6 used on low-power wireless personal area networks. It applies compress to the IPv6 packets so that 1024 bytes of packet is reduced to 127 bytes and ensures reliability and makes IPv6 efficient in wireless networks. It is especially suitable for IoT applications, where global networking and devices with low power consumption are used. It works for a short range with low memory usage and supports low data rates. It consists of an edge router and is responsible for connecting with other IP based Internet. The router also does appropriate 6LoWPAN packets to IPv6 packets. The main advantage of this protocol is interoperability as connectivity with other devices is possible through Wi-Fi. Security is ensured through the AES encryption mechanism. It is a more robust, scalable, and self-healing mesh network. It supports one-to-many and many-to-one routing.

10. *NB-IoT*

## APPLICATION LAYER PROTOCOLS

The application layer is responsible for providing services to the users. There are several protocols used at application layer.

## MQTT Protocol

### *Message Queuing Telemetry Transport*

Message queuing telemetry transport (MQTT) represents a lightweight protocol and is especially used for client–server communication. It is implemented in publisher/subscriber mode for communication. It is used along with the TCP/IP protocol.

The MQTT has the following three components:

1. Publisher: Generally it possesses the sensors.
2. Subscriber: Applications which are interested in collecting the data from sensors.
3. Broker: They connect the publisher and subscribers.

MQTT performs the following methods in establishing communication:

- Connect
- Disconnect
- Subscribe
- Unsubscribe
- Publish

### *Communication Procedure in Message Queuing Telemetry Transport*

MQTT protocol is a publish/subscribe architecture and it resembles a request/response paradigm. It is a kind of event-driven method, when an event occurs, it publishes the same as a message to its clients. To enable messaging between publisher and client, a controller called broker is deployed. The client message also includes a topic, which is used for routing

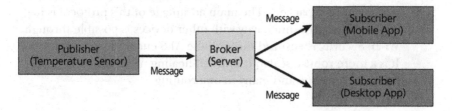

**Figure 10.2** MQTT publisher-broker-subscriber.

information. When a client wants to receive messages, it mentions through subscription and broker is responsible to deliver it with matching topic (Salman, 2016).

### Topics in Message Queuing Telemetry Transport

The topic is indicated as a string and hierarchical levels separated by slash.

*Example 1:* A topic used to send temperature data of a room can be represented as "house/ room/temperature." Suppose a mobile device is the client, which subscribed for this topic, then the subscription is represented with a wildcard as follows: "house/+/temperature."

The "+" sign indicates a single level wild card and only permits arbitrary values for one hierarchy level and a multilevel hierarchy can be represented through the wildcard symbol "#," which allows to subscribe to all underlying hierarchy levels in the given subtree .

*Example 2:* "house/#" represents subscribing to all topics that start with house.

Different QoS levels of MQTT makes it a suitable application level protocol for IoT applications:

1. *QoS 0-At Most Once:* As the lower layers such as TCP ensure reliable communication, MQTT allows the service *to send the message only once,* without any acknowledgement and no retries. There is no guarantee of message delivery, but lower layers will take care of this issue.
2. *QoS 1- At least Once:* If no acknowledgement from the receiver, the sender retransmits the message, in order to avoid duplicate messages flag bit is used.
3. *QoS 2-exactly Once:* It employs a four way handshaking mechanism to ensure the correct reception of the message and its acknowledgment. But, the message will be delivered only once. Therefore, this QoS mode is the slowest one compared to other two modes, and generally it needs, at least, 2 round trip times (RTTs).

### Application of Message Queuing Telemetry Transport

- MQTT protocol is used for online chat in Facebook messenger.
- AWS uses MQTT for Amazon IoT services.
- MSAzure uses MQTT protocol for telemetry messages in IoThub.
- EVRYTHNG IoT platform uses MQTT protocol to connect millions of devices, where MQTT works as M2M protocol.
- Adafruit uses MQTT cloud service called AdafruitIO for experimenter's purpose.

**Advantages**

- It requires low power consumption.
- It works at low bandwidth.
- Supports reliable communication.

**Disadvantages:**

- Interoperability is an issue.
- Security is not ensured.
- Not extendable.
- Message patterns are limited.

## Secure Message Queuing Telemetry Transport

It is an extension of MQTT, which adapts encryption to ensure security. In IoT applications broadcasting is an important feature, hence an encrypted message can be broadcasted to multiple recipients.

This protocol performs the following activities:

- *Setup:* The subscriber and publisher get master secret key.
- *Encryption:* It is done at the broker before publishing to the subscriber.
- *Decryption:* Done by the subscriber.

## Constrained Application Protocol

The Internet connectivity is needed in IoT applications, but HTTP becomes heavy for IoT communication. Constrained application protocol (CoAP) works with HTTP, where it works with short wake-up and long sleeping mode cycles to reduce the load on IoT devices. CoAP is a client–server-based Web transfer protocol used with constrained nodes in Internet of things. It is also called the Web of things protocol. It enables to connect hundreds of actuators, sensors, and other IoT devices to communicate through the Internet. It is designed to establish communication in machine to machine (M2M) applications such as smart energy, smart buildings, and automated manufacturing, and so on. It provides a request–response approach between end points. It is an asynchronous client–server communication and establishes a datagram service similar to UDP (Shelby et al., 2014). Though it is built based on the UDP concept, it provides reliable services.

Similar to HTTP, it is a RESTful service, where server's resources are available under an URL and clients are enabled to access these services through GET, PUT, DELETE, and POST methods for retrieve, create, delete, and update. Here, getting data from a sensor is treated as receiving a value from Web API. It supports different payload types such as XML, CBOR, JSON, and so on. It supports microcontrollers with low memory and works at lower bandwidths. Through CoAP directory we can find properties of nodes on the network (Karagiannis, 2015). It also meets low power constraints. It provides a simple caching mechanism based on the message's maximum age.

### CoAP Architecture Has Two Main Sub-Layers

*Messaging:* Responsible for reliability and duplication of messages.
*Request/Response:* Provides Communication.

CoAP has four categories of messages. They are:

- Confirmable
- Non-confirmable
- Piggyback
- Separate

Reliable and unreliable communication is represented by confirmable and non-confirmable modes. The piggyback and separate represent request/response communication.

As CoAP relies on a datagram approach, the reliability of data is ensured through datagram transport layer security (DTLS). It ensures reliability through sequence number during handshaking, packet retransmission, and replay detection, hence it avoids encryption and decryption overhead.

It allows HTTP clients to interact despite resource constraints and is perfectly suitable for automation applications with smart energy management. It provides machine-to-machine communication and supports devices with low availability and memory.

**Advantages:**

- DTSL parameters enable high security.
- Easily deployable.
- Supports communication among devices with constrained resource (i.e., low memory, speed, and bandwidth).

**Disadvantages:**

- As it works on UDP, sequence of messaging may not be possible.
- Due to dynamic IP address generation, network address translation may become difficult in establishing a connection among different devices.

## Extensible Messaging and Presence Protocol

This is an open source standard extensible markup language (XML) based middleware communication protocol used for real-time structured data exchange. It is a client–server model, and decentralization avoids server requirements. It enables finding services available either locally or across the network. Also, well suited for cloud computing, alternate source finding is a major challenge. Supports both M2M and P2P communication over a variety of networks.

The core extensible messaging and presence protocol (XMPP) technologies are as follows:

- *Core:* Supports XML streaming.
- *Jingle:* Supports multimedia messages—audio, video, and file transfer.
- *Multi-user chat:* Has flexibility of multi-user chatting.
- *PubSub:* Provides alerts and notifications for data syndication.
- *BOSH:* Provides HTTP binding to XMPP.

The features such as scalability, addressing, and security are suitable for IoT applications.

In spite of the above features, the XMPP has few drawbacks. It does not guarantee quality of service. It has higher overhead for text-based transmissions. Base-64 conversion is needed for binary data before transmission.

### Applications of XMPP

It has many applications such as publish–subscriber based systems, VoIP, multimedia transmission, file transfer, gaming, IoT, smart grid, social network based services, and so on.

## Advanced Message Queuing Protocol

Advanced Message Queuing Protocol (AMQP) is an open standard interoperability messaging protocol used between different systems, irrespective

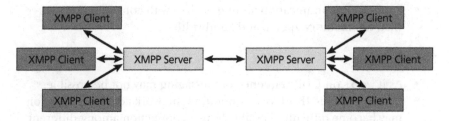

**Figure 10.3** XMPP communication architecture.

of platform or message broker vendor used. It provides a process to process communication among IP based networks. It is called compact protocol as it transfers everything in binary (Vinoski, 2006).

- Based on the exchange rules the routing key is generated in the message and the client or producer sends message to an exchange, and exchange distributes message copies to queues and through the service subscribed the consumer will get the message (Pratt, 2022).
- It supports transport layer security to ensure secure data transmission. *AMQP Components* (Fernandes et al., 2013):
  - Message Queue: Different queues are used for different business processes. The queue is a buffer, which stores messages which will be consumed later. The durable, exclusive, and auto-delete are the attributes used to declare the queues. A queue with an exclusive attribute is used only for one connection and this queue will be deleted when the connection is closed.
  - Exchange: The message routing is based on exchange type and the binding between exchange and queue. There are four kinds of exchanges namely direct, topic, fanout, and header exchanges.
  - Binding: It is a relationship between queue and exchange with a set of rules used to send messages to queues.
  - Message: It is an entity produced by the publisher and sent via to the subscriber. It also consists of headers to define the properties such as priority, durability, and life duration.
  - Connection: It represents a network connection between AMQP broker and application such as TCP/IP socket connection.
  - Channel: It is a virtual connectivity within a connection and it establishes a virtual path between two AMQP peers. The message

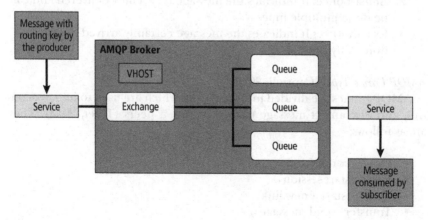

**Figure 10.4** AMQP architecture.

publishing as well as consumption are performed through an AMQP channel. Multiplexing is possible in a connection, where it can have multiple channels.

– Virtual Hosts: Also called as vhosts perform segregation of different applications in a broker. Users are provided with different access privileges to different hosts. The exchanges and queues exist within each vhost.

– AMQP methods: The methods are to declare a queue, open a channel, and delete an exchange (Johansson, 2019).

*Features of AMQP* (Bahashwan, 2018):
- Targeted QoS—Offers QoS to links selectively
- Persistence—Guaranteed message delivery
- One-to many exchange—Delivers messages to multiple consumers simultaneously
- Security—Ensures security through AES
- Reliability
- Interoperability
- Routing
- Queuing
- Open standard
- High-Speed
- Controlling multiple consumption of messages

*Message Delivery Guarantees*: AMQP ensures the successful delivery of messages through the following:

1. At-most-once: It indicates each message is delivered once or never.
2. At-least-once: It indicates the message is certainly delivered and can be done multiple times.
3. Exactly once: It indicates the message certainly arrived but can be done only once.

*AMQP Frame Types* (Caprioli, 2020):

AMQP frames are divided into nine types which are used to initiate, control, and disconnect message transfer between peers (Tezer, 2013). They are as follows:

- Open (connection open)
- Begin (start session)
- Attach (start a new link)
- Transfer (send messages)
- Flow (control flow rate of messages)

- Diagnosition (updates change of transfer state)
- Detach (terminate the link)
- End (close session)
- Close (close connection)

**Advantages:**

- Provides reliable communication
- Ensures secure communication.
- Supports different messaging patterns.
- Expandable with little effort.

**Disadvantages:**

- Memory requirements are heavy.
- Low data transmission rates.

***Data Distribution Service (DDS):***

It is a machine-to-machine communication standard used for scalable data exchange with publish–subscribe mode. It is mainly used in smart grid management, air-traffic control, smartphone operating systems, transportation systems, healthcare systems, and software-defined radio.

DDS applications are extensible. The application need not to configure end points as they are automatically discovered by DDS at run time. It supports plug-and-play connectivity without IP address configuration, irrespective of machine architecture, and supports different operating systems and hardware.

No broker is present, therefore all publishers and subscribers are connected to the same network, called *global data space* (GDS) and it avoids bottlenecks.

DDS is a reliable and scalable data exchange protocol with publish–subscribe messaging pattern, because dynamic discovery of publisher and subscriber is possible. It supports interoperable data communication, and therefore independent of software used among communicating devices. Also known as middle IoT standard.

**Advantages:**

- Supports scalability
- Ensures QoS and security
- Low-latency data transmission
- Supports interoperability

**Disadvantages:**

- High bandwidth requirement
- Works only with Web services based interfacing

### Transmission Control Protocol(TCP):

A popular protocol used in internet based communication. It supports host-to-host communication by breaking large data into packets and reassembling at the receiver.

### User Datagram Protocol (UDP):

It supports process-to-process communication and is suitable for data loss transmission.

### IP:

IoT protocols use IPv4 or IPv6. Helps for data routing and identifying and locating devices.

### LWM2M:

Lightweight M2M (LWM2M) protocol is designed for device management in sensor networks. It supports remote device management and M2M applications.

### Extensible Messaging and Presence Protocol:

XMPP is used for real-time machine-to-machine communication and supports data exchange between multiple entities in a network.

### QUIC:

It is a transport layer protocol using UDP and suitable for resource constrained environments such as IoT systems. It supports connection of devices in multiplexed mode in a secure manner. Its *connection migration* feature enables a client to switch over to a different interface. It provides security through end-to-end encryption and authentication via TLS protocol. It uses pluggable congestion control protocol. Therefore, a flexible communication is possible, where higher priority traffic may be allowed, data transmission rate is controllable, and an overloaded situation is manageable. Existing networks are supported without upgradation or retrofitting.

DLTS (datagram transport layer): Used to provide communication privacy in datagram protocol.

Nano-IP: Nano internet protocol was designed to bring internet services to sensors and embedded systems.

Radio Communication Technologies with IoT: Depending on IoT application deployment requirement characteristics different radio communications technologies have been evolved. The basic IoT applications are supported by 2G, 3G, Wi-Fi and LTE networks. Apart from end-to-end connectivity, IoT ecosystem should support low power consumption, and multiple connections at lower costs.

Bluetooth, Zigbee, and Wi-Fi protocols cover short and medium ranges with a constraint on power consumption, hence they are not suitable for all kinds of IoT applications. Similarly, traditional long-range communication is not suitable for battery operated IoT devices. To overcome these problems, long-power wide area networks are evolved to enable connection among massive numbers of IoT devices with battery life 5 to 10 years at lower price covering longer ranges.

The Characteristics of LPWAN:

- low power consumption
- short messages
- low price
- useful in building indoor and outdoor IoT applications
- scalable

Classification of LPWAN:

- LPWAN is classified as non-3GPP (non-third generation partnership project and 3GPP (third generation partnership project).

3GPP Technologies:

- These are classified as NB-IoT (narrow band IoT), LTE-M (LTE-machine-type communication), and EC-GSM (extendible-GSM IoT) and all these standards work with existing cellular networks with low-power and wide area.

Non-3GPP: These are unlicensed technologies and classified as follows: LoRaWAN (low range wide area network), weightless, RPMA (random phase multiple access), and Sigfox.

The main advantage of Sigfox, NB-IoT, and LoRaWAN is long device lifetime of approximately 10 years as they will be in sleep mode, when application requires considerable reduction in power consumption.

Sigfox communication covers a few meters to several thousands of meters with varied packet sizes of 4/8/12 bytes. Sigfox has more coverage area than LoRaWAN, but still LoRaWAN is preferred in many applications than Sigfox because it is an open protocol supporting dynamic data rate. RPMA works on 2.4 GHz allowing higher linking capacity. NB-IoT has extended design of LTE-M and reusable channels. Sigfox and LoRaWAN support nearly 5,000 end devices, whereas NB-IoT supports 100,000 end devices.

## CONCLUSIONS

IoT finds various applications in different sectors such as healthcare, manufacturing, security, and transport, and so on. The success of IoT based applications depends on various protocols used at different layers of its architecture. These IoT protocols enable structured ways of data exchange, and hence play a major role in IoT technology stack, without which the IoT hardware becomes useless. WiFi is simple and connects directly to the Internet with high speed. But power consumption is high and not suitable for battery operated devices. Bluetooth requires less power and opt for battery operated devices. It covers short distances of personal areas of networks, but a gateway is needed for the Internet. Zigbee works at low energy and supports mesh networks.

The protocols such as CoAP, MQTT, RESTful, and AMQT ensure security and QoS for the given application. In addition to this, CoAP also provides authentication, automatic key management, and data integrity. To ensure reliability, CoAP uses DTLS over UDP. Among the lightweight protocols MQTT and CoAP are popular and MQTT is preferably used for short message transmission constantly, whereas CoAP protocol is a choice for transferring a documented message. The MQTT and CoAP have low latency, low overhead, low computing, and less resource consumption. CoAP addresses the CPU-constrained nodes and memory limitations, and ensures reliable communication. Sigfox, LoRaWAN, and NB-IoT are highly scalable for the end devices. NB-IoT works at low energy and has good building penetration. Its drawbacks are limited mobility, long latency, and low speed. LoRaWAN works at low energy, and covers a wide area, but supports low speed and short messages. Sigfox works at low energy, and covers a wide area, but supports low speed and short messages.

This chapter provides a brief description on IoT architecture and protocol stack used at different layers. A detailed description of physical, network and application layer protocols, and the criteria such as type of network, data rate, specifications, topology, security, range of communication, and power consumption for building IoT applications is presented through this chapter.

## REFERENCES

Al-Fuqaha, A., Guizani, M., Mohammadi, M., Aledhari, M., & Ayyash, M. (2019). Internet of things: A survey on enabling technologies, protocols, and applications. *IEEE Communications Surveys & Tutorials, 17*(4), 2347–2376. https://doi.org/10.1109/comst.2015.2444095

Al-Masri, E., Kalyanam, K. R., Batts, J., Kim, J., Singh, S., Vo, T., & Yan, C. (2020). Investigating messaging protocols for the Internet of things (IoT). *IEEE Access, 8*, 94880–94911. https://doi.org/10.1109/access.2020.2993363

Caprioli, P. (2020). *AMQP standard validation and testing.* Open Access. https://openaccess.library.uitm.edu.my/Record/ndltd-UPSALLA1-oai-DiVA.org-kth-277850

Fernandes, J. L., Lopes, I. C., Rodrigues, J. J. P. C., & Ullah, S. (2013, July 2–5). *Performance evaluation of RESTful web services and AMQP protocol.* IEEE Xplore. https://doi.org/10.1109/ICUFN.2013.6614932

Johansson, L. (2019). *FAQ: What is AMQP and why is it used in RabbitMQ?* https://www.cloudamqp.com/blog/what-is-amqp-and-why-is-it-used-in-rabbitmq.html

Karagiannis, V., Chatzimisios, P., Vázquez-Gallego, F., & Alonso-Zárate, J. (2015). A survey on application layer protocols for the Internet of things. *Transaction on IoT and Cloud Computing, 3*(1), 9–18. https://www.researchgate.net/publication/303192188

Kulymbetov, V. A., Tukushev, T. K., & Nurlybayev, T. A. (2022). Коммуникационные протоколы и безопасность в Интернете вещей. *International Journal of Information and Communication Technologies, 1*(1), 65–67. https://doi.org/10.54309/ijict.2020.1.1.018

Postscapes. (2019). *IoT standards & protocols.* https://www.postscapes.com/internet-of-things-protocols/

Pratt, M. K. (2022, March 30). *Top 12 most commonly used IoT protocols and standards.* TechTarget. https://www.techtarget.com/iotagenda/tip/Top-12-most-commonly-used-IoT-protocols-and-standards

Salman, T., & Jain, R. (2016). Networking protocols and standards for Internet of things. In H. Geng (Ed.), *Internet of things and data analytics handbook* (pp. 215–238). Wiley. https://doi.org/10.1002/9781119173601.ch13

Sethi, P., & Sarangi, S. R. (2017). Internet of things: Architectures, protocols, and applications. *Journal of Electrical and Computer Engineering, 2017,* 1–25. https://doi.org/10.1155/2017/9324035

Shelby, Z., Hartke, K., & Bormann, C. (2014). *The constrained application protocol (CoAP).* RFC 7252, 1–112. https://doi.org/10.17487/RFC7252

Tezer, O. S. (2013). *An advanced message queuing protocol (AMQP) walkthrough.* DigitalOcean. https://www.digitalocean.com/community/tutorials/an-advanced-message-queuing-protocol-amqp-walkthrough

Vinoski, S. (2006). Advanced message queuing protocol. *IEEE Internet Computing, 10*(6), 87–89. https://doi.org/10.1109/mic.2006.116

# CHAPTER 11

# IoT ENABLED MONITORING OF SOLAR PLANTS IN AGRI LANDS

**P. Dhanalakshmi**
*Mohan Babu University*

**K. Srujan Raju**
*CMR Technical Campus, Hyderabad*

**Nagendra Panini Challa**
*SCOPE, VIT-AP University*

**B. Hemanth Kumar**
*Sree Vidyanikethan Engineering College*

**K. P. N. V. Satya Sree**
*Usha Rama College of Engineering and Technology*

*Innovations in Computational Intelligence, Big Data Analytics, and Internet of Things*, pages 199–214

# ABSTRACT

The electric distribution businesses receive a commission for the gadgets exported to the consumer. Hence, it's vital to display parameters like climate, windstorm, temperature, and rain to save you the panel from failure. When crossing the optimal level, those parameters ought to have an effect on the operating of the inverter and climate station, and lower their performance. Also, the gadgets exported are well mapped and tracked to generate invoices. IoT answers have severed influences on the solar plant. The integration improves performance via way of means of 20% and discovers low performance and failure in sun strings. Alerts are dispatched to the carrier team from the IoT Gateway, hence heading off the mishaps withinside the sun plant. The subsequent advantage is the capacity to display more than one plant life remotely and time table the panel cleaning.

The solar powered electrical device converts daytime into DC power to feed the located battery. This DC power is supplied to the battery via a star shape solar regulator that ensures the battery is fully charged and presently not damaged. DC domestic instrumentality might also be powered now from the battery. However, a converter is needed by the AC household system to transform the DC power into 240 capacity measure AC power. The DC household system frequently requires the appropriate component from some Low Voltage sources for the regulator indicates that the battery is unplugged. Famous person panels are labeled in line with each selected rated power output in the form of Watts. This rating represents the maximum power that an electrical panel device is anticipated to supply during a single peak hour of a well-known individual. Fully distinctive geographical locations gather the components of unusual place peak sun hours in step with day (Snegirev et al., 2019).

The Australia country figures the selection from as very little or noneas 3 in Tasmania to over half-dozen in spaces of QLD and WA. Every region of constellation despair in a field is spherical 5.6, and for as long as a period of time, it is not a unique spot. Every documented result for this area has an annual value that ranges from less than forty in June to a peak of sixty five in December. This vogue that associate 80 W electrical device might ideally manufacture spherical 320 W in step with a day in June and spherical 520 W regular with a day in December fully on the not unusual place affirm of 5.6, it might change before long as a period of time not unusual place of spherical 450W regular with day while not taking losses into thought (Goundar et al., 2020; Smita et al., 2014; Venkatraman et al., 2012).

Connecting solar panels in parallel means linking the positive terminals of all panels together and connecting all the negative terminals together. This configuration maintains the same voltage but increases the current capacity. It does not increase the voltage. The selected terminal voltage of a 12 capacity measured by solar panel is often spherical 17.0 volts, however via employing a regulator, the voltage is little to spherical 13 to 15 volts as needed for battery charging (Choras, 2007). Each panel output is plagued by the mobileular running temperature. The sealed panels are rated at a nominal temperature of 20 5 stage Celsius. The output of a most valued panel device might also be expected to require an issue through method of approach of 2.5% for every 5 stage variation in temperature (Dhiwaakar Purusothaman et al., 2013). Thanks to the actual fact that temperatures are increased and the final output is decreased.

With this selected panel output, values are recorded by manner totally worth noting, if the panels are terribly cool owing to cloud cover, and consequently the massive name bursts via the cloud, it's an extended method viable to exceed the rated output of the panel. Also the length is calculated as star regulator. The explanation of solar regulators, or worth controllers as they'll be more called, is to exchange the contemporary from the solar panels to stay aloof from losing you the batteries from overcharging. When solar panels overcharge batteries, it can lead to issues such as gassing and the electrolyte level in the batteries dropping. Gassing occurs when the charging process causes water to break down into hydrogen and oxygen gases. This can result in the release of potentially explosive gases.

Over time, if the batteries are consistently overcharged, it can lead to reduced battery life, electrolyte imbalance, and damage to the internal components.

- Regulating solar power is implemented to monitor the charging of batteries. Its purpose is to prevent or reduce the flow of excessive current to the battery (Raju et al., 2020).
- Many solar regulators also include a voltage disconnect feature. This feature cuts off the power supply to the load if the battery voltage becomes too low, serving as a mechanism to prevent voltage issues (Erosehenko et al., 2017).
- A powered solar regulator serves to prevent the battery from sending reverse power into the electrical panel device during nighttime, thus protecting the battery from potential damage.
- Regulators are rated based on the quantity of solar-powered panels connected in line. Each phase provides information on the efficiency and sizing of a solar regulator (Kumar Mittal, 2016).

## BACKGROUND STUDY

### S. Manikandan et al. (2021)

Associate converter is a tool that converts the DC strength throughout the battery to 240V AC electric power. Simple output designs, natural undulation, and modified square wave undulation are all available for the inverters. The majority of AC devices operate exceptionally well at the modified covered sinusoidal wave inverter, but numerous exceptions exist. Each selected device that contains optical maser printers is additionally broken whereas run on modified sine wave strength (Manikanta et al., 2020).

## Yan J. et al. (2016)

Motors and strength materials usually run hotter and far less efficiently; and a number of things, like amplifiers, electric fans, and reasonably priced fluorescent lights, offer off a loud buzz on modified sine wave strength (Yan et al., 2016). Modified sine wave electrical converters are incredibly affordable and highly effective in converting DC to AC. The AC strength produced by pure undulation electrical converters is frequently almost equal to, and occasionally more than, the strength of each grid.

## Renugadevi et al. (2019)

Inverters are typically rated through the quantity of AC strength they are going to deliver in a continuous manner. User can use the addition of 5 ordinal and 1/2 hour surge figures. An approximate amount of power is sent to the powered grids, but an additional amount of power is supplied by the electrical converter for five seconds and half an hour before the inverter's overload safety trip occurs and stops the power.(Renugadevi et al., 2019).

Unlike old car batteries, which may be made to provide a large amount of power for a short period of time, deep cycled batteries, which are used in solar energy systems, are intended to be charged and discharged over an extended period of time (such as 100 hours), and then recharged numerous times. Deep cycle batteries should currently not be depleted past 70% of their capability (i.e., 30 capability representations) in order to ensure long battery life.

## Hayes et al. (2015)

Discharging done in several stages can significantly cut back the existence of the sealed batteries. Batteries that undergo deep cycling are rated in ampere hours (Ah). A discharge price is included in these scored values as well, typically at 20 or 100 hours. According to Hayes and Ali (2015), this score indicates the maximum amps that the battery can produce over the intended number of hours.

A sun regulator must have the ability to control the newest trends that are developed via the use of solar panels. Specific temperature items correlated with mirrored daylight will increase output.

Design of a solar panel with the aid of exploitation as a degree sincere transaction with a 25% overrated output modem. The sun regulators are made to fit the larger, contemporary models. Regulators in the form of stars frequently speed up the sun panel's entry while controllingthis may not harm the sun panel right now, it suggests that the solar regulator should be made large enough to accommodate the 125% of sun panels that are classified as rapid circuit fashionable. A signal on the level of attentiveness at the burden unit sellers and grid agent linked letter of the alphabet sellers is provided by Purusothaman, SRR Dhiwaakar, et al. Sellers of weight units are similar to those of designated power resources, loads, garages, and subsequently grid sellers. The character agent acts as a result of the speech channel among the decigram sellers to the higher stage sellers that embody the managed agent.

## Li et al. (2018)

The implementation of the device has disbursed the usage of associated 8266 microcontroller. Alper Gorgun and Yasin Kabuli, among others, present an innovative tracking system for a renewable energy technology device, specifically an LED, coupled with a rotary engine and solar panel arrays. This tracking platform is entirely reliant on advanced technology, taking into account the voltage values observed in renewable energy sources for both devices. The recorded and connected components associated values are monitored and measured with the advanced connected metered circuits with associated degrees of processed via methodology of 18F4450 microcontroller with rectified microchip. Each recorded value is transmitted to a personal computing device with serial bus with general computing features to hold on variable information and look at the device as mentioned or specified interval duration/instantly (Li et al., 2018).

## Jannesari et al. (2020)

The connected and selected visible interface tracking system and computer codes program will manage the keep statistics to research daily, weekly, and month-to-month values of every size severally. Jiju, K. et al. (2019) gives the event web chase and manage device of assigned renewable energy source mostly on golem platform. This case makes use of the Bluetooth connected Android API with mobile phone, as a speech input for statistics modification with virtual of power learning unit. Yoshihiro et al. (2023) and colleagues recently disclosed an internal device designed to enhance and initiate the functioning of telecommunications power facilities for remote video monitors. The apparatus is utilized for the supervision and upkeep of more than 200,000 communication power facilities, including equipment like inverting rectifiers and air conditioners that are placed in about 8,000 communication buildings.

Choices of the marked device are the combination of managed and far-flung calculations into one device and configured interface values, used for analytics and speech era which embrace the Internet era. Ilya Galkin (2013) became aware of the value of the nonintrusive load pursuit technique of connected imbalanced load aggregation into separate connected components in rectified connected networks. When numerous mills primarily reliant on renewable energy sources are connected to the same grid, they are subject to fluctuations over time due to various variables. Nkoloma et al. (2012) and colleagues provide current data on the operation of a Wi-Fi-based remote tracking device for renewable energy facilities in Malawi.

The important purpose is to broaden a value powerful statistics acquisition device that constantly offers far off power values and overall performance factors. The challenges offer direct access from generated electrically powered strength at each agricultural web page via exploitation Wi-Fi device forums and matter content message transmission over mobile networks.

Antoine Bagula(2021) proposed a singular chase, a manipulate machine for reaching actual time pursuit and manipulation of a connection based on wind power PV battery of renewable strength machine. Powered and planned machine selected the superior manipulate and data acquisition SCADA machine field community of NCHU enclosed with computer programmable knowledge controlled components and virtual strength measured components or meters. The envisioned system is designed to provide real-time measurements of power-related data, facilitating seamless transmission to a remote monitoring center through the use of the Internet.

## PROCESS FLOW—MONITORING AND PREDICTION

The version was indisputable against four characteristic electrical phenomena presented in the open literature. The power records are generated using a single diode version containing range and shunt resistances. Although distinctive techniques have been designed to make you mind these records, Villalva et al. (2018) all complete their approach to some of the collection and parallel resistances that satisfy above all the electricity calculated by mishandling the version in STC from the values in the manufacturers datasheet should make the mapping of PV curve with IV curve for the experimental values and their pictures. However, the associate of discretion value of the pleasant element of the diode is chosen to change the version.

The accuracy is obtained from admirable experimental records for distinctive irradiance levels and temperatures. A 3-equation tool with 3 unknowns written from the derivatives of the IV curve in short-circuit and most electrical problems in addition to the current critical power factor equation converted to a numerical solution by ill-treatment (Sera et al., 2021). Carrera et al. (2020) suggested an ideal harmonic price for a pleasing element when the range of parallel resistance values are obtained using the results of various simulated experiments. Moreover, their results are an accurate determination of resistances that require complex calculation methods.

The implicit conversion equations for electric circuit voltage, connected short-circuit current, critical voltage and current are solved using the Newton-Raphson approach: calculated photocurrent and current saturation. Resistor values are a nice element of the diode array from distinctive methods then usually correct the reference version. It summarizes the calculated values of the resistances and the pleasant component of the diodes. The highest values of $n$ are calculated with the design approach.

Each result of the range and resistance parallel values are plotted in the calculations, $n$, won't have a constant connected physical value at this time. In fact, for an SP array of 100 and 50, a good element better than now no longer always means that multi-combination or multi-tunneling steps are occurring, as once discussed.

The I–V curve on the biggestquestion of energy work, the result of this by-product is additionally investigated. Using an implicit set of equations, the noninherited values in the created approach are compared to the specific values in the addition set from linked devices of the I–V curve at the $64,000 items Vm related degreed In. In addition, overall counseled errors of 7.67% are not inheritable among the I–V byproduct of the foremost

**Figure 11.1**  Solar plant fixing and operations.

energy issue for the popular version, yet the same referenced case (i.e., the poorest array). This error rate happens many times, in opposite cases this error is way smaller. Thus, acting as a byproduct of the foremost energetic question to estimate the strain beneath this issue appears to be a plausible hypothesis.

The operational I–V curves don't seem to be heritable, connected to the employment of constant calculations additionally to the popular version for the KC200GT array, shown in Figure 11.2. The results of controlled temperature of 25C and star irradiance of 200 W/m2 and 800 W/m2 are shown, respectively. Each record is obtained for recorded constant radiation of 1,000 W/m2 and for mobile temperatures of 10°C and 50°C are

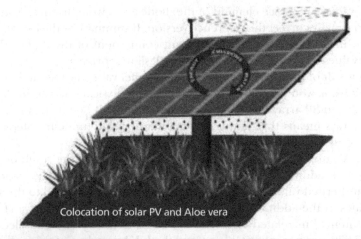

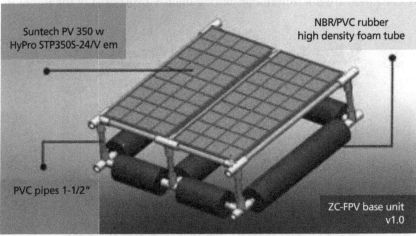

**Figure 11.2**   Solar plant operations and components.

illustrated in Figure 11.3—four and half-dozen, respectively. The planned technique is valid against reference values obtained from unvaried calculations performed on recognized star panels. Current activated performance of the version is calculable as a feature of well-known and weighted counseled errors placed among the referenced and expected values within the modern planned version, it's ready to offer quite correct results; it is simple to use and will be terribly helpful for style engineers to quickly and properly verify the overall performance of PV arrays as a feature of environmental constraints while not in-depth numerical calculations. Some unknown values which correspond to photo current values, actual saturation point and special face of the diodes, don't seem to be calculated, and also the knowledge is sometimes obtained with the assistance of electrical phenomenon panel manufacturers. The proposal lays out a replacement device for abusive electricity, based totally on IoT. This device includes star cells that convert daylight into energy which will be found in solar panels. Our fleet encompasses a junior clairvoyance 8266. Victimization sensors and current voltage parameter values are tracked. The selected current values are the same at various voltage levels. Everything displayed on the alphanumeric pad values displayed in IoT display. Because of the sensors it is connected to, the IoT tool can often exhibit parameters that the transfer shopper can additionally record its price from any network. Our favorite goal of this

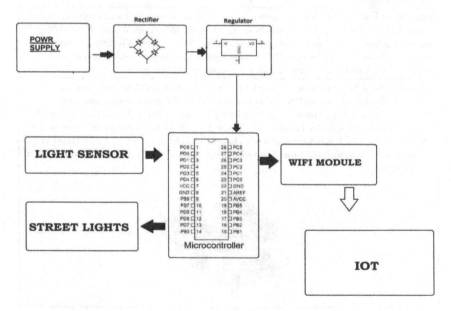

**Figure 11.3** IoT enabled service operation circuit.

**TABLE 11.1    Various Device Coded Representations**

It comprises solar cells. Once the star shape radiations fall on PV, cells retread those radiations into electrical energy to connect multiple connected components systems. The PV modules produce use of photons from the star mild and conveyed in different electric energy. They store energy in various batteries and utilize materials for household products and businesses. The solar energy radiation encompasses a range of services to monitor and manage these multiple variations, for which we employ specialized sensors.

| | |
|---|---|
| The circuit that models the rectifier converts AC power into DC for the linked components. The voltage provides a machine operating on a specified power supply with a constant level of voltage services. After using a controlled power source, the output is DC with infinite spherical shape. For regulated DC power delivery, each linear DC electricity delivery quantity is entirely distinct. This circuit determines the amount of power supplied to the regulator, DC filtered router, amplified rectifier, and diminution transformer at each block's face. | Another important issue to trust is that the speed stylish got to be more than the burden modern. Even though it functions as a backup battery-powered device that can handle up to 100 mA of load—quite a fast rate given today's standardsit still has the ability to create positive safety. Therefore, the charging trend should be at least five times faster than the load trend. |

However, in order for the microcontroller that is used to convert the battery voltage, it must be forced to be higher than necessary by using the conventional transformer input voltage. Simple example values are derived by assuming that a 74 V number 3 battery is connected to each of those 33 V Associate in 50 V voltage regulators. This is because linear regulators require a larger dropout voltage in addition to routing and switching.

The ESP 8266 IDE supports six analog I/O pins on the ATmega328P microchip on the controller board base by UNO, which is a model for the psychological phenomena 8266 Uno. To attach it to your computer's USB port, use a USB cable and the associated components board services. Combine any of the ESP 8266 Uno shown in the additional ESP 8266 Uno, which is made up of a reset button, an influence IoT, and a 16 MHz per second oscillator in a crystal form. It uses 5V to operate. For serving the microcontroller, it is appropriate.

ESP 8266 Uno

*(continued)*

**TABLE 11.1   Various Device Coded Representations (cont.)**

The voltage detector is indicated by a detector that may recognize optical or electrical signs or be prepared for police operations. This detector is used to measure the voltage that might be present in any given object, and it is made to look at it. Notably, the voltage steps are monitored and recognized during usage. It is supplied to the current sensored, and in addition, the output seen is a transfer or a portion of an analog sensor component with a model that has been saved. The signal voltage, the most recent signal, or a combination of the system A show module that is widely used in a variety of electrical devices and circuits might alternatively be called a liquid show.The system's alphanumeric display will be visible to the user. Digital displays typically employ delicate to block. We have a tendency to be prepared to use a 32 x 8 alphanumeric display show during this setup. Each episode's selection consists of sixteen personalities connected to a variety of models. Liquid crystals are employed to make LCD formation, which is the steady and liquid manufactured outcomes used to form a viewed photograph at the screen.

analysis is to induce reliable electric power generation with a scientific degree whereas the star panels get dirt buildup.

The analog inputs of a ESP8266 will measure up to a maximum of 5 volts Even while attached with a 5 V circuit and selected needy values to use the resistors to guard the ESP 8266 from stunning voltage ranges in IoT sensor record. The component circuit of the resistor is shown in Figure 11.4. The resistor's division function is frequently used to lower the voltage being computed to a level that the ESP 8266 can read. The circuit is constructed using a board that has a 10k ohm voltage circuit value. A 100k ohm sign up is utilized to lower the voltage circuit to 5 V. The Analog pin of clairvoyance

**Figure 11.4**   Panel activation and recording system in Agri Field system.

8266 offers the volt value. This clearly gives multiple variability which will be calculated as follows,

$$V_{out} = \left(R_2 / (R_1 + R_2)\right) \times V_{in}$$

In order for the ESP8266 voltmeter to operate properly, the divided value must have a maximum of 5V for the Vout value and a maximum of

$$V_{max} = X5.0 / \left(R_2 / (R_1 + R_2)\right)$$

We typically have a Hall result modern sensing ACS 712 with 30A degree and bad 30 amps ready to use for contemporary dimensions; the analog value output is 66mV/A. Contemporary connected sensor offers the readings from each powered device. Selected component values are used inside the projected device for conniving strength. The DC bulb is considered a full load during setup. The consequence of the strength provided representations is battery. Different selected and connected pins of sensors are noticed and connected to the ESP 8266. After testing and finishing the connections with the interior depicted in Figure 11.3, Clairvoyance 8266 displays the values of the most recent flow.

## PERFORMANCE EVALUATION

ThingSpeak is associated with open offer IoT utility values and API and retrieves knowledge from matters of the employment of the protocols over the Internet or online or via a local connected area network. The Thing-Speak permits the looks of detector work application and neighborhood observance applications and a social community of values with name updated features. The connected and recorded powered values got to be compelled to provide the connected values representation. Figure 11.5 shows the Pesudo Code for ThingSpeak representation.

This representation carries channels that are separated for extraordinary projects. Channel has the fields that are extraordinary for extraordinary parameters inside the pursuit device. Once assignment the parameter the devices are added the values in devices. The cloud has integrated choices in it that represent the values inside the shape of graphs. The following stages illustrate the artworks that are included in the shape of the solar electricity chase machine:

Step 1: 8266 controller shows energy utilization the usage of detected values via detector and voltage divider.

Step 2: Connected Raspberry Pi fetched the ESP 8266 output via port and showed the result using python script codes.

Step 3: Each Raspberry gives the stored records from the cloud.

Step 4: Cloud provides the recorded information to the user as a whole, shown as a graph.

The solar electricity saved in battery via means of a sun panel is DC modern. So, we tend to use connected DC bulbs as a result of the supply of energy utilization. Each terminal value of connected devices or bulbs is connected to the battery from energy supplied inputs. Different terminals are connected to the IoT detector with a date reading system. Circuit board is used for the divide and construct the circuit. It also allows for the construction of voltage dividers. Using analog pins, psychic phenomena 8266 sense the current and voltage. ESP 8266 programming is used to calculate the energy and electricity. The final resultant output is obtained from a

```
public partial class FileUpload: System.Web.UI.Page
//      Sql_Connection con2   =      new                        Sql_Connection
(ConfigurationManager.ConnectionStrings["connection"]. Connection String);
Sql_Connection con1   =     new
Sql_Connection1(ConfigurationManager.ConnectionStrings["connection"]. ToString ());
string filePath1, file-size, file-ext, date, file-con, val1, val2, val3; floatfilesiz= 0f; id id1 = new id()
protected void Page_Load (object sender, Eventers e)
{
Session["userid"] = lblID.Text;
lblID.Text = Convert.ToString(id1.idgeneration());
//Session["EncKey"] = txtEncKey.Text;
}
protected void Button1_Click(object sender, EventArgs e)
{
filePath =      Request.PhysicalApplicationPath      +      "FileUpload/"   +
System.IO.Path.GetFileName(FileUpload1.FileName);
FileUpload1.SaveAs(filePath);1];
byte []  file bytes    =    new   byte [FileUpload1.PostedFile. InputStream.Length    +
FileUpload1.PostedFile. InputStream.Read(file bytes, 0, file bytes. Length);
byte [] Key = Encoding.UTF8. Get Bytes("asdf! @#$1234ASDF"); FileStream fs3 = new FileStream
(filePath, FileMode.Create); RijndaelManagedrmCryp
= new RijndaelManaged ();
CryptoStream   cs   =   new   CryptoStream   (fs3,   rmCryp.CreateEncryptor(Key,   Key),
CryptoStreamMode.Write);
filecon = FileUpload1.PostedFile.ContentType
fileext      =      System.IO.Path.GetExtension(FileUpload1.PostedFile.FileName);      filesiz      =
(float)FileUpload1.PostedFile.ContentLength / 25600;
filesize = Convert.ToString(filesiz) + " KB"
date = Convert.ToString(DateTime.Now. ToString()); SqlCommandcmd
new SqlCommand ("INSERT INTO Upload
VALUES (@fileid,      @filename,                @filekey,                @filepath,
@files,@types,@fext,@fsizeinkb,@fdatetime, @enckey, @count)", con);
```

**Figure 11.5** Pesudo code for thing-speak representation.

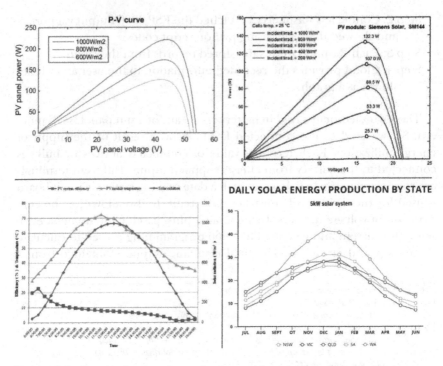

**Figure 11.6** Result of various interval solar panel operations from Matlab.

Raspberry via USB cable as shown in Figure 11.6. The Raspberry Pi's power is considered a consequence of the server. It shows the results via online website and cloud records.

The open-supply ESP 8266 integrated development surroundings or ESP 8266 coding system is utilized in machines to add the code to the board. The device's recoded gates are connected with the ESP 8266 to experience power and voltage. We have got an inclination to write down the code in C with sensed and schemed the energy associated electricity. Python is a high-level language that is represented as machine code, allowing it to function dynamically when employed within a computer. Python2 is used for taking psychic phenomena 8266 records. Python net packages have one vital owed item that implements the important utility. Victimization python associate in the flask, we've got an inclination to provide web website of pursuit machine as proved. The trailing website shows the tabled results with carries of voltage, energy, and electricity values. Below, the table date and time is displayed. The net page is recent for each 10 seconds. The cloud is enhanced with the help of a Python application that has been written. ThingSpeak cloud is used in this paper. It is linked to an open-source web of things (IoT) tool and API to prevent wasting time when obtaining data from this cloud. We introduced the social community of things with name updates in multiple connected layered service offered network model.

## CONCLUSION

Renewable energy technology is a galvanized manner of decreasing the environmental effect. Due to common electricity cut backs, it's crucial to select renewable electricity and pursue it. Observance classes are employed in the utilization of renewable energy sources. This device is price effective and performance is showed as 95%. It permits the inexperienced usage of renewable electricity, therefore decreasing the ability issues. This operation may be a task, might even be equally enhanced, through the usage of the results of this up-to-date task. The congenital trailing values are useful to predict the destiny values of the parameters considered for measuring the accuracy index and representations. The recorded and managed in cloud may also analyze the usage of the MatLab. The result of CSV report from the cloud is taken for evaluation and R tool analysis result is taken. Because of this, the web or the data we've gathered may even be enhanced for communication with the final customer; they may also anticipate future occurrences in the same way that we're prepared to go forward with golem software. Additionally, the equalized dataset might be utilized for additional styles or throughout the forecast to find every model's accuracy.

## REFERENCES

Choras, R. S. (2007). Image feature extraction techniques and their applications for CBIR and biometrics systems. *International Journal of Biology and Biomedical Engineering, 1*(1), 6–16. https://www.naun.org/main/NAUN/bio/bio-2.pdf

Dhiwaakar Purusothaman, S. R. R., Rajesh, R., Bajaj, K. K., & Vijayaraghavan, V. (2013). *Implementation of Arduino-based multi-agent system for rural Indian microgrids.* In *Proceedings for the 2013 IEEE Innovative Smart Grid Technologies-Asia* (pp. 1–5) . IEEE. https://doi.org/10.1109/isgt-asia.2013.6698751

Goundar, S., Avanija, J., Sunitha, G., Madhavi, K. R., & Bhushan, S. B. (2020). *Innovations in the industrial Internet of things (IIoT) and smart factory.* IGI Global.

Hayes, T., & Ali, F. H. (2015). Proactive highly ambulatory sensor routing (PHASeR) protocol for mobile wireless sensor networks. *Pervasive and Mobile Computing, 21,* 47–61. https://doi.org/10.1016/j.pmcj.2015.04.005

Hu, W., Tan, T., Wang, L., & Maybank, S. (2004). A survey on visual surveillance of object motion and behaviors. *IEEE Transactions on Systems, Man, and Cybernetics, Part C (Applications and Reviews), 34*(3), 334–352. https://doi.org/10.1109/TSMCC.2004.829274

Li, D.-D., Gao, F., Qin, S.-J., & Wen, Q.-Y. (2018). Perfect quantum multiple-unicast network coding protocol. *Quantum Information Processing, 17*(13). https://doi.org/10.1007/s11128-017-1781-x

Manikanta, S. P., Rameshchandra, K., & Santosh Kumar Patra, P. (2020). Performance comparison of optimized quantization in real-time distributed wireless network. *Journal of Critical Reviews, 7*(4), 1738–1741. https://www.jcreview.com/admin/Uploads/Files/61b3af2756cd34.94452765.pdf

Pal, A., Dasgupta, R., Saha, A., & Nandi, B. (2016). Human-like sensing for robotic remote inspection and analytics. *Wireless Personal Communications, 88*(1), 23–38. https://doi.org/10.1007/s11277-016-3239-3

Raju, K., Lavanya, R., Manikandan, S., & Srilekha, K. (2020). Application of GIS in COVID-19 monitoring and surveillance. *International Journal for Research in Applied Science and Engineering Technology, 8*(5), 1435–1440. https://doi.org/10.22214/ijraset.2020.5231

Renugadevi, R., & Vijayalakshmi, K. (2019). Modeling a novel network coding aware routing protocol for enhancement of network performance in wireless mesh network. *Wireless Personal Communications, 107*, 621–649. https://doi.org/10.1007/s11277-019-06293-2

Smita, H., Monika, G., & Shraddha, C. (2014). Content based image retrieval using HADOOP map reduce. *International Journal of Computer Science Trends and Technology, 2*(6), 94–96.

Snegirev, D. A., Eroshenko, S. A., Khalyasmaa, A. I., Dubailova, V. V., & Stepanova, A. I. (2019). *Day-ahead solar power plant forecasting accuracy improvement on the hourly basis.* In *Proceedings for the 2019 IEEE Conference of Russian Young Researchers in Electrical and Electronic Engineering* (1088–1091). IEEE. https://doi.org/10.1109/eiconrus.2019.8657024

Venkatraman, S., & Kulkarni, S. (2012). MapReduce neural network framework for efficient content based image retrieval from large datasets in the cloud. In *Proceedings for the 2012 12th International Conference on Hybrid Intelligent Systems* (pp. 64–68). IEEE. https://doi.org/10.1109/his.2012.6421310

Yan, J., Zhou, M., & Ding, Z. (2016). Recent advances in energy-efficient routing protocols for wireless sensor networks: A review. *IEEE Access, 4*, 5673–5686. https://doi.org/10.1109/access.2016.2598719

CHAPTER 12

# A SIMPLE AND EFFECTIVE APPROACH FOR IDENTIFICATION OF COLLABORATIVE CONCERNS AND RISKS UNDER DISTRIBUTED VERSION CONTROL

**K. Suneetha**
*Jain (Deemed-to-be-University), Bangalore, India*

**Jabeen Sultana**
*Majmaah University*

**Reddy Madhavi K.**
*Mohan Babu University*

**Gudavalli Madhavi**
*University College of Engineering*

**Naga Jyothi**
*Madanapalle Institute of Science and Technology*

# ABSTRACT

A single person or individual team in an organization is not responsible for creating an open source program. This requires collaborative preparation to separate and construct the item quickly and successfully. Collaborative filtering issues may arise between the end-user and the developer while enforcing a collaborative development process. Identifying and resolving such conflicts early leads to enhancement of product quality and also the programming capacity beneath the conveyed adapted prohibited surroundings. This technique can be executed by examining the data of adaptation in a controlled infrastructure and seven open-source frameworks with an extensive code-base, clashes arise frequently, manifesting not only as subtle literary edits but also as significant challenges in testing and constructing, leading to notable setbacks. In a controlled environment, a speculative method can be formulated by looking at the conflicts. Next the real improvement procedure starts to discriminate the differences, avoid and control the clashes in the early phases. Crystal is an open-source device consisting of Collaborative Version Control Systems (CVCS) and Distributed Version Control Systems (DVCS) to be used for getting assistance to the system. Detection of review clashes makes a difference to degree the seriousness and software system frameworks life span.

## COLLABORATIVE CONCERNS AND RISKS UNDER DISTRIBUTED VERSION CONTROL

Software engineering plays an important role in improving the performance and productivity of software. Many methodologies that focus on current and prior software development states are available to achieve this. The development of quality projects in an organization mainly depends on involvement of multidiscipline stakeholders. In a controlled environment, the development of good software, within time, cost, manpower, resources, is not an easy task. It all depends on how to manage the resources effectively, completing the right task at the right time, and deploying the product to the customer within deadlines, play an important role in the development of software.

Developing cutting-edge software is not easy and requires a controlled environment that manages time, resources, people, and costs to ensure on-time, on-budget delivery. The development of a project begins with the segmentation of a larger project into smaller modules, with each module's development assigned to different team members (Eisenberg et al., 2019). With required updates on the local databases, the individual team member continues his module development including source codes, list of files, and so on.

The same is eventually communicated with other project development teams. As a result of these sharing activities, the project's development is delayed, causing synchronization issues, disputes, and other challenges (Morrison-Smith et al., 2020). Consequently, the cost and time involved to develop a software project rises, and the project fails to meet its deadline. Conflict is often caused by pressure to complete a high-quality project in a short period, misunderstanding of project standards, variation in values, usage of available resources, variety of manpower, and various perspectives, and so on.

In advance, if a project manager identifies the conflicts and provides proper guidance and assistance to his team, then the quality project should be developed within time, budget, and as per user specifications. Textual and higher-order conflicts are two types of conflicts. A textual dispute (Brun et al., 2013) may happen if two developers attempt to make modifications to the same area of the software code in an inconsistent manner. The use of a version control system ([VCS]; Rao & Sekharaiah, 2016) can prevent this overwriting incompatibility, allowing the developer to make necessary changes while restricting the developer from publishing at the same time, until every conflict is resolved either by manual approach or with auto-generation of source code. To verify and validate the existing system and proposed systems, many software tools are available in the market which makes it easier for the developer to do his task.

A system or product can be handled properly in a short period of time with the use of software tools. With the use of evolutionary prototype models or techniques and with some genetic algorithms the quality and performance of the system can be improved. An abstract form representation doesn't identify and report the proper infractions of the project. At a time when two developers try to do modifications in the same source lines of code then textual or higher-order discrepancies exist (Brun et al., 2013).

Compilation errors, test failures (Brun et al., 2013), and other problems are faced by higher order conflicts, which are hard to detect and resolve in practice. Problems can emerge when developers have different copies of a shared project, which can make collaborative work difficult (Brun et al., 2013).

An approach is proposed to assist developers in identifying and fixing problems as quickly as possible, before the severity escalates and the developer's mind weakens. Suppose if a conflict occurs during the development of the project, then first we need to identify the type and impact of the conflict on the project and communicate with all the team members to understand the cause of the conflict. Always one should try to identify and resolve the conflicts at the earlier stages of the project life cycle. All projects completed on time, within budget, and as per user requirements always leads to project success.

Speculative analysis or speculative execution refers to any method for systematically discovering the potential future development stages of software. We presume that speculative analysis can help developers make better and more accurate decisions. Developers working in a collaborative environment may have conflicts with one another. These conflicts are frequently detected at the project implementation of tangible deliverables within the

VC repository. The conflicts can be identified at the earlier phases of the software development life cycle for better quality projects.

## BACKGROUND STUDY

In 1975, M. J. Rochkind proposed a mechanism to support the program related projects control switch to the source code. The code control system (CCS) is the name of the technique indicated above. It aids in the provision of services such as accumulating, renewing, and restoring all module adaptations. To uncover the reasons, this analyzes every module by its versioning identity number and keeps track of each program modification.

According to Peter Henderson and Mark (Henderson & Weiser, 1985), program implementation in a static mode is much better than in a dynamic mode in the early 1990s. Similarly, create a collective, amalgamation programming implementation situation that is largely self-contained. By applying this dynamic style of program development, testing, debugging, and user interfaces, all of the most commonly imported approaches are brought together. PECAN System (Reiss, 1984) is one example of such a methodology. PECAN is designed to make use of high-definition visual exhibits.

PECAN (Reiss, 1984) system components enable you to edit a project's text and sequencing, implode and modify acumen, seek input on syntactic and contextual discrepancies, and to use menus and windows rather than prompting commands to accomplish forward and backward processes, iterative arrangement, and filtering during execution of programs.

The PICT system does not use text to depict software programs and their interdependence; instead, pictorial representations are used. Data structures can be visually depicted using a combination of images and variables.

For intermediate-sized software projects, Mr. Dick Grune (1986) identified a challenge which states that disputes between employees working on the same set of files in parallel are common. They may have additional responsibilities, leading their working ability to fluctuate dramatically.

If a project simply has one file and we neglect effectiveness and efficiency, one of the simplest solutions for the observed problem is to evaluate two features like recording VCS and merging program differences.

Each VCS system collects files from the most recent versions of the software and tries to enhance the older versions based on end-user requirements. An action can be performed by preserving the total number of software versions or by utilizing the deltas method to determine the divergence between the files, this example is useless because it excludes attributes such as storage efficiency.

While the centralized version system (Grune, 1986) is used by a group of people, it may only benefit one user. The first one makes use of the version-recording system's intrinsic features: The user is attempting to troubleshoot his steps. Based on our time stamps and information, we can quickly react to the user's inquiry. This would allow users to view or confirm their adjustments in real time, prior to later commit. We use the version of the revision control system ([RCS]; Grune, 1986) to access the fields from scattered workstations; within the repository, as well as from separate machines where users may contribute. Configuration management tools helps organize all the development teams collaborating on the VCS system introduced in 1995.

The author says that to reduce the difficulties among the development teams and to identify the various factors like operating at different levels, visualization concerns, coordination conflicts, and so forth; the developers try to use this tool to support their work. This will cover a wide range of organizational themes, with a concentration on software development.

It is extremely difficult to handle the VCS software for the following three reasons: (a) if source lines of code can be changed frequently by the developers due to lack of requirements understanding; (b) lack of understanding of coupling and cohesion between the project modules that is if modules are having interdependency, then a change in one module gets reflected in another module; (c) a single modification in one module by a single team affects the other team modules. So the configuration management system (CMS) helps to focus on these issues and try to resolve the issues and control the programmers ability when trying to change the source code. Small and medium project teams, for example, frequently collaborate to maintain and manage the overall evolution of software. To develop a consistent software project, CMS will help the developers to build an efficient software project by considering standard organizational procedures, standards, and principles. This analysis describes how the system must interact with the coordination work, how the organizations are established among them, and what remains to be done. This type of analysis primarily provides the work's starting points. This type of analysis, which provides an interaction tool, will not support the entire articulation work required to build software. And there is still a considerable effort to be made to study, with the help of these technologies, how to support channel switching that allows stakeholders to access their completed project (Debreceni et al., 2017).

Harvey P. Siy and Thomas Ball (Ball et al., 1997) proposed the upgraded VCSs at Bell laboratories to overcome the flaws in CMS. This system helps to capture the contextual information on each and every change in the requirements. Also, it is used to reconstruct the earlier software versions and to be stored in the repositories effectively.

To discover the association between software development processes, a systematic and procedural structure to be used is VCS instead of only using source code.

Major variety of VCSs (Ball et al., 1997) operate on a collection of documents consisting of source lines of code (SLOC) in textual format. Each VCS system helps to monitor the relevant changes happening in a group with the help of modification record (MR). This helps to identify the reason for every change made in the system with detailed and descriptive information.

The main objective of VCS recording is to gain a better understanding of development decisions as system software evolves. To improve the concerned approach, time-series analysis, statistical techniques, and few emerging and important techniques were used. The proposed strategy to build a version management system that is used to generate distinct compiler versions relies heavily on abstract syntax trees (AST). Every VCS can keep track of how measurements change over time.

Concurrent versions system (CVS) is a basic part of a VC environment, and it is used specifically to work with all types of free source projects. CVS (Ball et al., 1997) has been incorporated into the open source software configuration management ([SCM]; Grinter, 1995) system source code control system (SCCS) and revision control system (RCS) are being phased down (Rochkind, 1975). With the help of VCS, project management has been more effective and faster. Rather than detecting faults, the monitoring procedure identifies the actual errors in the VCS.

The Version Control System (VCS) facilitates a range of operations on free software, with merging being particularly significant. In 2002, (Mens, 2022) conducted a survey on the concept of merging, emphasizing its importance. Merging of software is a critical component in the upkeep and large-scale software project evolution.

The initial method relies purely on textual merging in repositories; a more robust method can then consider the software's syntactic and semantic features.

This survey assisted in defining merging techniques that are as scalable, accurate, and customizable as possible. Merging of software plays an important role in larger development projects. There are primarily two types of merging techniques. They are 3-way and 2-way mergings.

Two-way merging: This project aims to combine two different versions of a computer program artifact without relying on a common ancestor (root hub or parent) through both—of which versions originated in a store.

Three-way merging: The information from a store's common ancestor is also used in the combining procedure. Literary consolidates, syntactic blends, semantic blends, and auxiliary consolidates come beneath this category. All sets of actions that lead to irregularity are summarized in a so-called strife table or combined framework in the case of confrontations (Mens, 2002). By doing a simple table search, it is now possible to distinguish consolidated clashes. Dewan and Hedge (2007) suggested a method that completely relies on blend network theory.

The main challenge for organizational leaders or managers is to properly balance the team, utilize the resources effectively, encourage innovation and creativity amongst the team members, understand the dynamics of conflict, learn how to resolve the conflicts, and provide a healthy environment, and so forth.

Reducing Conflicts: One of the foremost vital issues with computer program advancement is that little changes regularly have a large effect. This can be alluded to as change engendering or swell impact (Reiss, 1984), these clashes persistently dwell within the working duplicate of the store. If the conflicts in the project are well identified and managed, then it leads to producing a better project outcome within timelines.

Disadvantage: Identifying and effectively managing conflicts in a project can result in a more successful outcome within specified timelines. However, failure to address conflicts may lead to project failures. A notable disadvantage of this approach is the time and effort required to resolve conflicts, which could pose a significant challenge. Additionally, unattended changes may extend beyond the prescribed boundaries, impacting project outcomes beyond the intended scope.

Palantir's (Sarma et al., 2012) constant dissemination of data on all developers' operations raises awareness in the workplace. Events have been assigned to each operation, and an event notification system is utilized to interact with developers. Palantir displays which developers are making how many changes to which artifacts. When developers switch from one artifact to another, they are aware of other changes. When a modified artifact is checked in, Palantir determines and displays the degree of change (by differencing between old version and new version). Palantir reports the direct conflicts at the artifact level rather than at the level of particular programs or lines of code. It determines the class signature difference for indirect conflicts and broadcasts it. To ascertain whether this update causes issues with their local version, other developers interpret this information.

Visual studio's user interface is expanded by CollabVS (Dewan & Hegde, 2007). It offers a technique for conflict management during asynchronous software development. The model continuously scans for dependency issues and alerts developers to them. Classes, methods, and files are program elements where dependency conflicts are checked. The level of software components for which dependency conflicts are checked is up to the developers. Additionally, team members can quickly communicate via IM and audio/video meetings. Starting a code session will allow the developer to look at the version created by the remote developers and find any conflicts. Additionally, CollabVS has the option to set up a watch on a remote developer's work, which notifies you when the developer completes their editing task.

Conflict detection was done via continuous integration by Wecode (Guimarães & Silva, 2012), which is an Eclipse plug-in. Both direct and indirect conflicts are handled by Wecode. It continuously integrates developers' committed and uncommitted changes. This combined system has been evaluated, assembled, and tested. Changes made by developers are gathered to save time. Internally, each developer copy is represented as a tree. Every component of a program or file is a node in the system tree. Background merging makes use of recent changes made to nodes. Node change tracking information keeps tabs on conflicting nodes. Each disagreement is sent to the members of the node who have changed.

By actually producing a merged product, Crystal (Brun et al., 2013) is able to detect conflicts in version-controlled artifacts. The conflicts in this merged item are collated and examined. The developer is discreetly given the information on the resulting conflicts. The relationship between a developer's repository and that of other developers and the master repository can also be established. Crystal supports distributed environments and integrates with Mercurial.

## METHODOLOGY

### Speculative Analysis

Most computer program development, support instruments, and situations drive designers to analyze the progressing and past advancement states of their computer program frameworks in the early days of scattered form control systems. The standardization of computer hardware, inter-framework architectures, and cloud services will provide underused quality for communicating ostensibly-immediate criticism to the designers, to advise them on the consequences of any program modifications they may be exploring.

Modern improvement situations are regularly given arrangements that are within the shape of a fast settle proposition for settling and evacuating grouping mistakes. Simultaneously, the programmers must verify this type of list and choose the alternative that they are considering; this will resolve the issue of intricacy. Rather than this, the IDE ought to hypothetically acknowledge each of the recommendations within the foundation and deliver data that allows different designers to choose the finest choice for the given setting. This makes strides in program quality and developer's efficiency as well.

Creating and employing tools that conduct abstract analysis is highly feasible. This contributes to the advancement of cost-effective data processing through multi-core-designed models and cloud computation. According to the study, abstract analysis serves as a valuable source of information, aiding in the making of informed decisions. The control of version and instantaneous resolution cases present a challenging behavior for abstract analysis.

## Quick Fix on Speculative Analysis

The theoretical examination might be bolstered by employing the obscure instrument's quick settle. When a few compilation errors are discovered, Obscure will begin to suggest a change set (quick fixes) towards the code, which will naturally expose intricacy issues. As a result, it is possible to conclude that to resolve a problem, theoretical apparatus is required.

## Git Repository Mining

The forms in extracting the Git stores may govern the rapid development on the DSCM (distributed source code management) structure, in which each engineer has their own store that is independent of the others. This counteracts the current trend of cooperation in which work output flows sideways amongst collaborators rather than continually up and down through the central store. This process aids in finding definitions by exploring "how the continuous flow between official project repositories extends to the developers."

We're trying to keep track of commits, expulsions, and accumulations as they go from one store to the next. The distinction between centralized source code management (CSCMs) and distributed source code

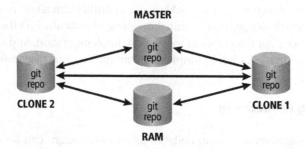

**Figure 12.1**  A model of decentralized usage on git.

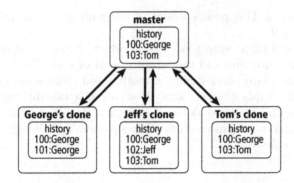

**Figure 12.2** Simple prototype with three developers collaborating parallel using distributed version control system.

management would be that in CSCM, changes and their respective commits are immediately visible to all customers or engineers, whereas in DSCM, it is as if appropriate for the neighborhood clone. The running picture is always in the checked-out position of the current duplicate of the repository in both Git (Bird et al., 2009) and SVN (subversion).

Tirelessness clashes from here on out, we intend to define the extent to which printed confrontations drive forward in dispersed scenarios. To quantify the duration of each change in DVC, we drew a timeline by passing information from two different sets of modifications, which were then integrated to determine the beginning position inevitably when one department conflicts with the other. The printed X remained in place for 3 days and 2 hours as usual and involved 18.3 series of changes within the dispersed conditions from the original ponder.

Changes done at 103 and 101 will result in a literal dispute, that's why we may state Jeff and Tom are in Linguistic X with Georges as well as among themselves, as seen in the diagram shown in Figure 12.2.

Figure 12.2 depicts among the most great examples the DVC framework and how to make changes to an image of a unique store. If any adjusted set differs from another, that change may quickly cause a conflict with all of the other software engineers or designers. The initial meaning of difficulty isn't the literary X mistake, rather than the errors in inspection, implementation, and design. We can eliminate such conflicts by employing continuous or relapse testing.

## Detecting Proactively

When disagreements occur, collaborative improvement can be constantly avoided since designers have discrepant duplicates of the same extent but even in sharing mode. We offered an approach that assists engineers in detecting and resolving disagreements early in the development process, and it has recently become more serious. In the development of a distributed creative environment, each module operates according to their own copy of the software ecosystem, which includes prerequisites, build records, and source code, among other things. Each engineer makes a few modifications in their replica of neighborhood records on a regular basis, and they share those changes with the rest of the group members, as well as coordinating changes from colleagues. We've identified seven of the most important connections that can be created between two duplicate repositories in shareable mode. SAME connection, AHEAD connection, BEHIND connection, Literary X connection, Construct connection, and TEST connection are a few examples.

## A Method for Identifying Disputes That Is Systematic

The following is an algorithmic depiction of identifying conflicts.

**START**
   // To recognize change sets, history of two repository copies were checked
   **For** Each copy← Repository
   Do   Int i←modi_set or chng-set;
      **If** (I belongs← SAME relation for all)
   //do the verification and compare on change sets of the two copies
         Relation: =SAME relation;
      **Else** Increment  i++;
      if (i← is greater)        //second copy of repository
         **Then** Relation: = AHEAD relation:
   // iterate all the other relations respectively
         **Else** Relation: = BEHIND relation;
   //Otherwise, if two copies of repositories contains change sets with the other do not have, i.e., new modifications are arrived into another repository.
         **Then Do Clone** ←Existing_Repository;  //Import
   //Here we are using version control system to integrate the changes
         **If** (Version Control System reports ←any_problem)
            Relation: =TEXTUALX_Relation;
            **Then Do** Generate ←Build_Script;
         **Else If** (Build_Script ←fails)
   |        Relation: =BUILDX_Relation;
         **Else** Relation: =TEST_Relation;
   //In other cases   Relation: =Test√_Relation;
   **End**

**Degree of Parallel Development**

In most cases, if more than one engineer is working on a project, there should be an opportunity for parallel development among the existing architects. With the help of formulae we proposed previously, this advancement was examined and quantified at the same time. Variables like integration rate and struggle rate might have a constant impact on parallel progress.

$$\text{Integration Rate} = (G + C) / (W + U + P + G + C)$$

Here,
G = Integration of automatic work
C = Result of conflicts
U = Updating and creating of new files
W= Remove the deleted files in repository
P = Log the updates which are done with the help of patch.
After calculate the conflict rate as follows,
  Conflict rate =C/(G+C)
Here,
G = Integration of automatic work
C = Result of conflicts
Additionally, we measured how many commits led to integration.

## OUTCOMES

The process of identifying conflicts will begin with the two following outcomes:

- detection of conflicts
- amount of human engagement necessary to resolve conflicts

**Detection of Conflicts**

As previously said, conflicts can be classified into a variety of categories depending upon the seriousness. Early detection of such disputes allows us to shorten the time it takes to progress and also the amount of human interaction needed to tackle them. When a dispute arises during the project development, our component will notify the engineer about the conflict situation and give advice on how to resolve it. The gem gadget can instantaneously do these two types.

When compared to traditional model control guidance, the speculation technology gives conflict data more quickly. The speculative method is used to construct the detection mechanism for developer conflicts. The speculative analysis is done by thinking about a few of the most popular jobs that can be found on http://github.com. Under the given environment, speculative assessments drive the complete dispute discovery procedure. The gear-making system that performs speculative evaluation is effective and feasible. One of the illustrations of the speculative method is the above discernment.

We deduced from Figure 12.3 that when the two constructors are synced, the picture depicted within the first tray may be represented. Some programmers tweaked their repository reproduction, which can be depicted with proper notations in Tray 2, in addition to Tray 3. Finally, the fourth tray will depict conflict resolution in better order, such as verify and construct incompatibilities.

**Figure 12.3** Representation of different types of conflicts under version control environment. Hollowness represents the severity of conflict level between the developers.

## Amount of Human Engagement Necessary to Resolve Conflicts

Conflict resolution methods are less intelligent than humans. We must, however, offer some support in addressing those that are still in the early stages of development. To evaluate this strategy, we must examine various open source projects that are frequently used by multiple developers. Only each developer's local repository's accessibility rights are necessary. The following is a list of open source projects that were considered from http://github.com. For several open source repositories, Table 12.1 shows the amount of manual work required to resolve textual disagreements.

The amount of human interaction necessary to resolve textual disagreements might be decreased by an average of 17% according to the above retrospective analysis table (Table 12.1). The user interface for a modeled retrospective analysis is depicted in the diagram in Figure 12.4.

We may choose the project name from several sources such as Git and Mercurial and evaluate the number of disputes using retrospective analysis.

## Conflicts: Their Incidence and Severity

The Crystal method, on average, identifies more conflicts than other approaches. In response, it has been chosen to focus on just a few statistics, primarily based on the number of implemented commits. The graph shown in Figure 12.5 depicts the severity of conflicts and their typical settlement.

The total number of conflicts identified with the Crystal can be calculated using the graph above. Despite the fact that we only made a few commits, the Crystal model is more appropriate for the greatest number of developer conflicts. Moreover, when programmers detect issues earlier

**TABLE 12.1 Amount of Manual Work Required to Resolve Textual Disagreements**

| System | Merges | Textual X | | Textual √ | |
|---|---|---|---|---|---|
| Bootstrap | 26,548 | 7,698 | 29.0 | 18,850 | 71.0 |
| Satellizer | 640 | 125 | 19.53 | 515 | 80.46 |
| Three20 | 1,788 | 235 | 13.14 | 1,553 | 86.83 |
| Tornado | 2,385 | 263 | 11.02 | 2,122 | 88.98 |
| PaperClip | 1,512 | 324 | 21.44 | 1,188 | 78.57 |
| ElasticSearch | 9,219 | 537 | 0.58 | 8682 | 99.42 |
| CarrierWave | 1,663 | 380 | 22.87 | 1,283 | 77.15 |
| Total | 54,637 | 9,562 | 17.5% | 45,075 | 82.5% |

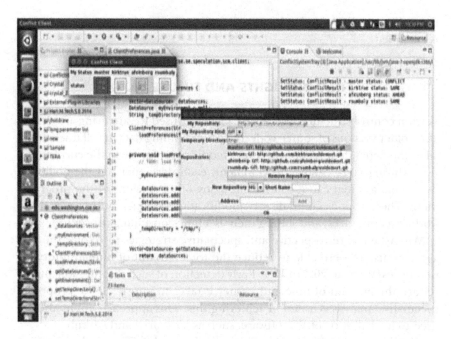

**Figure 12.4** Modeled GUI for retrospective analysis on multiple open source projects.

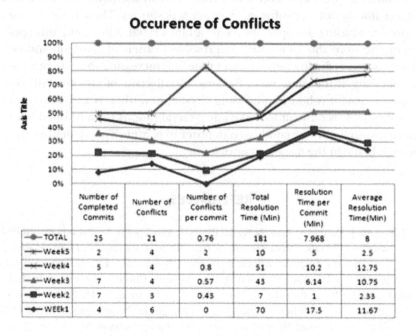

| | Number of Completed Commits | Number of Conflicts | Number of Conflicts per commit | Total Resolution Time (Min) | Resolution Time per Commit (Min) | Average Resolution Time(Min) |
|---|---|---|---|---|---|---|
| TOTAL | 25 | 21 | 0.76 | 181 | 7.968 | 8 |
| Week5 | 2 | 4 | 2 | 10 | 5 | 2.5 |
| Week4 | 5 | 4 | 0.8 | 51 | 10.2 | 12.75 |
| Week3 | 7 | 4 | 0.57 | 43 | 6.14 | 10.75 |
| Week2 | 7 | 3 | 0.43 | 7 | 1 | 2.33 |
| WEEk1 | 4 | 6 | 0 | 70 | 17.5 | 11.67 |

**Figure 12.5** Number of conflicts detected per each commit using the crystal.

than alternative methods, the time required for implementing a solution is extended.

## FINAL THOUGHTS AND FUTURE WORK

Version control structures (VCSs) are primarily used for archiving and recreating older versions of source code and programming data. It will track down all of the dependent records for every modification made in the current version. During collaborative development, each developer has the ability to make changes that cause conflicts in many other versions of the programming. These various contradictory modifications frequently appear in real-world circumstances, and solving them is a time-consuming procedure.

When we use retrospective and speculative strategies to resolve the disagreements, we were able to reduce the total amount of human intervention necessary from 20% to 17%. Early detection of such disputes will always reduce the amount of time and money it takes to improve. The proposed speculative analysis is useful in achieving this. This approach might also be used to lead all sorts of VC software, such as Mercurial and Github.

Distributed model control systems are classified into seven distinct conflict kinds, as previously noted, based on the consideration and analysis of a large number of free software program repositories. These categories are represented using the open source program Crystal. After using this application, we were able to identify and resolve a variety of common and persistent issues, reducing development time and increasing software program productivity at the same time. Because the diversity of conflicts will continue to grow, it is best to quit using Crystal; nevertheless, due to its small sample size, it is difficult to make any generalizations from it. In addition, more research must be conducted in order to provide a good identification of each battle in the dispersed environment.

## REFERENCES

Ball, T., Kim, J. M., Porter, A. A., & Siy, H. P. (1997, May 17–23). If your version control system could talk [Paper presentation]. 19th *ICSE Workshop on Process Modelling and Empirical Studies of Software Engineering*, Boston, MA. https://www.research gate.net/publication/2791666_If_Your_Version_Control_System_Could_Talk

Bird, C., Rigby, P. C., Barr, E. T., Hamilton, D. J., German, D. M., & Devanbu, P. (2009). The promises and perils of mining git. In *Proceedings for the 2009 6th IEEE International Working conference on Mining Software Repositories*. IEEE. https://doi.org/10.1109/MSR.2009.5069475

Brun, Y., Holmes, R., Ernst, M. D., & Notkin, D. (2013). Early detection of collaboration conflicts and risks. *IEEE Transactions on Software Engineering, 39*(10), 1358–1375. https://doi.org/10.1109/TSE.2013.28

Debreceni, C., Bergmann, G., Búr, M., Ráth, I., & Varró, D. (2017). The MONDO collaboration framework: Secure collaborative modeling over existing version control systems. In *Proceedings of the 2017 11th Joint Meeting on Foundations of Software Engineering* (pp. 984–988). https://doi.org/10.1145/3106237.3122829

Dewan, P., & Hegde, R. (2007). Semi-synchronous conflict detection and resolution in asynchronous software development. In L. J. Bannon, I. Wagner, C. Gutwin, R. H. R. Harper, & K. Schmidt (Eds.), *ECSCW 2007* (pp. 159–178). Springer. https://doi.org/10.1007/978-1-84800-031-5_9

Eisenberg, J., Post, C., & DiTomaso, N. (2019). Team dispersion and performance: The role of team communication and transformational leadership. *Small Group Research, 50*(3), 348–380. https://doi.org/10.1177/1046496419827376

Grinter, R. E. (1995). Using a configuration management tool to coordinate software development. In *Proceedings of Conference on Organizational Computing Systems* (pp. 168–177). https://doi.org/10.1145/224019.224036

Grune, D. (1986). *Concurrent versions systems, a method for independent cooperation.* Subfaculteit Wiskunde en Informatica.

Guimarães, M. L., & Silva, A. J. (2012). *Improving early detection of software merge conflicts.* In *Proceedings of the International Conference on Software Engineering* (pp. 342–352). https://doi.org/10.1109/ICSE.2012.6227180

Henderson, P. B., & Weiser, M. (1985). Continuous execution: The VisiProg environment. In *Proceedings of the International Conference on Software Engineering* (pp. 68–74). https://doi.org/10.5555/319568.319582

Mens, T. (2002). A state-of-the-art survey on software merging. *IEEE Transactions on Software Engineering, 28*(5), 449–462. https://doi.org/10.1109/tse.2002 .1000449

Morrison-Smith, S., & Ruiz, J. (2020). Challenges and barriers in virtual teams: A literature review. *SN Applied Sciences, 2*(6), 1–33. Springer. https://link.springer .com/article/10.1007/s42452-020-2801-5

Rao, N. R., & Sekharaiah, K. C. (2016). A methodological review based version control system with evolutionary research for software processes. In *Proceedings of the 2nd International Conference on Information and Communication Technology for Competitive Strategies* (Article 14). https://doi.org/10.1145/2905055.2905072

Reiss, S. P. (1984). Graphical program development with PECAN program development systems. *ACM SIGSOFT Software Engineering Notes, 9*(3), 30–41. https:// doi.org/10.1145/390010.808246

Rochkind, M. J. (1975). The source code control system. *IEEE transactions on Software Engineering, SE-1*(4), 364–370. https://doi.org/10.1109/TSE.1975.6312866

# CHAPTER 13

# LUNG DISEASE DETECTION USING HYBRID MACHINE LEARNING ALGORITHMS

**J. Avanija**
*Mohan Babu Univeristy*

**K. Srujan Raju**
*CMR Technical Campus*

**Gurram Sunitha**
*Mohan Babu Univeristy*

**Mohammad Gouse Galety**
*Catholic University*

**A. V. Sriharsha**
*Mohan Babu University*

*Innovations in Computational Intelligence, Big Data Analytics, and Internet of Things*, pages 233–248

## ABSTRACT

Lung disease is a worldwide issue. Among them includes chronic obstructive pulmonary disease, fibrosis, pneumonia, tuberculosis, asthma, and other disorders. It is critical to diagnose lung disease as soon as possible. Many machine learning methods and many image processing have been created to achieve this goal. Vanilla neural networks (VNN), convolutional neural networks (CNN), capsule networks and visual geometry group-based (VGG) neural networks are among the deep learning approaches used to predict lung sickness. The basic CNN performs poorly when images are rotated, tilted, or otherwise distorted. As a result, we propose a hybrid deep learning based architecture that integrates VGG, data augmentation, and STN with CNN. STN VGG Data Keras, Jupyter Notebook, and Tensorflow are examples of implementation tools. A dataset of "NIH chest X-ray" pictures from the Kaggle library is used to test the proposed model. The sample and complete versioned datasets are both taken into account. VDSNet surpasses conventional approaches in a range of parameters, including recall, precision validation accuracy, and F0.5 score, for both complete and sample datasets.

The demand for health care is increasing; adverse climate change is rising, terrain, and earthborn life significantly raise the danger of affection. Lung complications will be one of the contents covered in this chapter. 3.2 million individuals died of chronic obstructive pulmonary disease (COPD) in 2015—smoking and pollution were the primary causes—while 1.2 million people died of asthma (Centers for Disease Control and Prevention, 2020).

With so many various possibilities for lung problems, this is only one example of a sickness that can be avoided if discovered early. Preliminary diagnosis of difficulties, particularly lung complications, can be aided by technological machine and computer power, allowing us to determine ahead of time and more precisely, perhaps saving multiple individuals and reducing system pressure. The health care system has not evolved in lockstep with population growth. Now is a great time to find a solution to this problem, given the power of computers and the large amount of data that has been made public. In recent times, IT and e-health care systems have been introduced to the medical profession with the goal of allowing medical specialists to provide proper therapy for circumstances that are approaching their breaking point. Lung difficulties, also known as respiratory complications, are one of the most common complications in India, coming in second behind heart issues. Pneumonia, TB, and other corona contagion disease 2019 consequences are within the category of respiratory illness (COVID-19).

The COVID-19 outbreak, according to current research, affected many people and health care systems, resulting in huge human loss. In particular, lung illnesses are a leading cause of death and a global catastrophe. Early detection and treatment of lung problems enhance recovery prospects, although survival rates vary depending on when they are recognized and treated. Lung diseases were previously discovered using blood tests, skin tests, CT scan, and X-ray. The radiology department will review the report, and someone with appropriate competence will attempt to identify the analysis from the sample group, which will be difficult if the radiographer is not there at all times. Freshly acquired, profound information has drawn a lot of attention to the medical field in the hopes of detecting and avoiding abnormalities. As a result, we attempt to characterize the abnormality existing in the lungs utilizing chest X-ray examination employing our deep literacy approach to predict lung problems.

We can plainly see several types of examinations that are performed in order to find anomalies in human lungs from Figure 13.1. In general, in the medical field, we aim to apply deep learning to discover patterns in chest X-rays and then create probable learnt features from those images. Deep learning is swiftly becoming an art in a variety of medical applications, helping medical department employees and doctors detect and classify small medical irregularities more quickly and efficiently. There has been a lot of study done to identify lung ailments, but to our awareness, only one study piece based on previously published publications on the subject has been published. This chapter covers the entire history of deep learning as well

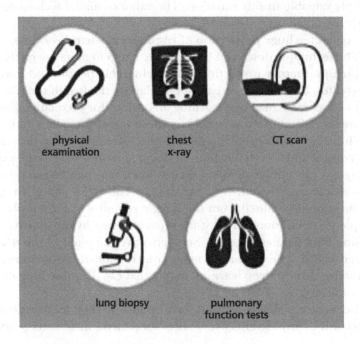

**Figure 13.1** Several methods for detecting lung diseases.

as how it is employed in pulmonary imaging applications. Deep learning algorithms are utilized to treat pulmonary embolism, pneumonia, interstitial lung disease, and pulmonary nodule disorders among other conditions.

With so many different options, lung issues that people might develop, this is only one example of a disease that can be avoided if caught early.

Due to the changes in climate, lifestyle, and other factors, the influence of disease on health is fastly increasing. This has elevated the likelihood of illness. Over 3.4 million people died of obstructive pulmonary disease (COPD)—which is mostly caused by "pollution" and "smoking"—and around "400,000" people died of asthma in 2016. Lung illnesses are a significant threat, specifically in the countries where the income is low and middle, where millions of people are poor and exposed to "pollution." According to World Health Organization each year around 4 million people die prematurely as a result of diseases induced by household air pollution, such as asthma and pneumonia. As a result, actions need to be taken to overcome pollution. It's also critical to put in place effective diagnostic technologies that can help diagnose lung problems. COVID-19, a new coronavirus disease, has been causing major lung problems and respiratory issues since late December 2019. As a result, early diagnosis of lung disorders is more critical than ever. Advanced analytics can be incredibly valuable in this situation. The value of digital technology has recently increased over the world.

As a dataset, a huge proportion of respiratory system X-ray images are used. The technique described here can also help to more correctly diagnose diseases, thereby protecting many vulnerable people and lowering sickness rates. Due to the increasing population, the health program has yet to be developed. Machine learning algorithms for predicting diagnostic information from X-ray pictures have been investigated by a number of researchers. Now is a key time to address this issue, with computers under public control and a vast collection of documents available to the public. This strategy can minimize medical costs when machine learning is used for health care and health research efforts. The "NIH" lung X-ray picture collection is obtained from the Kaggle repository, and the platform is completely open source. This study provides a new hybrid approach for classifying lung sickness that has been effectively applied to the datasets indicated above. The research's main contribution is the creation of a revolutionary hybrid deep learning system that can diagnose lung disease using X-ray images.

In the medical industry, e-health care systems attempt to provide medical specialists to provide effective services for patients in an emergency.

## BACKGROUND ANALYSIS

The goal of the proposed approach (American Thoracic Society, 2000) is to employ programming language data mining tools to use multiple categorization algorithms to diagnose lung cancer. For this work, the lung cancer dataset was collected from the UC Irvine machine learning repository. In the databases, abnormal cancers have been discovered. The ability and potentiality of logistic regression, random forest, tree, "K-nearest neighbors (KNN)," Naive Bayes, and neural network classifications to predict the presence of lung cancer with the greatest accuracy were investigated in this study. The algorithms were compared in terms of accuracy metrics such as precision, recall and F1 score. Naive Bayes has the highest overall accuracy of 57.047% and the highest kappa statistics value of 0.356, according to the confusion matrix data. With a total accuracy of 49.832%, random forest comes in second. It's also worth noting that Naive Bayes has the greatest proportion of ROC-controlled land (74.8%).

Pneumonia is one among the major and common causes of mortality around the globe. A virus, bacteria, or fungus can cause pneumonia. Also, relying simply on chest X-rays to diagnose pneumonia is risky (Bhandary et al., 2020). The purpose of this approach is to make influenza identification straightforward for experts and novices alike. Based on the principle of transfer learning, we offer a novel deep learning system for influenza identification. Several pretrained neural network models on ImageNet are used to extract picture attributes, which are then fed into a classifier for prediction. We experimented with five distinct models and compared the results. Then, to beat individual models and achieve state-of-the-art pneumonia recognition performance, an ensemble-based model was suggested in order to combine the outputs of all pretrained models.

The proposed approach compares CNN model performance for CXR COVID-19 identification using transfer learning. Because there has never been a study like this in the field of detecting COVID-19 cases using CXR photos, comparative study, which included 15 different deep learning models and an assessment system, is critical. Comparative studies have been contributed to by researchers from various fields. Plant species have been described using six different deep learning models. For example, various types of transferred deep learning models are explored to discriminate ultrasound breast masses. A total of 860 photographs (260 COVID-19 instances, 300 normal cases, and 300 influenza cases) were utilized to evaluate the proposed algorithm's performance, with 70% of each class's images suitable for training, 15% for validation, and the remainder for testing. The VGG19 achieves the greatest classification accuracy of 89.3%, with average precision, recall, and F1 scores of 0.90, 0.89, and 0.90, respectively. The efficient machine learning optimization approach (Adam), stochastic gradient descent, and root mean square propagation are the three optimization methodologies studied and tested (RMSprop). On a balanced dataset, preliminary computational results show that a model trained with Adam can accurately differentiate COVID-19 and non-COVID-19 individuals with 96.3% accuracy. The training with RMSprop surpassed all other models on the unbalanced dataset, with a correctness of 95.38%.

The ResNeXt feature extraction backbone was added to the UNet and LinkNet architectures, while the DenseNet architecture was added to the Tiramisu architecture. The ground-truth segmentation masks and accompanying contours were used to train all CNN architectures. Contour-based augmentation had been compared to contour-free architectures along with the 20 alternative lung field segmentation algorithms (Hu, 2018). The goal of the work (Kong et al., 2019) is to see how machine learning algorithms may be utilized to predict spine anomalies. Support vector machines (SVM), regression analysis (LR), and bagging ensemble techniques are among the machine learning algorithms used to diagnose spinal diseases. On a dataset of 310 observations that are publicly available in the Kaggle repository, the SVM, LR, bagging SVM, and bagging LR algorithms are used. During training and testing, the efficiency of the classification of aberrant and ordinary spinal patients is evaluated using accuracy, memory, and also miss rate. The classifier models were evaluated using the receiver operating characteristic (ROC) and pinpoint accuracy curves, as well as the kernel parameters. The obtained training accuracies for SVM, LR, bagging SVM, and bagging LR are 86.30%, 85.47%, 86.72%, and 85.06%, respectively, when 78% data is used for training. On the other hand, the test dataset accuracies for SVM, LR, bagging SVM, and bagging LR are all 86.96% (Marciniuk & Schraufnagel, 2017; Mohan et al., 2021). SVM, which has a greater recognition rate and a lower miss rate than the others, is the most enticing.

A deep learning algorithm was used to bridge the gap between reduced data collected by imaging equipment and elevated data preserved by people (Rahaman et al., 2020). A five-layer convolutional neural network consisting of one convolutional layer, one activation layer, along with a pooling layer, and a fully connected layer is presented, followed by a softmax layer that evaluates the likelihood of each genre's output. The authors (Madhavi et al., 2022) used the same dataset to train a VGG-16 model to solve this problem (a well-known CNN architecture trained on the Image Net dataset). Grad-CAM is a software that compares the model's performance with that of the test-image. The suggested methods were put to the test on the chest X-ray 14 dataset, yielding state-of-the-art results much better than the prior methods. A complete comparability with presently available studies was included.

For more than 50 years, the techniques such as computer-aided diagnoses (CAD) for chest X-rays (CXR) were used. CAD can help with early detection and treatment failure, reducing the number of people killed by late diagnosis and treatment failure. In recent years, deep machine learning approach for medical picture categorization have risen in importance. CNNs are a type of image classification and segmentation generative model. Deep neural network models such as AlexNet, VGG-16, and CapsNet were tested for detecting tuberculosis using the samples of CXR images. The bespoke models were developed using data from the National Institute for Health and private Thai sources. To avoid overfitting in established models, image enhancement with shuffle sampling is used. The VGG-16 classifier presently has the maximum sensitivity around the value 92.83% and the maximum value of specificity around 96.06% when using shuffle sampling of size 3310 (Rajaraman & Antani, 2020). Deep neural networks, contour-free designs (Yadlapalli et al., 2021), and 20 existing lung field processes may lead to correctly classify TB in X-ray images, according to our research. Furthermore, with an accuracy level of 73.6%, our proposed model outperformed a range of current deep learning models. But in this study the dataset that was used was rather small, and there were only four numerical and categorical variables considered.

## PROPOSED METHODOLOGY

The present system has no notion of how to detect lung cancer using CNN models. All of the forecasts were made from scratch or with the help of simple machine learning techniques. Although machine learning can classify lung cancer, these models cannot reliably and consistently categorize records. The proposed method uses deep learning to provide an excellent technique for expert identification of lung disorders using pretrained CNN models like VGG19 and VGG16. There are four partitions as layers such as "convolutional layer," "RELU," "pooling layer," and "fully connected layer."

### Convolution Layer

Convolution is a process with two functions. Both involve a set of numbers, with the first including adjacent pixels in the given position of the image and then involving a filter, otherwise a kernel. The result is obtained by taking the dot average of the two functions. The filter is then shifted to the next photo location, which is determined by the stride length. A feature (or activation) map is created by repeating the technique until the whole frame has been covered. The filter is active in this diagram, and it "sees" objects like a linear manner, a dot, or a crooked edge. When a CNN gets a facial image, the filters attempt to detect low-level details such as lines and edges. In successive levels of the CNN architecture, the component mappings build up to ever greater features, such as the inputs of human parts like ear, nose, and eye for the forthcoming level.

### Rectified Linear Unit Layer

Negative input values are converted to zero using the Rectified Linear Unit (RELU) function. This helps to avoid the degradation problem by reducing and speeding up calculations and training. $f(x) = \max$ is the mathematical formula $(0, x)$. The neuron receives $x$ as an input. Sigmoid, tanh, faulty RELUs, completely random RELUs, and dynamic RELUs are some of the other activation functions.

### Pooling Layer

To reduce the dimensionality to evaluate and the size of the image, the pooling layer is placed between the pooling layers and the RELU layers. Typically pooled and L2-normalization pooling are two other types of max pooling that are commonly employed. Maximum pooling aggregates the maximum activations over a neighborhood by selecting the maximum input value within such a filter and eliminating the other values. The concept is that the proximity of an extremely active feature to the next is more important than its specific placement.

### Fully Connected Layer

Every layer in the previous layer is linked to every layer in the CNN's fully connected layer. Depending on the desired level of component abstraction, there can be one or more entirely connected layers, similar to the inversion, RELU, and pooling layers. Using the output from the preceding layer, this layer generates probability values for classification into distinct classes (convolution, RELU, or pooling). This layer looks at the image's top dynamic attributes to see if it fits into a given category. Cancer cells, for example, have a greater DNA to cytoplasmic ratio on histopathology glass slides than normal cells.

## LIMITATIONS OF EXISTING METHODOLOGIES

There are only a few classes in all of the current classification schemes. All present methods for categorizing chest X-ray images and attempting to identify cancer signs fail. The goal of all modern machine learning algorithms is to classify patient data from an original dataset. There is no appropriate prediction for identifying true chest X-rays so that picture correctness may be detected and predicted.

The goal of the proposed work is to create an application that can predict lung cancer using chest X-ray images. In this proposed work, chest X-ray photographs with cancer signs from the KAGGLE website are collected to train the algorithm. After the system has been trained, the model productivity can be checked by the efficiency of each unique model. If a person has lung disease, deep learning could help them live longer by predicting it using chest X-rays. This is possible because the outcomes can be predicted accurately and in real time (Reddy et al., 2022). In the proposed work, hybrid deep learning models are used to provide an excellent technique for expert identification of lung disorders. The possible CNN model considered for detecting chest disease using pretrained CNN models like VGG19 and VGG16 in this part. There are four layers such as pooling layer, convolution layer, RELU layer, and fully connected layer.

## PROPOSED DEEP LEARNING ARCHITECTURE

The technique used in the proposed system is a challenging task with new datasets which have never been fully modeled: This is a difficult picture data processing algorithm. This is the ideal technique to utilize given the enormous amount of data in the entire dataset; nonetheless, some parameters must be reviewed and used: choosing the suitable architecture for your neural network; parameters for pre-processing; optimization; transformer of space; parameters for training; and not only photographs, but more data should be added to the network. The architecture is made up of the VGG16 pretrained model, consisting of the layers of spatial transformers. The first is lambda, which transfers routing features [−0.5 : 0.5], implying that the image's characteristics have an average value of 0 where, "lambda $x$: 2 * x − 1" is the lamda function. Batch normalization is the second process. The spatial transformer is the third layer, which uses the net localization of a small CNN to retrieve the most critical information for classification: Maxpooling is applied after the three convolution layers, with a doubling depth of 16 – 32 – 64 and a kernel size of 7 – 5 – 3, padding = "valid." Straighten the layer; then add three dense layers with reduced depth; activation = "relu"; extract features layers (VGG16 pretrained model). Extracting features requires a set of 13 layers, as indicated in the VGG sketch shown in Figure 13.2. There are numerous pretrained models, but we start with VGG16 because it's a simple model that takes less time to learn and train.

## Classification Layers (Last 3 layers)

The very first layer is a straightened layer made up of the output of layers VGG16 and 5 plus "Gender Male, Gender Female, Age, View position AP, and View position PA." These extra properties have been introduced to this layer since they will alter sorting, as we've seen as specified in Figure 13.3. The dropout layer comes after this one. After each layer, the next two levels are dense. With decreasing depth, the dropout 0.2. Because the chosen model did not have a small loss and a rapid convergence, there is still room for improvement in detecting the disease in the persons.

## RESULTS AND DISCUSSIONS

The proposed work makes use of a dataset available in Kaggle called sample. zip: sample labels.csv: Contains 5,606 photos at a resolution of 1024 x 1024. In the complete dataset, there are 15 classes (14 diseases and one for "No results"), but because this is a substantially reduced version of the whole dataset, several of the classes are sparse, 3,044 pictures were not found. As a preprocessing task to reduce the complexity, the images were resized (Setio et al., 2017); decreasing the image size minimizes the feature that allows for faster training. Grayscale and RGB images were created (Kuraparthi et al., 2021; Reshma et al., 2022). Both were employed in various models. Clinically, a chest X-ray, on either hand, may be more difficult to diagnose than a chest CT scan. With 4,143 images, Openi was the biggest publicly available collection of chest X-ray images prior to the start of this collection.

The National Institutes of Health's Chest X-ray Dataset contains 112,120 X-ray images from 30,805 patients, each with a medical indication. The authors employed natural language processing to text-mine disease classifications from correlated radiological data to construct these labels. The labels should be more than 90% correct and suitable for understanding without monitoring. Although the actual radiology reports are not generally accessible, "ChestX-ray8: Hospital-scale Chest X-ray Database and Benchmarks on Weakly-Supervised Identification and Segmentation of Common

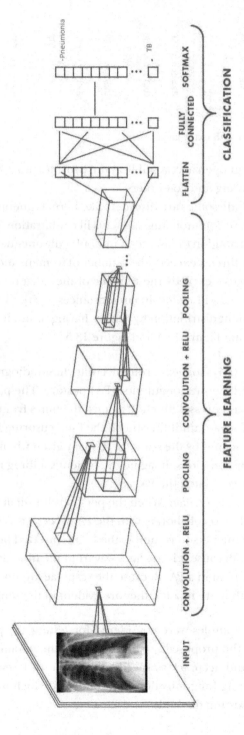

**Figure 13.2** VGG architecture.

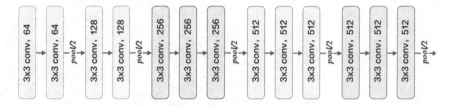

**Figure 13.3**   VDSNet with extra layers.

Thorax Diseases," an open access publication, provides more details on the labeling process (Wang and co-workers).

The images include some rare disorders like hernia, pneumonia, and fibrosis, as well as more common lung ailments like infiltration, effusion, and atelectasis. The distribution of diseases is undoubtedly unequal. The overall number of men on this list exceeds the number of women, and the number of confirmed instances exceeds the number of men diagnosed with lung illness. The difference will be less in circumstances where the condition is not confirmed. Patient distribution by gender having or not having disease, view position diagram Figure 13.4 and Figure 13.5.

*Posterior-Anterior (PA) Position:* A routine adult chest radiograph should be taken in the posterior-anterior (PA) posture. The patient stands up straight and presses his chest against the film's front. The arms are moved forward until they touch the film, ensuring that no lung areas are obscured by the scapulae. Usually given when the patient is completely conscious. Imagine the patient standing right in front of you while you watch the PA tape.

*Anterior-posterior (AP) Position:* When the person is hospitalized, immobile, or unable to collaborate with the PA process, this method is used. While the person is supine, the film is inserted behind his or her back. Because it is further away from the film, the heart appears larger than in a PA. Because the scapulae are not twisted out of vision as they are in a PA, they are evident in the lung fields.

Twenty random samples were considered for testing the proposed approach. Results of the proposed method based on the parameters such as precision, recall, and accuracy as specified in Table 13.1 reveals that the accuracy of predicting lung infection is around 76% which is better when compared to the existing methods.

## CONCLUSIONS AND FUTURE WORK

A deep learning CNN model is used and developed to diagnose chest or lung problems using chest X-ray photos. An application that can detect and locate problems in the human lungs or chest based on the image's impacted region is developed. The deep complex neural network (Optimized CNN), the most recent image recognition approach, is presently

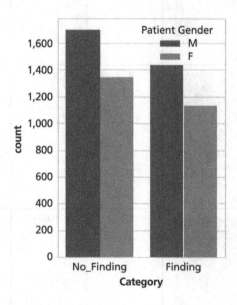

**Figure 13.4**   Distribution of disease based on gender.

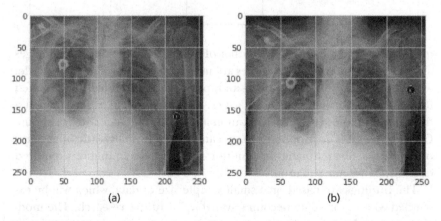

**Figure 13.5**   (a) Posterior-anterior position of image. (b) Anterior-posterior position of image.

**TABLE 13.1  Accuracy of Proposed Method for Sample Dataset**

| Sample Dataset | Precision | Recall | Accuracy |
|---|---|---|---|
| <br>Sample 1 | 0.50 | 0.82 | 56.9% |
| <br>Sample 2 | 0.72 | 0.45 | 58.0% |
| <br>Sample 3 | 0.71 | 0.62 | 76.0% |

quite exciting to create. A big number of diseased and healthy lung images are collected, the collected samples are used to train the system. The model with a typical chest X-ray image as an input is sent after it has been trained to determine if it has any irregularities. To this problem, we developed a deep learning model that detects anomalies in the human chest using the CNN approach. The proposed system can be used to analyze the lung status of covid patients, reducing the amount of physical examinations required during a pandemic situation.

The findings are based on a small sample size of data, which will be expanded when more data becomes available for future research. The models can then be tailored to a given country to provide even more information. The models were trained over a period of 20 epochs, which can be expanded on computers with better computing power. Various deep learning approaches and models could also be used to compare findings in multimedia medical picture screening. The models chosen and used in this work can serve as a foundation for future research in this field.

## REFERENCES

American Thoracic Society. (2000). *American Journal of Respiratory and Critical Care Medicine, 161*(4), 1376–1395. https://doi.org/10.1164/ajrccm.161.4.16141

Bhandary, A., Prabhu, G. A., Rajinikanth, V., Thanaraj, K. P., Satapathy, A. C., Robbins, D. E., Shasky, C., Zhang, Y.-D., Tavares, J. M. R. S., & Raja, N. S. M. (2020). Deep-learning framework to detect lung abnormality—A study with chest X-ray and lung CT scan images. *Pattern Recognition Letters, 129,* 271–278. https://doi.org/10.1016/j.patrec.2019.11.013

Centers for Disease Control and Prevention. (2020). Severe outcomes among patients with coronavirus disease 2019 (COVID-19)—United States, February 12–March 16, 2020. *Morbidity and Mortality Weekly Report, 69*(12), 343–346. https://www.cdc.gov/mmwr/volumes/69/wr/mm6912e2.htm

Hu, J., Tang, Z., Wang, Z., Zhang, K., Zhang, L., & Sun, Q. (2018). Deep learning for image-based cancer detection and diagnosis—A survey. *Pattern Recognition, 83,* 134–149. https://doi.org/10.1016/j.patcog.2018.05.014

Kong, W., Hong, J., Jia, M., Yao, J., Cong, W., Hu, H., & Zhan, H. (2019). YOLOv3-DPFIN: A dual-path feature fusion neural network for robust real-time sonar target detection. *IEEE Sensors Journal, 20*(7), 3745–3756. https://doi.org/10.1109/JSEN.2019.2960796

Kuraparthi, S., Reddy, M. K., Sujatha, C. N., Valiveti, H., Duggineni, C., Kollati, M., & Kora, P., & Sravan, V. (2021). Brain tumor classification of MRI images using deep convolutional neural network. *Traitement du Signal, 38*(4), 1171–1179. https://doi.org/10.18280/ts.380428

Madhavi, K. R., Kora, P., Reddy, L. V., Avanija, J., Soujanya, K. L. S., & Telagarapu, P. (2022). Cardiac arrhythmia detection using dual-tree wavelet transform and convolutional neural network. *Soft Computing, 26*(7), 3561–3571. https://doi.org/10.1007/s00500-021-06653-w

Mohan, E., Rajesh, A., Sunitha, G., Konduru, R. M., Avanija, J., & Ganesh Babu, L. (2021). A deep neural network learning-based speckle noise removal technique for enhancing the quality of synthetic-aperture radar images. *Concurrency and Computation: Practice and Experience, 33*(13), e6239. https://doi.org/10.1002/cpe.6239

Rahaman, M. M., Li, C., Yao, Y., Kulwa, F., Rahman, M. A., Wang, Q., Qi, A., Kong, F., Zhu, X., & Zhao, X. (2020). Identification of COVID-19 samples from chest X-Ray images using deep learning: A comparison of transfer learning approaches. *Journal of X-ray Science and Technology, 28*(5), 821–839. https://doi.org/10.3233/XST-200715

Reddy, M. K., Kovuri, K., Avanija, J., Sakthivel, M., & Kaleru, S. (2022, September). Brain stroke prediction using deep learning: A CNN approach. In *Proceedings for the 2022 4th International Conference on Inventive Research in Computing Applications* (pp. 775–780). IEEE. https://doi.org/10.1109/ICIRCA54612.2022.9985596

Reshma, G., Al-Atroshi, C., Nassa, V. K., Geetha, B., Sunitha, G., Galety, M. G., & Neelakandan, S. (2022). Deep learning-based skin lesion diagnosis model using dermoscopic images. *Intelligent Automation & Soft Computing, 31*(1), 621–634. https://doi.org/10.32604/iasc.2022.019117

Setio, A. A. A., Traverso, A., De Bel, T., Berens, M. S., Van Den Bogaard, C., Cerello, P., Chen, H., Dou, Q., Fantacci, M. E., Geurts, B., van der Gugten, R., Heng, P. A., Jansen, B., de Kaste, M. M. J., Kotov, V., Lin, J. Y.-H., Manders, J. T. M. C., Sóñora-Mengana, A., García-Naranjo, J. C., & Jacobs, C. (2017). Validation, comparison, and combination of algorithms for automatic detection of pulmonary nodules in computed tomography images: The LUNA16 challenge. *Medical Image Analysis, 42*, 1–13. https://doi.org/10.1016/j.media.2017.06.015

Yadlapalli, P., Reddy, M. K., Gurram, S., Avanija, J., Meenakshi, K., & Kora, P. (2021). Breast thermograms asymmetry analysis using gabor filters. In *E3S Web of Conferences, 309*, 01109. https://doi.org/10.1051/e3sconf/202130901109

# CHAPTER 14

# AN INVESTIGATION OF FUTURE RESEARCH DIRECTIONS IN SECURE INTERNET OF THINGS SYSTEMS AND APPLICATIONS

**M. Bharathi**
*Mohan Babu University*

**M. Dharani**
*Mohan Babu University*

**Sivaram Rajeyyagari**
*Shaqra University*

**B. M. Rajeswari**
*Mohan Babu University*

*Innovations in Computational Intelligence, Big Data Analytics, and Internet of Things*, pages 249–263
Copyright © 2024 by Information Age Publishing
www.infoagepub.com
**249**

## ABSTRACT

Internet of things (IoT) is a most exhilarating and enabling technology which has been creating more noise in this revolution. Based on smart connectivity with present networks and context-aware computation of the usage of community resources becomes a crucial part of IoT. There is a cutthroat in present technological evolution with the presence of Wi-Fi and 4G LTE. For the IoT vision to fully come to life, the way we use computers needs to go beyond just using smartphones and portable devices. It should extend to connecting our daily lives with smart gadgets and incorporating intelligence into our surroundings. There are numerous applications of IoTs. Some of them are smart cities, connected cars, wearable safety monitoring, wireless inventory tracking, biometric safety security, autonomous agriculture equipment, smart home surveillance, shipping containers and logistics, IoT controls and trading. This chapter is about IoT and the useful tools and websites that professionals can use to learn and create applications. The chapter also discusses practical applications related to diverse fields related to IoT.

Internet technology and wireless sensor networks are increasing rapidly in the process of modernization. A new trend is realized in an era of evolution and ubiquity (Yang et al., 2017). The rise in numbers is because more people use the internet, and they apply it to connect everyday objects that need communication between people or between people and computers. Internet of things (IoT) enables the exchange of information between devices or things. The IoT is a network of physical objects, devices, vehicles, buildings, and other objects that incorporate electronics, software, sensors, and networks connections that allow these objects to collect and share data, and so on—refrigerators, clocks, fans, air conditioners, cars, and so forth; communication between man and machine, machine and machine. Thanks to the flexibility and low cost of the Internet, the popularity of things (IoT) is increasing day by day. People who say the Internet has already changed society might be right, but the biggest changes might still be on the way. New technologies are coming together in a way that suggests the internet is about to grow a lot. Things of all sizes are connected to each other and have their own identity on the web. While we're used to our computers being linked to the internet, soon, everyone being connected through mobile internet will become the norm, making everything more accessible and connected. The following improvement for phones and other versatile gadgets is the Web of things. When nearly everything within the virtual world is associated and controlled. This revolution is the largest arranged development to date, with far-reaching impact across all businesses—and our whole everyday life. In smart network with display systems and context-conscious computation, the utilization of organized resources is a basic portion of IoT. With the creating nearness of Wi-Fi and 4G LTE Wi-Fi Web gets to, the advancement toward omnipresent insights and communication systems is as of now apparent. Be that as it may, for the Web of things creative and prescient to proficiently develop, the computing worldview will need to move past expected cellular computing outcomes that utilize intelligent phones and portables, and advance into interfacing ordinary show things and implanting insights into our environment. For time to disappear from the recognition of the client, the Web of things requests: a shared skill of the scenario of its clients and their apparatuses, program structures and inescapable communication networks to procedure and bring the relevant truths to wherein it's miles important, and the analytics hardware withinside the Web of things that objective for self-adequate and intelligent behavior. With these 3 basic grounds input, intelligent network and context-conscious computation can be accomplished. A radical advancement of the modern-day Web right into a range of interconnected contraptions that now not most compelling harvests realities from the environment (detecting) and interatomic with the physical world (activation/command/control), be that as it may also make utilization of current Web prerequisites to offer offerings for truths exchange, analytics, applications, and communications (Ahanger, 2018). Fueled by the prevalence of gadgets empowered by open remote innovation such as Bluetooth, radio recurrence identification (RFID), Wi-Fi, and telephonic information administrations as well as inserted sensor and actuator hubs, IoT has ventured out of its earliest stages and is on the skirt of changing the current inactive Web into a fully coordinated future Web.

## APPLICATIONS OF IOT: DETAILED

The uniqueness Internet of things has became a real thing at the end, to its selection over a wide variety of applications, indeed, in businesses as well. The flexibility of IoT makes it an attractive choice for so many businesses, organizations, and government offices that it doesn't make sense to disregard it (Lu & Da Xu, 2018). Learn more about his IoT applications in different businesses underneath.

IoT in Agriculture
IoT in Intelligent Management System
IoT Applications in Healthcare
Smart Firefighting Drone Using IoT
Security Applications Using IoT
IoT in Consumer Usage
5G Mobile Communication Using IoT
IoT Applications in Insurance
IoT Applications in Industries

IoT Applications in Online and Retail Shopping
IoT Applications in Transportation

## IOT in Agriculture

Engineering the proper conditions for plants and their productivity is a key component of agricultural accuracy. The agricultural industry today employs a wide range of sensors in networked engineering to gather data on the precise needs of the plants and their output (Rishitha & Ullas., 2019). Since the IoT was developed, agriculture may now be implemented rather methodically. Agriculture is without a doubt one of the most important financial industries in the world. It is a crucial market for the developing world (Sunitha et al., 2022). Food, clothing, and shelter are just a few of the daily necessities that are directly tied to farming. In recent years, developing countries have faced a variety of horticulture-related problems, including a water shortage. The monitoring and management of microclimate conditions for indoor planting is made possible by IoT, which increases output (Shakir et al., 2019). With the help of IoT-enabled devices, irrigation and fertilizer systems for outdoor planting may be better managed by keeping an eye on soil moisture, nutrients, and weather data. For instance, if sprinkler systems only discharge water, when necessary, this prevents resource waste (Ullas & Vishwas, 2019).

To fulfill rising demands and reduce output losses, IoT applications in agriculture focus on conventional farming activities (Shereesha et al., 2022). Robots, drones, remote sensors, computer imagery, and ever-evolving machine learning and analytical tools are used in IoT in agriculture to monitor crops, survey and map fields, and give farmers information they may use to make time- and money-saving farm management decisions (Nennuri et al., 2022; Routray et al., 2019; Sunitha et al., 2023).

## IoT in Intelligent Management System

Due to advent in mechanical advancement, road lights are built with typical devices commonly used by commuters. When you approach the goal, the light will turn on, unlike road lights which ensure safety while people are walking down the road and helping others to stay safe (Rajput et al., 2013). When nobody uses it, nobody takes off and may be eliminated intelligently. This is possible with the aid of advanced sensors. Choosing to switch on the light is viable. Power IoT may be used to monitor and track device status. This archive illustrates a competent and practical discovery technique. Unusual or odd behavior as well as recommendations are given to the supervising authority to demand essential activity.

## IoT Applications in Healthcare

Medical big data electronic health information regarding specific patients is kept in electronic medical records (EHR; Rizwan et al., 2018). The EHR keeps track of a variety of electronic health information, including personal information, demographics, medical history, prescriptions, and allergies. Age and weight-based IoT data from the outdated Sanjeevani EHR are stored and used to monitor patient health information (Sunitha et al., 2021). High availability and security for patient data against unauthorized individuals making effective use of a lot of data. Most importantly, wearable IoT gadgets let clinics screen their patients' well-being at home, consequently lessening emergency clinic stays while giving expert ongoing data that could save lives (Jindal et al., 2018). In medical clinics, shrewd beds keep the staff educated with regards to the accessibility, subsequently cutting sit tight time with the expectation of complimentary space (Arunachalam et al., 2023). Putting IoT sensors on basic gear implies less breakdowns and expanded unwavering quality, which can mean the distinction among life and demise (Karthika et al., 2020).

Older considerations turn out to be altogether more OK with IoT. Notwithstanding the previously mentioned ongoing home checking, sensors can likewise decide whether a patient has fallen or is experiencing a coronary failure.

Many people are waiting in a dull waiting area, eager to see the doctor as soon as possible. Then again, there were blue patients present who were crying in misery. Indeed, a couple of years prior, emergency clinics were in this situation. Things are presently changing rapidly on account of innovation. Present day medical services offices, medical services versatile applications, and the fresh out of the box new IOT thought are changing the medical services industry in general. In the wake of grabbing hold in various enterprises, including business, retail, government, and industry, IOT is presently flourishing in the medical services area. Maybe no industry has profited from the IoT more than medical care. IOT is a strong power in the medical services industry, helping everybody from specialists, to scientists, to patients, to protection. Patients can now effectively speak with their primary care physicians and be ceaselessly observed utilizing IOT, while specialists can now constantly follow patients' well-being and improvement. Subject matter experts and specialists get the opportunity to talk with each other in regards to complex clinical issues from one side of the planet to the other. Despite the fact that innovation can't invert populace maturing or end persistent illnesses, it can essentially make admittance to medical services more helpful.

In the past couple of years, we have seen numerous improvements that will clearly shape the future of medical care and observing frameworks. So, it's fair to say that healthcare is one of the most exciting yet challenging areas for IoT transformation, offering significant potential for the future of IoT in healthcare. Utilizing extra sensors generally, conceivable security issues could be checked like gases, dust, vibrations, fire, and so forth (Alemdar & Ersoy, 2010). Other significant information can be imparted through this framework making it plausible where wired correspondence is an obstruction. We can transfer the information to the server utilizing Wi-Fi (Karnik et al., 2008). We can likewise execute to peruse other information utilizing various sensors like smoke, dust, and so forth. We can likewise carry out sending message alarms to the closest accessible emergency vehicle.

## Smart Firefighting Drone Using IoT

The IoT is the interconnection of actual things. Since the framework's parts are interconnected, significant information can be imparted to the end client to assist them with choosing what to do and when. The abilities of the Web of things can be utilized to oversee hazardous and perilous conditions that call for human activity. A fire setback can bring about property harm and fatalities at a production line, business complex, or lodging society. Even though firefighters take precautions, they can still be exposed to dangerous gases and high temperatures. Robots have as of late arisen as the best method for finishing explicit exercises in contrast with people when critical gamble is involved. Formation of an independent robot that can identify and quench fire simultaneously, screen with a camera, send results by means of the Internet of things (IoT), and furthermore be controlled from a distance from anyplace. This work utilizes IoT innovation to fabricate and foster a firefighting robot that can extinguish fires without the requirement for human intercession on the scene. The framework comprises of a temperature sensor to find the fire and a water siphon to put it out.

The IoT is a quickly growing industry. This technology has advanced in many different domains. We must get regular reports on the status of skyscraper or high-rise fires in order to provide efficient and secure firefighting. Due to certain restrictions or limitations, ground vehicles are often unable to enter high-rise fires. Due to slower technological innovation, the majority of skyscrapers lack adequate fire monitoring and prevention systems. To solve this issue, this chapter suggests that drones are emerging as a promising solution to prevent these types of events. In this system, the Fire Control Unit may launch UAVs (FCU). When a fire is present, sensors located in the skyscraper immediately relay stress signals to the command and control center, where additional possible action can be done (Malfante et al., 2018). The fire control unit's pilot continuously keeps an eye on the flight route while also receiving video and fire scan data from the UAV. Global Positioning System (GPS) is used to locate the skyscraper in the event of a stress signal or fire signal, and permission to launch the extinguisher vehicle is requested from the appropriate security agency. When permission is given, the system is updated with the location's coordinates, and the closest station sends a UAV there. Once the firefighting substance is used, the vehicle goes back to the nearest landing spot. It gets refilled with more firefighting material before being taken back to the fire location. The quality of service should increase thanks to this suggested methodology.

**Security Applications Using IoT**

The wrongdoing of youngster misuse has been continuously expanding in India, with an absence of security and insurance being the primary driver. A study discovered that girls aged 5 to 12 experience sexual abuse more than 53% of the time. Our proposed plan consolidates a security and well-being confirmation framework. A savvy band with various sensors and programmable gadgets will be conceivable with this association savvy arm band that conveys remotely with a cell phone (Sridhar & Smys, 2017). Applications for brilliant groups have been planned, downloaded, and introduced by an important number of advanced cell clients. The savvy band produces a sign that is sent to the cell phone. A PDA will in a flash send the message: "Help me and save me, I'm in a peril circumstance." Alongside the area to the closest police headquarters/watch/control room, as well as send the message to significant contacts that you saved and send ready SMS to who are utilizing this application (i.e., shouting caution and GPS following). This assistance is presented by GSM and naturally sends SMS messages to contacts who are utilizing it. It likewise contains an uproarious caution and GPS. The brilliant band will then begin to shout after that.

**IoT Applications in Consumer Use**

IoT devices like wearables and sumptuous homes make life more straightforward for the undercover inhabitant. Furthermore, wearables incorporate extra items like Fitbit, cell phones, Apple watches, and thriving presentations, to give some example types. These gadgets advance organization availability, achievement, and prosperity notwithstanding redirection. Lovely homes deal with subtleties like setting up standard controls to guarantee your house is at its most agreeable when you return home. Suppers that require a broiler or a stewpot can be begun ahead of time so everything is prepared when you return home. Moreover, security is improved on the grounds that the client may remotely oversee machines and lights as well as approving a brilliant lock that mainly allows the suitable people to enter the home (Zhou & Piramuthu, 2014).

A wearable monitoring gadget called a "smart band" has a geo-fencing feature to assure safety (precise location updating). If something unusual happens and there's not enough help around, our smartphone app will send a free text message and share the location with the police. It also stores contacts and similar situations for all users of the application (Jung et al., 2017).

The application and the devices it is deployed on are the main differences between consumer electronics IoT and other types of IoT. The IoT connects different systems, networks, and gadgets for user convenience and communication. A smart home is the perfect illustration of consumer IoT. It applies and obtains consumer-friendly communication and usage by integrating all smart devices with the same network. The consumer IoT is created by a wide range of consumer categories, such as fitness, healthcare, automobiles, and the house. Further component level reduction, improved sensor accuracy, and data analysis are paving the way for connected medical devices as smartwatches, earphones, and TVs have become more popular in recent years.

## 5G Mobile Communication Using IoT

The routine operations of the current 3G and 4G organizations generate a significant amount of estimate, control, and board data. In general, this amount is meant to significantly build something different for the upcoming 5G mobile network. It is likely that billions of remote IoT physical hubs with extended applications and services could come into daily reality using 5G communication frameworks given the foundation's rapid development (Jabbar et al., 2017). Although there are no official details of 5G organizations, there is general agreement on the vision that the technology should be able to realize: more machine and client-driven communications where access to data and sharing of information is available wherever and whenever to any device; depicts the key potential requirements for 5G communication networks from this perspective. It is frequently observed that the 5G innovation can integrate distributed energy resources (DERs), smart meters, and heterogeneous things through various organizations including the web, hand-off, and base station. The majority of the time, this structure can be applied to convey data between the shipper and distant target devices or frameworks. The fifth era (5G) innovation will be the prospective framework that will support the IoT's aspirations in order to achieve the goals starting with 5G organizations aspirations and needs for the IoT (Manikandan & Sakthi, 2018). A scattered methodology was put up by numerous investigations for assessing microgrid state. After the microgrid is demonstrated, it is linearized around the working point so that the suggested distributed state estimation using the IoT with 5G organizations can be used. A correspondence system based on a distant sensor network to identify, communicate, and assess the microgrid states. In the end, it should have the opportunity to accurately examine the framework state using IoT with 5G companies.

## IoT Applications in Insurance

The IoT insurgency could help the protection area. Protection firms might give limits to policyholders to IoT wearables like Fitbit. Wellness following empowers the protection to give customized inclusion and advance better way of life decisions, which at last advantages both the backup plan and the buyer.

## IoT Applications in Manufacturing

The world of manufacturing and industrial automation is another big winner in the IoT sweepstakes. RFID and GPS technology can help a manufacturer track a product from its start on the factory floor to its placement in the destination store, the whole supply chain from start to finish (Ranjith et al., 2019). These sensors can gather information on travel time, product condition, and environmental conditions that the product was subjected to.

Sensors attached to factory equipment can help identify bottlenecks in the production line, thereby reducing lost time and waste. Other sensors mounted on those same machines can also track the performance of the machine, predicting when the unit will require maintenance, thereby preventing costly breakdowns (Rani et al., 2017).

## Applications in Retail

The retail business has a ton to acquire from IoT innovation. Deals information from both on the web and disconnected retail can oversee stockroom advanced mechanics and mechanization utilizing information from IoT sensors. This is reliant by and large on RFIDs, which are at present broadly utilized.

Shopping center areas are hazardous speculations in light of the fact that their organization is inclined to high points and low points, and as a result of the ascent of web-based shopping, there is less interest for actual stores. IoT, then again, can help with dissecting shopping center traffic to let shopping center found retailers cause the expected changes to further develop the client shopping experience while bringing down above.

IoT empowers traders to target clients in view of past buys, which is connected with client commitment. A business could make a designated advancement for their committed clients utilizing the information presented by IoT, getting rid of the necessity for expensive mass-showcasing advancements with low achievement rates. Clients' cell phones can be utilized for the overwhelming majority of these missions, particularly assuming they have an application for the important store.

## IoT Applications in Transportation

A great many people have heard at this point about the headways being made in self-driving cars. However, that mainly starts to expose transportation's colossal potential. The GPS, one more illustration of IoT, is utilized to help transportation organizations in arranging faster and more compelling courses for vehicles conveying cargo, diminishing conveyance times.

Route has proactively taken incredible steps, a gesture again to a telephone or vehicle's GPS. Notwithstanding, those insights can likewise be utilized by metropolitan organizers to design street building and upkeep, as well as traffic examples and parking spot interest.

In the future, there might be apps that stop a car from starting if the driver is drunk!

## PRACTICAL TOOLS AND WEBSITES RELATED TO IOT

Aerial.ai: Broadcom's Private 6 GHz WiFi passageway (AP) and network configurations are now compatible with Aeronautical Advancements' award-winning Wi-Fi detecting knowledge apps, the industry leader and pioneer in Wi-Fi detection.

Nest.com: Nest is currently Google Nest, however you can in any case arrive at this page to find all that you could have to deal with your current Nest items.

Josh.ai: Josh is a voice-controlled home mechanization framework. Like Siri or Google Now, the Josh programming language is used to help regular language voice orders. This incorporates good tidings, questions, guidelines, and that's only the tip of the iceberg.

Further, Josh is used to control and associate any "shrewd" gadget, from any gadget.

Zenbo Asu.com: ASUS makes use of some testing, focusing, advertising, and video-implanted incentives provided by ASUS or third parties.

Cubic.ai: Cubic is an innovation driven, market-driving supplier of incorporated arrangements that increment situational understanding arrangements range of Full Movement Video (FMV); knowledge, observation and surveillance (ISR); and man-made consciousness/AI (simulated intelligence/ML).

Voice flow.com: Voice flow is the collaboration tool that lets conversational computer-based intelligence groups model, arrange, and quickly send off amazing conversational interactions. Voice flow is typically the preferred tool for accelerating and sizing application conveyance. Utilize effective tools like drag-and-drop planning, rapid prototyping, continuous input, and pre-assembled code to accelerate your work process. To design, model, and develop conversational associates collaboratively, quickly, and at scale, Voice flow engages conversational computer-based intelligence groups.

Bridge.ai: The extension to artificial reasoning (Bridge2AI) initiative of the NIH Normal Asset will advance biomedical research by paving the path for the inevitable acceptance of artificial consciousness (simulated intelligence) that solves complex biomedical problems beyond the capability of human instinct.

Sleep.ai: The principal adage is to determine wheezing and tooth crushing to have your telephone. Our Enemy of Wheeze Wearable assists you with halting wheezing.

PTC.com: Modern organizations are confronted with critical issues that call for (industrial Internet of things (IIoT) arrangements. PTC (Parametric Technology Corporation) has spent a lot of time developing the ThingWorx IIoT platform to meet various manufacturing, service, and engineering needs. Thing Worx resolves normal issues across various ventures, from administration to laborer viability and resource improvements. Building Modern IoT arrangements is much of the time referenced as a trouble spot, and Thing Worx is made to bring down these hindrances. Utilizing pre-assembled applications and designer apparatuses, change from pilots to big business scale arrangements.

Vergidris.co: The NASA Ames Exploration Center in the core of Silicon Valley is home to the endeavor supported manmade reasoning innovation fire up Verdigris Advances, which was sent off in 2011 by Imprint Chung, Thomas Chung, and Jonathan Chu. An IIoT clean-tech stage for energy the board in business and modern shrewd structures, Verdigris is controlled by manmade intelligence.

Sleeptrackers.io: This is the latest, rest following innovation for wearables and in beds. Checking your rest can furnish you with priceless data about your overall well-being and health. Find the top rest screens to improve your well-being and rest quality. Look at the freshest wearable wellness/rest trackers as well as independent rest checking gadgets, which can screen different physical processes as you rest, for example, development, breathing, wheezing, pulse, and even cerebrum action.

## SUMMARY AND FUTURE

These days, a tremendous scope of administrations is offered through the Internet of Services, including data search, video real time, document sharing, internet shopping, banking, long range interpersonal communication, and so on. This chapter highlights several applications of IoT in diverse areas. In this section, we looked at the obstacles and untapped opportunities that may stand in the way of achieving the goal of workable correspondence. We looked at research on the quality of workmanship in a variety of industries, including farming, healthcare, and other fields. The section uses IoT a couple times in various locations. A couple of the models in this area make use of the vast number of pieces. The fact that dramatically different developments use the same basic component arrangement is also advantageous. Upcoming 5G cell IoT is anticipated to benefit from flexible communication networks with multiple administrations. In order to do this, 5G has to work with a number of powerful technologies. The biggest challenge here is to organize many significant advancements and provide constant availability with excellent quality.

## REFERENCES

Ahanger, T. A. (2018). Defense scheme to protect IoT from cyber attacks using AI principles. *International Journal of Computers Communications & Control, 13*(6), 915–926. https://doi.org/10.15837/ijccc.2018.6.3356

Alemdar, H., & Ersoy, C. (2010). Wireless sensor networks for healthcare: A survey. *Computer networks, 54*(15), 2688–2710. https://doi.org/10.1016/j.comnet.2010.05.003

Arunachalam, R., Sunitha, G., Shukla, S. K., Pandey, S. N., Urooj, S., & Rawat, S. (2023). A smart Alzheimer's patient monitoring system with IoT-assisted technology through enhanced deep learning approach. *Knowledge and Information Systems, 65*(12), 5561–5599. https://doi.org/10.1007/s10115-023-01890-x

Jabbar, S., Ullah, F., Khalid, S., Khan, M., & Han, K. (2017). Semantic interoperability in heterogeneous IoT infrastructure for healthcare. *Wireless*

*Communications and Mobile Computing, 2017*, Article ID 9731806. https://doi .org/10.1155/2017/9731806

Jindal, A., Dua, A., Kumar, N., Das, A. K., Vasilakos, A. V., & Rodrigues, J. J. (2018). Providing healthcare-as-a-service using fuzzy rule based big data analytics in cloud computing. *IEEE Journal of Biomedical and Health informatics, 22*(5), 1605–1618. https://doi.org/10.1109/JBHI.2018.2799198

Jung, D., Zhang, Z., & Winslett, M. (2017, April 19–22). Vibration analysis for iot enabled predictive maintenance. In *Proceedings for the 2017 IEEE 33rd International Conference on Data Engineering (ICDE)* (pp. 1271–1282). IEEE. https:// doi.org/10.1109/ICDE.2017.170

Karnik, A., Iyer, A., & Rosenberg, C. (2008). Throughput-optimal configuration of fixed wireless networks. *IEEE/ACM Transactions on Networking, 16*(5), 1161– 1174. https://doi.org/10.1109/TNET.2007.909717

Karthika, P., Ganesh Babu, R., & Karthik, P. A. (2020). Fog computing using interoperability and IoT security issues in healthcare. In D. Kumar Sharma, S.-L. Peng, R. Sharma, & D. A. Zaitsev (Eds.), *Micro-electronics and telecommunication engineering* (pp. 97–105). Springer.

Lu, Y., & Da Xu, L. (2018). Internet of things (IoT) cybersecurity research: A review of current research topics. *IEEE Internet of Things Journal, 6*(2), 2103–2115. https://doi.org/10.1109/JIOT.2018.2869847

Malfante, M., Dalla Mura, M., Métaxian, J. P., Mars, J. I., Macedo, O., & Inza, A. (2018). Machine learning for volcano-seismic signals: Challenges and perspectives. *IEEE Signal Processing Magazine, 35*(2), 20–30. https://doi.org/ 10.1109/MSP.2017.2779166

Manikandan, G., & Sakthi, U. (2018, August 30–31). A comprehensive survey on various key management schemes in WSN. In *Proceedings for the 2018 2nd International Conference on I-SMAC (IoT in Social, Mobile, Analytics and Cloud)* (pp. 378–383). IEEE. https://doi.org/10.1109/I-SMAC.2018.8653656

Nennuri, R., Kumar, R. H., Prathyusha, G., Tejaswini, K., Kanishka, G., & Sunitha, G. (2022). A multi-stage deep model for crop variety and disease prediction. In *International Conference on Soft Computing and Pattern Recognition* (pp. 52–59). Springer Nature.

Rajput, K. Y., Khatav, G., Pujari, M., & Yadav, P. (2013). Intelligent street lighting system using GSM. *International Journal of Engineering Science Invention, 2*(3), 60–69. http://www.ijesi.org/papers/Vol(2)3%20(Version-3)/J236069.pdf

Rani, P. J., Bakthakumar, J., Kumaar, B. P., Kumaar, U. P., & Kumar, S. (2017, March 23–24). Voice controlled home automation system using natural language processing (NLP) and internet of things (IoT). In *Proceedings for the 2017 Third International Conference on Science Technology Engineering & Management (ICONSTEM)* (pp. 368–373). IEEE. https://doi.org/10.1109/ ICONSTEM.2017.8261311

Ranjith, R., Krishna Prakash, N., Prasanna Vadana, D., & Pillai, A. S. (2019). Smart home energy management system—A multicore approach. In R. Kamal, M. Henshaw, & P. S. Nair (Eds.), *International conference on advanced computing networking and informatics* (pp. 363–370). Springer.

Rishitha, K., & Ullas, S. (2019, March 27–29). IoT based automation in domestic sewage treatment plant to optimize water quality and power consumption. In

*Proceedings for the 2019 3rd International Conference on Computing Methodologies and Communication (ICCMC)* (pp. 306–310). IEEE. https://doi.org/10.1109/ICCMC.2019.8819700

Rizwan, A., Zoha, A., Zhang, R., Ahmad, W., Arshad, K., Ali, & Abbasi, Q. H. (2018). A review on the role of nano-communication in future healthcare systems: A big data analytics perspective. *IEEE Access, 6,* 41903–41920. http://eprints.gla.ac.uk/165289/7/165289.pdf

Routray, S. K., Javali, A., Sharma, L., Ghosh, A. D., & Sahoo, A. (2019, November 27–29). Internet of things based precision agriculture for developing countries. In *Proceedings for the 2019 International Conference on Smart Systems and Inventive Technology (ICSSIT)* (pp. 1064–1068). IEEE. https://doi.org/10.1109/ICSSIT46314.2019.8987794

Shakir, A. A., Hakim, F., Rasheduzzaman, M., Chakraborty, S., Ahmed, T. U., & Hossain, S. (2019, February 7–9). Design and implementation of SENSEP ACK: An IoT based mushroom cultivation monitoring system. In *Proceedings for the 2019 International Conference on Electrical, Computer, and Communication Engineering (ECCE)* (pp. 1–6). IEEE. https://doi.org/10.1109/ECACE.2019.8679183

Shereesha, M., Hemavathy, C., Teja, H., Reddy, G. M., Kumar, B. V., & Sunitha, G. (2022, December 25–17). Precision mango farming: Using compact convolutional transformer for disease detection. In A. Abraham, A. Bajaj, N. Gandhi, A. M. Madureira, & C. Kahraman (Eds.), *Proceedings of the 13th International Conference on Innovations in Bio-Inspired Computing and Applications (IBICA 2022)* (pp. 458–465). Springer. https://doi.org/10.1007/978-3-031-27499-2_43

Sridhar, S., & Smys, S. (2017, January 19–20). Intelligent security framework for IoT devices cryptography based end-to-end security architecture. In *Proceedings of the 2017 International Conference on Inventive Systems and Control (ICISC)* (pp. 1–5). IEEE. https://doi.org/10.1109/ICISC.2017.8068718

Sunitha, G., Pushpalatha, M. N., Parkavi, A., Boyapati, P., Walia, R., Kohar, R., & Qureshi, K. (2022). Modeling of chaotic political optimizer for crop yield prediction. *Intelligent Automation and Soft Computing, 34*(1), 423–437. https://doi.org/10.32604/iasc.2022.024757

Sunitha, G., Sasikumar, G., Madhan, E. S., Reeba, R., & Supriya, L P. (2021). Intelligent system to find the health care centers for senior citizens based on disease and nearest locations using GPS. *Turkish Journal of Computer and Mathematics Education, 12*(2), 2140–2150. https://pdfs.semanticscholar.org/0509/192a81 14192a47c515ac816432e2dc575fd3.pdf

Sunitha, G., Sudeepthi, A., Sreedhar, B., Shaik, A. B., & Farooq, C. (2023). RetinaNet and vision transformer-based model for wheat head detection. In *Proceedings of the 5th International Conference on Inventive Research in Computing Applications* (ICIRCA) (pp. 151–156). IEEE. https://doi.org/10.1109/ICIRCA57980.2023.10220614

Ullas, S., & Vishwas, H. N. (2019, November 27–29). Flow management and quality monitoring of water using Internet of things. In *Proceedings of the 2019 International Conference on Smart Systems and Inventive Technology (ICSSIT)* (pp. 477–481). IEEE. https://doi.org/10.1109/ICSSIT46314.2019.8987862

Yang, C., Puthal, D., Mohanty, S. P., & Kougianos, E. (2017). Big-sensing-data curation for the cloud is coming: A promise of scalable cloud-data-center mitigation for next-generation IoT and wireless sensor networks. *IEEE Consumer Electronics Magazine, 6*(4), 48–56. https://doi.org/10.1109/MCE.2017.2714695

Zhou, W., & Piramuthu, S. (2014, June 18–21). Security/privacy of wearable fitness tracking IoT devices. In *Proceedings of the 2014 9th Iberian Conference on Information Systems and Technologies (CISTI)* (pp. 1–5). IEEE. https://doi.org/10.1109/CISTI.2014.6877073

# CHAPTER 15

# AN EFFECTIVE PEDESTRIAN DETECTION USING CONVOLUTIONAL NEURAL NETWORK

## Computer Vision Applications

**N. Ashokkumar**
*Mohan Babu University*

**T. Kavitha**
*Vel Tech Rangarajan Dr. Sagunthala R&D Institute of Science and Technology*

**P. Nagarajan**
*SRM Institute oF Science and Technology, Vadapalani Campus*

**M. Bharathi**
*Mohan Babu University*

**K. Neelima**
*Sree Vidyanikethan Engineering College*

**M. Dharani**
*Mohan Babu University*

*Innovations in Computational Intelligence, Big Data Analytics, and Internet of Things*, pages 265–282
Copyright © 2024 by Information Age Publishing
www.infoagepub.com

## ABSTRACT

Automated techniques must be used to handle the vast amounts of data provided by today's big number of surveillance cameras since they are unable to analyze the information manually. For pedestrian detection, the vast majority of presently known techniques cannot handle this volume of data in real time. A new strategy based on the maximum search problem theorem is proposed in this paper to improve pedestrian detection algorithms by randomly selecting a limited number of detection windows from among all available detection windows. Although random filtering may choose areas that catch every individual in a picture, certain windows can only cover sections of a person, reducing the accuracy. Using a regression model, the windows may be resized based on their position. The suggested technique does not need any processing when picking windows. Partial least squares-based pedestrian identification is successful in accuracy and less computational cost, according to the studies.

Pedestrian detection offers a wide range of scientific and technical application possibilities as a vital component of an intelligent transportation system. Many intelligent robotics rely on target identification, which is a challenging problem in computer vision that must be solved (Arunachalam et al., 2023). As pedestrian detection technology improves, the precision and speed of its detection are getting more and more feasible, and the database of pedestrians is growing in size as a result. There are still a lot of issues with pedestrian identification because of the wide range of variations in pedestrian posture, size, clothes, and deformation, as well as the wide range of lighting conditions, backdrop complexity, and occlusion (Ashokkumar et al., 2022). An overview of pedestrian detection techniques from both classical and deep learning approaches will be presented in this study.

Intelligence in video surveillance and intelligent transportation relies heavily on the ability to recognize and follow people (Charan et al., 2023). Counting pedestrians, catching people running red lights, and other types of behavior analysis depend heavily on their work. A specific feature of the software is that it automatically identifies and locates targets of interest in a picture sequence, and does so in consecutive images (Cheng et al., 2020). Banks, military bases, transit hubs, retail establishments, and other high-security facilities are just a few of the places where this technology is now in use. Since the presence of people in a scene gives important information for activity identification and interpretation, applications like video surveillance and monitoring place a high value on pedestrian detection (Isermann et al., 2008).

Because of this, in order to process the huge data offered by several surveillance cameras, pedestrian detection methods must first be used to reduce the volume of data in order to focus only on the areas that are of interest in solving problems such as face recognition (García et al., 2012).

Pedestrian detection faces a number of difficulties. Changes in light and the look of the person, position fluctuations, and poor quality data make the identification procedure more difficult (Gao et al., 2019). Many applications need high performance and trustworthy detection findings, which necessitates efficient and accurate pedestrian detection systems.

Numerous pedestrian recognition methods have been developed in recent years, however the approaches now available do not provide enough of a challenge for real-time processing of pedestrian data (Guo et al., 2023). Because of this, the development of strategies to drastically lower the computing cost is desired. Focusing on optimization methodologies is one way to accomplish this. However, in most circumstances, these methods fall short of achieving real-time processing (Xu et al., 2017). This study presents a new way to improve sliding window-based pedestrian detection algorithms. As a first step, we'll randomly choose a few detection windows from the picture and reject the rest.

Slightly displaced from the person's body, the picked windows may need to be adjusted before being presented to a classifier due to the random nature of their selection (Li et al., 2021). As a result, each detection window is subjected to a regression, known as location regression, to alter its position in the picture. A previous study used a similar method, but with a different goal: identifying superfluous windows (Hu, 2016). To get an estimate of a set's maximum by selecting a tiny subset, the maximum search problem theorem claims that it is extremely likely to obtain the best approximation. Zhu already used this theorem for a different purpose. Reliable findings may be obtained using the publicly accessible INRIA pedestrian dataset (which is commonly used to evaluate pedestrian detection). Using location regression to fix the detection window locations has also shown to be quite beneficial (Ho et al., 2022). As a result, the cost of calculation may be significantly reduced.

## METHOD

### Pedestrian Detection

Pedestrian detection is to recognize pedestrians in each frame of a video and to sequentially put them into a container. For video processing of a fixed camera, pedestrian identification in general may be tackled by: optical flow technique, inter-frame difference method, and background removal method. Background subtraction approach is basic and straightforward to be implemented, which is employed in this study. The block diagram of the pedestrian detection method, consisting of two modules; namely, a main thread module and a support thread module.

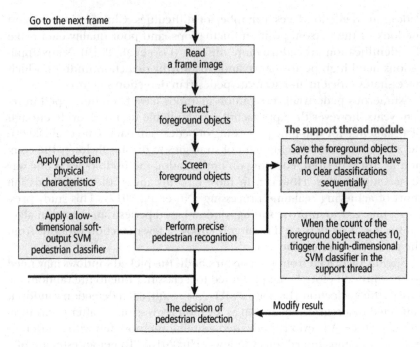

**Figure 15.1** Pedestrian detection method.

## PEDESTRIAN DETECTION ALGORITHMS BASED ON HOG AND SVM

For pedestrian identification, Dalal and Triggs introduced a groundbreaking approach in 2005, based on histogram of oriented gradients (HOG) features and support vector machine (SVM) classifiers (Kannan et al., 2022).

### Histogram of Oriented Gradients Feature

A commonly used method for detecting pedestrians is called HOG (Histogram of Oriented Gradients.) . With HOG, you can create features by figuring out and representing local objects in images, like edges. The HOG descriptor focuses on the structure or form of the thing being described (Kavitha et al., 2018). You may be wondering how this is different from the edge characteristics that are extracted from photos at this point. When it comes to edge features, all that has to be determined is whether or not the pixel in question is an edge (Li, 2017). HOG is also able to offer information on the edge direction. In order to do this, the gradient and orientation of the edges,

HOG features          Flipping the image          Flipping the features

**Figure 15.2** Histogram of oriented gradient.

sometimes referred to as their magnitude and direction, are extracted. In addition to that, these orientations are computed in "localized" chunks of the whole. This results in the whole picture being segmented into smaller sections, and the gradients and orientation of each segmented portion are then determined individually. In the next parts, we will go into much more depth about this topic. In the end, the HOG would produce a histogram for each of these areas on their own. Because the histograms are produced by making use of the orientations and gradients of the pixel values, this kind of histogram is known as a "histogram of oriented gradients." The frequency distribution of a collection of continuous data may be seen using a figure called a histogram (Luo et al., 2014). On the $x$-axis, we have the variable represented as bins, and on the $y$-axis, we have the frequency of occurrence.

## Support Vector Machine Classifier

The SVM algorithm invented by Vapnik and separated into linear and nonlinear SVM methods is a two-class algorithm (Mendiluce & Schipper, 2011). The SVM method aims to improve classification accuracy. Classification mistakes cannot be avoided when using the linear classification technique on linear inseparable samples. Errors are penalized to increase the time period during which they are permitted. The data is initially transformed into a linear issue in a high-dimensional space for nonlinear situations (Mohan et al., 2021).

## Algorithm Effect

It is important to modify the size of the target picture to identify pedestrians of various sizes since Dalal uses a $64 \times 128$ fixed-size window to detect pedestrians. This technique necessitates the storage of pictures at various scales, which raises the level of complexity in the system. Nevertheless, its huge dimensions and sluggish computing speed make it unsuitable for real-time detection (Neelima et al., 2022). The SVM is one of the most widely used supervised learning algorithms. It may be used for issues involving classification as well as regression. However, its primary use is in the field of machine learning, namely for classification difficulties.

The purpose of the SVM technique is to generate the optimal line or decision boundary that can divide an $n$-dimensional space into classes (Ouyang & Wang, 2012). This will allow us to simply place any new data points in the appropriate category in the future. A hyperplane is the term used to describe this optimal decision boundary (Qiang & Huang, 2016).

The extreme points and vectors that contribute to the creation of the hyperplane are selected using SVM. These exceptional circumstances are referred to as support vectors, which is how the method got its name: the support vector machine (Savelonas et al., 2022). Take a look at the picture below, which shows how two distinct groups may be differentiated from one another with the use of a decision boundary or a hyperplane:

## Pedestrian Detection Based on HOG Features and AdaBoost

Later researchers replaced the SVM with the AdaBoost cascade classifier since the HOG + SVM algorithm's computation is too massive and the calculation speed is too sluggish.

## Training AdaBoost Classifier

Combining numerous weak classifiers into a single strong classifier is an ensemble learning approach known as "boosting." AdaBoost is the most widely used and well-known boosting algorithm. To get the final classification result, AdaBoost uses "weighted voting" to merge all of the weak classifiers. The AdaBoost algorithm is seen in Figure 15.3.

## Image Edge Feature Detection

- Recognition and matching of picture features is a key part of image processing and machine vision. In our study (Suma et al., 2023), we introduce new methods for recognizing and matching these features. We describe new approaches to feature identification and matching in this study. For feature identification, we've employed edge points and the collected curvature information they acquire.

A novel approach, dubbed "fuzzy-edge based feature matching," is used to match the discovered features. A novel multi-resolution-based technique and edge pyramids are offered to speed up matching algorithms. Algorithms that have been tested and shown to work well in noisy and changing-illumination situations have demonstrated to be quick and dependable. Target tracking, picture registration, and stereovision may all benefit from the presented techniques (Sunitha, Geetha et al., 2022).

- Noise and changes in lighting of pictures might affect the effectiveness of feature matching algorithms, as was previously noted in this article. As a result, feature recognition and matching algorithms must be less sensitive to noise and light variation. Consequently, edge points are less susceptible to image noise and light change. Aperture issues arise when the edge points create straight lines or lines with less curvature, causing the matching points to be inaccurate. In order to address an aperture problem and identify the precise position of connected points, images should be selected as edge features (Tian et al., 2015). In order to extract the corners of an image from the edges that have been identified, a CSS corner detector is a good choice. Here are the details of the CSS corner detector's operation:
  - Take the input picture and use a decent edge detector such as Canny to extract the edge contours.
  - Fill in the tiniest of spaces around the edges. Mark the T-junction as a T-corner if the gap has become a T-junction.
  - Calculate the curvature of the edge contours at a high resolution.
  - Absolute curvature maxima over a certain threshold are what are considered the corner points.
  - Improve localization by following the corners across numerous lower scales.
  - This is a simple way of removing any corners that are too near to the T-corners.

Edge curvature is an excellent property for edge matching, however only one contour is examined by the CSS corner detector (Victor et al., 2017). In other words, corner detection is conducted on a per-contour basis. In order to provide excellent corner localization qualities for the CSS algorithm while missing out on some of the attributes that are necessary for matching, this method is used. We have developed an edge feature detector technique that takes into account the cumulative curvature of edge pixels in the match window in order to discover more relevant edge features. For accurate edge matching, an algorithm takes into account the amount of edge pixels in a match window.

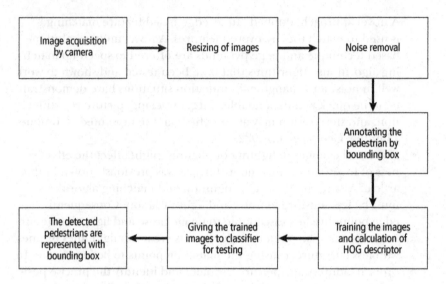

**Figure 15.3** Stages of algorithm.

The following are the stages that make up our algorithm:

- Use a decent edge detector like Canny to extract the image's edge outlines.
- Fill up minor gaps in the edge outlines.

Mark the T-junction as a T-corner if the gap has become a T-junction. These little windows (usually 5 × 5) are used to fill in any minor gaps that may exist in the edge contour. T-junctions occur when two or more edge contours intersect at or near an end point.

## Histogram of Oriented Gradient

However, the simplest method of calculating gradients is the most effective in terms of detector performance (Wang et al., 2019). We experimented with several discrete derivative masks after Gaussian smoothing to see which ones produced the best results. Sobel masks, 3 × 3 Sobel masks, and 2 × 2 diagonal Sobel masks were among the masks that were examined for their 1-D point derivatives (the most compact centered 2-D derivative masks). [1, 0, 1] masks are the most effective at = 0. For Gaussian derivatives, increasing from = 0 to = 2 decreases the recall rate from 89% to 80% at 104 FPPW—1% poorer at 104 FPPW for cubic adjusted 1-D width 5 filters and 1.5% worse for 22 diagonal masks. Uncentered [1, 1] derivative

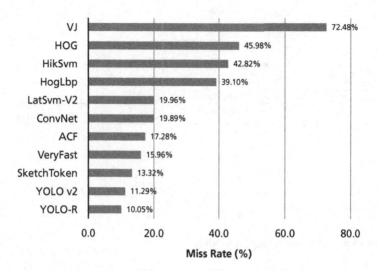

**Figure 15.4** Comparison of missing detection rate of pedestrian detection algorithm.

masks also reduce performance (by 1.5% at 104 FPPW), likely because orientation estimation suffers since the $x$ and $y$ filters are placed at different centers. Gradients are computed separately for each color channel in photos in order to provide a more accurate pixel-by- by-pixel representation of brightness and hue (Yang et al., 2019).

## Support Vector Machine

When it comes to classification and regression, the SVM is a machine learning approach that may be employed. Data points are represented by $n$-dimensional coordinates ($n$ is the number of features you have) in the SVM method, where each feature is represented by a specific coordinate value (Liu et al., 2024). In order to classify the data, we first look for a hyperplane that makes a clear distinction between the two sets of data.

## Pedestrian Detection Algorithm Based on SSD

In 2016, Liu introduced the SSD algorithm. Direct regression of boundary and categorization probability is used in YOLO. This is how it works. Aside from Faster R-CNN, it employs anchors to increase recognition accuracy, and it also relates to the latter. A greater MAP and better recognition speed are achieved by the SSD via the combination of these two structural elements (Meng et al., 2022).

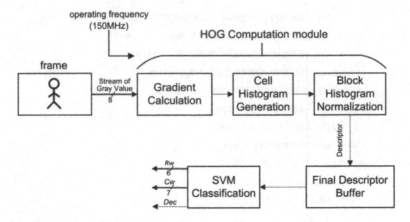

**Figure 15.5**   HOG computation module.

It is similar to YOLO, but unlike YOLO, SSD does not have a complete connection layer, and it does not restrict the size of the objects it may detect. Large and small items emerge in the output images of the front and back convolution layers, respectively.

## Overview of SSD

Full convolution networks are used to build the multi-target detection network of the SSD, which can identify and categorize individual objects in photos. Convolution networks are used to identify and regress the borders of default boxes in an SSD detection framework, which leads to high detection speed and accuracy (Ren et al., 2020). VGG16 is used to simulate the SSD network. Replacement of two entire connection layers of VGG16 with convolution layer stacks for the first five. In addition, the VGG1 network has four convolution stacks added to it in order to extract more sophisticated semantic information.

## Design Default Box

The identification of meta-objects in complicated settings has grown to be a significant area of study in computer vision. Traditional single shot multibox detector (SSD) algorithms had a number of flaws, including a poor tiny item detection effect and a dependency on human setup for default box construction. As a result, the detection results in complicated scenarios were not optimal. An improved approach based on the adaptive default box mechanism (ADB) is presented to address the drawbacks of the SSD technique. Allows for a more even distribution of positive and negative samples and avoids having to manually define default box super settings by introducing an adaptive approach. Researchers have conducted tests to evaluate the upgraded SSD algorithm's detection performance and accuracy in more complicated scenarios with that of the old method.

## Border Regression and Loss Classification

The target position's rectangular box is returned for each default box specified on the detection layer using the convolution process. The network's self-learning ability corrects the default box, making it more accurate at representing the target location, and convolution may be used to determine the level of confidence in the learning default box for each category. In this way, the detection network's full convolution may be achieved. Border offset and category confidence may be learned using the convolution core of $3 \times 3$ in this study.

To accurately determine the SSD network's loss, the input data must be compared to the network's output. Different default boxes of all sizes and proportions are calculated for each ground truth to find the default box with the highest degree of matching. As a result, each kind of sample's ground truth will have a default box that matches it exactly. In order to calculate the total loss function of the SSD detection network, we must take into account both the target location and the classification losses.

## Pedestrian Vehicle Distance Algorithms

Cars have become a necessity for many individuals in our nation as the economy has grown and people's living conditions have improved. Cities' sustainable development has been severely hampered by the fast rise of vehicles, which has resulted in a persistent increase in carbon dioxide emissions as well as a major reduction in the quality of urban air. Ultimately, electric cars will displace existing fuel vehicles and usher in a new age of personal mobility thanks to the implementation of the national air quality protection program. Traffic accidents have increased in frequency and severity with an increase in the number of cars on our roads. Drivers are provided with a more sophisticated driving environment in order to better protect pedestrians. Researchers have used image processing to develop an algorithm for detecting pedestrians and estimating their distance from a vehicle. It is possible to evaluate the method's practicality and effectiveness by comparing its performance with that of the standard HOG + SVM technique. Researchers may use this algorithm as a starting point for future work on electric vehicle pedestrian detection algorithms because of its shown feasibility and practicality.

## EXPERIMENT AND RESULTS

We experimented with SVM and Random Forest classifiers to see which one produced the most accurate model. A validation collection of 1,000 pedestrian photos served as the basis for our evaluation of our models. We tested several regularization settings (C) for the SVM classifier in order to get the best accuracy. Each training sample has a regularization parameter that informs the SVM optimizer how much we want to prevent misclassifying it. The optimization will vary if C is really high.

You may choose to select a hyperplane with a narrower margin if it performs a better job of classifying all training points. This means that even if a hyperplane misclassifies more points, a very small value of C will lead the optimizer to search for a greater margin separating hyperplanes. The SVM model performed best when the regularization parameter was set at 0.001.

In the case of Random Forest, we looked at multiple training models with varying numbers of trees. Random Forest grows a tree using bagging (selecting a subset of observations) and random subspace technique (selecting a subset of features). As a result, certain observations will only be predicted once or not at all if the number of trees is too low. Some characteristics may be overlooked if the number of predictors is too great and the number of trees is too small. The predictive power of random forests decreases in both circumstances. Nevertheless, this is a somewhat severe instance, as the selection of subspace is done at each node in the network. We obtain better outcomes when we utilize more trees. Because more trees mean more computation time, a certain point will be reached in which the benefits of learning more trees outweigh the costs in prediction performance. Random Forest was the most accurate model for our dataset, with an average of 1,000 trees. The hyper parameters for HOG features were also retrieved using multiple block sizes and cell sizes in order to fine-tune them. The results of these tests are explained in results section. According to this data, the block and cell sizes have a big impact on our models' accuracy. Accordingly, the models' performance is greatly influenced by the HOG feature settings. SVM outperforms random forest in all except one scenario (block size is 2 x 2 and cell size is 4 x 4), in this case random forest beats SVM by a wide margin. Conclusion: There is no ideal HOG feature setup, and it depends on the dataset we are using. These results confirm our previous findings. After searching through all 2,100 negative photos and removing false positive objects the size of 64 x 128 pixels, we retrained our model using this new augmented set in order to minimize the number of false positives. No false positives were found in the new model with hard negative mining that was validated using 1,000 photos of previously unseen negative images. Poles and trees were the most common sources of false positive results. Many false positives were removed by our hard negative mining model. This enhancement may be observed in action.

Due to the fact that each item has several bounding boxes, we employed non-maximal suppression to get rid of the unnecessary ones. The reference image for the background removal was created using a Gaussian mixture-based technique based on background and foreground segmentation. As a result, we calculated a foreground mask by subtracting each frame from this picture. In the end, the picture is binary segmented, highlighting areas with moving items. Moving areas in images might be segmented in real time thanks to this method.

After subtracting the backdrop and obtaining the foreground mask, we used contour analysis to determine the bounding boxes for each frame in order to follow the pedestrian. This is because all of our training photos are 64 x 128, therefore we had to resize any contours that were too tiny for the photographs. The heights and widths of the curves were padded to achieve this. After that, we used our classifier to determine whether or not that line represents a pedestrian. For each item, we next utilized the non-maximal suppression approach to eliminate all of its bounding boxes.

## Experimental Evaluation Criteria

The suggested method's performance is evaluated in this section. Experimentation is focused on two primary aspects: a classifier-free random filtering, and a classifier-followed random filtering (using just ground truth). As a comparison to using the detector's initial version, we provide and explain the execution costs (without discarding detection windows). Random filtering is tested in the first experiment to see whether it misses pedestrians when employed on its own. Using a random filter and comparing the results to what really happened might demonstrate this. In addition, we investigate whether location regression after random filtering improves detection performance. If you take into account ground reality, the technique has a good recall, but when it comes to classifying people, windows may be somewhat off center. Because of this, we'd want to see how well a detector does in areas where there are a lot of people walking by. Pedestrian detection results and the number of randomly selected subwindows are traded off in this investigation. The location regression is also done to determine whether it can be utilized to correct the detection window positions and increase the recall.

### Experimental Platform

Workstation Dell Tesla K20c is used as the server in this algorithm. A library of more than 20,000 learning aids is stored on the server for use in classrooms throughout the world. It takes roughly 5 hours to complete the model.

### Results 1

Comparison of pedestrian test results. There are four contrast maps based on the recognition results of HOG, SVM, and SSD, which are picked from the test results.

### Results 2

The MR–FPPI curve. It is thus possible to compute and plot an association between the MR and FPPI values obtained from the two pedestrian detection methods.

### Results 3

A pedestrian–vehicle distance algorithm has been tested and the results are in. These pedestrian recognition and distance algorithm systems will be used to operate an electric car throughout the area. As a driver, you can monitor the distance between you and other cars and pedestrians in real time.

## Discussion

SVM or Random Forest features paired with negative hard mining and HOG feature descriptors may be used to identify pedestrians and track them. As a result, our model is unable to follow a wide range of human postures and can only track pedestrians after some delay is inserted into a video because of the high complexity of HOG extraction. Pedestrians are typically obscured by occlusion in many films, making it difficult to identify them. Other methods of pedestrian tracking, such as optical flow and Kalman filtering, may be included into our system in the future. To be sure, it is tough to track people in today's computer vision culture. However, improving surveillance systems at home and at work may considerably decrease the number of yearly car accidents and criminal activity rates.

## CONCLUSIONS

Representative pedestrian detection methods are reviewed and discussed from the viewpoints of classical methods and deep learning methods. This is a review article. There is a description of the new algorithms and enhancements. It is also examined in terms of its efficacy, benefits, and downsides.

Even though computer hardware and algorithms have improved, it's apparent that the detection of blocked pedestrians and small-scale pedestrians is still missing after analyzing the approach for pedestrian identification. In the realm of pedestrian testing, there is still a great deal of potential for improvement and an abundance of tasks to be accomplished.

Additionally, we developed a low-dimensional SVM pedestrian classifier. The classifier and support thread working together may increase the accuracy and speed of pedestrian detection.

Using random filtering, this study developed a detection optimization method that eliminates a large number of detection windows and then applies regression to adjust the window placement so that it matches the people in the picture better.

Detectors based on sliding windows may use this method as a first step. As an example, it might be used as the initial step in a chain of rejection. In contrast to only relying on detector approaches, we discovered that valid conclusions could still be reached using our strategy even when a significant number of detection windows were deleted. To get the same findings at much lower processing costs, we're going to expand our understanding of how window displacements affect the classifiers in future work to improve location regression even more.

## REFERENCES

Arunachalam, R., Sunitha, G., Shukla, S. K., Pandey, S. N., Urooj, S., & Rawat, S. (2023). A smart Alzheimer's patient monitoring system with IoT-assisted technology through enhanced deep learning approach. *Knowledge and Information Systems, 65*(12), 5561–5599. https://doi.org/10.1007/s10115-023-01890-x

Ashokkumar, N., Meera, S., Anandan, P., Murthy, M. Y. B., Kalaivani, K. S., Alahmadi, T. A., Alharbi, S. A., Raghavan, S. S., & Jayadhas, S. A. (2022). Deep learning mechanism for predicting the axillary lymph node metastasis in patients with primary breast cancer. *BioMed Research International, 2022*, Article ID 86616535. https://doi.org/10.1155/2022/8616535

Charan, N. S., Narasimhulu, T., Bhanu Kiran, G., Sudharshan Reddy, T., Shivangini Singh, T., & Sunitha, G. (2023). Solid Waste Management using Deep Learning. In A. Abraham, T. Hanne, N. Gandhi, P. Manghirmalani Mishra, A. Bajaj, & P. Siarry (Eds.), *Proceedings for the 14th International Conference on Soft Computing and Pattern Recognition* (pp. 44–51). Springer.

Cheng, G., Cheng, R., Xu, L., & Zhang, W. (2020). Risk assessment of roadside accidents based on occupant injuries analysis. *Journal of Jilin University* (Engineering and Technology Edition) *51*.

Gao, Z., LaClair, T., Ou, S., Huff, S., Wu, G., Hao, P., Boriboonsomsin, K., & Barth, M. (2019). Evaluation of electric vehicle component performance over eco-driving cycles. *Energy 172*(2019), 823–839.

García, F., Jimenez, F., Naranjo, J. E., Zato, J. G., Aparicio, F., Armingol, J. M., & de la Escalera, A. (2012). Environment perception based on LIDAR sensors for real road applications. *Robotica, 30*(2), 185–193. https://doi.org/10.1017/S0263574711000270

Geng, H. (2017). My opinions on the bottlenecks and countermeasures of the development of electric vehicles in China. *Scientific Chinese, 2Z*, 135–135.

Guo, Y., Bruno, G., Zhang, D., & Han, K. (2023). Analysis of low-carbon technology innovation efficiency and its influencing factors based on triple helix theory: Evidence from new energy enterprises in China. *Heliyon 9*(10).

Ho, J. C.,& Huang, Y-H. S. (2022). Evaluation of electric vehicle power technologies: Integration of technological performance and market preference. *Cleaner and Responsible Consumption 5*(2022), 100063.

Hu, Z. (2016). Advantages and prospects of hybrid electric vehicles. *Development Reform Theoretical Practice, 11*, 10–15.

Isermann, R., Schorn, M., & Stählin, U. (2008). Anticollision system PRORETA with automatic braking and steering. *Vehicle System Dynamics, 46*(S1), 683–694.

Kannan, K. S., Sunitha, G., Deepa, S. N., Babu, D. V., & Avanija, J. (2022). A multi-objective load balancing and power minimization in the cloud using bio-inspired algorithms. *Computers and Electrical Engineering, 102*(5), 108225. https://doi.org/10.1016/j.compeleceng.2022.108225

Kavitha, A., Ashok Kumar, N., & Revathy, M. (2018). Automatic identification of maritime boundary alert system using GPS. *International Journal of Engineering & Technology, 7*(3), 20–22. https://doi.org/10.14419/ijet.v7i3.1.16788

Li, B., Huang, H., Zhang, A., Liu, P., & Liu, C. (2021). Approaches on crowd counting and density estimation: A review. *Pattern Analysis and Applications, 24*(2021), 853–874.

Liu, J. (2020). Research on pedestrian detection and vehicle distance algorithms of electric vehicle based on image processing. *International Journal of Pattern Recognition and Artificial Intelligence, 34*(5), 2054014.

Luo, P., Tian, Y., Wang, X., & Tang, X. (2014). Switchable deep network for pedestrian detection. In *Proceedings of the 2014 IEEE Conference on Computer Vision and Pattern Recognition* (pp. 899–906). IEEE. https://doi.org/10.1109/CVPR.2014.120

Mendiluce, M., & Schipper, L. (2011). Trends in passenger transport and freight energy use in Spain. *Energy Policy, 39*(10), 6466–6475. https://doi.org/10.1016/j.enpol.2011.07.048

Meng, X., Chen, M., Gu, A., Wu, X., Liu, B., Zhou, J., & Mao, Z. (2022). China's hydrogen development strategy in the context of double carbon targets. *Natural Gas Industry B, 9*(6), 521–547.

Mohan, E., Rajesh, A., Sunitha, G., Konduru, R. M., Avanija, J., & Ganesh Babu, L. (2021). A deep neural network learning-based speckle noise removal technique for enhancing the quality of synthetic-aperture radar images. *Concurrency and Computation: Practice and Experience, 33*(13), e6239. https://doi.org/10.1002/cpe.6239

Neelima, K., Nagarajan, A. K., & Vikram Teja, N. (2022). Digital twin technology characteristics design implications and challenges for healthcare applications. In S. N. Kumar, S. Suresh, P. Vivekananth, & S. Zafar (Eds.), *Advancement, opportunities, and practices in telehealth technology* (pp. 105–115). IGI Global.

Ouyang, W., & Wang, X. (2012). A discriminative deep model for pedestrian detection with occlusion handling. In *Proceedings of the 2012 IEEE Conference on Computer Vision and Pattern Recognition* (pp. 3258–3265). IEEE Computer Society. https://doi.org/10.1109/CVPR.2012.6248062

Qiang, M., & Huang, W. (2016). Comparison of emission of hybrid electric car and traditional gasoline car based on PEMS test. *Environmental Engineering, 34*(4), 166–171.

Ren, X., Dong, L., Xu, D., & Hu, B. (2020). Challenges towards hydrogen economy in China. *International Journal of Hydrogen Energy, 45*(59), 34326–34345.

Savelonas, M. A., Veinidis, C. N., & Bartsokas, T. K. (2022). Computer vision and pattern recognition for the analysis of 2D/3D remote sensing data in geoscience: A survey. *Remote Sensing 14*(23), 6017.

Suma, K. G., Sunitha, G., & Avanija, J. (2023). SegMatic: A deep neural network learning model for semantic segmentation. *SSRG International Journal of Electronics and Communication Engineering, 10*(10), 40–48. https://doi.org/10.14445/23488549/IJECE-V10I10P104

Sunitha, G., Arunachalam, R., Abd-Elnaby, M., Eid, M. M. A., & Rashed, A. N. Z. (2022). A comparative analysis of deep neural network architectures for the dynamic diagnosis of COVID-19 based on acoustic cough features. *International Journal of Imaging Systems and Technology, 32*(5), 1433_1446. https://doi.org/10.1002/ima.22749

Sunitha, G., Geetha, K., Neelakandan, S., Pundir, A. K. S., Hemalatha, S., & Kumar, V. (2022). Intelligent deep learning-based ethnicity recognition and classification using facial images. *Image and Vision Computing, 121*(5), 104404. https://doi.org/10.1016/j.imavis.2022.104404

Sunitha, G., Prathima, B., Yadav, C. C., Sudeepthi, A., Charitha, C. L., & Berinath, V. S. (2022). Speech recognition based assistant bee: Vision to the impaired. In 4th *International Conference on Inventive Research in Computing Applications* (ICIRCA), pp. 1535–1540. IEEE. doi: 10.1109/ICIRCA54612.2022.9985022.

Tian, Y., Luo, P., Wang, X., & Tang, X. (2015). Pedestrian detection aided by deep learning semantic tasks. In *Proceedings of the 2015 IEEE Conference on Computer Vision and Pattern Recognition* (pp. 5079–5087). IEEE. https://doi.org/10.1109/CVPR.2015.7299143

Victor, D., Akimoto, K., Kaya, Y., Yamaguchi, M., Cullenward, D., & Hepburn, C. (2017). Prove Paris was more than paper promises. *Nature News, 548*(7665), 25–27. https://doi.org/10.1038/548025a

Xu, Y., Yu, G., Wang, Y., Wu, X., & Ma, Y. (2017). Car detection from low-altitude UAV imagery with the faster R-CNN. *Journal of Advanced Transportation 2017*.

Xu et .al., (2017).

Yang, C., Ge, H., Yao, G., & Ma, L. (2019). Core and attribute reduction algorithms based on compatible discernibility matrix. *International Conference on*

*Computational Intelligence and Natural Computing*, 2, 103–106. https://doi.org/10.1109/CINC.2009.212

Yu, W., Wang, X., Hou, Z., Wang, P., & Qin, X. (2019). Deep discriminative correlation tracking based on adaptive feature fusion. *Microprocessors and Microsystems* 71, 102854.

CHAPTER 16

# CHRONIC KIDNEY DISEASE PREDICTION USING HYBRID MACHINE LEARNING MODELS

**K. Reddy Madhavi**
*Mohan Babu University*

**J. Avanija**
*Mohan Babu University*

**Shivaprasad Kaleru**
*Juniper Networks Inc.*

**K. Arun Kumar**
*Sree Vidyanikethan Engineering College*

**R. Hitesh Sai Vittal**
*Royal Holloway University of London*

*Innovations in Computational Intelligence, Big Data Analytics, and Internet of Things,* pages 283–298
Copyright © 2024 by Information Age Publishing
www.infoagepub.com
**283**

# ABSTRACT

The prevalence of chronic kidney disease has steadily increased, becoming a significant issue. Researchers and medical professionals from the Department of Nephrology, the All India Institute of Medical Sciences, and the director general of health services Ministry of Health and Family Welfare, and the Government of India published a report. The estimated prevalence of CKD is 800 per million people. Early detection and characterization are regarded as critical factors in chronic kidney disease management and control. Using effective data mining techniques, physicians can uncover and extract hidden insights from clinical and laboratory patient data, allowing them to accurately identify disease severity stages. This chapter aims to develop a model for predicting risk levels in CKD while taking into account all of the symptoms and causes. Certain solutions can be provided in terms of the dominant characteristics in order to prevent the progression of CKD. Various machine learning approaches can be used to build a model for risk prediction of kidney disease, and their effectiveness can be contrasted in terms of accuracy, specificity, and sensitivity. Before applying any machine learning technique, feature selection must be performed in order to understand the dominant attributes. To select dominant attributes, a feature selection method known as random forest is used.

A severe and spreading public health issue is chronic kidney disease (CKD). When the kidneys suffer damage and are unable to adequately filter the blood, kidney disease occurs. As a result of this damage, wastes may accumulate in the body. Stage 5 CKD is the most severe, with the kidneys unable to perform the majority of their functions. Determining a patient's CKD stage can be challenging, particularly in the initial stages. It is also associated with a high risk of death in a short period of time, which necessitates hospitalization and proper treatment. The most frequent causes of kidney disease are diabetes and high blood pressure.

A subfield of computer science called "machine learning" allows computers the ability to learn without being explicitly programmed. Research reveals that the diagnosis of disease is accurate through the use of machine learning algorithms through the use of better methods of computation. These methods provide useful information for medical practitioners through the representation of unidentified patterns which helps in making correct decisions.

Eight to sixteen percent of people worldwide have CKD, which is associated with a higher risk of cardiovascular disease (CVD), muscle atrophy, impaired physical function, and a generally worse quality of life (QOL). Exercise is increasingly being recognized for its therapeutic benefits in CKD patients, including improved physical fitness, cardiovascular health, and quality of life. The majority of research on such benefits has been done in dialysis patients, but exercise's ability to modulate a number of disease progression factors as well as address comorbidities makes it an especially interesting and theoretically important treatment for all CKD patients. International guidelines currently recommend that CKD patients engage in 30 minutes of cardiovascular-healthy exercise per day.

Regardless, CKD patients are known to be sedentary. A common technique used in behavior change interventions is identifying barriers and asking participants to strategize ways to overcome them. Data preparation, a missing value handling method with collaborative filtering, and attribute selection are all part of the workflow proposed in this chapter for predicting CKD status based on medical data. The study emphasizes the value of adding domain expertise when using machine learning to predict the presence of CKD while also taking into account the practical issues of data collection.

CKD is widespread and associated with a higher risk of CVD and end-stage renal disease, both of which may be avoided if those at risk are recognized and receive early treatment. This approach will create models that will aid in disease prediction at an early stage, allowing patients to receive adequate health care. The proposed work is divided into three stages: preprocessing, implementation, and conclusion. The preprocessing stage is the most important because the database may contain redundant and noisy data. In the implementation stage, we will map the results using three common neural network algorithms (probabilistic neural networks, multilayer perceptron algorithm, and support vector machine algorithm) and visualization tools; in the conclusion stage, different results can be drawn by analyzing the graphs. The proposed method requires less time and can be used to forecast CKD delivering precise and effective results

## BACKGROUND ANALYSIS

Data from modern electronic health records (EHRs) can be used to answer clinically relevant questions. The growing amount of data in EHRs makes healthcare ripe for machine learning applications. Learning in a clinical setting, on the other hand, presents unique challenges that make the application of common machine learning methodologies more difficult. In EHRs, for example, diseases are poorly labeled, conditions can have multiple underlying endotypes, and healthy people are underrepresented. This chapter serves as an introduction to the challenges and opportunities for members of the machine learning community to contribute to healthcare.

Renal insufficiency is characterized by the loss of kidney function, which is responsible for filtering blood residues, salts, and liquids. It is classified as a silent disease because symptoms are frequently detected only in advanced stages of the disease. Those involved in public health should strive for early detection. Until now, fuzzy logic has been developed for the management of CKD patients. Information mining procedures are used to arrive at a specific solution relating to the characteristics of various types of patients with kidney infections. We discovered that some of the machine learning approaches being considered are not viable for large volumes of data after analyzing the currently available models. When a unique situation arises, a few classifiers do not have to fit the informational index. The disadvantages were the process's complexity and time consumed.

Artificial intelligence techniques were used for early detection of CKDs. The authors (Senan et al., 2021) proposed methodologies using machine learning algorithms such as "support vector machines," "decision trees," and "random forest" to detect kidney diseases. The method as specified by the authors can be used by physicians for early diagnosis of kidney problems and to prevent patients from reaching critical situations by providing appropriate treatment to them. The accuracy of the proposed approach was also promising as stated in the article. The dataset used was based on the samples collected from around 350 patients—around 25 features were pre-processed and used for analysis.

Machine learning algorithms play a vital role in the early detection of kidney diseases. The proposed work (Almansour et al., 2019) was based on "support vector machine" and "artificial neural network" to diagnose kidney problems. These two techniques proved to be better to diagnose diseases and the same was proven by several researchers. The dataset considered was from UCI machine learning repository. The authors analyzed the dataset by performing statistical analysis after preprocessing the dataset. Experimentation was performed to analyze the performance of the two methodologies support vector machines (SVM) and artificial neural networks (ANN) to diagnose the problems in the kidney. Optimal parameters were derived by the authors to get better accuracy of prediction. The performance of the proposed approach had been measured using the metrics such as the confusion matrix and ROC curve.

An automated system has been proposed by authors for early diagnosis of kidney disease to reduce the mortality rate by providing proper treatments (Ilyas et al., 2021). Machine learning algorithms were used for the diagnosis of kidney failure (Ramadan et al., 2021). Automated detection of kidney failures helps physicians in making decisions about the failure of kidneys and give proper treatment to patients. The algorithms used were random forest and J48 to improve the accuracy of diagnosis. The dataset was from UCI machine learning repository with 400 number of instances and attributes count of 25 along with classes specified as a class with CKD and not with CKD. These classes were expanded further as different stages such as normal function of kidney, mild failure of kidney, moderate failure of kidney, a severe problem in kidney function and finally failure of kidney. The dataset was preprocessed before applying the machine learning model. The models were applied for predicting the occurrence of kidney failure. The performance was evaluated using metrics such as precision, recall, F-measure, sensitivity, specificity and ROC curve. According to the results specified by authors, J48 performed better than random forest and can be used by physicians for early diagnosis of kidney problems. The authors further concluded that machine learning algorithms perform better in the case of larger datasets.

Machine learning algorithms were used to predict the failure of the kidney using the features formed as subsets (Almasoud & Ward, 2019). The features that are redundant had been removed using various statistical methods like ANOVA. The algorithms used for prediction were "SVM," "logistic regression," "random forest," and "gradient boosting." The authors used a dataset collected from the hospital over a period of 2 months also available in UCI machine learning repository. The authors identified several problems with the dataset such as noisy data, imbalance, and overfitting of data. The analysis of data reveals that over 300 observations consist of missing values and noise. These problems were overcome through the use of statistical methods for data preprocessing to identify missing values, detect outliers and reduce the number of features by applying data reduction methods. The methods such as ANOVA, and Pearson correlation had been used to find how the variables were related. After performing the data preprocessing in order to enhance the model-building process, the feature selection process had been carried out using mutual information. After applying data transformation machine learning algorithms were used to train the model. Ensemble learning technique with "bagging" and "boosting" methods was used to improve the accuracy of prediction. The model was evaluated through various performance metrics such as cross-validation, accuracy, specificity, precision, recall and F1-score. The accuracy of the model was better for smaller data samples.

The authors (Bai et al., 2022) analyzed the feasibility of using machine learning to predict kidney disease at the end stage. The attributes used for prediction include the patient's health data and their blood sample results. The dataset used was collected from 748 patients. Data preprocessing was performed to identify and remove missing values through the imputation method to improve the performance of the model. Traditional statistical methods were also applied by authors to pre-processed data. However, the authors observed that the prediction was accurate through the use of machine learning methods. The study also reveals that albuminuria forms a good predictor for kidney disease which will not be considered in most cases while testing the samples in the lab. Instead, the age, BMI, gender of patients and blood results specifying creatinine, and blood urea nitrogen were used as the predictor variables for the algorithm and the accuracy was around 83%. The machine learning model was trained using the algorithm's "naïve bayes," "logistic regression," "random forest," "decision tree" and "K-nearest neighbor. The method used a kidney failure risk equation to compare the prediction accuracy of the algorithms used. Performance metrics such as accuracy, precision, recall, specificity, and F-measure along with 5-fold cross-validation have been used to evaluate the algorithms. The study revealed that machine learning algorithms perform better and can be used for patient screenings in case of kidney failures.

Recently, the rate of persons affected with kidney disease increases drastically leading to difficulty in predicting the disease accurately (Lei et al., 2022). In nephrology, various prediction models built using machine learning models were used for early diagnosis. The study reveals that the accuracy was not consistent even after applying machine learning models for predicting the prevalence of disease. Considering these facts, the authors conducted a systematic analysis of the use of machine learning algorithms to predict the progression of kidney disease accurately. Around 15 articles were considered by the authors for review among 185,042 records. For data synthesis and prediction around seven research papers were considered in which 20 machine learning algorithms were considered for predicting the disease (Singh et al., 2022). The diagnosis of kidney disease using blood and urine samples also provides better accurate results. The study specified that the algorithms "ANN" and "XGBoost" provided better results in terms of accuracy as compared to other methods. The authors concluded that machine learning algorithms can help physicians to diagnose early stage high-risk kidney failures and can also be used in the diagnosis of other chronic diseases.

The prediction of chronic kidney disease using machine learning models plays a vital role in disease diagnosis. The accuracy of the prediction depends on the approach for selecting features and using data reduction methods to minimize the size of the data. Further, the authors (Ma et al., 2020) specified that the deep learning-based approach modeled using a hybrid approach combining ANNs with SVMs resulted in accurate prediction. The input considered consists of ultrasound images to which image segmentation is applied. Image filters had been applied in order to smoothen the images (Mohan et al., 2021; Reshma et al., 2022). The noise in the image had been reduced through the wavelet method. After the removal of noise, image restoration was applied then the region of interest can be identified through the segmentation process (Katz et al., 2022; Yadlapalli et al., 2021). After applying feature extraction classification performed using SVMs combined with multilayer perceptron to identify the presence of kidney stones and cysts. The model for predicting the occurrence of kidney failures was trained using ANNs. Feed-forward network was used in the proposed hybrid-based model (Avanija et al., 2021). The performance metrics such as accuracy, sensitivity, ROC curve, and prediction ratio used in the proposed approach and the results reveal that the accuracy and computation time was better compared to other state of art methods used for kidney disease diagnosis.

Recent studies reveal that the use of a deep learning model provides better results for predicting kidney injury caused due to cardiothoracic (Rank et al., 2020) surgery. The main cause of the injury is the raise in the levels of serum creatinine. This leads to death in most cases and the cost of treatment is also high. The authors developed a deep learning model using recurrent neural networks with various architectures involving different cell types to predict kidney injury following a week's time after undergoing cardiothoracic surgery. Around 300 patients' data was considered to train the model after performing necessary preprocessing. Time series analysis was performed by applying probabilistic measures to predict the severity of injury within 1 week after surgery. The performance of the trained model was compared with the diagnosis of the physicians. The metrics used were sensitivity and accuracy and the predictors used were around 85 features. The hyperparameters were tuned using 10-fold cross validation. Automated diagnosis of disease becomes a major application of machine learning algorithms (Reddy et al., 2022).

Most of the existing methods focus on the accuracy of prediction but in the case of kidney disease special care and treatment are required which incurs costs (Ali et al., 2020). To enhance the usage of machine learning models in automated diagnosis factors such as cost had been considered by the proposed system. The ensemble method based on the heuristics was used for the classification of CKD (Kuraparthi et al., 2021; Madhavi et al., 2022). The accuracy of the proposed approach was better than other state-of-art methods. The authors proposed an automated approach for the diagnosis of kidney problems using recursive feature elimination. The algorithms such as "SVM," and "random forest" (Kong et al., 2019) were used for the classification of CKD. The proposed method was accurate and helped physicians in the early detection of kidney problems (Hu et al., 2018).

## PROPOSED METHODOLOGY

Early detection of CKD helps to save the patient's kidney and reduces the risk of heart attacks and strokes. CKD detection takes less time and allows doctors to begin treatment for patients sooner. It aids in the diagnosis of more patients in less time. This procedure employs five stages (data preprocessing, feature selection, classifier application, SMOTE, and classifier performance analysis) to improve the algorithm's ability to detect CKD at a higher level. To identify kidney disease, machine learning models like ANN, SVM, and random forest are implemented in order to increase prediction accuracy and decrease time complexity. The authors also revealed that there may be a possibility of getting false negatives and false positives.

The dataset collected from the UCI repository. Snapshot of the data, as well as the dataset's features and attributes, were specified in Figure 16.1.

| | age | bp | sg | al | su | rbc | pc | pcc | ba | bgr | bu | sc | sod | pot | hemo | pcv | wbcc | rbcc | htn | dm | cad | appet | pe | ane | class |
|---|---|---|---|---|---|---|---|---|---|---|---|---|---|---|---|---|---|---|---|---|---|---|---|---|---|
| 0 | 48 | 80 | 1.02 | 1 | 0 | ? | normal | notpresent | notpresent | 121 | 36 | 1.2 | ? | ? | 15.4 | 44 | 7800 | 5.2 | yes | yes | no | good | no | no | ckd |
| 1 | 7 | 50 | 1.02 | 4 | 0 | ? | normal | notpresent | notpresent | ? | 18 | 0.8 | ? | ? | 11.3 | 38 | 6000 | ? | no | no | no | good | no | no | ckd |
| 2 | 62 | 80 | 1.01 | 2 | 3 | normal | normal | notpresent | notpresent | 423 | 53 | 1.8 | ? | ? | 9.6 | 31 | 7500 | ? | no | yes | no | poor | no | yes | ckd |
| 3 | 48 | 70 | 1.005 | 4 | 0 | normal | abnormal | present | notpresent | 117 | 56 | 3.8 | 111 | 2.5 | 11.2 | 32 | 6700 | 3.9 | yes | no | no | poor | yes | yes | ckd |
| 4 | 51 | 80 | 1.01 | 2 | 0 | normal | normal | notpresent | notpresent | 106 | 26 | 1.4 | ? | ? | 11.6 | 35 | 7300 | 4.6 | no | no | no | good | no | no | ckd |
| 5 | 60 | 90 | 1.015 | 3 | 0 | ? | ? | notpresent | notpresent | 74 | 25 | 1.1 | 142 | 3.2 | 12.2 | 39 | 7800 | 4.4 | yes | yes | no | good | yes | no | ckd |
| 6 | 68 | 70 | 1.01 | 0 | 0 | ? | normal | notpresent | notpresent | 100 | 54 | 24 | 104 | 4 | 12.4 | 36 | ? | ? | no | no | no | good | no | no | ckd |
| 7 | 24 | ? | 1.015 | 2 | 4 | normal | abnormal | notpresent | notpresent | 410 | 31 | 1.1 | ? | ? | 12.4 | 44 | 6900 | 5 | no | yes | no | good | yes | no | ckd |
| 8 | 52 | 100 | 1.015 | 3 | 0 | normal | abnormal | present | notpresent | 138 | 60 | 1.9 | ? | ? | 10.8 | 33 | 9600 | 4 | yes | yes | no | good | no | yes | ckd |
| 9 | 53 | 90 | 1.02 | 2 | 0 | abnormal | abnormal | present | notpresent | 70 | 107 | 7.2 | 114 | 3.7 | 9.5 | 29 | 12100 | 3.7 | yes | yes | no | poor | no | yes | ckd |

**Figure 16.1** Snapshot of CKD dataset.

The dataset consists of around 24 features such as "age," "albumin," "sugar," "blood pressure," and so on, with 450 rows of data as samples. Around 12 nominal and 13 numeric attributes were identified in the dataset. The samples of patients considered for analysis consist of two classes such as patients affected with CKD and not affected with CKD. Among 450 rows of data 270 were CKD affected and the rest around 180 not affected with CKD.

## Limitations of Existing Methodologies

There are only a few classes in all of the current classification schemes. All present methods for categorizing chest x-ray images and attempting to identify cancer signs fail. The goal of all modern machine learning algorithms is to classify patient data from an original dataset. There is no appropriate prediction for identifying true chest x-rays so that picture correctness may be detected and predicted.

The goal of proposed work is to create an application that can predict lung cancer using chest x-ray images. In this proposed work, chest X-ray photographs with cancer signs from the KAGGLE website are collected to train the algorithm. After the system has been trained, the model productivity can be checked by giving results drastically and checking the efficiency of each unique model. If a person has lung disease, deep learning could help them live longer by predicting it using chest X-rays. This is possible because the outcomes can be predicted accurately and in real time. In the proposed work, hybrid deep learning models are used to provide an excellent technique for expert identification of lung disorders. The possible CNN model is considered for detecting chest disease using pre-trained CNN models like VGG19 and VGG16 in this part. There are four layers such as pooling layer, convolution layer, rectified linear unit (RELU) layer and fully connected layer.

## Proposed CKD Classification Architecture

Overall architecture for the CKD prediction system is depicted in Figure 16.2. The system takes a dataset, preprocesses it, trains a model, and then uses it to build a classifier.

Initially, CKD dataset collected from UCI repository was preprocessed using statistical analysis. Utilizing mean values, the missing values were located and substituted. Next, feature selection of attributes was performed using the recursive feature elimination method, an optimal method using the greedy-based approach. The features were prioritized based on their importance through the metric support and accuracy value. Based on these values the

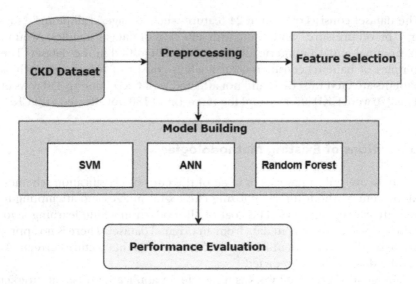

**Figure 16.2** Proposed CKD classification architecture.

features will be prioritized and sent to the model to proceed with the training process. The model building process considers the algorithms ANN, SVM, and random forest. During the process, the dataset will be split for training and testing the model. Proposed work considers 70% of the dataset for training and 30% for testing the model. The model was applied for test data and the performance had been evaluated using metrics such as accuracy, confusion matrix, sensitivity, and specificity. Results revealed that the accuracy was better and the proposed model outperformed other state of art models.

ANN is a computer system encouraged by the function of biological neurons in order to create an artificial network through the connections formed by artificial neurons. The network has the capability of analyzing and predicting the data as if the human brain functions. As more data is available, ANNs can self-learn and produce better results. The data is transformed using necessary libraries in python. Then the model is built using a tensor. Once the model is built then the evaluation process is applied. Based on the results the model shall be enhanced till the accuracy of the results are good.

SVM is a method using a supervised learning approach and solves problems related to classification and also regression. Basically, the algorithm works on the principle of identifying the best decision boundary in order to categorize the points in $n$-dimensional representation. If this approach is used then the data points shall be positioned in suitable categories using the hyperplane to separate the decision boundary.

The SVM algorithm functions by labeling the classes either as positive value 1 or as negative value −1. The method uses a loss function termed a hinge to identify the margin which is maximum. In order to apply optimization for weights partial derivatives are used to compute the gradients. Based on the classification the updating of gradients takes place using the regularization parameter. In case of classification error, the loss function shall be used.

Random forest method can be used to find a solution to problems related to classification and can also be used for regression problems. The method uses the learning process through ensembles combining different approaches for classification in order to derive solutions for complex problems. An arbitrary forest algorithm consists of a huge number of decision trees. Training will be carried out for the forest through the bagging methodology so as to improve the accuracy of the algorithm applied. Results are predicted by methodology using the concept of decision trees. The accuracy shall be increased by building more decision trees.

The random forest algorithm reduces overfitting in the dataset while increasing precision. It generates predictions without requiring multiple package configurations.

- Step 1: Start by randomly choosing samples from a dataset.
- Step 2: This method will produce a decision tree for each sample. The outcome of each decision tree's forecast will then be determined.
- Step 3: Every predicted result will be voted on in this stage.
- Step 4: Choose the most common prediction result as the last prediction. Every predicted result will be voted on in this stage.

## RESULTS AND DISCUSSIONS

Considering a large volume of data without preprocessing will degrade the performance of the algorithm. In order to overcome this problem, data samples should be analyzed and the required information should be extracted using proper mining methodologies. In turn, data should be cleaned and then preprocessed after which data should be transformed. The intermediate data after completing these process patterns should be identified and evaluated. Finally, proper methods should be used for presenting the data. Data can be visualized using data exploration methods.

Initially, load the dataset into the work environment and check for any null values. After checking for null values, divide the data into train and test sets. After splitting, run the algorithm on the train and test data. Finally, the entire process will be completed using the Flask framework. The user can access the home, about, training, and results pages. Following detection, we can predict the CKD, which will aid in decision-making.

The proposed work consists of the home page of the CKD web application. In order to obtain results, the user must enter values into specific fields. The model's generated results are displayed to the user. Working on a dataset for CKD the system checks for data availability and loads it into CSV files. Preparation data must be preprocessed in accordance with the models; this improves the model's accuracy and provides more information about the data. The model construction option will assist the user in developing a model that predicts CKD with greater accuracy. The data preparation option will perform preprocessing, and the data will be divided into two parts: train data and test data, which will be used to train the given algorithms. Then the model will be trained using the proposed method. After completion of training, the result of the model was tested using test data and performance of the model was measured using various measures.

Figure 16.3 shows the age distribution based on presence of kidney disease. Results reveal that the minimum age of persons having kidney problems is around 3 and the maximum age is around 88 years. The correlation between age and blood pressure based on occurrence of kidney disease is shown in Figure 16.4. The results specify that high blood pressure has more risk of getting diagnosed with kidney problems. The model was also examined using 10-fold cross validation and the accuracy was shown in Figure 16.5.

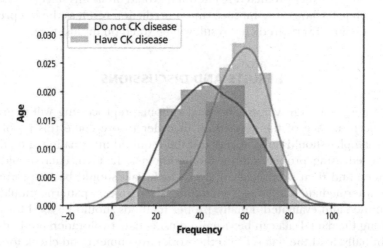

**Figure 16.3** Age distribution based on CKD.

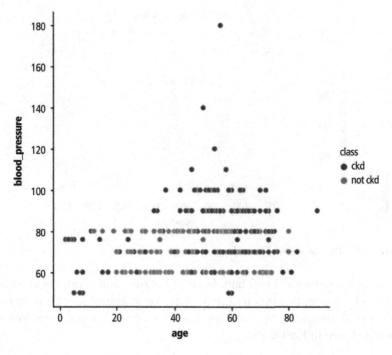

**Figure 16.4**  Correlation between age and blood pressure.

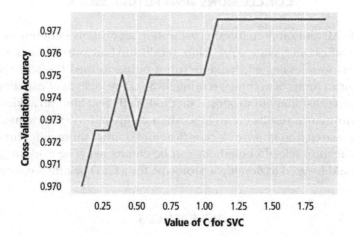

**Figure 16.5**  Cross-validation accuracy of the model.

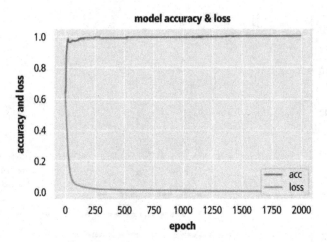

**Figure 16.6**  Plot of accuracy and loss vs epochs.

The proposed system can handle large datasets and produces accurate results. The system can predict the occurrence of kidney problems and assist in decision-making by physicians.The plot of the accuracy and loss vs. epoch is shown in Figure 16.6.

## CONCLUSIONS AND FUTURE WORK

ANN, SVM, and random forest classification algorithms were investigated. The classification accuracy, precision, recall, and f-measure of each of these classifiers were evaluated. Random forest outperformed the other two algorithms in terms of accuracy, scoring 98.3%. The analysis of experimental results revealed that our proposed method is efficient and can achieve better performance results on average when compared to existing methods. More research into improving classification accuracy using different classifiers or feature selection methods can be conducted. The work proposed here could be used to develop a prototype for a CKD healthcare system.

## REFERENCES

Ali, S. I., Bilal, H. S. M., Hussain, M., Hussain, J., Satti, F. A., Hussain, M., Park, G. H, Chung, T., & Lee, S. (2020). Ensemble feature ranking for cost-based non-overlapping groups: A case study of chronic kidney disease diagnosis in developing countries. *IEEE Access, 8,* 215623–215648. https://doi.org/10.1109/ACCESS.2020.3040650

Almansour, N. A., Syed, H. F., Khayat, N. R., Altheeb, R. K., Juri, R. E., Alhiyafi, J., Alrashed, S., & Olatunji, S. O. (2019). Neural network and support vector machine for the prediction of chronic kidney disease: A comparative study. *Computers in biology and medicine, 109*, 101–111. https://doi.org/10.1016/j .compbiomed.2019.04.017

Almasoud, M., & Ward, T. E. (2019). Detection of chronic kidney disease using ma-chine Learning algorithms with least number of predictors. *International Jour-nal of Soft Computing and Its Applications, 10*(8). https://doi.org/10.14569/ IJACSA.2019.0100813

Avanija, J., Sunitha, G., Reddy Madhavi, K., & Hitesh Sai Vittal, R. (2021). An auto-mated approach for detection of intracranial haemorrhage using DenseNets. In K. S. Raju, R. Senkerik, S. P. Lanka, & V. Rajagopal (Eds.), *Data Engineering and Communication Technology* (pp. 611–619). Springer.

Bai, Q., Su, C., Tang, W., & Li, Y. (2022). Machine learning to predict end stage kidney disease in chronic kidney disease. *Scientific Reports, 12*(1), 1–8. https:// doi.org/10.1038/s41598-022-12316-z

Hu, Z., Tang, J., Wang, Z., Zhang, K., Zhang, L., & Sun, Q. (2018). Deep learning for image-based cancer detection and diagnosis—A survey. *Pattern Recognition, 83*, 134–149. https://doi.org/10.1016/j.patcog.2018.05.014

Ilyas, H., Ali, S., Ponum, M., Hasan, O., Mahmood, M. T., Iftikhar, M., & Malik, M. H. (2021). Chronic kidney disease diagnosis using decision tree algorithms. *BMC Nephrology, 22*(1), Article 273. https://doi.org/10.1186/s12882-021-02474-z

Katz, S., Suijker, J., Hardt, C., Madsen, M. B., Meij-de Vries, A., Pijpe, A., Skrede, S., Hyldegaard, O., Solligard, E., Norrby-Teglund, A., Saccenti, E., & Dos Santos, V. A. M. (2022). Decision support system and outcome prediction in a cohort of patients with necrotizing soft-tissue infections. *International Journal of Medi-cal Informatics, 167*, 104878. https://doi.org/10.1016/j.ijmedinf.2022.104878

Kong, W., Hong, J., Jia, M., Yao, J., Cong, W., Hu, H., & Zhan, H. (2019). YOLOv3-DPFIN: A dual-path feature fusion neural network for robust real-time so-nar target detection. *IEEE Sensors Journal, 20*(7), 3745–3756. https://doi .org/10.1109/JSEN.2019.2960796

Kuraparthi, S., Reddy, M. K., Sujatha, C. N., Valiveti, H., Duggineni, C., Kollati, M., Kora, P., & Sravan, V. (2021). Brain tumor classification of MRI images using deep convolutional neural network. *Traitement du Signal, 38*(4). https://doi .org/10.18280/ts.380428

Lei, N., Zhang, X., Wei, M., Lao, B., Xu, X., Zhang, M., Chen, H., Xu, Y., Xia, B., Zhang, D., Dong, C., Fu, L., Tang, F., & Wu, Y. (2022). Machine learning algo-rithms' accuracy in predicting kidney disease progression: A systematic review and meta-analysis. *BMC Medical Informatics and Decision Making, 22*(1), 1–16. https://doi.org/10.1186/s12911-022-01951-1

Ma, F., Sun, T., Liu, L., & Jing, H. (2020). Detection and diagnosis of chronic kid-ney disease using deep learning-based heterogeneous modified artificial neu-ral network. *Future Generation Computer Systems, 111*(15), 17–26. https://doi .org/10.1016/j.future.2020.04.036

Madhavi, K. R., Kora, P., Reddy, L. V., Avanija, J., Soujanya, K. L. S., & Telagarapu, P. (2022). Cardiac arrhythmia detection using dual-tree wavelet transform and

convolutional neural network. *Soft Computing, 26*(4), 3561–3571. https://doi
.org/10.1007/s00500-021-06653-w

Mohan, E., Rajesh, A., Sunitha, G., Konduru, R. M., Avanija, J., & Ganesh Babu, L.
(2021). A deep neural network learning-based speckle noise removal technique for enhancing the quality of synthetic-aperture radar images. *Concurrency and Computation: Practice and Experience, 33*(13), e6239. https://doi
.org/10.1002/cpe.6239

Ramadan, M. A., Abdelgwad, M., & Fouad, M. M. (2021). Predictive value of novel
biomarkers for chronic kidney disease among workers occupationally exposed to silica. *Toxicology and Industrial Health, 37*(4), 173–181. https://doi
.org/10.1177/0748233721990304

Rank, N., Pfahringer, B., Kempfert, J., Stamm, C., Kühne, T., Schoenrath, F., Falk, V.,
Eickhoff, C., & Meyer, A. (2020). Deep-learning-based real-time prediction of
acute kidney injury outperforms human predictive performance. *NPJ Digital
Medicine, 3*, 139. https://doi.org/10.1038/s41746-020-00346-8

Reddy, M. K., Kovuri, K., Avanija, J., Sakthivel, M., & Kaleru, S. (2022, September).
Brain stroke prediction using deep learning: A CNN approach. In *Proceedings of the 2022 4th International Conference on Inventive Research in Computing Applications (ICIRCA)* (pp. 775–780). IEEE. https://doi.org/10.1109/
ICIRCA54612.2022.9985596

Reshma, G., Al-Atroshi, C., Nassa, V. K., Geetha, B., Sunitha, G., Galety, M. G., &
Neelakandan, S. (2022). Deep learning-based skin lesion diagnosis model using dermoscopic images. *Intelligent Automation & Soft Computing, 31*(1), 621–
634. https://doi.org/10.32604/iasc.2022.019117

Senan, E. M., Al-Adhaileh, M. H., Alsaade, F. W., Aldhyani, T. H., Alqarni, A. A.,
Alsharif, N., Uddin, M. I., Alahmadi, A. H., Jadhav, M. E., & Alzahrani, M.
Y. (2021). Diagnosis of chronic kidney disease using effective classification
algorithms and recursive feature elimination techniques. *Journal of Healthcare
Engineering, 2021.* https://doi.org/10.1155/2021/1004767

Singh, J., Agarwal, S., Kumar, P., Rana, D., & Bajaj, R. (2022, August). Prominent features based chronic kidney disease prediction model using machine learning.
In *Proceedings of the 2022 3rd International Conference on Electronics and Sustainable Communication Systems (ICESC)* (pp. 1193–1198). IEEE. https://doi.org/
10.1109/ICESC54411.2022.9885524

Yadlapalli, P., Reddy, M. K., Gurram, S., Avanija, J., Meenakshi, K., & Kora, P. (2021).
Breast thermograms asymmetry analysis using gabor filters. In *E3S Web of
Conferences* (Vol. 309). EDP Sciences. https://doi.org/10.1051/e3sconf/
202130901109

CHAPTER 17

# CYBER SECURITY CONSTRAINED POWER SYSTEM WITH TCSC UNDER *n*-1 CONTINGENCY CONDITION

**Suresh Babu Daram**
*Mohan Babu University*

**Kumar Reddy Cheepati**
*KSRM College of Engineering*

**Killada Sesi Prabha**
*Sree Vidyanikethan Engineering College*

**Venkatesh P.**
*Mohan Babu University*

*Innovations in Computational Intelligence, Big Data Analytics, and Internet of Things*, pages 299–321
Copyright © 2024 by Information Age Publishing
www.infoagepub.com

## ABSTRACT

Cybersecurity uses technology, processes, and policies to safeguard systems, networks, programs, devices, and data. Power system security means keeping the system running when components fail. Thyristor controlled series compensation (TCSC) is a flexible AC transmission system (FACTS) device attached to an AC transmission network to increase power transfer, stability, and controllability. The utilization of a series-connected FACTS device to observe system performance during a single transmission loss is presented in this chapter. A systemic data transfer involving data encryption and decryption using software tools is utilized to safely transport the required amount of data to the destination based on cyber security ideas. A conventional IEEE-30 bus system is utilized to comprehend and simulate the proposed solution.

Electricity is generated, transmitted, and consumed. A power plant generates energy, a transmission line and distribution system transport it, and customers utilize it to power lights, TVs, air conditioners, and motors. Low-voltage electricity is produced. Low-voltage has benefits. Low voltage lowers armature stress. Low voltage allows for smaller, thinner alternators. Beyond a certain threshold, insulation prices increase and line-supporting buildings become prohibitively expensive. Power transmits voltage. Surge impedance loading determines the system's transmission voltage. Our society depends on several infrastructures.

Ideal power system has three networks. Generation, transmission, and distribution networks. The power system has various loads and networks. Power flow analysis improves normal and abnormal system operation. Power flow analysis is required for power system expansion and contingency planning. In this process, bus voltage profiles, active and reactive power flows, the effect of rearranging circuit configurations and installing regulating devices, and so on, for different loading conditions are efficiently analyzed. Modern power systems are so large and complex that they should be analyzed by computer.

Security assessment is important because it reveals the system's state in an emergency. Off-line analysis of a power system's many components to predict individual contingencies is tedious. Only certain events will cause severe power system problems. Using performance indices, "contingency selection" identifies severe contingencies. Load flow analysis of a real-time power system with many buses is complex because many data points are required, including power, voltage, circuit breaker condition, transformer tap position, reactive power source condition, and sink. First formulate the system's network model to proceed systematically. Transmission lines connect several buses in a power system. Power flow analysis can determine the magnitude and angles of all steady-state buses.

## FACTS AND COMPENSATION

Flexible AC transmission system (FACTS) is a power electronic system where static devices improve power transfer and controllability. FACTS devices are used in AC transmission networks. Mechanical switches were used to connect capacitors, reactors, and synchronous generators before power electronics switches. Mechanical switches are problematic. Mechanical switches wear out quickly and respond slowly. There aren't reliable ways to improve transmission line controllability and stability. After the invention of power electronics switches like the thyristor, FACTS controllers were developed.

### What Is the Need of Facts Devices in Power Systems?

Coordination between power production and consumption is essential to any functioning power grid. The need for electricity is constantly growing. All parts must be running at peak performance if we're going to keep up with this demand. The FACTS devices are simply devices used to improve the transmission system's efficiency and to have active power, reactive power, and apparent power. The power aimed is to transmit active power, which is also known as true power. However, reactive power is caused by the load's collection of energy stores. Types of reactive power include inductive and capacitive.

Therefore, the methods used to equalize inductive and capacitive reactive power are known as compensation methods. These techniques supply or absorb reactive power inductively and capacitively. The transmission network's efficiency and power quality are both enhanced as a result.

### Cyber Security

The term "cyber security" is used to describe the practice of guarding computer systems and networks against threats such as hacking, data loss, and service disruption. These days, cyber security is an absolute must for any industry that uses the internet or other forms of electronic communication. In today's world, everything from communication to financial transactions to entertainment relies on some combination of the internet, computers, and other electronic devices run by various programs. Internet-connected devices are essential to the daily operations of all banking, healthcare, monetary, governmental, and industrial infrastructure.

Hacking the system and other security attacks are now a global concern and could threaten the global economy due to the widespread nature of the internet. Therefore, having a solid cybersecurity strategy in place to guard against publicly disclosed data breaches is crucial. In addition, as the number of cyberattacks increases, it is more important than ever for businesses and other organizations to employ stringent cybersecurity measures and processes to safeguard their customers' private information and data.

### Why do we need Cyber Security in Power Systems?

Because of their reliance on networked computers and the internet, power grids are an easy target for hackers. False information inserted by malicious actors during information exchange can lead to blackouts, financial losses, and system instability. Power system flaws can also be hidden with the help of false data injection (FDI). In turn, the operator's ability to see the problems and take corrective action will be diminished. In 2015, for instance, hackers attacked the Ukraine's power grid and tripped substation breakers. Understanding the effects of FDI on the power grid is critical for designing effective safeguards that will increase the system's resilience. Therefore, there has been a lot of study into the means and results of FDI attacks. FDI can lead to erroneous control instructions being generated because it targets economic dispatch. By injecting erroneous load data into a security-constrained economic dispatch, it is possible to cause a line outage and even a cascade failure. Intentional interference with economic dispatch drives up operating costs and yields illicit gains in the power markets. Economic dispatch is analyzed in relation to the potential threat of FDI attacks when attackers lack complete network knowledge. The security of power system state data is vulnerable to FDI because it can penetrate the system through attacks on system state estimation and measurement. This makes it harder for the operator to see the system in its true working condition and makes it more likely that the operator won't take adequate countermeasures.

## Literature Survey

Power system infractions are quantified using a contingency analysis, and both the offenses and the ensuing corrective measures are detailed in (Freitas & Morelato, 2001). Its primary function is to supply the operator with data relevant to the power system in the event of an emergency, making it an indispensable tool in the planning and operation of power grids. In the event that the compensator detects a transmission line failure, transformer failure, or generator failure, studies of the system are performed. Outages of individual components can have varying degrees of impact on the entire power grid, so a performance index and severity index were used to determine how seriously each event should be taken. When combined, these two indices reveal data on active power flows and bus system voltages, allowing for a ranking of transmission lines' severity (Vasquez-Arnez & Zanetta, 2005). In order to increase precision and foresee additional factors in the power system, artificial neural networks (ANN) perform contingency analysis (Vasquez-Arnez & Zanetta, 2007). The revised definition of a contingency and its use in analyzing the safety of power systems were presented. It reveals which circuit breakers are required to switch on the emergency gear. We simulate each scenario by turning on the circuit breakers in the areas that would be affected. Because of this, corrective measures can be taken after a disaster has occurred (Bharathi & Rajan, 2011).

Big data analytics can be used to determine the potential impact of a single transmission line failure. Calculating the line voltage stability index under varying load conditions reveals the system's severity (LVSI). DC load flow studies and an expert system work together to assess the gravity of potential disasters and collect data on potential branch overheating. Turbo-prolog is used for symbolic operations and reasoning (Huang et al., 2018). Each line loss in a network can be quickly calculated and analyzed using the proposed methods (Ghorbani et al., 2016; Ghorbani et al., 2018). To reduce the scope of a simulation, we can use a technique called "contingency searching" or "contingency screening." The recursive nature of the calculation procedure informs the choice of the sorting algorithm used. The results show a nearly twofold gain in computational efficiency compared to the conventional contingency sorting process (Angadi et al., 2020; Angadi, Daram, & Venkataramu, 2020; Angadi, Venkataramu, & Daram, 2020).

At the outset, a bus impedance matrix is built element by element with an algorithm that doesn't call for any further manipulations or inversions. Matrix inversion and transformation are thus rendered unnecessary. Added elements, in the form of regular shifts in the bus impedance matrix, will be considered for the possibility of various outcomes. Since the base-case currents were used to calculate the system voltages, only approximations can be made (Ghorbani et al., 2018).

After a line failure, Musirin et al. (2009) presented a novel approach to automatic contingency analysis and ranking. The algorithms' processes have been combined into a single program, making for a thorough and efficient answer to the problem. Based on experimental results, it appears that this method is not only more efficient than the standard method, but also significantly less prone to human error.

Researching fuzzy logic's applicability to contingency choices for voltage ranking is the primary objective. The primary objective is to research fuzzy logic's potential application in contingency choice for voltage ranking. The paper demonstrates how the exponent index and weighting factors can be adjusted using fuzzy logic. Some examples of fuzzy control rules include the Mamdani rule and the Sugeno rule. It is shown that the Sugeno method is significantly more flexible, applicable, and effective.

Musirin et al. (2009) discussed a method provided for analyzing the safety of power systems. This research produced a method that simultaneously accounts for both apparent power overloads and voltage violations. The validation of the number of security breaches in each scenario by applying the proposed approach. The proposed method is grounded in a practical strategy that accounts for practical considerations.

According to studies, FACTS technology is meant to alter the transfer capacity and voltage regulation of the network (Peruthambi, V et al., 2022). Implementing FACTS has the technological benefit of decreasing power losses in network hardware. Using FACTS tools to solve several issues at once can increase productivity significantly (Bharathi & Rajan, 2011). Modern SVC and STATCOM devices are tested in a wide range of voltage surge scenarios to evaluate their performance and effects (Kankane et al., 2014; Khederzadeh & Ghorbani, 2011).

The FACTS device family consists of solid-state power converters capable of controlling diverse transmission circuit electrical characteristics. Several power flow simulation programs were created to model the operation of different FACTS devices. Three main generic types of FACTS devices are integrated into power flow studies, wheeling studies, and interchange power flow control.

When it comes to managing and optimizing power flow and modifying the voltage profile of transmission systems, the unifying power flow regulator (UPFC) is the most useful piece of power electronic equipment. Voltage stability describes how well a power system is able to keep all of its underlying voltages at safe levels after being subjected to disturbances. As power systems have improved, so has the difficulty of accurately measuring voltage fluctuations. One way to ensure stability is by using the L index. In order to increase power transfer capability, decrease system losses, and enhance system stability, FACTS devices have been proposed for use in electrical power transmission lines and bus voltage regulation. Two machines and five buses are tested for efficiency. In this research, we detail how to use FACTS within a Newton-Raphson load flow (NRLF) framework (Venkatesh & Visali, 2023).

According to the researchers, the system's most unstable bus was pinpointed with the help of the P-V curve and eigenvalue analysis. It is possible to locate a critical line at the point where the index reaches its maximum value. Numerous studies have examined the weaknesses of smart grid systems, potential malicious assaults, and recommended defenses against these dangers (Kim & Tong, 2013). These cyberattacks on automatic devices that are connected through communication networks could hurt the reliability of the power system's large infrastructure.

Multiple indicators were developed to monitor for load fluctuations and suspicious branch flow changes. There is a two-step process laid out here that can help you spot FDI cyberattacks. The first phase identifies if the system is under attack, and the second phase selects the assaulted node. The proposed two-stage false data injection detection (FDID) method is effective, and numerical simulations demonstrate that FDI can lead to severe system violations. The proposed FDID method is able to find FDI cyberattacks and figure out which branch is being attacked. This makes operators much more aware of the situation in real time (Lim et al., 2009).

The effects of FDI attacks on power grids were studied from three different angles. One way that bad data injection can affect economic dispatch is by increasing the price of running the power grid or setting off a chain reaction of overloads and blackouts (Liu et al., 2015). Second, adversaries may introduce bogus information into the power system status estimator, hiding the true operating conditions from operators (Liu & Li, 2014, 2016). Third, an imbalance in power supply can result from a bogus data injection attack on a distributed generator or microgrid. This article lists all of the ways that power systems could be vulnerable to cyberattacks so that system operators can understand the risk and put in place the right solutions.

Concerning cyber security focused on vulnerable entry points in a substation. Issues pertaining to cyber security, as well as the development and categorization of power system communication systems, the evolution of power system control systems, and other related topics, are discussed in detail (Cho et al., 2015).

Frequency and voltage disturbances caused by a cyberattack on an isolated power system and a neural network-based defense strategy against such attacks. It has been shown that an artificial neural network trained with a genetic algorithm can be used to create adaptive proportional–integral–derivative (PID) controllers, which can then be used to automatically regulate the voltage and frequency of the load. These inputs were used to teach the neural network. There are three input switches that regulate the speed of the governor and the amplifier gain. Compared to PID controllers tuned by humans, PID controllers tuned by a neural network can reduce frequency disturbance by 48% and voltage disturbance by 70% during a cyberattack. The safety of any future smart grid depends on fixing the cyber-security flaws in the country's existing power grid. There are many different kinds of older infrastructure and technology that will be put to use by the smart grid. In order to increase the safety and effectiveness of the smart grid, it is necessary to fix the existing holes in the legacy systems currently in use.

Cyber security threats, such as deception attacks that feed false data into the control center, were examined, with a focus on state estimators in SCADA systems used in power grids. When the attacker has complete knowledge of the model, similar attacks on linear state estimators have been studied (Phillips et al., 2009). Ignoring the possibility of an actual compromised model and assuming the attacker merely has a disrupted one. The system it represents may only be partially captured by this model, or it may be an outdated representation. Deception attacks were defined in terms of the attacker's goals, and rules were proposed for synthesizing such attacks for linear and nonlinear estimators. It was shown that the attacker's ability to conduct a large deception attack without being detected increases in proportion to the accuracy of the model at his disposal. The relative importance of model accuracy and potential attack impact is quantified for a number of BDD systems.

Concerns, trends, and future research directions for bolstering the cyber security of control systems used in electric power system operations are highlighted by Ten et al. (2008) who also analyzed the difficulties associated with securing these systems. McLaughlin et al.'s (2016) examination of the ICS cyber security landscape covered key principles and distinguishing features of ICS operation, a brief history of cyber-attacks on ICS, an overview of ICS security assessment, a survey of "uniquely ICS" test beds that capture the interactions between the various layers of an ICS, and current trends in ICS attacks and defenses.

Zhang et al. (2017) briefly proposed a novel type of secure power system data encryption solution and outlined the encryption requirements of real-time data transfer in the power system. High-speed quantum key distribution (QKD)-based encryptions can provide end-to-end network security by guarding against sophisticated eavesdropping threats. For the future of power system data encryption, QKD holds great promise.

Vichare et al. (2017) presented an Android app that performs all three of these tasks automatically, encrypts and decrypts data, and backs up data to the cloud. The AES-256 protocol is used for this purpose. Because of its high computational complexity and security, AES is widely used for both encryption and decryption. Therefore, the time required for the intruder to decode the data will increase.

To examine the real-world scenario of merging physical and cyber systems, Ameli et al. (2018) reviewed a comprehensive framework. Modeling, simulation, and analysis methods, along with cyberattacks and cybersecurity measures for contemporary CPPS, have all been thoroughly investigated. A variety of cyberattack detection and mitigation control techniques are discussed, with an emphasis on their applicability to the real-world power grid.

Online tools were presented by Zonouz et al. (2012) to quantify the dangers posed to businesses by cyberspace and their ability to run smoothly. Better management of the power grid is made possible by cyber technologies, but these innovations may also introduce new risks that must be mitigated. Introducing cyber-induced or cyber-enabled disturbances to physical component operation is one possible repercussion. Large-scale cyber-physical system understanding and evaluation are greatly aided by this idea.

Combining the RSA and RC4 algorithms was proposed as a method of cryptography (Zonouz et al., 2013). The key quality for the RSA algorithm is determined by multiplying two prime numbers, p and q, together. The encryption key can only be used to encrypt a single byte of data. Some adjustments must be made to the RSA algorithm before the key can be used with bytes in files. Combine the RSA method with the RC4 algorithm to add an extra layer of protection to the file. The effectiveness of the proposed algorithm was measured in terms of entropy, the number of avalanches produced, the bit error ratio (BER), and the time required for the computation. It was proved that there was an increase in file security using the proposed method because it yielded a positive result in the testing (Zonouz et al., 2013).

## SECURITY ANALYSIS

Examining how a power grid operates with some of its components disabled. Power system problems can be caused by a number of different things, such as the failure of an internal part or an outside event like lightning or an overload of equipment.

### Contingency Analysis

A power system contingency is a situation where something unexpected happens, such as the failure or loss of a component or a change in the device's condition. Because of their importance to our daily lives, the connections include the power grid, the phone network, and the water supply. Data is transmitted via both wide-area and local networks and managed by sophisticated distributed software systems (Ericsson, 2010; Ghalib, 2017).

Power flow analysis is used to enhance regular and emergency power system operations. Enhancing, analyzing for contingencies, and expanding power systems all necessitate an understanding of power flow (Daram et al., 2016). Due to the size and complexity of modern power grids, these analyses really need to be done with the help of computers. This software and its subsequent evaluation of power flow are known as a load flow analysis. Finding a steady-state solution for power grids as a whole is the purpose of load flow analysis.

Engineers in the power sector have the unenviable task of ensuring the safety of the grid. The security evaluation is crucial because it reveals the health of the system in the event of a catastrophe. For the purpose of estimating the impact of outages like equipment failures, transmission line failures, and others and for the purpose of taking the necessary steps to keep the power system secure and reliable, the contingency analysis technique is frequently used. Offline analysis to estimate the effect of individual contingencies is a time-consuming operation due to the large number of moving parts in a power system. A few extreme power system conditions are unlikely to occur in actual practice. Finding these extreme cases is the goal of contingency selection, and it can be accomplished by developing performance indices for each potential outcome. The primary objective of this work is to engage in contingency planning by computing the active power performance index (APPI) and the reactive power performance index (RPPI) for single transmission line outages. Using the Newton-Raphson method in the MATLAB environment, we have computed the APPI and developed a contingency ranking. It's a useful method for assessing the potential impacts of various power system loading and generation scenarios. IEEE 30 bus testing systems have confirmed the method's efficacy.

Power, voltage, circuit breaker status, transformer tap position, and reactive power source and sink conditions are just some of the data points needed for a comprehensive load flow analysis of a real-time power system with many buses (Sinagham & Kumar, 2013). As a result, starting with the creation of a model of the system's network, a methodical approach is necessary. Transmission lines connect multiple buses that make up a power grid. Power flow analysis can be used to determine the steady-state voltage magnitude and voltage angle for all buses. For optimal power flow along the transmission line, it is important to maintain the buses at a constant voltage. Real and reactive power flow through the lines can be computed with the aid of MATLAB once the bus voltages and angles have been determined.

## SERIES COMPENSATION

Users can control one or more of the system's parameters to achieve optimal performance via the compensation devices' placement. Many power system operational features, including tiny signal stability, transient stability, dampening of oscillations, security of the power system, less active power loss, voltage profile, congestion management, and load ability, are improved by large-scale growing power system networks.

### Thyristor Controlled Series Capacitor (TCSC)

The power supply was linked in series with the capacitive reactance. A bank of capacitors coupled in series and parallel make up the structure. The thyristor-controlled reactor is connected in parallel with the capacitor bank. It provides a series capacitance that is constantly variable. It is the thyristors' job to control the impedance of the system. By adjusting the thyristor's firing angle, the impedance of the entire circuit can be changed. A basic block diagram is presented in Figure 17.1.

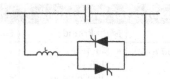

**Figure 17.1**   Block diagram of TCSC.

## CYBER SECURITY

Cybersecurity refers to the measures taken to safeguard information technology resources from intrusion or attack. Cybersecurity is another name for protecting computer systems and other forms of information technology. The goal of cyber security is to protect an online device's data, programs, and hardware from unauthorized access. Without a security strategy in place, hackers can break into your network and steal sensitive information, including customer data and business secrets.

### Cryptography

To safeguard information from intruders, one cyber security measure that can be implemented is cryptography, which involves the simultaneous use of encryption and decryption at every stage of the data's journey. File encryption and decryption using a shared secret key is a cryptographic technique used to protect sensitive information stored in files using algorithms from symmetric and asymmetric cryptography. Cryptography makes use of both symmetrical and asymmetrical keys.

#### Symmetric Key Cryptography
This form of cryptography employs a single key for both encrypting and decrypting messages. Both parties need to settle on a key before any sort of conversation can begin. Ideally, only the two of them would have access to this key. This is why it is also known as secret or private key cryptography.

#### Asymmetric Key Cryptography
In this type of encryption, the message is encrypted using a public key that is available to all users, and it is decrypted using a private key that is known only to the intended recipient. Even if the recipient generates both keys, only the public key will be shared with the sender for encryption purposes. A message encrypted with a public key can be read by anyone, but only the recipient can read a message encrypted with their private key. Thanks to this function, only the recipient can read the message. Therefore, the formal name for this field is "public key cryptography."

| TABLE 17.1 Rounds for Encryption | | |
|---|---|---|
| **Initial Round** | **Main Round** | **Final Round** |
| • XOR With Round KEY0 | • Sub Byte<br>• Shift Rows<br>• Mix Columns<br>• Add Round Key | • Sub Byte<br>• Shift Rows<br>• Add to Last Round |

## Advanced Encryption Standard

The most popular and widely implemented symmetric encryption algorithm is the advanced encryption standard (AES). It offers at least a six-fold improvement in speed over triple DES in terms of detection. It takes 128 bits of input data and produces 128 bits of encrypted cypher text. The substitution-permutation network concept, which is used in AES, is a series of linked operations that replace and shuffle the input data. With a 128-bit key, 10 rounds are required, while 192-bit and 256-bit keys require 12 and 14 rounds, respectively. The steps of encryption are as follows:

1. Key Generation:
   a. ROT word of last column
   b. Sub byte of ROT word
   c. XOR with RCON and 1st column of key and subbyte
   d. Result becomes 1st column of Round Key1
2. Performing rounds for encryption specified in Table 17.1.

## PROPOSED ALGORITHM

### Algorithm to Perform Contingency Analysis

Step 1: Read the line data, Bus data.

Step 2: From line data provided, compute the admittance matrix.

Step 3: Set iteration count as kk = 0.

Step 4: Create a high impedance condition on the line on which outage occurs.

Step 5: The Jacobian matrix in equation is used for the computation of the real and reactive power mismatch.

Step 6: Calculate the change in voltage magnitude, voltage angles, and power flows using the N-R method.

Step 7: Tabulate them and plot the graphs.

Step 8: Set kk = kk + 1, next to Step 4.

## Algorithm to Perform Compensation

Step 1: To read the data for load flow technique.

Step 2: Compute the admittance matrix from the given line data.

Step 3: Create a high impedance condition on the line on which outage occurs.

Step 4: The Jacobian matrix in equation is used for the computation of the real and reactive power mismatch.

Step 5: Compensate the impedance value.

Step 6: Calculate the change in voltage magnitude, voltage angles, and power flows using the N-R method.

Step 7: Tabulate these values.

## CASE STUDY AND RESULTS

### Single Transmission Line Outage

The analysis was carried out on the IEEE 30 bus system and there are 41 lines and 6 generators. The considered contingencies are listed in Table 17.2. Table 17.2 shows the contingencies are 17. The voltage magnitudes and the voltage angles of the single line outage are given in Figure 17.2 and Figure 17.3. The real power and the reactive power flow in the transmission lines are given in Figure 17.4 and Figure 17.5.

| TABLE 17.2 Considered Contingencies | |
|---|---|
| Line Number | Line Outage |
| 4 | 3–4 |
| 7 | 4–6 |
| 9 | 6–7 |
| 20 | 14–15 |
| 21 | 16–17 |
| 22 | 15–18 |
| 23 | 18–19 |
| 24 | 19–20 |
| 29 | 21–22 |
| 30 | 15–23 |
| 31 | 22–24 |
| 32 | 23–24 |
| 33 | 24–25 |
| 35 | 25–27 |
| 37 | 27–29 |
| 39 | 29–30 |
| 41 | 6–28 |

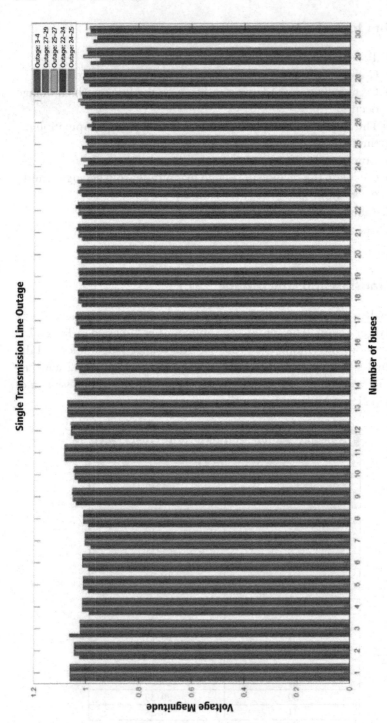

**Figure 17.2** Voltage magnitude of single line outage.

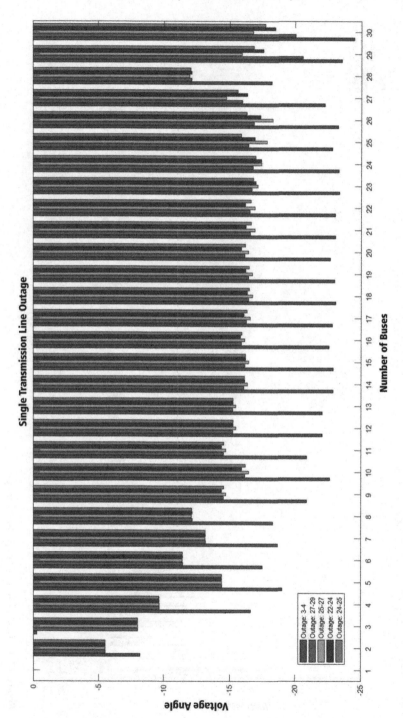

**Figure 17.3** Voltage angle of single line outage.

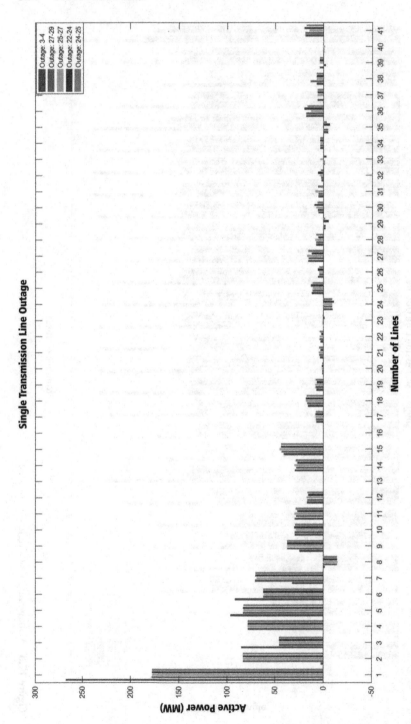

**Figure 17.4** Real power of single line outage.

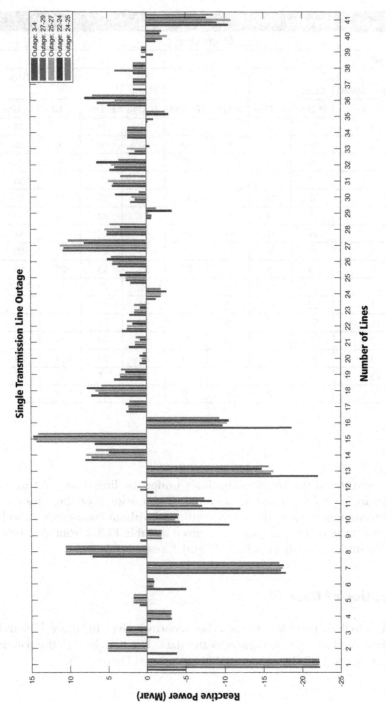

**Figure 17.5** Reactive power of single line outage.

| TABLE 17.3 Severity Table | | | | | | | | |
|---|---|---|---|---|---|---|---|---|
| **Single Line** | | | | | | | | |
| **Outages** | 32 | | | | 4 | | | |
| **Compensation** | No Comp | 5% | 10% | 15% | No Comp | 5% | 10% | 15% |
| **Severity No.** | Tr. Line | Tr. Line | Tr. Line | Tr. Line | Tr. Line | Tr. Line | Tr. Line | Tr. Line |
| 1 | 31 | 31 | 31 | 31 | 31 | 31 | 31 | 31 |
| 2 | 30 | 30 | 30 | 30 | 30 | 30 | 30 | 30 |
| 3 | 35 | 35 | 35 | 35 | 32 | 32 | 32 | 32 |
| 4 | 4 | 4 | 4 | 4 | 35 | 35 | 35 | 35 |
| 5 | 37 | 37 | 37 | 37 | 37 | 37 | 37 | 37 |
| 6 | 24 | 24 | 24 | 24 | 24 | 24 | 24 | 24 |
| 7 | 41 | 41 | 41 | 41 | 41 | 41 | 41 | 41 |
| 8 | 29 | 29 | 29 | 29 | 29 | 29 | 29 | 29 |
| 9 | 23 | 23 | 23 | 23 | 23 | 23 | 23 | 23 |
| 10 | 21 | 21 | 21 | 21 | 21 | 21 | 21 | 21 |
| 11 | 22 | 22 | 22 | 22 | 22 | 22 | 22 | 22 |
| 12 | 33 | 33 | 33 | 33 | 33 | 33 | 33 | 33 |
| 13 | 39 | 39 | 39 | 39 | 39 | 39 | 39 | 39 |
| 14 | 20 | 20 | 20 | 20 | 20 | 20 | 20 | 20 |
| 15 | 7 | 7 | 7 | 7 | 7 | 7 | 7 | 7 |
| 16 | 9 | 9 | 9 | 9 | 9 | 9 | 9 | 9 |

The severity of the transmission lines under the line outage 32 and 4 is given in Table 17.3. The severity number is provided for the lines considered. Among 16 lines, the severity with and without compensation with TCSC is provided. The compensation given in Table 17.3 is from 5% , 10%, and 15% under two different lines 32 and 4, respectively.

## Encryption of Data

The actual file provided for the cyber security is given in Figure 17.6 and this file is used for the encryption of the data. The key given to the data is given in Figure 17.7. The encrypted file is given in Figure 17.8.

| 31 | 30 | | 32 | | 35 | | 4 | | | |
|----|----|----|----|----|----|----|----|----|----|----|
| 30 878.1861131 | | 31 113253208.6 | | 31 113253208.6 | | 31 113253208.6 | | 31 113253208.6 | |
| 32 657.805859 | | 32 657.805859 | | 30 878.1861131 | | 30 878.1861131 | | 30 878.1861131 | |
| 35 587.4421172 | | 35 587.4421172 | | 35 587.4421172 | | 32 657.805859 | | 32 657.805859 | |
| 4 489.8693203 | | 4 489.8693203 | | 4 489.8693203 | | 4 489.8693203 | | 35 587.4421172 | |
| 37 487.2809666 | | 37 487.2809666 | | 37 487.2809666 | | 37 487.2809666 | | 37 487.2809666 | |
| 24 470.7818546 | | 24 470.7818546 | | 24 470.7818546 | | 24 470.7818546 | | 24 470.7818546 | |
| 41 470.3364356 | | 41 470.3364356 | | 41 470.3364356 | | 41 470.3364356 | | 41 470.3364356 | |
| 29 447.8627982 | | 29 447.8627982 | | 29 447.8627982 | | 29 447.8627982 | | 29 447.8627982 | |
| 23 444.0797821 | | 23 444.0797821 | | 23 444.0797821 | | 23 444.0797821 | | 23 444.0797821 | |
| 21 440.0828027 | | 21 440.0828027 | | 21 440.0828027 | | 21 440.0828027 | | 21 440.0828027 | |
| 22 429.9115302 | | 22 429.9115302 | | 22 429.9115302 | | 22 429.9115302 | | 22 429.9115302 | |
| 33 426.2463307 | | 33 426.2463307 | | 33 426.2463307 | | 33 426.2463307 | | 33 426.2463307 | |
| 39 424.664208 | | 39 424.664208 | | 39 424.664208 | | 39 424.664208 | | 39 424.664208 | |
| 20 423.9570403 | | 20 423.9570403 | | 20 423.9570403 | | 20 423.9570403 | | 20 423.9570403 | |
| 7 417.0224935 | | 7 417.0224935 | | 7 417.0224935 | | 7 417.0224935 | | 7 417.0224935 | |
| 9 400.4397428 | | 9 400.4397428 | | 9 400.4397428 | | 9 400.4397428 | | 9 400.4397428 | |

**Figure 17.6** Actual file.

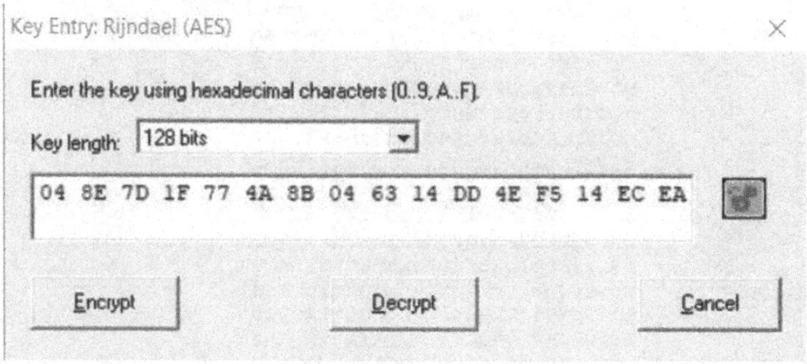

**Figure 17.7** Giving key for encryption.

## CONCLUSION

The data sets are produced by taking various IEEE 30 bus system characteristics into account. Many scenarios involving line outages and generator outages are taken into consideration when observing the security circumstances. It must be sent securely in order to communicate the pertinent info to the other network user. Cybersecurity is thus a powerful instrument. When data is encrypted and decrypted with a key and transferred from one user to another user with that previously shared pass key, the DES algorithm is employed in cryptography. Since DES is a block cypher, it operates on blocks of 64-bit plaintext and outputs blocks of the same size as cypher text.

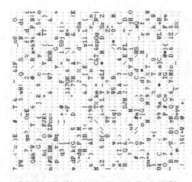

**Figure 17.8** Encrypted file.

# REFERENCES

Ameli, A., Hooshyar, A., El-Saadany, E. F., & Youssef, A. M. (2018). Attack detection and identification for automatic generation control systems. *IEEE Transactions on Power Systems, 33*(5), 4760–4774. https://doi.org/10.1109/TPWRS.2018.2810161

Angadi, R. V., Daram, S. B., Pravallika, D., & Venkataramu, P. S. (2020, December). Contingency ranking through big data analytics with GIPFC in power system under n-1condition. In *2020 IEEE 17th India Council International Conference (INDICON)* (pp. 1–6). IEEE. https://doi.org/10.1109/INDICON49873.2020.9342527

Angadi, R. V., Daram, S. B., & Venkataramu, P. S. (2020, October). Contingency analysis of power system using big data analytic techniques. In *Proceedings of the 2020 5th International Conference on Computing, Communication and Security (ICCCS)* (pp. 1–7). IEEE. https://doi.org/10.1109/ICCCS49678.2020.9276796

Angadi, R. V., Daram, S. B., & Venkataramu, P. S. (2022). Role of big data analytic and machine learning in power system contingency analysis. In R. Sehgal, N. Gupta, A. Tomar, M. Dutt Sharma, & V. Kumaran (Eds.), *Smart electrical and mechanical systems* (pp. 151–184). Academic Press.

Angadi, R. V., Venkataramu, P. S., & Daram, S. B. (2020). Role of big data analytics in power system application. In *E3S Web of Conferences, 184*, 01017. https://doi.org/10.1051/e3sconf/202018401017

Bharathi, R., & Rajan, C. C. A. (2011, July 20–22). An advanced FACTS controller for power flow management in transmission system using IPFC. In *Proceedings of the 2011 International Conference on Process Automation, Control and Computing* (pp. 1–6). IEEE. https://doi.org/10.1109/PACC.2011.5978982

Cho, C. S., Chung, W. H., & Kuo, S. Y. (2015). Cyberphysical security and dependability analysis of digital control systems in nuclear power plants. *IEEE Transactions on Systems, Man, and Cybernetics: Systems, 46*(3), 356–369. https://doi.org/10.1109/TSMC.2015.2452897

Daram, S. B., Venkataramu, P. S., & Nagaraj, M. S. (2016). An improved steady-state model of an interline power flow controller for the multi-transmission system. *International Journal of Grid and Distributed Computing, 9*(5), 13–24. https://doi.org/10.14257/ijgdc.2016.9.5.02

Ericsson, G. N. (2010). Cyber security and power system communication—Essential parts of a smart grid infrastructure. *IEEE Transactions on Power delivery, 25*(3), 1501–1507. https://doi.org/10.1109/TPWRD.2010.2046654

Freitas, W., & Morelato, A. (2001). A generalised current injection approach for modelling of FACTS in power system dynamic simulation. *Seventh International Conference on AC and DC Transmission*, 175–180.

Ghalib, M. T. (2017). *Improvement of real and reactive power control by putting unified power flow controllers (UPFC) in the optimal locations of transmission lines* [Unpublished master's thesis]. Fen BilimleriEnstitüsü.

Ghorbani, A., Ebrahimi, S. Y., & Ghorbani, M. (2018). Modeling generalized interline power-flow controller (GIPFC) using 48-pulse voltage source converters. *Journal of Electrical Systems and Information Technology, 5*(1), 68–82. https://doi.org/10.1016/j.jesit.2017.01.002

Ghorbani, A., Soleymani, S., & Mozafari, B. (2016). A PMU-based LOE protection of synchronous generator in the presence of GIPFC. *IEEE Transactions on Power Delivery, 31*(2), 551–558. https://doi.org/10.1109/TPWRD.2015.2440314

Huang, G., Wang, J., Chen, C., & Guo, C. (2018). Cyber-constrained optimal power flow model for smart grid resilience enhancement. *IEEE transactions on smart grid, 10*(5), 5547–5555. https://ieeexplore.ieee.org/ielaam/5165411/8809237/8558579-aam.pdf

Kankane, P., Shukla, R., & Khare, A. (2014). Review on the research and developments of FACTS controller in improving power system stability. *International Journal on Emerging Technologies, 5*(2), 83–88. https://www.researchtrend.net/ijet/ijet31/16%20PRIYA%20KANKANE%20RISHABH%20SHUKLA%20AND%20ANULA%20KHARE.pdf

Khederzadeh, M., & Ghorbani, A. (2011). Impact of VSC-based multiline FACTS controllers on distance protection of transmission lines. In *Proceedings of the IEEE transactions on Power delivery, 27*(1), 32–39. https://doi.org/10.1109/TPWRD.2011.2168428

Kim, J., & Tong, L. (2013, July). On topology attack of a smart grid: Undetectable attacks and countermeasures. *IEEE Journal on Selected Areas in Communications, 31*(7), 1294–1305. https://doi.org/10.1109/JSAC.2013.130712

Lim, I. H., Hong, S., Choi, M. S., Lee, S. J., Kim, T. W., Lee, S. W., & Ha, B. N. (2009). Security protocols against cyber attacks in the distribution automation system. *IEEE Transactions on Power Delivery, 25*(1), 448–455. https://doi.org/10.1109/TPWRD.2009.2021083

Liu, R., Vellaithurai, C., Biswas, S. S., Gamage, T. T., & Srivastava, A. K. (2015). Analyzing the cyber-physical impact of cyber events on the power grid. *IEEE Transactions on Smart Grid, 6*(5), 2444–2453. https://doi.org/10.1109/TSG.2015.2432013

Liu, X., & Li, Z. Y. (2014). Local load redistribution attacks in power systems with incomplete network information. *IEEE Transactions on Smart Grid, 5*(4), 1665–1676.

Liu, X., & Li, Z. (2016). Local topology attacks in smart grids. *IEEE Transactions on Smart Grid, 8*(6), 2617–2626. https://doi.org/10.1109/TSG.2016.2532347

Musirin, I., Ismail, N. H. F., Kalil, M. R., Idris, M. K., Rahman, T. K. A., & Adzman, M. R. (2009). Ant colony optimization (ACO) technique in economic power dispatch problems. In P. K. Wai, X. Huang, & S. I. Ao (Eds.), *Trends in communication technologies and engineering science.* (Lecture Notes in Electrical Engineering, vol 33). Springer, Dordrecht. https://doi.org/10.1007/978-1-4020-9532-0_15

Peruthambi, V., Cheepati, K. R., Kumar, D. P., Daram, S. B., Angadi, R. A., & Prabha, K. S. (2022, December 1–3). Forecasting the open pool energy market with FACTS devices and alternative energy sources under contingency conditions. In *Proceedings of the 6th International Conference on Electronics, Communication, and Aerospace Technology (ICECA 2022)* (pp. 416–420). IEEE. doi: 10.1109/ICECA55336.2022.10009419

Phillips, L. R., Richardson, B. T., Stamp, J. E., & LaViolette, R. A. (2009). *Final Report: Impacts analysis for cyber attack on electric power systems (National SCADA*

*Test Bed FY08)* (No. SAND2009-1673). Sandia National Laboratories. https:// www.osti.gov/servlets/purl/983693

Ten, C. W., Liu, C. C., & Manimaran, G. (2008). Vulnerability assessment of cyber-security for SCADA systems. *IEEE Transactions on Power Systems, 23*(4), 1836–1846. https://doi.org/10.1109/TPWRS.2008.2002298

Vasquez-Arnez, R. L., & Zanetta, L. C. (2005, June 27–30). Operational analysis and limitations of the GIPFC (generalized interline power flow controller). In *Proceedings of the 2005 IEEE Russia Power Tech Conference* (pp. 1–6). IEEE. https:// doi.org/10.1109/PTC.2005.4524836

Vasquez-Arnez, R. L., & Zanetta, L. C. (2007). A novel approach for modeling the steady-state VSC-based multiline FACTS controllers and their operational constraints. *IEEE transactions on Power Delivery, 23*(1), 457–464. https://doi .org/10.1109/TPWRD.2007.905564

Venkatesh, P., & Visali, N. (2023). Investigations on hybrid line stability ranking index with polynomial load modeling for power system security. *Electrical Engineering & Electromechanics, 1,* 71–76. https://doi.org/10.20998/2074-272X.2023.1.10

Vichare, A., Jose, T., Tiwari, J., & Yadav, U. (2017). Data security using authenti-cated encryption and decryption algorithm for Android phones. In *2017 International Conference on Computing, Communication and Automation (ICCCA),* pp. 789–794, doi: 10.1109/CCAA.2017.8229903

Zhang, X., Liu, D., Zhan, C., & Chi, K. T. (2017). Effects of cyber coupling on cascading failures in power systems. *IEEE Journal on Emerging and Selected Topics in Circuits and Systems, 7*(2), 228–238. https://doi.org/10.1109/ JETCAS.2017.2698163

Zonouz, S., Davis, C. M., Davis, K. R., Berthier, R., Bobba, R. B., & Sanders, W. H. (2013). SOCCA: A security-oriented cyber-physical contingency analysis in power infrastructures. *IEEE Transactions on Smart Grid, 5*(1), 3–13. https:// doi.org/10.1109/TSG.2013.2280399

Zonouz, S., Rogers, K. M., Berthier, R., Bobba, R. B., Sanders, W. H., & Overbye, T. J. (2012). SCPSE: Security-oriented cyber-physical state estimation for power grid critical infrastructures. *IEEE Transactions on Smart Grid, 3*(4), 1790–1799. https://doi.org/10.1109/TSG.2012.2217762

CHAPTER 18

# TRENDING OPPORTUNITIES AND CHALLENGES IN ENABLING TECHNOLOGIES OF INDUSTRY 5.0

**S. Sreenivasa Chakravarthi**
*Amrita School of Computing*

**Jagadeesh Kannan**
*VIT University*

**S. Sountharrajan**
*Amrita School of Computing*

**Saravana Balaji B.**
*Lebanese French University*

**J. Avanija**
*Mohan Babu University*

*Innovations in Computational Intelligence, Big Data Analytics, and Internet of Things*, pages 323–342
Copyright © 2024 by Information Age Publishing
www.infoagepub.com

**ABSTRACT**

In the industrial revolution, we are emerging through Industry 5.0 and creating Society 5.0 which is technologically strong enough to solve day-to-day living issues. Its goal is to provide resource-efficient and user-preferred industrial products relative to Industry 4.0 by harnessing the inventiveness of human experts in combination with effective, intelligent, and reliable machines. Industry 5.0 is anticipated to benefit from a variety of innovative technologies and applications that will enable increased production and spontaneous delivery of customized products.

European Commission interprets Industry 5.0 as "value driven" and hence expects it to create a society with values, powered by technology. This would be a boon for the human race to keep up their living style with ethical values and technological strength as two edges of a sword. Industry 5.0 embraces the capacity of industry to fulfill social goals beyond jobs and growth, transforming it into a resilient source of wealth by enabling manufacturing to respect our planet's limitations and putting the well-being of industry workers at the core of the production cycle.

In this chapter, we aim to provide a brief survey on enabling technologies of Industry 5.0. Also, the chapter discusses the opportunities to sustain in Society 5.0 leading to Industry 5.0 and potential challenges on which the researchers geared up to provide effective and feasible solutions.{/ABS}
Industry 5.0 emphasizes the collaboration between humans and technology, utilizing cognitive computing to create products and services that prioritize the needs and capabilities of the user. It utilizes advanced technologies like Internet of things (IoT) and big data to enhance human work and augment human abilities.

The vision of Industry 5.0 is as shown in Figure 18.1, which can be interpreted in the following brief statements (Berg, 2022).

- Industry 5.0 places a strong emphasis on the integration of human labor and technology in industrial settings.
- Instead of viewing robots as a replacement for human workers, Industry 5.0 focuses on utilizing technology to enhance and support human capabilities in the workplace.
- Human workers in manufacturing are reallocated to roles that involve problem-solving and decision-making, moving away from repetitive tasks.
- Industry 5.0 aims to recognize the limitations and drawbacks of excessive automation and find a balanced approach for optimized manufacturing processes.
- The goal is to deliver the highest quality customer experience and offer personalized options for consumers through "mass customization."

**Figure 18.1**  Vision of Industry 5.0.

- Building flexible and adaptable supply chain systems is a key aspect of Industry 5.0.
- Industry 5.0 prioritizes the design and production of interactive consumer products that enhance the user experience.
- Security and safety concerns associated with the increasing interconnectedness of industrial systems are addressed in Industry 5.0.
- Designing and manufacturing so-called "experience-activated" (interactive) consumer products.

## ENABLING TECHNOLOGIES OF INDUSTRY 5.0

The Enabling Technologies of Industry 5.0 are as under (Müller, 2020):

1. Individualized human–machine interaction
2. Bio-inspired technologies and smart materials
3. Digital twins and simulation
4. Data transmission, storage, and analysis technologies
5. Artificial intelligence
6. Energy-efficiency, renewables, storage, and autonomous technologies

On a broader note, the enabling technologies from the computer science domain are grouped together as under, based on their importance in the existence and survival of Industry 5.0:

1. Big data
2. Internet of things
3. Computational intelligence

In the forthcoming section of the chapter, we shall look into a detailed study on the contributions of the aforesaid enabling technologies.

## BIG DATA, IOT, AND COMPUTATIONAL INTELLIGENCE IN INDUSTRY 5.0

### IoT

In the IoT ecosystem, data is collected from various devices and appliances through IoT-enabled gateways and sent to a cloud-based server for analysis. Advanced analytic tools and machine learning (ML) techniques are used to process the data and generate recommendations for optimal actions. These recommendations are then implemented by actuators, which control the flow of information to the IoT appliances for further processing. The implementation of innovative IoT standards is essential for transitioning from traditional sensor networks to systems of intelligent sensors with actuation capabilities. This evolution towards the "Internet of intelligent things (IIoT)" involves creating intelligent, connected devices that can understand their surroundings and make decisions independently (Goundar et al., 2020). This allows for faster response times in time-critical situations as decisions are made in a decentralized manner.

The IoT enables the collection of large amounts of data, which has become a valuable asset for businesses and organizations. When this data is combined with the power of AI, as illustrated in Figure 18.2, it allows for the efficient analysis of unstructured data to reveal valuable insights and inform decision-making processes.

### Decision Tree in IoT

By ordering instances according to their features, a decision tree is a technique used to solve categorization issues. The most pertinent attribute

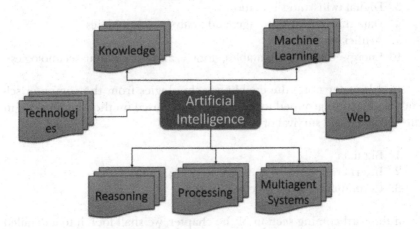

**Figure 18.2** The classification of AI based on its power when merged with data.

to divide the training instances is found using a variety of methodologies, including knowledge gain and Gini index. Building a decision tree entails pre- and post-pruning to minimize its size, modifying the search space between items, utilizing an optimal search model to eliminate duplicate features, and finally turning the finished tree structure into a usable data format, such as a set of rules. Decision trees are often used in real world applications such as pattern recognition, decision-making, tracking, safety, and health management in the IoT.

## Random Forest in IoT

One of the most appreciated supervised learning is random forest which uses multiple decision trees to make a prediction. Every tree in the forest is constructed at random before being learned to make a vote for the best class. The final classification result is determined by the class with the most votes. One of the benefits of random forest is that it doesn't require a lot of input parameters but is still able to achieve high computational accuracy. This makes it well-suited for use in IoT devices across various domains. For example, using features obtained from network traffic, a random forest model can accurately identify different types of IoT devices, even unauthorized ones.

## Clustering

The K-means clustering technique divides data points into a predetermined number of clusters according to how similar they are. K-means is a valuable tool for analyzing huge, unlabeled datasets since it aims to find patterns in the data. This technique is fast and efficient, and can even be used in distributed computing environments to process large amounts of data. Researchers have also applied K-means to analyze travel patterns and identify consistencies in the data.

DBSCAN is a density-based clustering algorithm that groups together data points that are closely located to each other in the feature space. It is a well-liked technique for grouping unlabeled data, and it is frequently applied in a number of real-world applications, including spotting temperature anomalies, traffic management systems, emotion identification, and X-ray crystallography. It's suitable for datasets with varying densities, and it does not require the user to specify the number of clusters in advance.

## Support Vector Machine in UIoT

Support vector machines (SVMs) are a type of supervised learning algorithm that separates data into different classes by creating a hyperplane that maximizes the distance between the classes. They are particularly useful for datasets with a large number of features but a small number of samples. The primary benefit of SVMs is their ability to perform real-time intrusion detection and adapt to changing patterns. Variants of SVMs, such as QS-SVM, CESVM, including SVDD, are commonly utilized in applications of security such as detection of anomaly and intrusion. All of them are also efficient in terms of memory usage and computation time.

## One Class Support Vector Machine

One class support vector machines (OCSVM) following a semi-supervised method is a very strong extension of SVMs. It establishes a barrier between the training data and any new data that deviates from this limit is referred to as an outlier or anomaly. Due to its ability to identify unusual patterns, OCSVMs are useful in scenarios such as detection of anomaly in wireless sensor networks, detection of intrusion in networks, and evaluating the performance of IoT-based equipment.

## Ensemble Learning Models in IoT

Ensemble learning (EL) is a method that combines multiple basic classification models to create a more effective and efficient output. Studies have shown that different models perform better for different applications. As a result, researchers have begun to combine different classifiers to increase precision. Additionally, EL models use various techniques to reduce variance and are less prone to overfitting. Along with online intrusion, detection of anomaly in an IoT-based environmental information as well as the assessment of real-world datasets for precise decision-making in IoT devices have successfully used EL.

## Neural Networks

Since neural networks (NNs) have condensed representations, they are effective models for processing new data instances. NNs come in a variety of forms with a range of uses. The multilayer perceptron, usually referred to as a feed-forward neural network (FFNN), is one form that is frequently used. In an FFNN, a nonlinear or activation function controls the activity of each layer. Providing there are enough hidden units, an FFNN with at least two hidden layers may roughly approximate a randomized transfer of space from a limited input to a limited output. However, choosing the best weights for an FFNN is a computationally challenging task. The weights can be learned using a variety of methods, including Nesterov's accelerated gradient, stochastic gradient descent, and adaptive moment estimation. FFNNs may be utilized in IoT applications for energy management, decision-making, feature selection, and computing complexity reduction.

## Social Networks and the Internet of Intelligent Things

Social media has become a vital aspect of modern society, with millions of individuals regularly engaging, connecting, and sharing their thoughts, opinions, and ideas. This allows for collective problem-solving, where a group of people can come to solutions more efficiently than a single individual. With the rise of the IoT, intelligent sensors are now able to categorize the actions of large groups of people in real-time. IoT has also enabled new forms of networking, such as IoIT and robotics as a service, which adds intelligence to connected devices and allows for the use of robots and collaborative robots (COBOTs) as services. By applying principles of social networking to the IoT, significant changes and benefits can be achieved. In the IoT, groups can be formed by humans, robots, or a combination of both, creating virtual communities. Continuous research is also being conducted on incorporating other intelligent beings into social networks in the IoT. Examples of this include relationships between co-located objects, social objects, and ownership objects, which are all part of the social Internet of things (SIoT).

## Principal Component Analysis

Principal Component Analysis (PCA) is a dimensionality reduction technique that aims to project high-dimensional data onto a lower-dimensional linear subspace, called the principal subspace. It uses an iterative eigenvalue decomposition method to achieve this goal. This method is widely used for data visualization and compression, making it an important pre-processing step in ML. A variant of PCA, called canonical correlation analysis, deals with multiple variables, and aims to find the most highly correlated linear subspaces among them. This allows for a relationship to be established between the variables within one subspace and a single component from the other subspace.

## Bagging

Bagging, often referred to as bootstrap aggregating, is a technique for enhancing the stability and accuracy of ML techniques by reducing overfitting. By randomly choosing data points from the initial training set with replacement, several training datasets are created. Then, an ML technique is trained on each generated dataset. This method can be applied to various ML approaches, such as decision trees, random forests, and NNs, and has been shown to improve their performance.

## Artificial Intelligence in Analytical Skills for IoT

Businesses have been utilizing analytical techniques for many years, and now they are focused on developing their AI capabilities. In the past, companies focused on using data and statistical analysis to improve decision-making, but now they are primarily focused on utilizing AI to enhance these capabilities. AI is not limited to statistical methods like ML and deep learning (DL; Chander et al., 2022), which are rapidly gaining popularity and becoming in high demand. Organizations that value analytics should invest in these technologies and develop new nonstatistical abilities.

The innovative metrics has seen several changes, some of which are listed here:

1. Analytics 1.0 is the first stage of data analysis and refers to the use of traditional methods and tools for decision-making. This stage is characterized by the use of manual analysis and the reliance on internal decision-making.
2. Analytics 2.0 is the next stage of data analysis, characterized by the emergence of big data analytics tools like Hadoop, and the development of data-driven products and services for external clients.
3. Analytics 3.0 is the stage where companies began to focus on creating data and analytics-based products and services, using advanced ML models. Analytics 4.0 is the current stage, where organizations are heavily incorporating AI and cognitive-based models into their analytical processes. This stage also includes the use of automated ML and the integration of various AI models to improve accuracy and efficiency.

The use of AI in analytics is driven by a combination of skill gaps and the need for internal partnerships to support AI development.

Unsupervised learning, on the other hand, deals with unknown results and is used to identify patterns and relationships in data. This method is often used in clustering and dimensionality reduction techniques. Furthermore, semi-supervised learning combines both supervised and unsupervised techniques, where a small portion of the data is labeled and the rest is unlabeled. This method is useful in scenarios where labeled data is scarce. Overall, the integration of AI and analytics has the potential to improve the accuracy and efficiency of decision-making processes in various industries. As more organizations adopt these technologies, it is important for companies to stay up-to-date with the latest developments in AI and analytics to remain competitive in the market.

In summary, Analytics 4.0 is the latest evolution in data analytics, which heavily relies on AI and cognitive-based models to improve analytical sophistication. It is expected to have a greater impact than previous automation evolutions, and organizations that adopt it quickly will have a competitive advantage. To fully understand and utilize the potential of AI in Analytics 4.0, businesses must consider the effects of AI on creativity, the new skills required, and the implementation of a practical action plan. Additionally, organizations that have a strong foundation in their current analytical abilities will have a head start in the implementation of AI in their analytics.

## Deep Learning for Analytics for IoT

IoT based devices and systems are becoming increasingly popular in various industries and applications. These devices are able to collect large amounts of data from their surrounding environments, which can be used to gain valuable insights and make predictions. As a result, deploying analytical models on these data streams is crucial for extracting meaningful information, forecasting future trends and taking appropriate actions. This makes IoT applications a valuable tool for businesses and can enhance the quality of life in various ways.

In recent years, IoT-based devices have been collecting large amounts of sensor data from their surrounding environments. This data can be used to extract valuable insights, make predictions, and take control of the results. This has made IoT applications a valuable tool for businesses and has greatly improved the quality of life. The use of intelligent learning mechanisms such as DL and ML has been critical to the success of these applications. Future applications are thought to benefit greatly from the convergence of DL and IoT as it can quickly address the analytical needs of real-time IoT applications. The growth of IoT has also led to the expansion of big data, and it is important for stakeholders to understand the meaning, building blocks, capabilities, and challenges of both IoT and big data. The relationship between IoT and big data is strong, with IoT being a significant source of data for big data and big data being a valuable tool for expanding the capabilities and services of IoT applications (Chander et al., 2022).

1. The characteristics of IoT data and how they differ from those of large standard data were necessary to identify in order to better understand the needs for IoT-based data analytics (Fortino & Trunfio, 2014; Hassan et al., 2017; Jha et al., 2017; Yang et al., 2017) a few of them are listed below:

2. Large-Scale Streaming Data: IoT applications collect tremendous amounts of data when deployed with a large number of dispersed devices, creating a large amount of ongoing streaming data.

3. Heterogeneity: IoT is a heterogeneous linked network, and as a result, various IoT data collecting devices together with disparate results provide heterogeneous data.

4. The link between time and space: At this time, the majority of IoT appliances are situated in the real world. Here, sensor devices are placed in a specific location, and each piece of data has a time and location stamp.

5. High noise data: It is vital to remove them from any decision-making systems prior to implementing them since doing so would affect the results. This is because IoT queries result in noisy data because of the dynamic changing environments, minute incorrect bits, and outliers that the IoT generates.

Obtaining meaningful insights from large amounts of data is a complex task that requires advanced techniques, innovative strategies, and modern infrastructure. However, with the advancements in ML and DL, it is now possible to effectively analyze and extract information from big data in the context of IoT devices. For example, Speedy and constant streaming data is necessary for IoT gadgets like detection of fire and vehicle recognition to operate successfully. For genuine data stream analysis, researchers have created a variety of techniques and strategies that make use of cloud-based systems' capabilities.

Additionally, for certain applications, it may be more efficient to perform analytics on smaller scale platforms, such as fog/edge computing, in order to achieve fast and accurate decision-making. For example, in healthcare-related applications, quick and accurate identification is crucial to prevent negative outcomes.

## Edge Computing in IoT

The huge quantity of data generated by connected IoT devices are often gathered and analyzed at the suitable objects to yield needful information.

As a result, today's IoT setups all rely heavily on data activities. Since the courts of massive detecting then boost data maintained in IoT, big data enables IoT applications. The diverse connections in IoT also result in the collection of unstructured, multivariate data that requires further analysis to be able to extract the useful information (Davenport & Kirby, 2016; Davenport & Harris, 2017; Davenpoprt & Mahidhar, 2018). IoT is the next technology revolution because of the rapid growth of many technologies, but it will be complicated by the need for extensive data processing, storage, and analytical knowledge. IoT uses real-world applications which are used to handle continuous and constant streaming, which disrupts the data storage capacities among many companies. As a result, more data centers are required to manage the information gathered by IoT devices. Utilizing the application platform as a service to send the data to the cloud is one likely solution. These days, cloud computing is a well-known technology that provides computer resources or online data storage.

A variety of services are provided by cloud computing providers including Google Cloud, Amazon Web Services, and IBM Cloud Analytics, which include proficiency, capability, and flexibility for storing and utilizing data from IoT devices. However, managing and analyzing large amounts of data from various objects in different geographical locations can be challenging for IoT-related appliances. To address this, new technologies like fog or edge computing are being implemented to improve the efficiency and effectiveness of cloud computing in IoT. These technologies provide computing and storage capabilities at the edge of the system, allowing for efficient data storage, computation, and connectivity in heterogeneous networks. This enables connected devices and objects to be placed in various locations and assemble IoT devices with connected applications (Aslam et al., 2020; Chander, 2020; Nahavandi, 2020; Özdemir & Hekim, 2018; Qiu et al., 2019).

According to the particular requirements of the application, the data gathered from IoT devices is often moved to appropriate objects or places for further evaluation. Fog or edge computing nodes that are closer to IoT devices may handle high priority data that has to be processed right away, while lower-priority information can be sent to other objects or nodes for processing and analysis additionally. While fog and edge computing offer many advantages, they also have limitations and challenges when integrated with IoT.

One of the key challenges in integrating IoT with fog or edge computing is ensuring that each fog or edge computing node is optimally configured and equipped to provide the necessary resources for IoT devices. This includes managing and allocating resources effectively between nodes, as well as addressing issues such as energy consumption, cost, and service availability. Additionally, ensuring the security and privacy of data in a fog or edge computing environment is also a critical concern.

## AI-Based Trustworthiness in IoT Systems

Many of us assumed that the IoT would make human life more pleasant and stress-free as a result of its integration (Chander & Kumaravelan,
2021). Because it contains malware, copyrights, spam, and other unwanted
content, some experts have claimed that IoT stands for "Internet of gar-
bage." On the other hand, it develops with better community administrations, rigorous moderation, greater communications, and better addresses.
The most important task is identifying the right value, which comes after
gathering data from a network of people who adore junk. IoT's quick expansion and unique needs are well-known facts (Samie et al., 2019). From
the discussion above, it is clear that big data analytics, real-time monitoring
with streaming data, and another crucial topic are effective communication
capabilities and meeting security needs in such a vast network. A secure network connection should be used with the deployed software applications.
Since their data is available on a network, customers and employees of
smart IoT products will be particularly vulnerable. Data privacy, trust, and
secrecy are the three main problems with IoT devices and services. Before
exchanging data or gaining access to a service, an IoT item or device must
obtain authorization from a party. Cybersecurity is a method for protecting
IoT systems and the components that go with them. IoT-based cybersecurity
solutions primarily prevent hackers from obtaining critical data, making cybersecurity rules particularly crucial when working with small devices. Numerous cybersecurity techniques exist, including secure socket layers, fire-
walls, antivirus software, and cryptographic protocols. IoT security is greatly
improved by ML, DL, Blockchain, and quantum-resistant crypto methods.

There have also been some new problems, such as the collection of user
data by tiny IoT wearable devices that link to the databases of device suppliers (Lee & Lee, 2015; Lv et al., 2020; Pianini et al., 2018; Vesnic-Alujevic
et al., 2020). Then, without the customer's consent, these device providers sell the user data they have gathered to other commercial enterprises.
Through social networks, business organizations provide specific individual
ongoing notifications and adverts depending on the information. The biggest problem with IoT-based systems, other than security constraints, is how
to prevent this sort of data ethics.

## INFLUENCE OF TECHNOLOGICAL DOMAINS
## ON ENABLING TECHNOLOGIES OF INDUSTRY 5.0

Industry 5.0 is an advanced production model that leverages various technological advancements such as edge computing, digital twin, Internet
of everything, big data analysis, COBOTs, 6G, and blockchain to increase

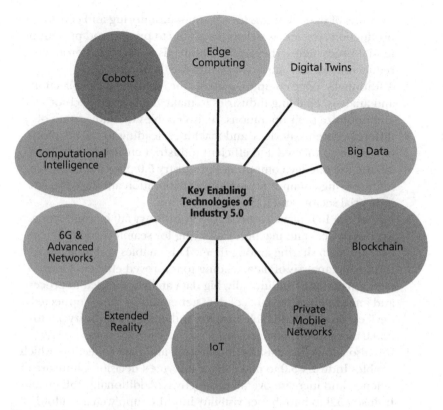

**Figure 18.3**   Impact based key enabling technologies of Industry 5.0.

efficiency and deliver personalized products more quickly (Maddikunta et al., 2022). The integration of these technologies with cognitive skills and innovation enhances the collaboration between machines and humans, making human tasks more productive and automatable for small businesses and individuals. Figure 18.3 briefs the key enabling technologies of Industry 5.0.

Industry 5.0 is a cutting-edge production model that incorporates various technological advancements, including EC, Digital Twin (DT), IoE, big data analytics, COBOTs, 6G, blockchain, network slicing, XR, and XR private mobile networks, to enhance the interaction between machines and humans.

The integration of the mentioned technologies allows for increased efficiency and productivity in industries, as well as the ability to deliver personalized products faster, as discussed below:

1. DT enables Industry 5.0 to improve the efficiency of production processes and optimize performance by analyzing and utilizing vast

amounts of data. It allows for real-time monitoring and control of production systems, as well as the ability to predict and prevent potential issues before they occur. This leads to increased productivity, reduced downtime, and cost savings for the industry.

2. Additionally, edge computing allows for real-time data collection and analysis, enabling industries to make data-driven decisions and optimize their operations. It also enables the integration of different systems, devices, and machines, leading to the creation of a more connected and efficient industrial environment. Overall, the use of edge computing in Industry 5.0 plays a crucial role in improving communication and collaboration among different industrial sectors and fostering innovation.

3. IoE, or the IoT, plays a crucial role in Industry 5.0 by connecting various devices and machines, allowing for seamless communication and data sharing among them. This enables real-time monitoring and analysis of data, leading to improved efficiency and decision-making. Additionally, big data analytics is used to process and analyze large amounts of data generated by these connected devices, providing valuable insights and enabling Industry 5.0 to make more informed decisions.

4. IoE also allows for real-time monitoring and data collection, which enables Industry 5.0 to make more informed decisions, improve efficiency, and increase overall productivity. Additionally, IoE enables Industry 5.0 to have better visibility into the supply chain, allowing for better forecasting and inventory management. Overall, the integration of IoE in Industry 5.0 leads to improved communication, automation, and data-driven decision-making, resulting in increased efficiency and productivity.

5. Blockchain technology in Industry 5.0 offers secure and transparent data sharing, tracking and traceability of products, and efficient supply chain management. It also enables secure and decentralized decision-making and automation of business processes, reducing the need for intermediaries and increasing trust among stakeholders.

6. In Industry 5.0, the integration of blockchain technology and smart contracts provide a secure and efficient way to manage and automate agreements between various stakeholders. This enhances the flexibility and transparency of the contracting process, allowing for more dynamic interactions and security enforcement through authentication and automated service-oriented actions.

7. In Industry 5.0, network slicing technology is utilized to provide dedicated network resources to specific Industry 5.0 applications and services, allowing for the creation of virtual networks that can be tailored

**TABLE 18.1  Role of Enabling Technologies on Industry 5.0 Applications**

| Enabling Technologies | Industry 5.0 Applications | | | | | | |
|---|---|---|---|---|---|---|---|
| | Intelligent Healthcare | Cloud Manufacturing | Supply Chain Management | Manufacturing/ Production | Education | Human-Cyber-Physical Systems | Disaster Management |
| Edge Computing | H | H | M | H | H | H | H |
| Digital Twins | M | H | L | H | M | H | M |
| Cobots | L | H | L | H | L | H | M |
| IoT | H | H | H | H | M | H | H |
| Computational Intelligence | H | H | H | H | M | H | H |
| Big Data | H | H | H | H | M | H | H |
| Blockchain | H | H | H | H | M | H | M |
| 6G and Advanced Networks | H | H | H | H | H | H | H |
| Extended Reality | H | H | L | H | H | H | H |
| Private Mobile Networks | M | M | L | H | M | H | M |

*Note:* H = High Influence; M = Medium Influence; L = Low Influence

    to specific requirements. This allows for the efficient use of network resources and improved performance for Industry 5.0 applications.
8. In Industry 5.0, the integration of technologies such as NS and extended reality (XR) allows for the creation of virtualized networks at a low cost, with optimal network resource utilization for monitoring in IIoT networks. XR can be used for various applications such as remote assistance, assembly line monitoring, health education, and remote healthcare. Additionally, private mobile networks can be used to deliver location-specific connectivity solutions in various settings such as factories, hospitals, schools, and universities.

Table 18.1 gives the influence measure of technological domains on enabling technologies of Industry 5.0.

## COMMON ISSUES AND LIMITATIONS IN INDUSTRY 5.0

Most of the production problems brought on by eliminating human labor from various processes are solved by Industry 5.0. However, it must also have more futuristic abilities because in the near future, humanity could develop innovative manufacturing abilities. Many abilities are still in the development stage, some of them are mentioned in this section.

1. It is necessary to comprehend how an autonomous system might include ethical standards before integrating sophisticated abilities into industrial management.
2. It is crucial to make sure that the autonomous system model's ethical behavior is properly validated and verified.
3. Implementing operation transparency, effective manufacturing techniques, and skilled manufacturing may significantly affect overproduction reduction.
4. The answer should be a clear ethical conduct policy for an autonomous system. Adapting and putting these suggestions into practice may be difficult for industry experts.
5. Proper tuning and validation can prevent potential problems between technology, experts, stakeholders, society, and businesses.

## TECHNOLOGICAL OPPORTUNITIES AND CHALLENGES IN INDUSTRY 5.0

### Opportunities of Industry 5.0

- Automation in industry will have a positive impact on employment through the use of advanced technology.
- Largely automated production processes provide clients more options for personalization.
- For creative people, Industry 5.0 offers the opportunity to maximize their productivity and abilities.
- Machines can be adapted to meet the needs of employees, offering a higher level of choice and assistance in managing repetitive tasks.
- Industry 5.0 creates higher-value employment, empowering individuals with more responsibility for construction and design (Naveen, 2019).
- In Industry 5.0, operators within the production process become more involved in the planning process compared to traditional automated manufacturing methods.
- Industry 5.0 allows for greater flexibility in design and the creation of more personalized products.
- Automation in manufacturing can be improved by using real-time data from the industry.
- The use of COBOTs in Industry 5.0 can increase safety for employees by taking on hazardous tasks.

- Personalized products and services can lead to increased customer satisfaction, loyalty, and profits for companies.
- Industry 5.0 presents opportunities for start-ups and entrepreneurs to develop new products and services, given adequate funding and infrastructure.
- Industry 5.0 places greater emphasis on the field of human–machine interaction and provides a platform for research and development in this area.
- Quality services can be provided remotely, particularly in the healthcare industry, through the use of Industry 5.0, such as medical surgeries in rural areas performed by robots.

## Challenges of Industry 5.0

- The increased automation in Industry 5.0 may lead to a decrease in middle-skill employment, creating a divide between highly trained and qualified workers and low-paid and unqualified employees.
- Adopting advanced and cutting-edge technologies in highly automated manufacturing systems can be a difficult task, requiring significant training and effort to develop the necessary skills.
- Collaborative robotics, a method of automation, can present a risk on the shop floor due to the potential for accidents or errors.
- Smart manufacturing systems require increased autonomy and social capabilities, but the shift from current systems to Industry 5.0 can be difficult due to a lack of integrated decision-making abilities.
- Acquiring high-quality and integrity data from manufacturing systems can be challenging, as well as accommodating diverse data repositories.
- The increased connectivity and use of standard communication protocols in Industry 5.0 can lead to an increased risk of cyber-security threats in critical industrial systems and manufacturing lines.
- Industry 5.0 requires a significant amount of investment to fully implement all its pillars, which can be difficult for industries and small and medium-sized enterprises to adopt.
- The healthcare industry, in particular, presents potential opportunities with Industry 5.0, but it requires a high degree of precision and accuracy, and research in this field is still in its early stages.
- Startups and entrepreneurs may find it challenging to adopt Industry 5.0 due to the high investment and infrastructure requirements with cutting-edge technology.

- Regulating Industry 5.0 can be difficult due to the high level of automation present, as it can be challenging to determine accountability in case of failures.
- Existing business strategies and models may need to be modified and customized to meet the requirements of Industry 5.0, with a focus on customer-centric operations. However, this can be difficult as customer preferences may change over time.
- Business strategies in Industry 5.0 require a high level of dynamism to sustain competition due to varying customer preferences.

## CONCLUSION

The fourth industrial revolution has now transitioned into Industry 5.0, which is defined by better human–machine interaction and more personalization (Naveen, 2019). This is accomplished by combining technologies like big data, AI, the IoT, cloud computing, and COBOTS. Industry 5.0 is anticipated to produce high-value job possibilities and grant more freedom for creative thinking and design. However, there are drawbacks to the use of this cutting-edge technology, including the requirement for worker skill development and a rise in cyber security concerns. Additionally, while Industry 5.0 provides greater autonomy to robots, important and moral based decision making remains the responsibility of humans. Overall, Industry 5.0 is anticipated to transform production methods and procedures by enabling more interaction between people and machines to deliver customized products to clients.

The current global pandemic of COVID-19 has presented many challenges for businesses in terms of meeting customer demands for goods and services, managing production, and addressing daily needs (Maddikunta et al., 2022). This crisis has forced manufacturers, companies, and service providers to reevaluate their current production strategies, delivery of services to customers, customer engagement, supply chain management, circular economy, integration of products, green transition, and digitalization. However, it has been observed throughout history that during times of industrial upheaval, businesses have shown the ability to adapt and undergo significant transformations. Going forward, companies will continue to be ready to adapt to changes in environmental sustainability and digital governance in a flexible and predictable world (Das & Pan, 2022).

India is aspiring to become a manufacturing hub through initiatives such as Make in India, Skill India, and Start-up India. Industry 5.0 has great potential to integrate with these programs and initiatives in making India the forerunner in smart and collaborative manufacturing systems.

## REFERENCES

Aslam, F., Aimin, W., Li, M., & Rehman, K. U. (2020). Innovation in the era of IoT and Industry 5.0: Absolute innovation management (AIM) framework. *Information*, *11*, 124. https://doi.org/10.3390/info11020124

Berg, C. (2022, November 9). Industry 5.0: Industrial revolution with a soul. Clarify. *Retrieved November 30, 2022, from https://www.clarify.io/learn/industry-5-0.*

Chander, B. (2020). Clustering and Bayesian networks. In F. P. Marquez (Ed.), *Handbook of research on big data clustering and machine learning* (pp. 50–73). IGI Global.

Chander, B., & Kumaravelan, G. (2021). Cyber security with AI—Part I. In M. Chakraborty, M. Singh, V. E. Balas, & I. Mukhopadhyay (Eds.), *The "essence" of network security: An end-to-end panorama* (pp. 147–171). Springer.

Chander, B., Pal, S., De, D., & Buyya, R. (2022). Artificial intelligence-based Internet of things for industry 5.0. In S. Pal, D. De, & R. Buyya (Eds.), *Artificial intelligence-based internet of things systems* (pp. 3–45). Springer.

Das, S., & Pan, T. (2022, May 9). *A strategic outline of Industry 6.0: Exploring the future.* http://dx.doi.org/10.2139/ssrn.4104696

Davenport, T. H., & Harris, J. G. (2017). *Competing on analytics, updated, with a new introduction: The new science of winning.* Harvard Business Review Press.

Davenport, T. H., & Kirby, J. (2016). *Only humans need to apply: Winners and losers in the age of smart machines.* Harper Business.

Davenport, T. H., & Mahidhar, V. (2018, May 10). What's your cognitive strategy? *MIT Sloan Management Review.* https://sloanreview.mit.edu/article/whats-your-cognitive-strategy/

Fortino, G., & Trunfio, P. (2014). *Internet of Things based on smart objects: Technology, middleware, and applications.* Springer.

Goundar, S., Avanija, J., Sunitha, G., Madhavi, K. R., & Bhushan, S. B. (2020). *Innovations in the industrial internet of things (IIoT) and smart factory.* IGI Global.

Hassan, Q. F., Khan, A. R., & Madani, S. A. (2017). *Internet of things: Challenges, advances, and applications.* CRC Press.

Jha, S., & Seshia, S. A. (2017). A theory of formal synthesis via inductive learning. *Acta Informatica*, *54*, 693–726. https://doi.org/10.1007/s00236-017-0294-5

Lee, I., & Lee, K. (2015). The Internet of things (IoT): Applications, investments, and challenges for enterprises. *Business Horizons* 58, 431–440. https://doi.org/10.1016/j.bushor.2015.03.008

Lv, Z., Han, Y., Singh, A. K., Manogaran, G., & Lv, H. (2020). Trustworthiness in industrial IoT systems based on artificial intelligence, *17*(2), 1496–1504. https://doi.org/10.1109/TII.2020.2994747

Maddikunta, P. K. R., Pham, Q. V., Prabadevi, B., Deepa, N., Dev, K., Gadekallu, T. R., Rukhsana, R., & Liyanage, M. (2022). Industry 5.0: A survey on enabling technologies and potential applications. *Journal of Industrial Information Integration*, *26*, 100257. https://doi.org/10.1016/j.jii.2021.100257

Müller, J. (2020). *Enabling technologies for Industry 5.0: Results of a workshop with Europe's technology leaders.* Publications Office of the European Union. https://op.europa.eu/en/publication-detail/-/publication/8e5de100-2a1c-11eb-9d7e-01aa75ed71a1

Nahavandi, S. (2020). Industry 5.0—A human-centric solution. *Sustainability, 11*(16), 4371. https://doi.org/10.3390/su11164371

Naveen, B. R. (2019). *Management challenges and opportunities of Industry 5.0.* Niruta Publications.

Qiu, T., Zhao, Z., Zhang, T., Chen, C., & Chen, C. L. P. (2019). Underwater Internet of things in smart ocean: System architecture and open issues. *IEEE Transactions on Industrial Informatics, 16*(7), 4297–4307. https://doi.org/10.1109/TII.2019.2946618

Özdemir, V., & Hekim, N. (2018). Birth of Industry 5.0: Making sense of big data with artificial intelligence. "The Internet of things" and next-generation technology policy. *OMICS A Journal of Integrative Biology, 22*(1). https://doi.org/10.1089/omi.2017.0194

Pianini, D., & Salvaneschi, G. (2018). Proceedings first workshop on architectures, languages and paradigms for IoT. *arXiv* preprint arXiv:1802.00976. http://dx.doi.org/10.4204/EPTCS.264

Samie, F., Bauer, L., & Henkel, J. (2019). From cloud down to things: An overview of machine learning in Internet of things. *IEEE Internet of Things Journal, 6*(3). https://doi.org/10.1109/JIOT.2019.2893866

Vesnic-Alujevic, L., Nascimento, S., & Polvora, A. (2020). Societal and ethical impacts of artificial intelligence: Critical Notes on European policy frameworks. *Telecommunications Policy, 44*(6), 101961. https://doi.org/10.1016/j.telpol.2020.101961

Yang, L. T., Di Martino, B., & Q. Zhang, Q. (2017). Internet of everything. *Mobile Information Systems, 2017,* Article ID 8035421. https://doi.org/10.1155/2017/8035421

# CHAPTER 19

# BIG DATA ANALYSIS TO CATEGORIZE AGRICULTURAL LAND ACCORDING TO CLIMATIC INFORMATION

**M. Sirish Kumar**
*Mohan Babu University*

**Kurakula Arun Kumar**
*Mohan Babu University*

**Avula chitti**
*CVR College of Engineering*

**B. Panduranag Raju**
*Annamacharya Institutee of Technology & Sciences*

**Sivaram Rajeyyagari**
*College of Computing and Information Technology*

*Innovations in Computational Intelligence, Big Data Analytics, and Internet of Things*, pages 343–360
Copyright © 2024 by Information Age Publishing
www.infoagepub.com
**343**

The realm of analytics is rapidly transforming with the growing and changing scope of big data. This constantly evolving field offers both huge challenges and business opportunities due to the sheer volume and structure of data being generated. Big data refers not just to the large amounts of data, but also the entire process of collecting, storing, and analyzing it, with the goal of improving the world (Dugane & Raut, 2014). The term big data is relatively new and emerged in the latter part of the last decade, but its significance to various companies has become clearer.

Big data comes in many different forms and variations, with the most obvious difference being between structured data (organized in rows, columns, and fields like operation records), unstructured data (with no uniform format [Fisher et al., 2012]), and semi-structured data (having a partial format that allows for specialized processing, but still considered unstructured). The key objective is to create a method for identifying differences, enabling comparison, and comparison of different sets of big data (Arunachalam et al., 2023).

The growth of unstructured data, such as photos, videos, and social media, has led to the development of a new type of nonrelational databases that can uncover their own patterns and trends (Charan et al., 2023). This shift from simply gathering data to connecting it has helped businesses to better understand the relationships between datasets, leading to more informed decision-making based on actionable insights (Davidian, 2011). Though big data is relatively new, its rapid evolution and improvement in a short period of time is evident. This points to even greater changes to come in the future. Big data is moving beyond being just a buzzword known to a select few and becoming more mainstream. Those who are utilizing big data are seeing significant success.

Big data has a significant impact on various industries, including product development, marketing, human resources, banking, finance, telecom, retail, healthcare, and more (Brown et al., 2011). The challenges posed by big data require advanced techniques in modeling, analysis, capture, storage, transfer, visualization, querying, information privacy, and more.

Many organizations seek to collect, store, and analyze data as it greatly enhances decision-making. Big data analytics is crucial in handling unstructured data, which makes up 85% of all data. It must be analyzed in accordance with the organization's needs. A key component of big data applications is the data itself.

## THE BIG DATA

*Big data* refers to the large volume of structured and unstructured data that is generated and collected by organizations (Bhargavi et al., 2018). It can be difficult to manage and analyze this data quickly and effectively, but the benefits of doing so can be significant. By analyzing big data, organizations can gain insights that can help them improve their operations, increase efficiency, and make better-informed decisions. The use of big data has become increasingly important in recent years across a wide range of industry sectors, including finance, healthcare, and retail.

The study explores the challenges of ensuring the quality of big data in the context of agriculture data. It highlights that the main factors affecting big data quality related to the difficulties in managing and maintaining the reliability of the data throughout its lifecycle—from gathering to processing and storage (Forsyth, 2012). The study specifically mentions that these challenges are heightened by the complexity of the data pipelines and the real-time nature of crop growing data (Kannan et al., 2022; Reshma et al., 2022). These factors have a more significant impact compared to the age of the data, the methods used to process it, and the tools applied to manage it (Sunitha et al., 2023).

## What Is the Definition of Big Data?

Big data refers to an immense and intricate set of datasets that surpasses the ability of traditional database management tools to capture, preserve, manage, and interpret.

Big data is a term used to describe a vast and intricate set of datasets that challenge the ability of current database management systems and data processing tools to effectively handle the data.

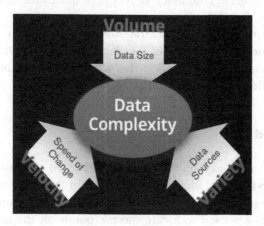

**Figure 19.1** The three V of Big Data.

The term big data is often used interchangeably with related concepts such as business intelligence (BI) and data mining. While all three focus on analyzing data, and in many cases, advanced analytics, big data is distinct due to the huge and complex nature of the data—requiring unique technology and approaches to process it, unlike traditional data warehouse solutions that may be insufficient.

## DATA ON LOCATION AND ELEVATION

Big data analysis and programming languages R and MongoDB are used to classify agricultural land in England and Wales based on the climate in that region. This classification system, known as *agricultural land classification* (ALC), assesses how the physical and chemical properties of the land limit its long-term use for agriculture and provides a framework for this classification. Unit climate, site, and soil are the three primary physical elements affecting agriculture production. The most limiting element determines the grade or subgrade of land, which can be categorized into grades ranging from 1 (*good*) to 5 (*very poor*). These criteria, along with their interactions, constitute the basis for classifying land into one of five grades.

- Grade 1 refers to very good agricultural land.
- Grade 2 refers to farmland that is of very high quality and caliber.
- Sub-Grade 3a represents farmland that is of high quality.
- Sub-Grade 3b refers to agricultural land that is of fair quality.
- Grade 4 refers to land that is of low quality for agricultural use.
- Grade 5 refers to land that is of very poor quality for agricultural use.

The algorithm for determining temperatures and moisture deficits for grid locations was devised by studying the data from the station dataset. The rainfall and field capacity duration datasets were created using a dataset that was compiled from several thousand rain gauges.

### National Grid

The statistics are based on the national grid system provided by the Ordnance Survey, which includes an error located in the southwest of the Isles of Scilly at the point where 0 degrees east and 0 degrees north intersect. Grid references are used to locate specific points on the grid and determine the distance between these points and other locations.

## Altitude (ALT)

The Meterological Office, Bracknell's 0.5 km resolution dataset of representative elevations was used to obtain the altitude data (ALT). Values are provided in meters (m)

## Rainfall

To calculate the average rainfall data in millimeters (mm), the recordings from thousands of rain gauges spanning the period from 1941 to 1970 were utilized. This is currently considered the worldwide standard period.

### Average Annual Rainfall

On a topographic base map at a scale of 1:250,000, the average annual rainfall (AAR) data were plotted, and isohyets were manually drawn (Arockia Panimalar & Subhashri, 2017). Using this base map as an interpolator, grid point values were derived. The 1:250,000 base map was also used to create the 1:625,000 map that AAR published. AAR was utilized to calculate the altitude adjustments for moisture shortage and is employed in the assessment of the overall climatic limitations.

### The Decrease in Average Annual Rainfall Over Time (LR_AAR)

To estimate the AAR for locations that fall between grid points, taking into account altitude differences, the method of using the rate at which rainfall changes with elevation is employed (Prakasam, 2010). The lapse rate data, which gives the rate of decrease in rainfall for each 5 km grid point, was generated by utilizing the AAR and altitude data sets (Bhadani & Jothimani, 2016).

### Average Summer Rainfall

For the months of April through September, the average summer rainfall (ASR) was computed. According to the method used by the producer for determining AAR, grid point data was calculated and rain gauge measurements were plotted on a topographic with a scale of 1:625,000. By using a set method, the temperature information from the entire agromet collection was gathered above freezing point. The median values for days with temperatures at $0°$ C were calculated for the period of January to June (AT0) and April to September (ATS).

## Accumulated Temperature, January to June (AT0)

Altitude, latitude, and longitude all play a significant role in determining temperature. Equation 1 is a mathematical model that can be used to express this relationship and was developed using data from the entire agromet dataset. This method of using a regression model was found to be more accurate for computing gridpoint temperature data than trying to analyze and extrapolate data from maps.

### Equation 19.1

The formula for calculating the temperature of a specific location on the grid (AT0g) is 1708 – 1.14 times the altitude (ALTg) of the location –0.023 times the easting (EASTg) and –0.044 times the northing (NORTHg) of the location on the national grid.

Where, AT0g is the grid point value for inserting temperature into the dataset (in degrees Celsius), ALTg is the altitude of the grid point as determined by the dataset (in meters), EASTg is the national grid easting measurement to 100 m, and NORTHg is the national grid northing measurement to 100.

## Accumulated Temperature, April to September (ATS)

Equation 19.2 was utilized to compute the ATS values for specific grid points directly from AT0 and the national grid easting. This equation, which explains 95% of the fluctuations in ATS, was developed from a comprehensive analysis of data from all the agromet stations and the equation:

$$: ATSg = 611 + 1.11AT0g + 0.042 \ EASTg$$

where:
   ATSg—grid value of ATS to be inserted into the dataset (measured in degrees Celsius)
   AT0g—grid value of AT0 to be inserted into the dataset (measured in degrees Celsius)
   EASTg—national grid easting measured to 100 meters in its full numerical form
   ASR (automated soil monitoring) and CATS (crop and soil temperature sensor) are used together to identify moisture levels that are below what is needed.

## CONSTRAINTS OF THE CLIMATE

The spectrum of viable agricultural uses, as well as the price and amount of production, are all significantly and in some locations predominantly influenced by climate, which also has an impact on soil quality. Its most fundamental impact is on a plant's capability to grow by determining the energy provided for photosynthesis and the availability of water to the roots of the plant. The interaction of site and soil qualities, which control soil moisture and doughtiness, has an impact on plant growth in part (Mohan et al., 2021). More immediate effects on crops or livestock include exposure to corrosive wind, prolonged moisture or high humidity, and frost, which can result in physical harm, illness, or stress. Therefore, in addition to the interaction limits, the ALC must also include an assessment of the general climatic limitations.

## Evaluation of the Overall Impact of the Climate on the Land

A standardized data source is necessary for the accurate and consistent evaluation of the relationship between AAR and average temperature (AT) for each agricultural land grade and subgrade. To this end, grid point data sets with a 5 km spacing have been developed to cover all of England and Wales and a standardized method has been created to estimate the value of each parameter at any location (Swarupa Rani et al., 2017). The grid point information is stored in the computerized land information system (Land IS) and can be utilized to retrieve both grid point and estimated values for designated grid references (Suma et al., 2023). The full set of data will also be disclosed by the Meteorological Office and the process for getting interpolated values will be described in their publication.

## Collection of Data on the Climate

The five agroclimatic parameters used by the ALC system are listed in Table 19.1, along with the associated restriction factors. The FCD dataset was developed by the SSLRC in collaboration with the Meteorological Office,

**TABLE 19.1  Factors That Restrict Crop Growth and Related Meteorological Data**

| Limitation Factor | Parameter | Observation period |
|---|---|---|
| Climate | Average Annual Rainfall (AAR) | 1941–1970 |
| | Median Accumulated Temperature above 0°C, January to June (AT0) | 1961–1980 |
| Soil Wetness | Median Duration of Field Capacity Days (FCD) | 1941–1970 |
| Soil Droughtiness | Average Summer Rainfall, April to September (ASR) | 1941–1970 |
| | Median Accumulated Temperature above 0°C, April to September (ATS) | 1961–1980 |

who provided and processed the data before its incorporation into Land IS. Additionally, Land IS includes datasets of elevation and average yearly rainfall that vary across elevation, which are used to interpolate from grid point values to site values.

The data resources are as follow:

### Average Annual Rainfall

The grid point values for AAR in millimeters were estimated by using a map with a scale of 1:250,000, which was more detailed than the previously available map with a scale of 1:625,000, and covering the period of 1941–1970.

### Average Summer Rainfall

The grid point values for ASR in millimeters were estimated by using a physical interpolation method on an unpublished map with a scale of 1:625,000, which covered the period of 1941–1970.

The median temperature during the period from January to June (AT0) was above 0 °C.

The dataset for median accumulated temperature above 0 °C for the months of January to June (AT0) was generated by analyzing temperature data from 94 stations in the Agromet Database (Bhargavi & Jyothi, 2018)). The data covers the period of 1961 to 1980. The median values of accumulated temperatures for each station were computed by using daily measurements of maximum and minimum temperature. A regression equation was then used to extrapolate these median values to grid points, taking into account factors such as altitude, latitude, and longitude. The equation used is:

$$AT0 \ (day \ °C) = 1708 - 1.14A - 0.023E - 0.044N$$

where
$A$ is altitude above mean sea level (meters),
$E$ is national grid easting to 100 m, and
$N$ is national grid northing to 100 m.

The equation explains about 90% of the variation in AT0 for the 94 agrometeorological record stations.

At the local level, variations in the terrain such as slope, incline, and altitude can greatly affect the climate, particularly with regards to temperature, exposure, and risk of frost. The orientation of a slope can significantly impact the amount of energy received by a site. In general, mean daily temperatures and accumulated temperatures during the growing season tend to be higher on slopes with a south-facing aspect that faces north. The intensity of radiation also varies with the angle of the slope, with variations

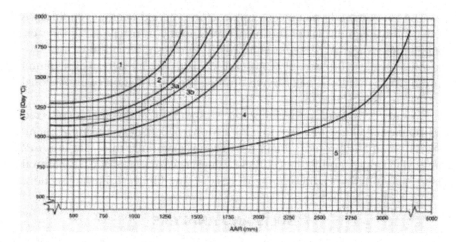

**Figure 19.2** Illustrates the average annual rainfall (AAR) and median accumulated temperature above 0°C for the months of January to June (AT0) for different grades and sub-grades of agricultural land in relation to local climate factors.

due to aspect being more noticeable on steeper slopes. In valleys, the effects of geography on climate can be more complex, with shading potentially reducing the advantages of a south-facing slope and increasing the disadvantages of a north-facing slope.

The benefits of having a favorable direction of the sun's rays on ATs can be diminished or eliminated due to exposure. In some instances, exposure to persistent strong winds or freezing winds can harm crops or cause stress to livestock, particularly during wet weather. Upland regions and land that is elevated in the surrounding landscape are often exposed. Coastal areas are often exposed to strong winds carrying salt, and these winds can affect the region several miles inland. The speed of wind is heavily influenced by the location. In general, wind speed increases with altitude and decreases as you move away from the west coast, as winds are channeled through valleys, particularly in upland areas, resulting in consistently high wind speed.

The danger of detrimental frost is strongly tied to location and can be specific to a certain area (Chi et al., 2016). Frosts that occur in the spring can cause severe harm to fruit crops and can impact the growth of other crops (James et al., 2001). A slope angle of 2 degrees is enough to cause the movement of cold air downhill, and areas at the bottom of valleys and basins are particularly susceptible to frost. Assessing the risk of frost is particularly important for land with high agricultural potential, where crops that are more delicate are likely to be grown (Gallagher & Biscoe, 1978). The type of soil also affects the risk of frost, with sandy and dry peat soils being more likely to experience late spring frosts than other soils.

The connection between geographical location and weather conditions is often intricate and it is not feasible to give specific instructions for their examination (Nagaraja & Sreeramulu, 2013). In cases where local factors have a considerable influence on the overall climate, the impact on agricultural productivity should be determined through the consultation of professional agrometeorological experts.

To categorize land, information on AAR and AT of the area is collected and analyzed. This data is stored in a MongoDB database using a client-server command prompt. Then, the image is examined to obtain the AAR and ATO values, and based on these values, the quality of the agricultural land is classified into different grades as discussed in the following section.

## RESULTS AND ANALYSIS

### Grade 1

This land has soil that is suitable for growing a variety of crops (see Figure 19.3).

### Grade 2

The top and subsoil of this land are generally of medium quality; however, the slight tendency towards droughtiness may limit its potential for cultivation (see Figure 19.4).

### Grade 3a

The soil in this land is not well-drained and has a tendency to be wet, which may negatively impact its suitability for farming as it may cause difficulty in working the soil (see Figure 19.5).

### Grade 3b

The soil in this land is poorly drained, and has a severe tendency towards wetness which greatly limits its suitability for farming due to the difficulty in working the soil (see Figure 19.6).

### Grade 4

The soil in this land is poorly drained, and has a more pronounced tendency towards wetness compared to other areas of the site, which greatly limits its suitability for farming (see Figure 19.7).

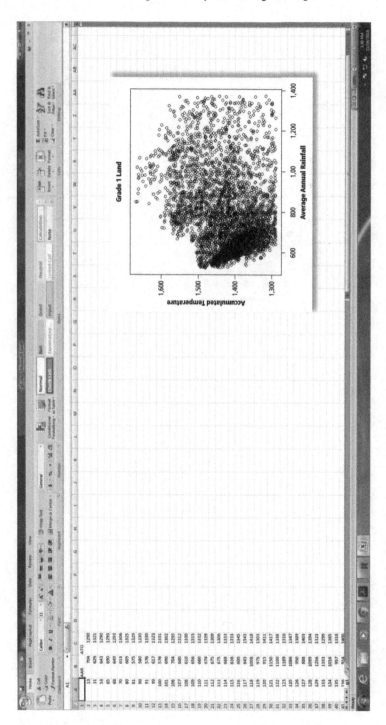

**Figure 19.3** Grade 1 data.

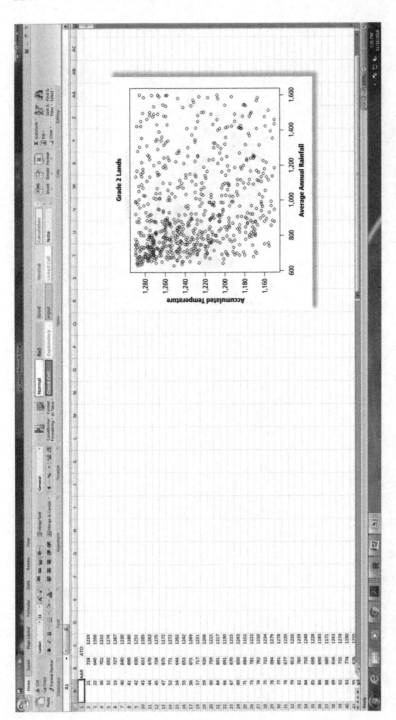

**Figure 19.4** Grade 2 data.

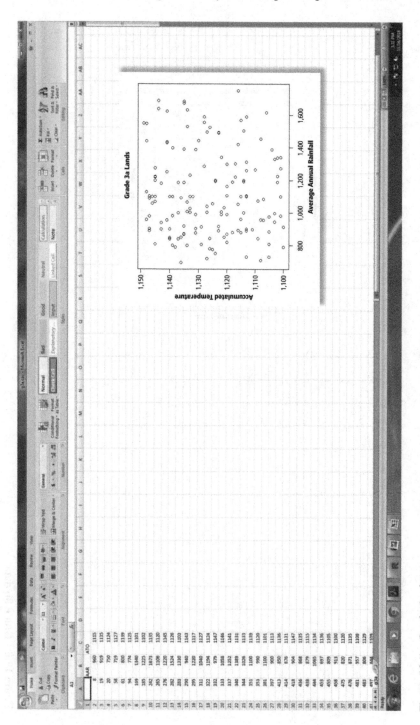

**Figure 19.5** Grade 3a data.

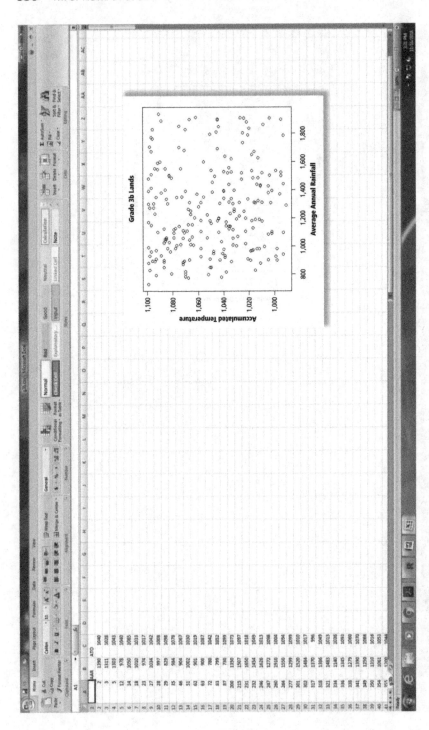

**Figure 19.6** Grade 3b data.

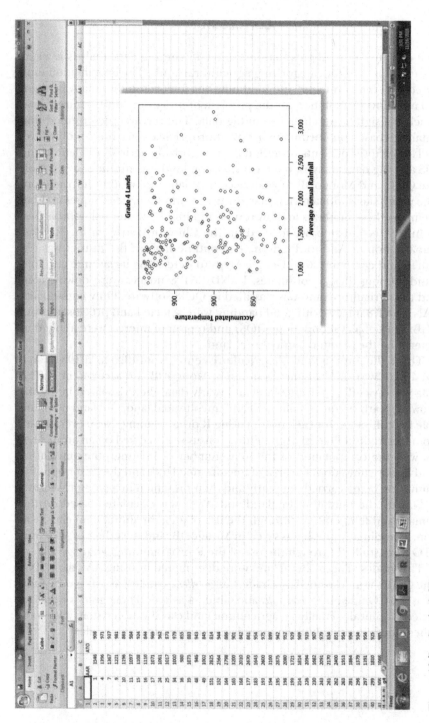

**Figure 19.7** Grade 4 data.

## CONCLUSION

The conclusion highlights that utilizing GIS and big data analysis is a successful approach for categorizing agricultural lands. The examination evaluated different strategies and methods, but discovered that many of them did not provide a solution for the problem of processing unstructured data, which is a significant challenge in big data. The research determined that databases based on documents are an appropriate choice for this objective.

This chapter presents a method for categorizing agricultural land using GIS and big data analysis. It concentrates on land classification, using tools like QGIS and MongoDB to analyze census data and weather information. The paper starts with a review of existing data modeling techniques and implements these methods to draw results and highlight the best approaches.

In the second step, we focused on the Chittoor district in the Rayalaseema region of Andhra Pradesh. The outline map of the district was obtained and compared with Google Maps to determine its latitude and longitude. Using these coordinates, LAND SAT 8 images were downloaded and the agriculture land was classified in QGIS software. Only high-quality LAND SAT 8 images with good banding were selected and processed using RGB. Dark object subtraction (DOS) and region of interest were applied to determine the extent of agricultural land.

Third, the Andhra Pradesh agriculture census from 1995 to 2010 was analyzed year by year. The data was stored in MongoDB and accessed in R. The data was divided into district-level and yearly data, then visualized in graphs showing yearly holdings, cultivated and uncultivated land, and land not available for cultivation for each district using R programming. Next, overall data from the Andhra Pradesh Agriculture Census was analyzed on an annual basis, with the computation of the total number of holdings, the amount of land under cultivation, the area of uncultivated land, and the land not fit for cultivation being carried out yearly and then presented in a graphical form.

Fourth, the rainfall in England and Wales was calculated based on the climate and temperature through the use of an agricultural land classification. The climatic graph was saved in MongoDB, and the values of AAR and ATO were studied through the use of the R programming language.

The grades of agricultural land were determined by using AAR and ATO. The grades were classified as: Grade 1 as *excellent*, Grade 2 as *very good*, Grade 3a as *good*, Grade 3b as *moderate*, and Grade 4 as *poor*. These grades were depicted graphically. Finally, an agricultural land classification system was established, incorporating both cultivated and uncultivated land grades.

## REFERENCES

Arockia Panimalar, S., & Subhashri, K. (2017). Big data architecture for remote sensing applications. *International Research Journal of Engineering and Technology, 4*(10), 57–61. https://www.irjet.net/archives/V4/i10/IRJET-V4I1012.pdf

Arunachalam, R., Sunitha, G., Shukla, S. K., Pandey, S. N., Urooj, S., & Rawat, S. (2023). A smart Alzheimer's patient monitoring system with IoT-assisted technology through enhanced deep learning approach. *Knowledge and Information Systems, 65*(12), 5561–5599. https://doi.org/10.1007/s10115-023-01890-x

Bailey, J. T., & Boryan, C. G. (2010). *Remote sensing applications in agriculture at the USDA National Agricultural Statistics Service.* USDA. https://www.fao.org/fileadmin/templates/ess/documents/meetings_and_workshops/ICAS5/PDF/ICASV_2.1_048_Paper_Bailey.pdf

Bhadani, A., & Jothimani, D. (2016). Big data: Challenges, opportunities and realities. In M. K. Singh & D. G. Kumar (Eds.), *Effective big data management and opportunities for implementation* (pp. 1–24). IGI Global.

Bhargavi, P., & Jyothi, S. (2018). Big data and Internet of things for analysing and designing systems based on hyperspectral images. In A. V. Krishna Prasad (Eds.), *Exploring the convergence of big data and the Internet of things* (pp. 240–260). IGI Global Publications.

Brown, B., Chui, M., & Manyika, J. (2011, October 1). Are you ready for the era of big data? *McKinsey Quarterly.* http://www.mckinsey.com/insights/strategy/are-you-ready-for-the-era-of-big-data

Charan, N. S., Narasimhulu, T., Bhanu Kiran, G., Sudharshan Reddy, T., Shivangini Singh, T., & Sunitha, G. (2023). Solid waste management using deep learning. In *Proceedings of the 14th International Conference on Soft Computing and Pattern* (vol. 648, pp. 44–51). Springer.

Chi, M., Plaza, A., Benediktsson, J. A., Sun, Z., Shen, J., & Zhu, Y. (2016). Big data for remote sensing: Challenges and opportunities. *IEEE, 104*(11), 2207–2219. https://doi.org/10.1109/JPROC.2016.2598228

Craull, P. J. (1985). A description of urban soils and their desired characteristics. *Journal of Arboriculture, 11*(11), 330–339. https://doi.org/10.48044/jauf.1985.071

Dugane, R. A., & Raut, A. B. (2014, April). A survey on big data in real-time. *International Journal on Recent Innovative Trends on Computer Communication, 2*(4), 794–797. https://www.academia.edu/9156825/A_Survey_on_Big_Data_in_Real_Time

Fisher, D., Deline, R., Czerwinski, M., & Drucker, S. (2012). Interactions with big data analytics. *Interactions, 19*(3), 50–59. https://doi.org/10.1145/2168931.2168943

Forsyth, C. (2012). *For big data analytics there's no such thing as too big* [Cisco WhitePaper]. https://www.cisco.com/c/dam/en/us/solutions/data-center-virtualization/big_data_wp.pdf

Gallagher, J. N., & Biscoe, P. V. (1978, August). Radiation absorption, growth, and yield of cereals. *The Journal of Agricultural Science, 91*(01), 47–60. https://doi.org/10.1017/S0021859600056616

James, R., Anderson, E., & Hardy, E. (2001). *A land use and land cover classification system for use with remote sensor.* U.S. Department of the Interior. (Original work published 1976)

Kannan, K. S., Sunitha, G., Deepa, S. N., Babu, D. V., & Avanija, J. (2022). A multi-objective load balancing and power minimization in cloud using bio-inspired algorithms. *Computers & Electrical Engineering, 102*(5), 108225. https://doi.org/10.1016/j.compeleceng.2022.108225

Majumdar, J., Naraseeyappa, S., & Ankalaki, S. (2017). Analysis of agriculture data using data mining techniques: application of big data. *Journal of Big Data, 4*, Article 20. https://doi.org/10.1186/s40537-017-0077-4

Mohan, E., Rajesh, A., Sunitha, G., Konduru, R. M., Avanija, J., & Ganesh Babu, L. (2021). A deep neural network learning-based speckle noise removal technique for enhancing the quality of synthetic-aperture radar images. *Concurrency and Computation: Practice and Experience, 33*(13), e6239. https://doi.org/10.1002/cpe.6239

Nagaraja, P., & Sreeramulu, R. (2013). Land use management in Andhra Pradesh (1960-61–2009-10): A critical analysis. *Journal of Research in Agriculture and Animal Science, 1*(2), 1–8. https://www.questjournals.org/jraas/papers/vol1-issue2/A120108.pdf

Prakasam, C. (2010). Land-use and land-cover change detection through remote sensing approach: A case study of Kodaikanal Taluk, Tamil Nadu. *International Journal of Geomatics and Geosciences, 1*, 150–158.

Reshma, G., Al-Atroshi, C., Nassa, V. K., Geetha, B., Sunitha, G., Galety, M. G., & Neelakandan, S. (2022). Deep learning-based skin lesion diagnosis model using dermoscopic images. *Intelligent Automation & Soft Computing, 31*(1), 621–634. https://doi.org/10.32604/iasc.2022.019117

Suma, K. G., Sunitha, G., & Avanija, J. (2023). SegMatic: A deep neural network learning model for semantic segmentation. *SSRG International Journal of Electronics and Communication Engineering, 10*(10), 40–48. https://doi.org/10.14445/23488549/IJECE-V10I10P104

Sunitha, G., Sudeepthi, A., Sreedhar, B., Shaik, A. B., & Farooq, C. (2023). RetinaNet and vision transformer-based model for wheat head detection. In *Proceedings of the 5th International Conference on Inventive Research in Computing Applications (ICIRCA)* (pp. 151–156). IEEE.

CHAPTER 20

# BINAURAL HEARING AID NOISE REDUCTION USING AN EXTERNAL MICROPHONE

**G. Naga Jyothi**
*Madanapalle Institute of Technology and Science*

**K. Vijetha**
*Matrusri Engineering College*

**K. Reddy Madhavi**
*Mohan Babu University*

**K. Suneetha**
*Jain (Deemed-to-be University)*

**S. Sreenivasa Chakravarthi**
*Amrita School of Computing*

*Innovations in Computational Intelligence, Big Data Analytics, and Internet of Things*, pages 361–373
Copyright © 2024 by Information Age Publishing
www.infoagepub.com

## ABSTRACT

A hearing aid (HA) is an electronic gadget used by people with hearing loss. Generally, several algorithms have been enhanced in the past to remove the noise signal occurring in the hearing aids. A binaurally linked single microphone device is used in HA to remove the noises occurring due to lower back directional interference. Using an emic as an HA attachment is commonplace. This book chapter describes the method for "HA signal augmentation" that combines the "signals of a microphone from the HAs and external-device." The advantages of the emic's body shielding for increasing HA signal are discussed in the book's first part. The proposed design is implemented in MATLAB tool and has taken several frequencies with noises and is passed to the pre and post FIR filters which will remove the maximum noises and make the signal with high accuracy when compared with the other existing designs. The ratio between the signal and noise is also much less when compared with the other circuits.

## BINAURAL HEARING AID NOISE REDUCTION USING AN EXTERNAL MICROPHONE

Hearing loss is the inability to hear sound. The hearing loss will vary from person to person and is influenced by age. Several people affected by hearing impairment are older adults—with roughly one-third of seniors 65 and older reporting hearing loss. One example of an assistive device that can benefit someone with hearing loss is hearing aids.

Mild hearing loss affects more than 6% of individuals globally, and as the world's population ages, this number is expected to increase. Consequently, improving HA technology can result in a significant section of the population having a higher level of living.

ITE devices, which are considerably smaller, are located in the ear canal, the main unit comprising all the HA components for BTE devices is situated behind the ear. This is one of the key differences between BTE and ITE devices. The most popular ITE and BTE realizations are:

1. Completely-in-canal (CIC) ITE devices
2. Receiver-in-canal (RIC) BTE devices

Figure 20.1 shows the relative sizes of these devices. In comparison to ITEs, BTEs currently hold a greater market share. According to estimates, BTEs made up 77% of the HA sold in the United States of America in 2014.

The size of ITE devices is currently trending downward. Invisible-in-canal (IIC) devices—a smaller version of the CIC—are said to offer better

**Figure 20.1** Types of hearing aids.

localization, less occlusion nuisance, and less wind noise than BTEs and CICs. The smaller size restricts the ability to house several microphones in a single device, even if it is also chosen for comfort and aesthetics. Due to the bigger housing of BTE devices, it is possible to use many microphones within a single device to conduct spatial filtering. The size of ITE devices has recently been on the decline.

Several wireless technologies are used to HA with an external device. For instance, a wire-free connection allows an external remote to transmit volume changes to the HA. As an alternative, an audio signal may be received by the external device and then sent directly to the HAs. As cellphones become more and more popular, it is typical to see them close in numerous circumstances.

## Literature Review

Accardi and Cox (1999) explained about the modular approach to speech enhancement with several speech coding techniques. In this they explained about the modular approach. Later, Ali et al. (2017) explained about noise reduction strategy for hearing devices using an external microphone. By having an external device we can reduce the noise but an extra device may occupy more area and power consumption. Boothroyd (2004) has explained the accessories of HA for adults. In this they also explained advantages and disadvantages of using HA gadgets. Bertrand and Moonen (2009) described and eliminated the high distributed noise present in HA with external acoustic sensor nodes. The integration of integrating a remote microphone with hearing-aid processing was described by Kates et al. (2019). Plomp (1978) explains about the auditory handicap of hearing impairment and their limitation and advantages of HA. The archeology of deafness and its etic and emic identity of construction was discussed by Reagan (2002). Binaural hearing in the virtual world and real world used to increase the children's listening experience in the schools and colleges (Ramírez et al., 2022). Buck et al. (2008) elaborate about microphone calibration for multi-channel signal processing. The next adaptive binaural filtering for a multiple-talker listening system using remote and on-ear microphones has been explained by authors (Corey & Singer, 2021). In this, the noise reduction can be done by using MVDR beamformers. Haukedal et al. (2022) describes HA in detail. HA controllers for binaural speech enhancement using a model-based approach is discussed in Kavalekalam et al. (2019). Moradi et al. (2016) explains about the comparison of gated audiovisual speech identification in elderly hearing aid users and elderly normal-hearing individuals.

Nagajyothi and Sridevi (2017) explained about various types of FIR filters to remove noises in the HA. Lisan et al. (2022) explains the prevalence of hearing loss and HA uses among adults in various countries.

Kates et al. (2019) and Kim et al. (2006) described the integration of integrating a remote microphone with hearing-aid processing. Reagan (2002) explained about the archeology of deafness and its etic and emic identity of construction. Ramírez et al. (2022) discussed the binaural hearing in the virtual world and real world to increase the children's listening experience in the schools' and colleges' communication between audiologist, patient, and patient's family members during initial audiology consultation and rehabilitation planning sessions described by Manchaiah et al. (2019). Tasell (1993) explained about the loss of speech hearing and hearing aids.

"A Relative-Transfer-Function-Based Post-Filter for Speech Enhancement in Hearing Aids Using a Nearby External Microphone" is discussed by Yee et al. (2017). Migirov et al. (2010) explained the Cochlear implantation in elderly patients—the surgical and audiological outcome. HA plays a paramount role these days because many people were suffering from hearing loss. Ferdousi et al. (2018) explained about correlation-based pre-filtering for context-aware recommendation. Other researchers—Stanisavljevic et al. (2000), Xie et al. (2022), Yee et al. (2018), and Zheng et al. (2015)—explained about the various types of pre- and post-filter techniques for the HA to remove the noise signals. Parvin and Hussain (2018) have explained about the HA and the filter bank for the removal of noise signals.

The contribution of this chapter is as follows: The first section describes the introduction of the literature survey of the "HA and emic." The advantages and disadvantages of the pre-filter and post-filter in binaural BF have been explained. Next, the proposed design for the HA using the emic post filter has been explained. Finally, the result analysis and comparison of the proposed and existing designs has been explained. When we observed the result analysis, there was less signal noise ratio present when compared with the other HA devices. Also the proposed design is more useful when compared with the other designs and the architectures. Lastly, the conclusion is explained.

## USING THE EMIC, POST-FILTER THE BINAURAL BEAMFORMER

When employing the suggested placement method, the body-related transfer function (BRTF) of frontal and back target speakers are very different. Following that, a variety of probability models are created using this property to characterize the many conditions under which medial sources can arise.

The frontal target source presence probability (FTSPP) then uses probability models to identify which source—from the front or the back—is more likely to be at fault for the media coverage. The generalized sidelobe canceller (GSC) structures depicted in Figure 20.2 are used to estimate the variance parameters of the likelihood models. HA microphones are used by the GSC, also known as HA microphone development, to perform dual-channel adaptive BF as seen in Figure 20.2. The suggested FTSPP requires front–back differentiation to first estimate the medial source presence probability (MSPP) in order to address front–back ambiguity. The possibility of medial presence for a specific medial source presence must also be evaluated. The HA signals are used to calculate the MSPP because HA microphones can distinguish between lateral and medial sources. The FTSPP estimator then uses the emic to differentiate between the front and the back. Emic post-filtering is performed to the output following the binaural HA BF. As can be observed, the target and noise signal components are estimated more precisely by the FTSPP estimator.

### Correlation-Based Post-Filtering

Emic signals are used as the target signal when the body-shielding effect has significantly increased their signal-to-noise ration (SNR). Figure 20.3 shows the post filtering correlation. When we observe the Figure 20.4, the

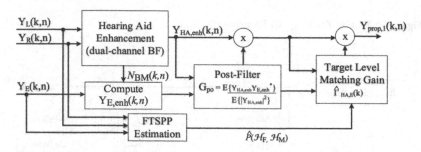

**Figure 20.2** Proposed design.

input $Y_L$ and $Y_R$ are passed to the HA BF, $Y_E$ is passed to compute the cell design, where $Y_L$ and $Y_R$ are given to the FTSPP. After that, these three inputs are passed and compared with the post filter signal. There, the error can be removed and if it is matched with the target cell then there is no problem, and again if more errors are present it means it will be sent back until final noise is removed.

### Noise Estimation-Based Post-Filtering

Emic is utilized in a new way to evaluate the acoustic power spectrum (PS) in the HA. A longer monitoring of the l PS can be used to measure stable noise with lesser standard error, whereas a faster monitoring of the signals PS would be employed during front goal absences to estimate the noise PS more precisely.

### Target RTF-Based Post-Filtering

The target signal is assumed to be the main source of correlations between the increased mic signal and binaural BF o/p in the target post-filtering based on RTF developed using Method 1 mentioned in the section "Correlation-Based Post-Filtering" (Figure 20.5).

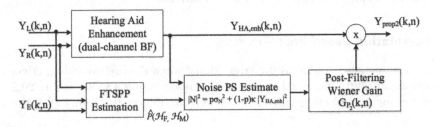

**Figure 20.3** Post-filtering HA BF using the Emic.

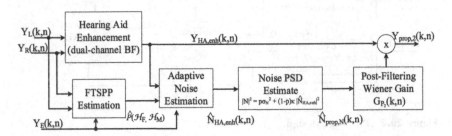

**Figure 20.4** RTL based noise estimation.

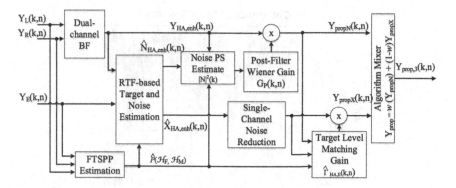

**Figure 20.5** Post-filtering channels of binaural HA BF through the Emic.

When it comes to speech frequencies that are immune to diffuse noise, the RTF-based target estimator is more useful. It is challenging to distinguish between speech and noise because diffuse noise exhibits correlation for low frequencies. As a result, single-channel improvement techniques are used to post-filter the o/p of the RTF-based speech estimator.

## SIMULATION RESULTS

The proposed design is designed in MATLAB and finds the microphone configuration in Figure 20.6. The white noise data is broadcasted from the loud speaker from 0th position direction to run the target signal, and eight evenly spaced surrounding loudspeakers play a diffuse babbling noise.

Using a window period of 12.1 ms and 50% overlap, the HA and emic signals are segmented to estimate the MSC between them. The intended signal is held constant while the noise level is raised in this process for varying SNR conditions. Figure 20.7 displays the experimental MSC measurement results. In diffuse babbling noise, the low frequencies contain the majority of the signal power when the amount of diffuse noise rises.

When we observe Figure 20.7 the various SNR ratios of proposed and existing designs are present. The proposed design has 10% less noise when compare with the yoo (2020). Also the convergence of various signals has been taken from 0dB, 10dB, 20dB, and so on.

The drop of minimum sampling error (MSE) between $Y_{HA}$ and $Y_E$ as a o/p of normalized least mean square (NLMS) design, corresponds to the convergence metric previously described. To put it another way, the convergence value calculates how much the MSE between YHA and bYHA is less than the MSE between YHA and $Y_E$. The NLMS filter converges for all frequencies and experimental conditions studied, which depends on frequency. For frequencies under 800.0 Hz, NLMS convergence is comparatively

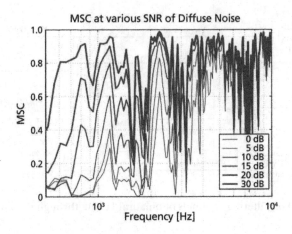

**Figure 20.6** Coherence between HA and Emic.

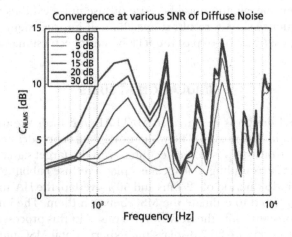

**Figure 20.7** Various SNR of diffuse noise.

weak. Additionally, NLMS performance suffers if the algorithm's learning rate is too slow to keep up with the changing dynamics of the environment. Figure 20.8 shows the various misadjustments present at various frequency levels.

## The Noise Estimation Performance

Figure 20.9 shows bars with a total height that represents the sum of the log overestimation and underestimation errors and a lower component

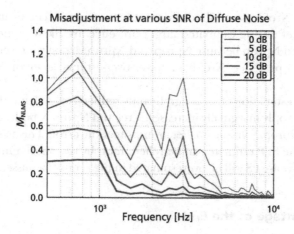

**Figure 20.8**  Misadjustments at various SNR.

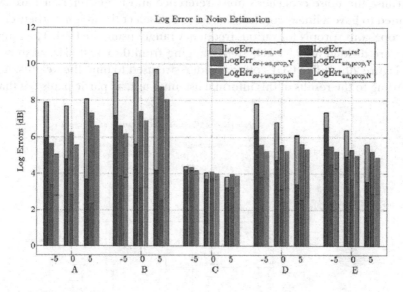

**Figure 20.9**  Noise estimator.

that represents the log underestimation error for each bar—the terms "log over estimate error" and "under estimate error." Given that noise reference (Nref) is often used to estimate stationary noise, the Figure 20.9 demonstrates that it has a very low overestimation error and a large underestimation error. When FTSPP is low, proposed noise (Nprop) and Nprop expand Nref to follow the noisy signal PS. The suggested estimators therefore outperform Nref for a smaller under-estimation error. The overestimation errors of Nref during estimated target presence are likewise incorporated in Nprop and Nprop because Nprop and Nprop virtually converge to Nref during target presence. Nref has a lower over-estimation error than Nprop as a result.

The total estimation error is significantly reduced overall, but the overestimation error only marginally increases. Nref and Nprop,N both extend each other, but Nprop,N has a smaller overestimation error. This is so that the veracity of the SPP estimate can be relied upon by the offered noise PS estimators. The noise PS will be overestimated in the event of a missed detection.

## SNR Advantage of the Emic

The GUI noise reduction is as shown in Figure 20.10. This is partially because the noise canceller's noise reference and target reference are assumed to have a linear connection. Users can select the weights $w$ between YpropX and YpropN for various frequency ranges using the GUI. The ranges were divided into 1.1 kHz steps, ranging from 0 to 4.00 kHz, as shown in Figure 20.10. The GUI's offered sliders are used to tune the weights. According to the results of this informal listening test, all participants felt that

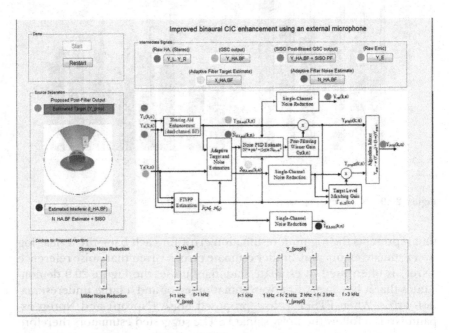

**Figure 20.10**   GUI image of binaural CIC enhancement.

YpropX was able to reduce interference and noise more effectively while YpropN was able to produce residual ambient noise that sounded more naturally. However, YpropX is chosen over YpropN for the application of interferer suppression. User-dependent appears to be the way that YpropX and YpropN were weighted. The majority of users concur that YpropN is recommended for higher frequencies. The majority of users concurred that YpropN was best at higher frequencies. Two parametrizations of Yprop3 are used in a formal testing technique to assess how well the suggested methods outperform the state-of-the-art.

## CONCLUSION

The application of emic for HA signal is discussed in this chapter. Body-shielding causes the inherent in emic data which is used to address front–back ambiguity using the strategic emic placement described in the book and the FTSPP estimator suggested. To enhance the decrease of interference from the rear direction, a post-gain filter's function is controlled by the FTSPP. Three distinct augmentation scheme designs were presented, and their effectiveness was assessed.

## REFERENCES

Accardi, A. J., & Cox, R. V. (1999). A modular approach to speech enhancement with an application to speech coding. *1999 IEEE International Conference on Acoustics, Speech, and Signal Processing*. Proceedings. ICASSP99 (Cat. No. 99CH36258) https://doi.org/10.1109/icassp.1999.758097

Avanija, J., Konduru, S., Kura, V., NagaJyothi, G., Dudi, B. P., & S., M. N. (2022). Designing a fuzzy q-learning power energy system using reinforcement learning. *International Journal of Fuzzy System Applications, 11*(3), 1–12. https://doi.org/10.4018/ijfsa.306284

Boothroyd, A. (2004). Hearing aid accessories for adults: The remote FM microphone. *Ear and Hearing, 25*(1), 22–33. https://doi.org/10.1097/01.AUD.0000111260.46595.EC

Bertrand, A., & Moonen, M. (2009). Robust distributed noise reduction in hearing aids with external acoustic sensor nodes. *EURASIP Journal on Advances in Signal Processing, 2009*, 1–14. https://doi.org/10.1155/2009/530435

Buck, M., Haulick, T., & Pfleiderer, H. J. (2008). Microphone calibration for multichannel signal processing. In E. Hänsler & G. Schmidt (Eds.), *Speech and Audio Processing in Adverse Environments* (pp. 417–467). Springer.

Corey, R. M., & Singer, A. C. (2021, October). Adaptive binaural filtering for a multiple-talker listening system using remote and on-ear microphones. In *2021 IEEE Workshop on Applications of Signal Processing to Audio and Acoustics* (WASPAA; pp. 1–5). IEEE.

Ferdousi, Z. V., Colazzo, D., & Negre, E. (2018, March). Correlation-based pre-filtering for context-aware recommendation. In *2018 IEEE International Conference on Pervasive Computing and Communications Workshops* (PerCom Workshops; pp. 89–94). IEEE.

Haukedal, C. L., Wie, O. B., Schauber, S. K., Lyxell, B., Fitzpatrick, E. M., & von Koss Torkildsen, J. (2022). Social communication and quality of life in children using hearing aids. *International Journal of Pediatric Otorhinolaryngology, 152*, 111000. https://doi.org/10.1016/j.ijporl.2021.111000

Kates, J. M., Arehart, K. H., & Harvey, L. O., Jr. (2019). Integrating a remote microphone with hearing-aid processing. *The Journal of the Acoustical Society of America, 145*(6), 3551–3566. https:/doi.org/10.1121/1.5111339

Kavalekalam, M. S., Nielsen, J. K., Christensen, M. G., & Boldt, J. B. (2019, May). Hearing aid-controlled beamformer for binaural speech enhancement using a model-based approach. In *ICASSP 2019-2019 IEEE International Conference on Acoustics, Speech and Signal Processing* (ICASSP; pp. 321–325). IEEE.

Kim, H. H., & Barrs, D. M. (2006). Hearing aids: A review of what's new. *Otolaryngology—Head and Neck Surgery, 134*(6), 1043–1050. https://doi.org/10.1016/j.otohns.2006.03.010

Lisan, Q., Goldberg, M., Lahlou, G., Ozguler, A., Lemonnier, S., Jouven, X., Zins, M., & Empana, J. P. (2022). Prevalence of hearing loss and hearing aid use among adults in France in the CONSTANCES Study. *JAMA Network Open, 5*(6), e2217633–e2217633. https://doi.org/10.1001/jamanetworkopen.2022.17633

Manchaiah, V., Bellon-Harn, M. L., Dockens, A. L., Azios, J. H., & Harn, W. E. (2019). Communication between audiologist, patient, and patient's family members during initial audiology consultation and rehabilitation planning sessions: A descriptive review. *Journal of the American Academy of Audiology, 30*(09), 810–819. https://doi.org/10.3766/jaaa.18032

Migirov, L., Taitelbaum-Swead, R., Drendel, M., Hildesheimer, M., & Kronenberg, J. (2010). Cochlear implantation in elderly patients: Surgical and audiological outcome. *Gerontology, 56*(2), 123–128. https://doi.org/10.1159/000235864

Moradi, S., Lidestam, B., & Rönnberg, J. (2016). Comparison of gated audiovisual speech identification in elderly hearing aid users and elderly normal-hearing individuals: Effects of adding visual cues to auditory speech stimuli. *Trends in Hearing, 20*, 2331216516653355. https://doi.org/10.1177/2331216516653355

NagaJyothi, G., Debanjan, K., & Anusha, G. (2020). ASIC implementation of fixed-point iterative, parallel, and pipeline CORDIC algorithm. In *Soft Computing for Problem Solving: SocProS 2018* (Vol. 1, pp. 341–351). Springer Singapore.

NagaJyothi, G., & SriDevi, S. (2017, March). Distributed arithmetic architectures for fir filters-a comparative review. In *2017 International Conference on Wireless Communications, Signal Processing and Networking* (WiSPNET) (pp. 2684–2690). IEEE.

NagaJyothi, G., & Sridevi, S. (2020). High speed low area OBC DA based decimation filter for hearing aids application. *International Journal of Speech Technology, 23*, 111–121. https://doi.org/10.1007/s10772-019-09660-3

Parvin, K. N., & Hussain, M. Z. (2018, January). Multiplication techniques for an efficient FIR filter design for hearing aid applications. In *2018 2nd International Conference on Inventive Systems and Control* (ICISC; pp. 964–968). IEEE.

Plomp, R. (1978). Auditory handicap of hearing impairment and the limited benefit of hearing aids. *The Journal of the Acoustical Society of America, 63*(2), 533–549. https://doi.org/10.1121/1.381753

Ramírez, M., Kowalk, U., Arend, J. M., Bitzer, J., Pörschmann, C., & Plotz, K. (2022, September 12). *Binaural hearing in the real and virtual world to improve school-aged children's listening experience (ViWer-S)*. GMS German Medical Science. https://doi.org/10.3205/22dga205

Reagan, T. (2002). Toward an "archeology of deafness": Etic and emic constructions of identity in conflict. *Journal of Language, Identity, and Education, 1*(1), 41–66. 10.1207/S15327701JLIE0101_4

Stanisavljevic, V., Kalafatic, Z., & Ribaric, S. (2000, May). Optical flow estimation over extended image sequence. In *2000 10th Mediterranean Electrotechnical Conference. Information Technology and Electrotechnology for the Mediterranean Countries. Proceedings*. MeleCon 2000 (Cat. No. 00CH37099; Vol. 2, pp. 546–549). IEEE.

Tasell, D. J. V. (1993). Hearing loss, speech, and hearing aids. *Journal of Speech, Language, and Hearing Research, 36*(2), 228–244. https://doi.org/10.1044/jshr.3602.228

Yee, D., Kamkar-Parsi, H., Martin, R., & Puder, H. (2017). A noise reduction post-filter for binaurally linked single-microphone hearing aids utilizing a nearby external microphone. *IEEE/ACM Transactions on Audio, Speech, and Language Processing, 26*(1), 5–18. https://doi.org/10.1109/TASLP.2017.2727684

Yee, D., Kamkar-Parsi, H., Martin, R., & Puder, H. (2018, October). A relative-transfer-function-based post-filter for speech enhancement in hearing aids using a nearby external microphone. In *Speech Communication; 13th ITG-Symposium* (pp. 1–5). VDE.

Zheng, Y., Mobasher, B., & Burke, R. D. (2015, July). Incorporating context correlation into context-aware matrix factorization. In *CPCR+ ITWP@ IJCAI* (p. 7).

# ABOUT THE EDITORS

**Sam Goundar** is an international academic having taught at twelve different universities in ten different countries. He is editor-in-chief of the *International Journal of Blockchains and Cryptocurrencies* (IJBC; Inderscience Publishers), editor-in-chief of the *International Journal of Fog Computing* (IJFC; IGI Publishers), section editor of the *Journal of Education and Information Technologies* (EAIT; Springer), and editor-in-chief (emeritus) of the *International Journal of Cloud Applications and Computing* (IJCAC; IGI Publishers). He is also on the editorial review board of more than 20 high-impact factor journals. Professor Goundar is a senior member of IEEE; a member of ACS; a member of the IITP, New Zealand; Certication Administrator of ETA-I, USA; and past president of the South Pacific Computer Society. He also serves on the IEEE Technical Committee for Internet of Things, Cloud Communication and Networking, Big Data, Green ICT, Cybersecurity, Business Informatics and Systems, Learning Technology, and Smart Cities. He is a member of the IEEE Technical Society and a panelist with the IEEE Spectrum for Emerging Technologies.

**J. Avanija** completed her PhD at Anna University Chennai, India, currently working as professor in the School of Computing, Mohan Babu University, Andhra Pradesh, Tirupati, India. Her research area of interest: semantic web mining, machine learning, artificial intelligence, big data, and cloud computing. She has 23 years of experience in academia and has 10 patents and 7 books published to her credit. She has published more than 70 papers in

*Innovations in Computational Intelligence, Big Data Analytics, and Internet of Things*, pages 375–376
Copyright © 2024 by Information Age Publishing
www.infoagepub.com

reputed international journals and conferences. She has been serving as a reviewer and editorial board member for various international journals.

**Gurram Sunitha** is currently working as professor at School of Computing, Mohan Babu University, Tirupati, India. She received her PhD in computer science and engineering from S.V. University, Tirupati. She has 22 years of experience in academia. Her research interests include: data mining, spatio-temporal analytics, machine learning, and artificial intelligence. She has 13 patents and 6 books published to her credit. She has published around 70 research papers in reputed journals and conferences. She has been serving as reviewer for several journals; and has served on the program committees and co-chaired for various international conferences.

**K. Reddy Madhavi**, completed BTech from S.V. University, Tirupati, M. Tech from JNTU Hyderabad and PhD from JNTU, Anantapur and currently working as professor, school of computing, Mohan Babu University, Tirupati. She has filed and published 21 national and international patents and few of them granted too. To her profile she has more than 100 papers in international journals/conferences indexed in SCI/Scopus/Web of Science and published edited/authored books and book chapters. She has undergone a course on design Thinking in collaboration with IUCEE EPICS Purdue University, USA. She is also an innovation ambassador associated with IIC, MHRD, government of India. She is the convener of many international conferences, ICDIC 2021, NCKITS-2022, ICIHCNN-2022, ICTIS-2023. She received funds from DST SERB for organizing the same. She is acting as a reviewer and program committee member for many international and national conferences and journals. She is acting as session chair/co-chair for many symposia and conferences, delivered expert talks too. She has received Young Women Scientist award by Dr. Abdul Kalam Educational Trust during the academic year 2019–20 and Young Researcher Award at CHSN-2020 at JNTUK and Woman Researcher Award by INSO, International Scientist Award on Engineering, Science, and Medicine 2022, October 2022.

Printed in the United States
by Baker & Taylor Publisher Services